CHRONICLES OF THE CURSED SWORD

Volume 6

Story by
YEO BEOP-RYONG

Art by
PARK HUI-JIN

WITHDRAWN

TOKYOPOP®

Los Angeles • Tokyo • London

Translator - Yongju Ryu
English Adaptation - Matt Varosky
Copy Editor -Tim Beedle
Retouch and Lettering - Yoohae Yang
Cover Layout - Gary Shum

Editor - Paul Morrissey
Digital Imaging Manager - Chris Buford
Pre-Press Manager - Antonio DePietro
Production Managers - Jennifer Miller and Mutsumi Miyazaki
Art Director - Matt Alford
Managing Editor - Jill Freshney
VP of Production - Ron Klamert
President & C.O.O. - John Parker
Publisher & C.E.O. - Stuart Levy

E-mail: info@TOKYOPOP.com

Come visit us online at www.TOKYOPOP.com

A  Manga

TOKYOPOP Inc.
5900 Wilshire Blvd. Suite 2000
Los Angeles, CA 90036

Chronicles of the Cursed Sword Vol. 6
©2001 YEO BEOP-RYONG and PARK HUI-JIN.
First printed in Korea in 2001 by Daiwon C.I. Inc. English translation rights in
North America, UK, NZ and Australia arranged by Daiwon C.I. Inc.

English text copyright ©2004 TOKYOPOP Inc.

ISBN: 1-59182-423-0

First TOKYOPOP printing: May 2004

10 9 8 7 6 5 4 3 2 1

Printed in the USA

The story so far...

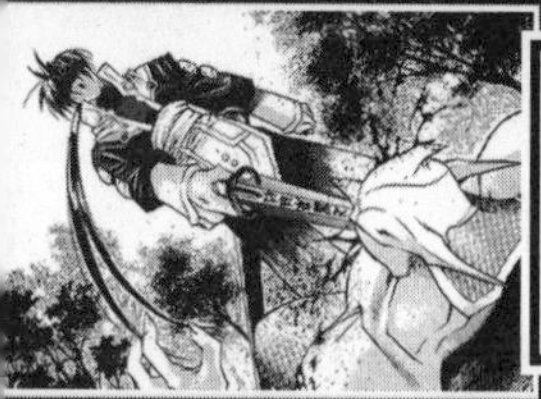

Rey Yan and Shyao Lin rescued Jaryoon using Rey's cursed PaSa sword.

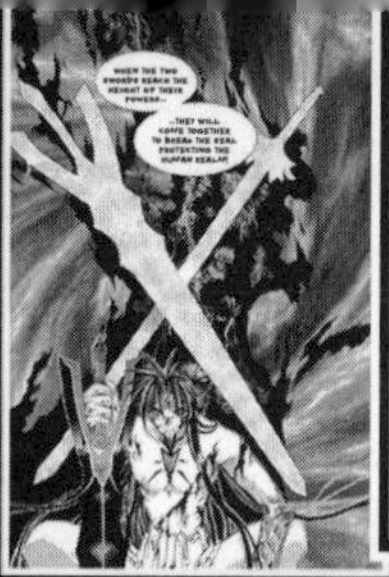

WHEN THE TWO SWORDS REACH THE HEIGHT OF THEIR POWERS...
...THEY WILL COME TOGETHER TO BREAK THE SEAL PROTECTING THE HUMAN REALM!

The demon possessing Rey conspires with the Sorceress of the Underworld to summon the Demon Emperor by combining the powers of the PaSa and PaChun swords.

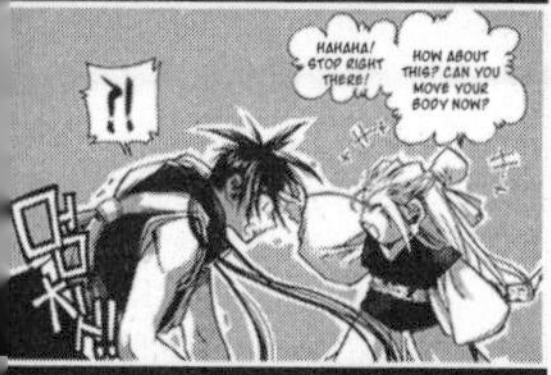

HAHAHA! STOP RIGHT THERE!
HOW ABOUT THIS? CAN YOU MOVE YOUR BODY NOW?
?!

Rey begins rigorous training with chen Kaihu—a diminuitive martial arts master with powerful techniques.

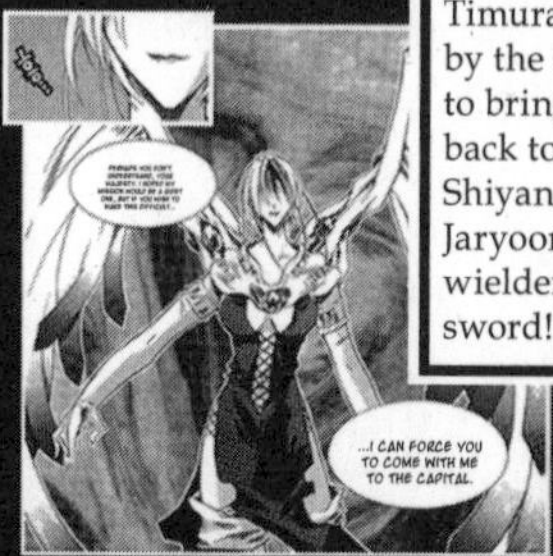

...I CAN FORCE YOU TO COME WITH ME TO THE CAPITAL.

Timura Oshu is sent by the sinister Shiyan to bring Jaryoon back to the capital. Shiyan has plans for Jaryoon—as the new wielder of the PaChun sword!

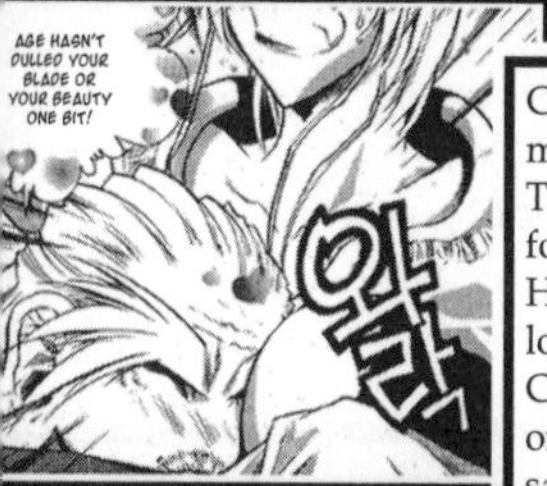

AGE HASN'T DULLED YOUR BLADE OR YOUR BEAUTY ONE BIT!

Chen Kaihu mistakes Timura Oshu for Lady Hwaren, his long-lost love. Could they be one and the same?

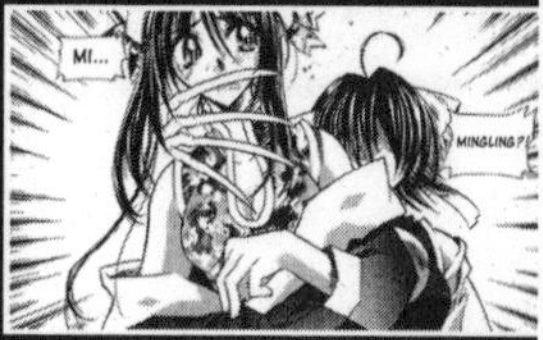

MI...
MINGLING?!

Timura Oshu possesses Mingling, usi her to threate Shyao's life. Given no choi Jaryoon reluctantly accompanies Timura to the capital...

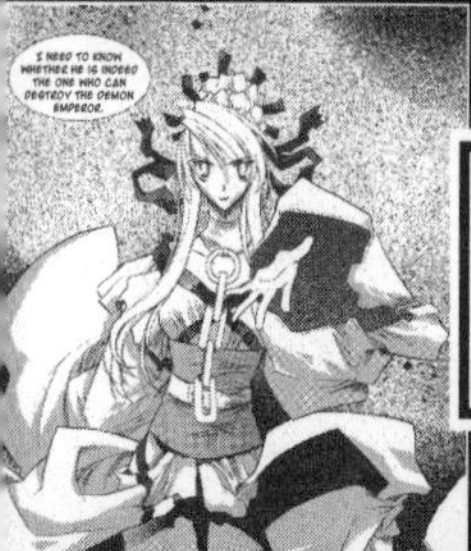

I NEED TO KNOW WHETHER HE IS INDEED THE ONE WHO CAN DESTROY THE DEMON EMPEROR.

The powerful woman warrior Hyacia tracks down Rey. She wants to test his mettle in order to determine if he's powerful enough to defeat the Demon Emperor.

Rey battles Shouren—the Sorcerer of the Dark—whose true form is that of a dragon!

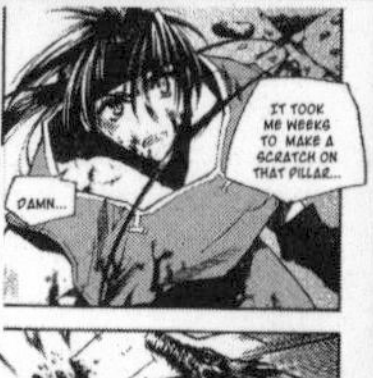

IT TOOK ME WEEKS TO MAKE A SCRATCH ON THAT PILLAR...
DAMN...

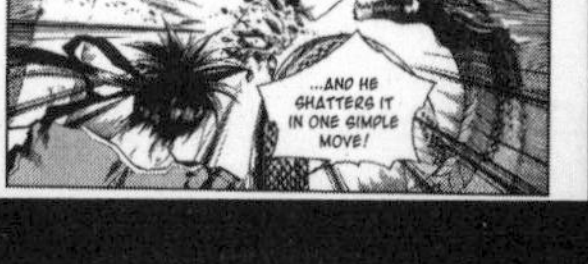

...AND HE SHATTERS IT IN ONE SIMPLE MOVE!

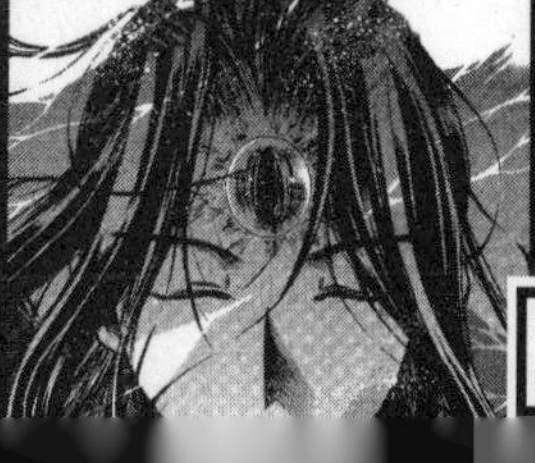

Shyan implants a demon stone in the captive Jaryoon's forhead...

CHRONICLES OF THE CURSED SWORD

the cast of characters

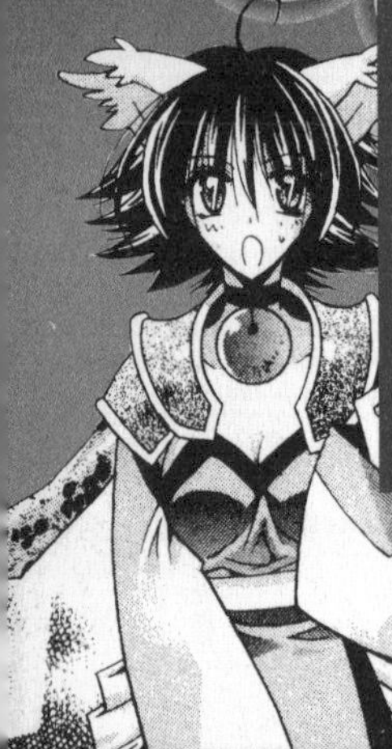

MINGLING

A lesser demon with feline qualities, Mingling is now the loyal follower of Shyao Lin. She lives in fear of Rey, who still doesn't trust her.

THE PASA SWORD

A living sword that hungers for demon blood. It grants its user incredible power, but at a great cost—it can take over the user's body and, in time, his soul.

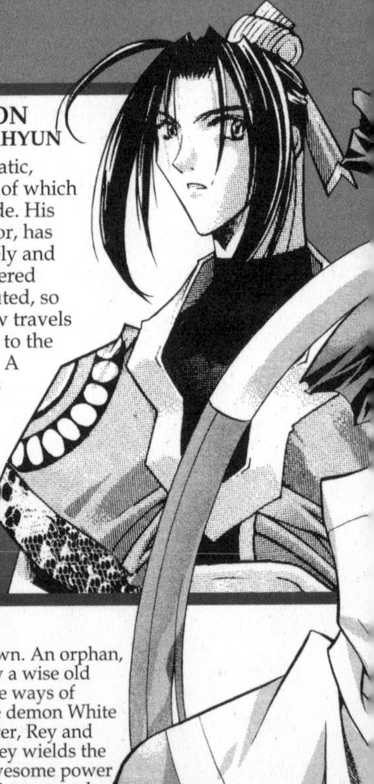

JARYOON
KING OF HAHYUN

Noble and charismatic, Jaryoon is the stuff of which great kings are made. His brother, the emperor, has been acting strangely and apparently has ordered Jaryoon to be executed, so the young king now travels to the capital to get to the heart of the matter. A great warrior in his own right, he does not have magical abilities and is unaccustomed to battling demons.

SHYAO LIN

A sorceress and Rey Yan's traveling companion. Shyao grew fond of Rey during their five years of study together with their master, and thinks of him as her little brother. She's Rey's conscience—his sole tie to humanity. She also seems quite enamored with the handsome Jaryoon.

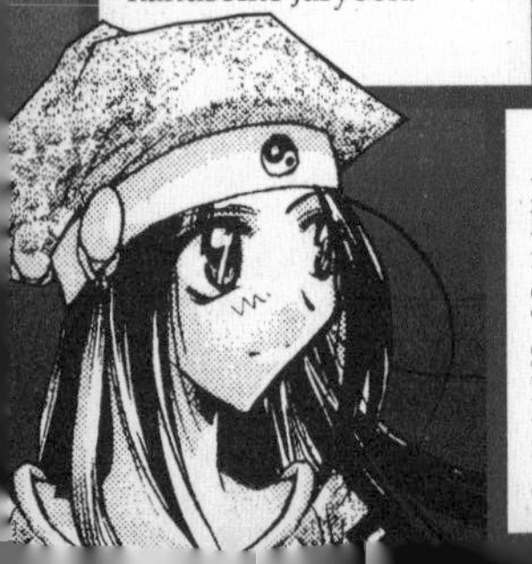

REY YAN

Rey's origins remain unknown. An orphan, he and Shyao were raised by a wise old man who trained them in the ways of combat and magic. After the demon White Tiger slaughtered their master, Rey and Shyao became wanderers. Rey wields the PaSa sword, a weapon of awesome power that threatens to take over his very soul. Under the right circumstances, he could be a hero.

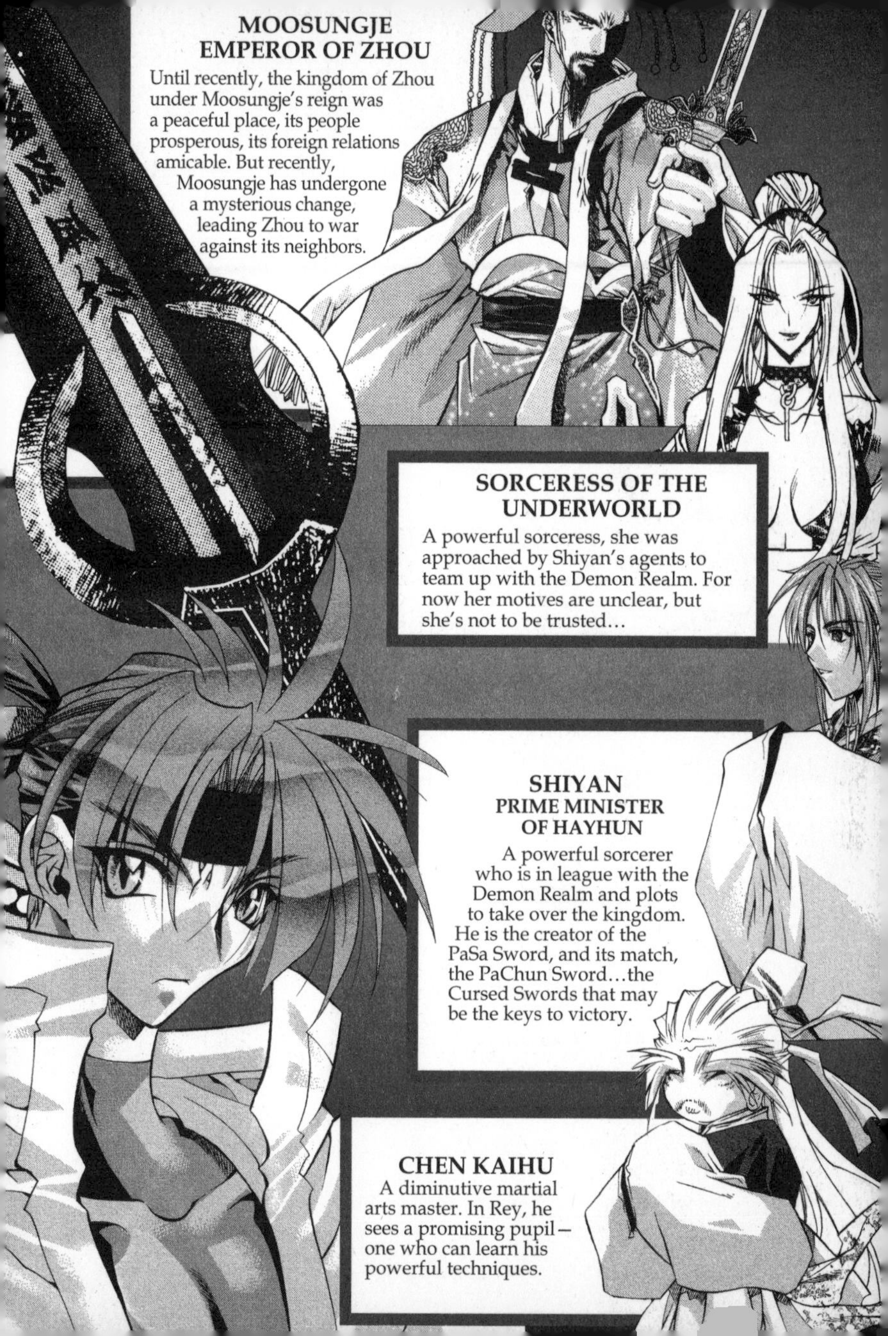

MOOSUNGJE
EMPEROR OF ZHOU

Until recently, the kingdom of Zhou under Moosungje's reign was a peaceful place, its people prosperous, its foreign relations amicable. But recently, Moosungje has undergone a mysterious change, leading Zhou to war against its neighbors.

SORCERESS OF THE UNDERWORLD

A powerful sorceress, she was approached by Shiyan's agents to team up with the Demon Realm. For now her motives are unclear, but she's not to be trusted...

SHIYAN
PRIME MINISTER OF HAYHUN

A powerful sorcerer who is in league with the Demon Realm and plots to take over the kingdom. He is the creator of the PaSa Sword, and its match, the PaChun Sword...the Cursed Swords that may be the keys to victory.

CHEN KAIHU

A diminutive martial arts master. In Rey, he sees a promising pupil—one who can learn his powerful techniques.

Chronicles

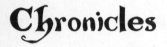

Chapter 24: The PaSa Sword Reborn . . . 9

Chapter 25: The Armor of Dead Souls . . 49

Chapter 26: Jaryoon's Change of Heart . . 89

Chapter 27: An Achilles' Heel 129

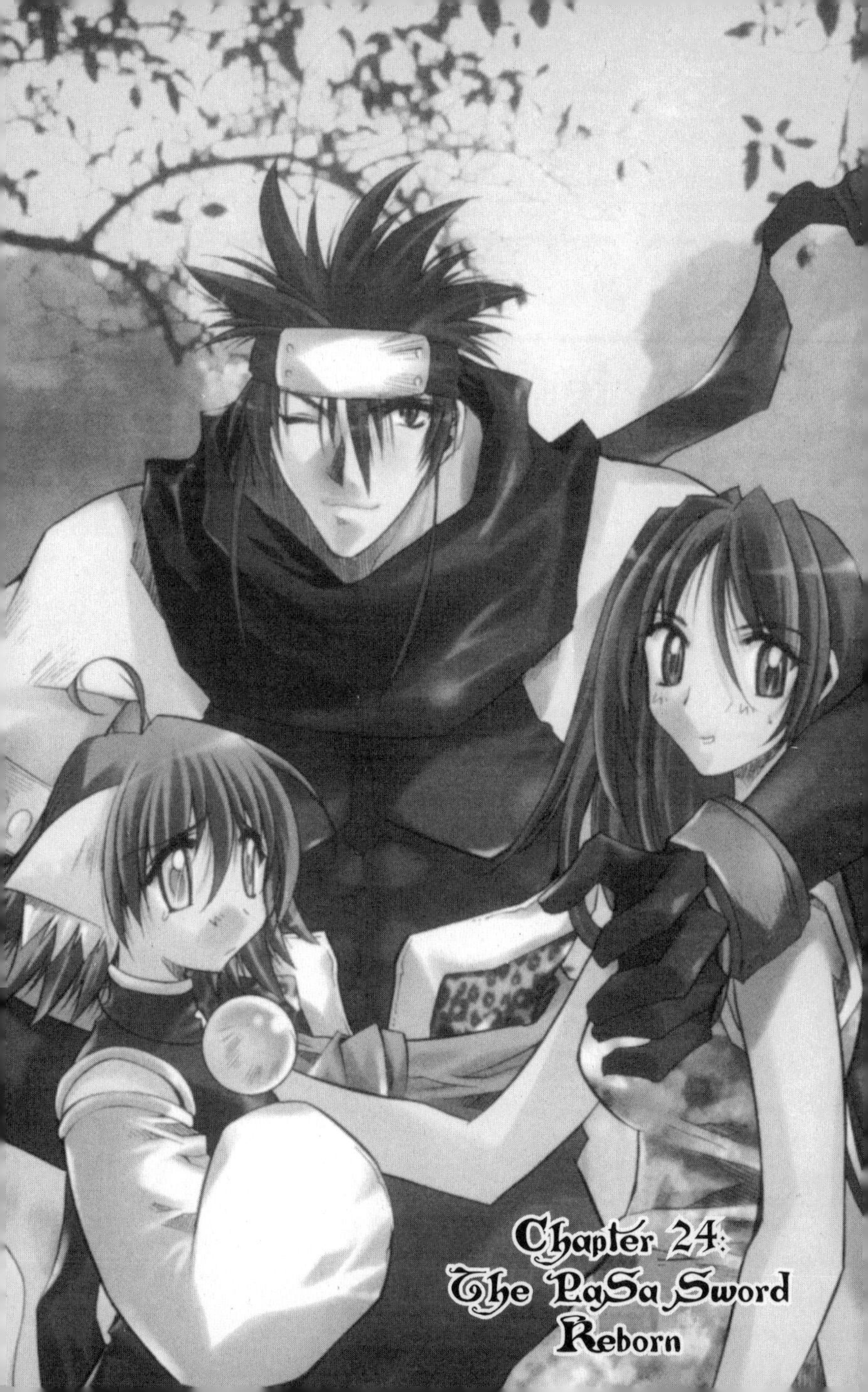
Chapter 24:
The LaSa Sword
Reborn

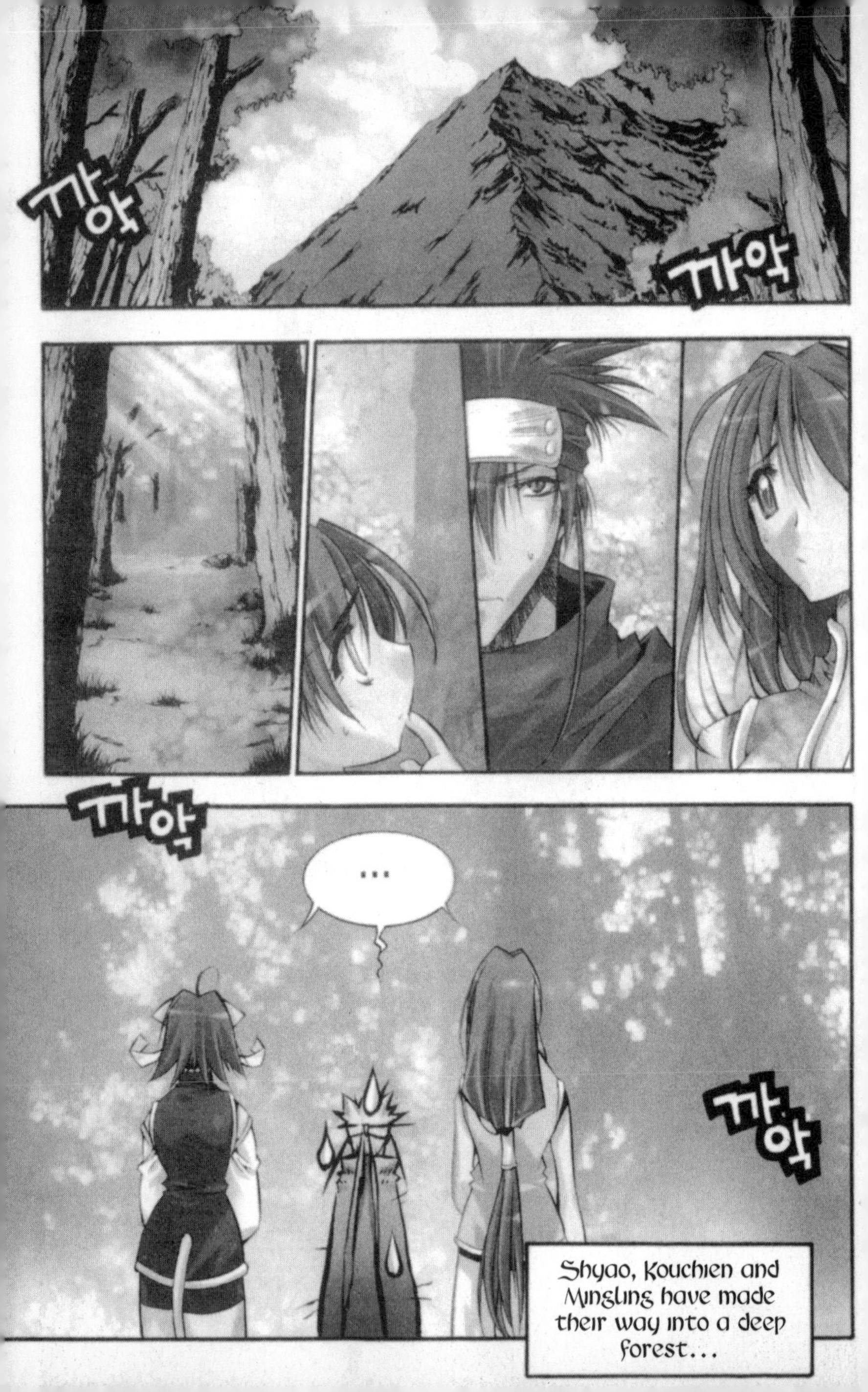
까약
까약
까약
...
까약
Shyao, Kouchien and Mingling have made their way into a deep forest...

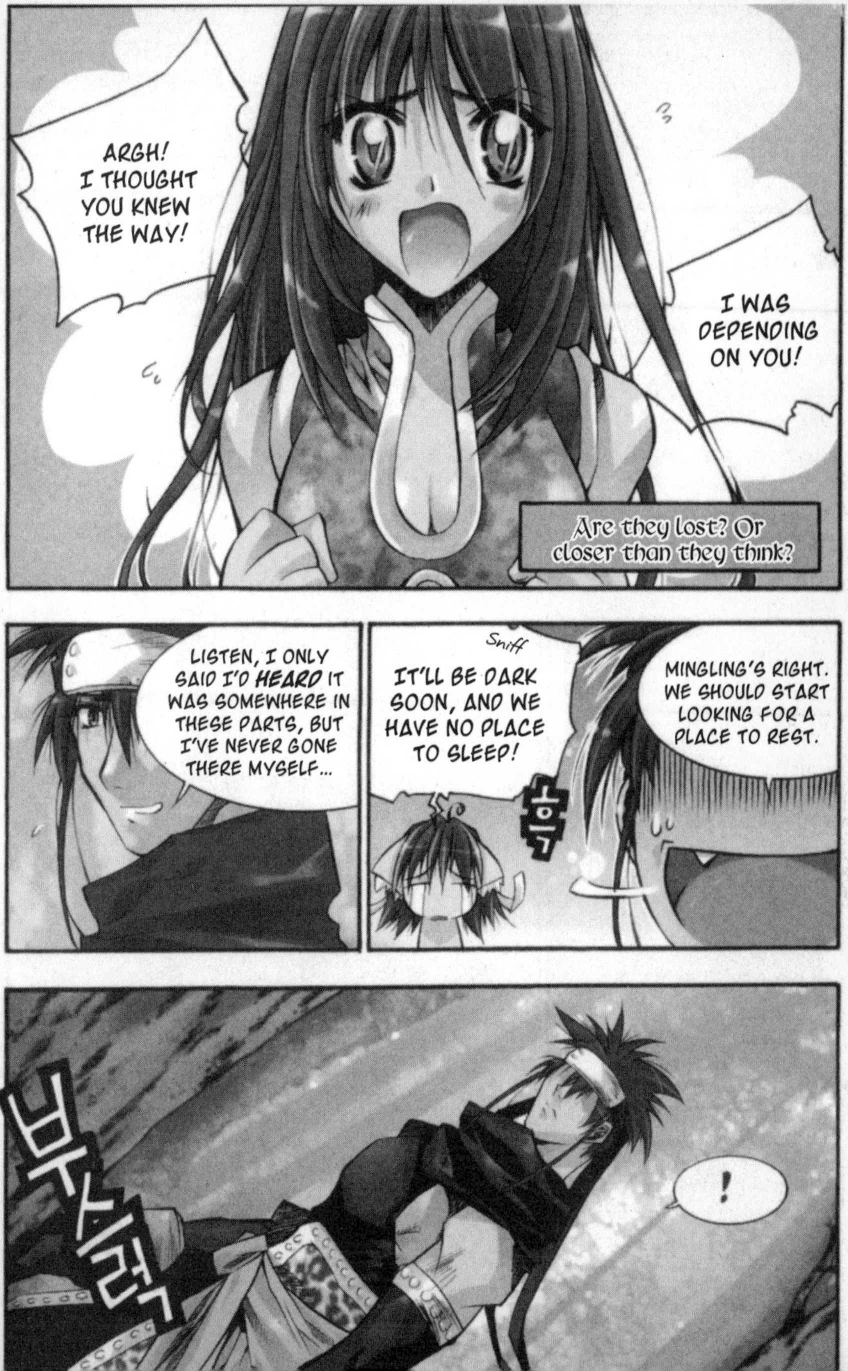
ARGH! I THOUGHT YOU KNEW THE WAY!
I WAS DEPENDING ON YOU!
Are they lost? Or closer than they think?
LISTEN, I ONLY SAID I'D **HEARD** IT WAS SOMEWHERE IN THESE PARTS, BUT I'VE NEVER GONE THERE MYSELF...
Sniff
IT'LL BE DARK SOON, AND WE HAVE NO PLACE TO SLEEP!
MINGLING'S RIGHT. WE SHOULD START LOOKING FOR A PLACE TO REST.
!

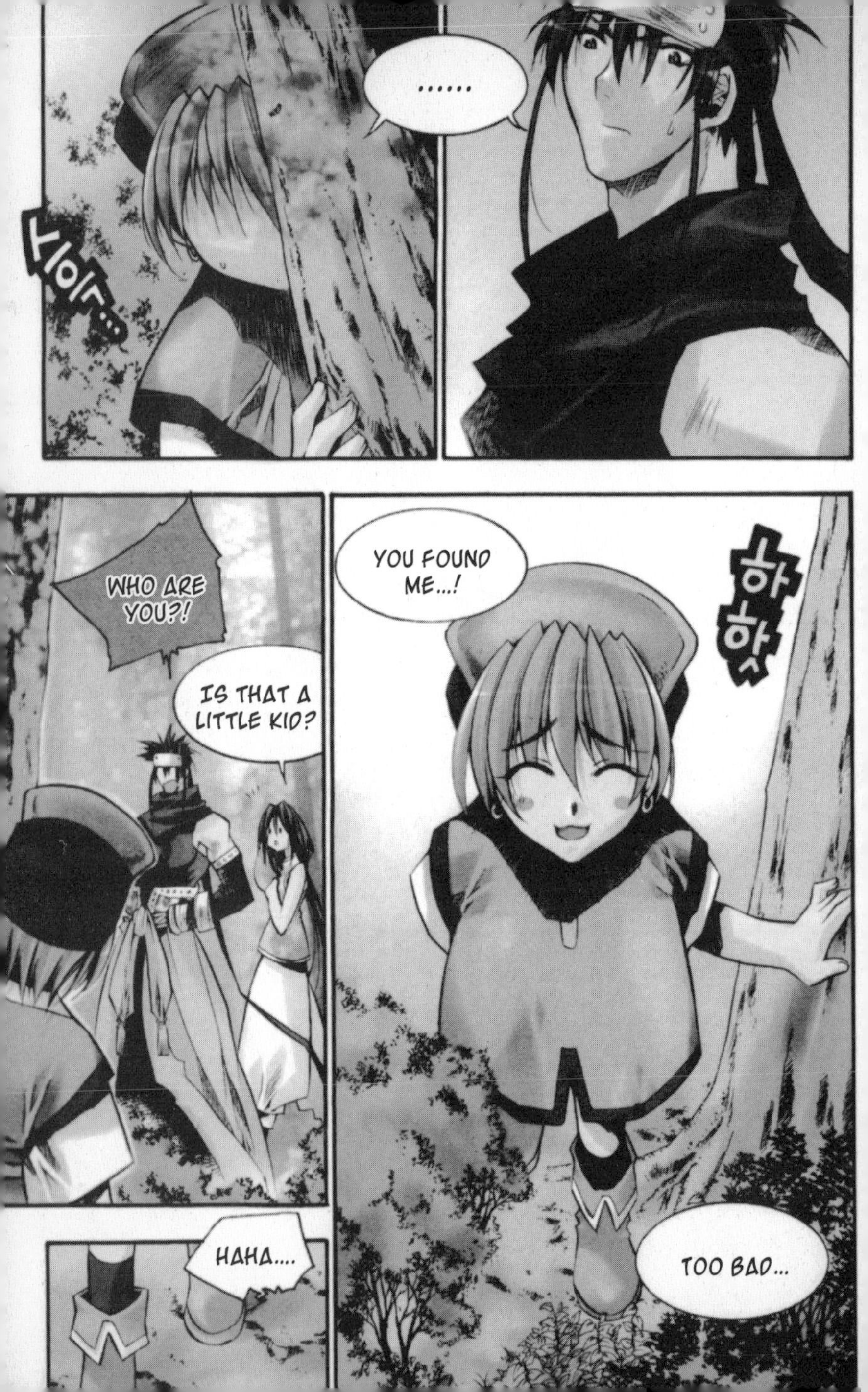
......
WHO ARE YOU?!
IS THAT A LITTLE KID?
HAHA....
YOU FOUND ME...!
하핫
TOO BAD...

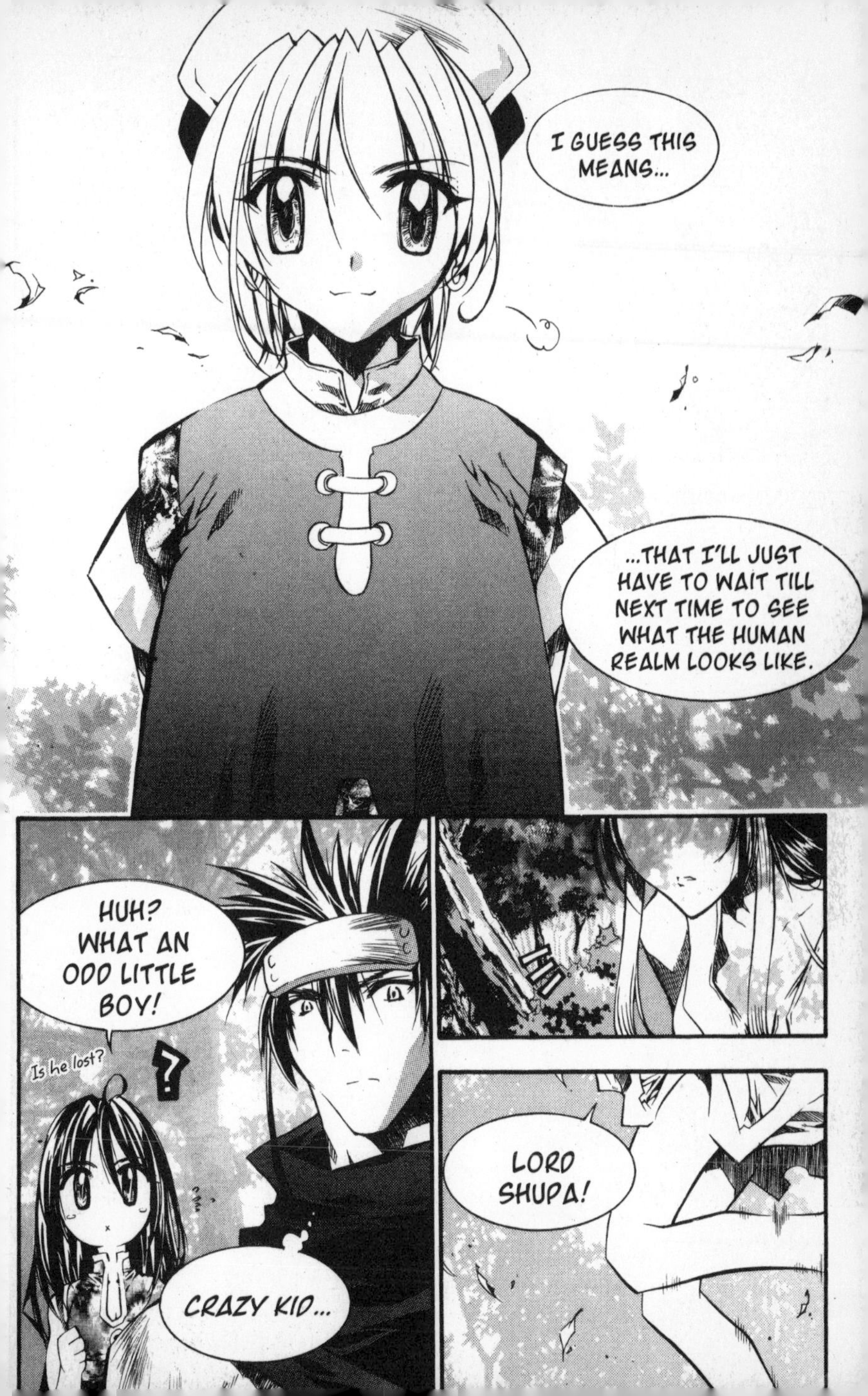
I GUESS THIS MEANS...
...THAT I'LL JUST HAVE TO WAIT TILL NEXT TIME TO SEE WHAT THE HUMAN REALM LOOKS LIKE.
HUH? WHAT AN ODD LITTLE BOY!
Is he lost?
?
CRAZY KID...
LORD SHUPA!

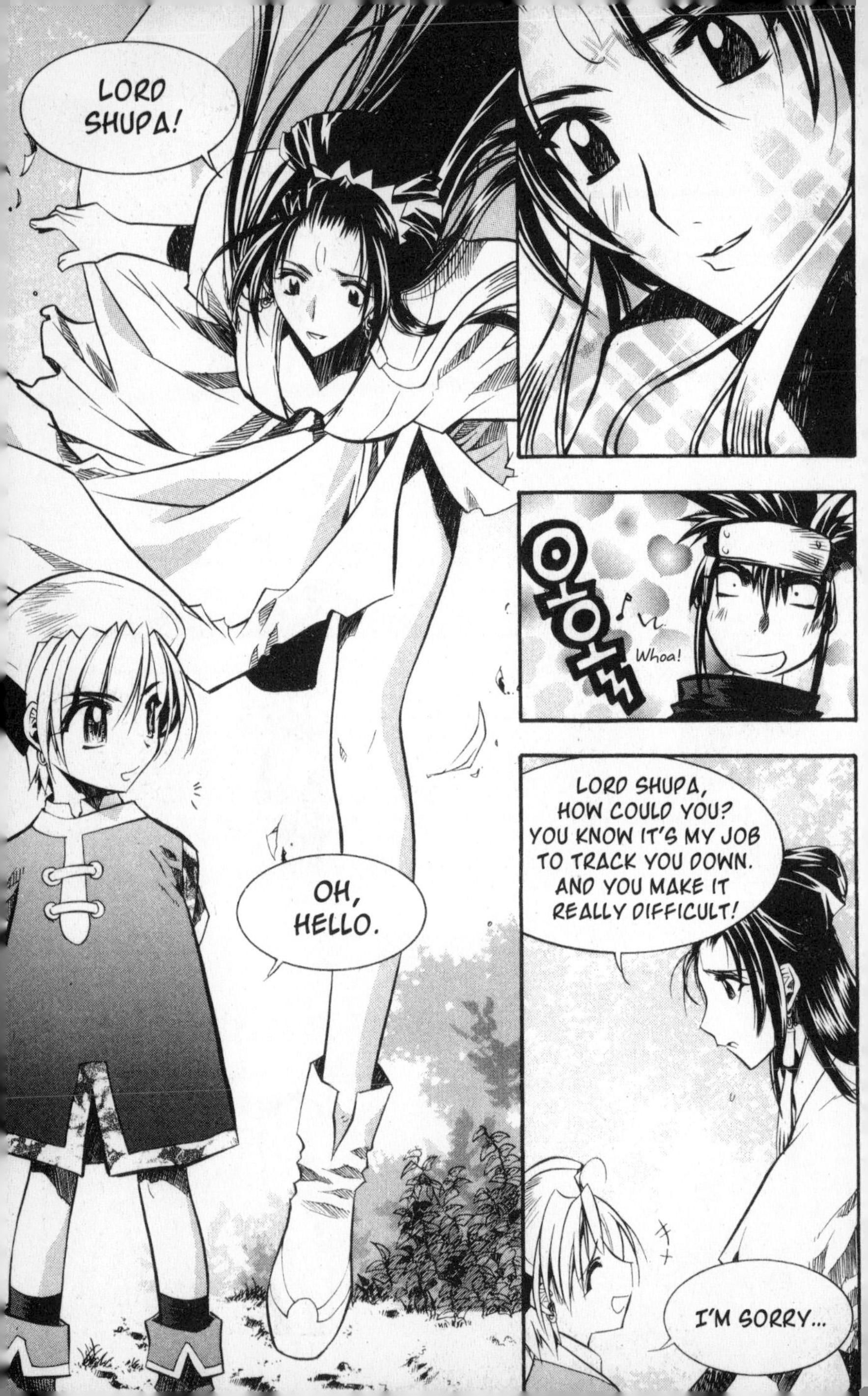
LORD SHUPA!
OH, HELLO.
Whoa!
LORD SHUPA, HOW COULD YOU? YOU KNOW IT'S MY JOB TO TRACK YOU DOWN. AND YOU MAKE IT REALLY DIFFICULT!
I'M SORRY...

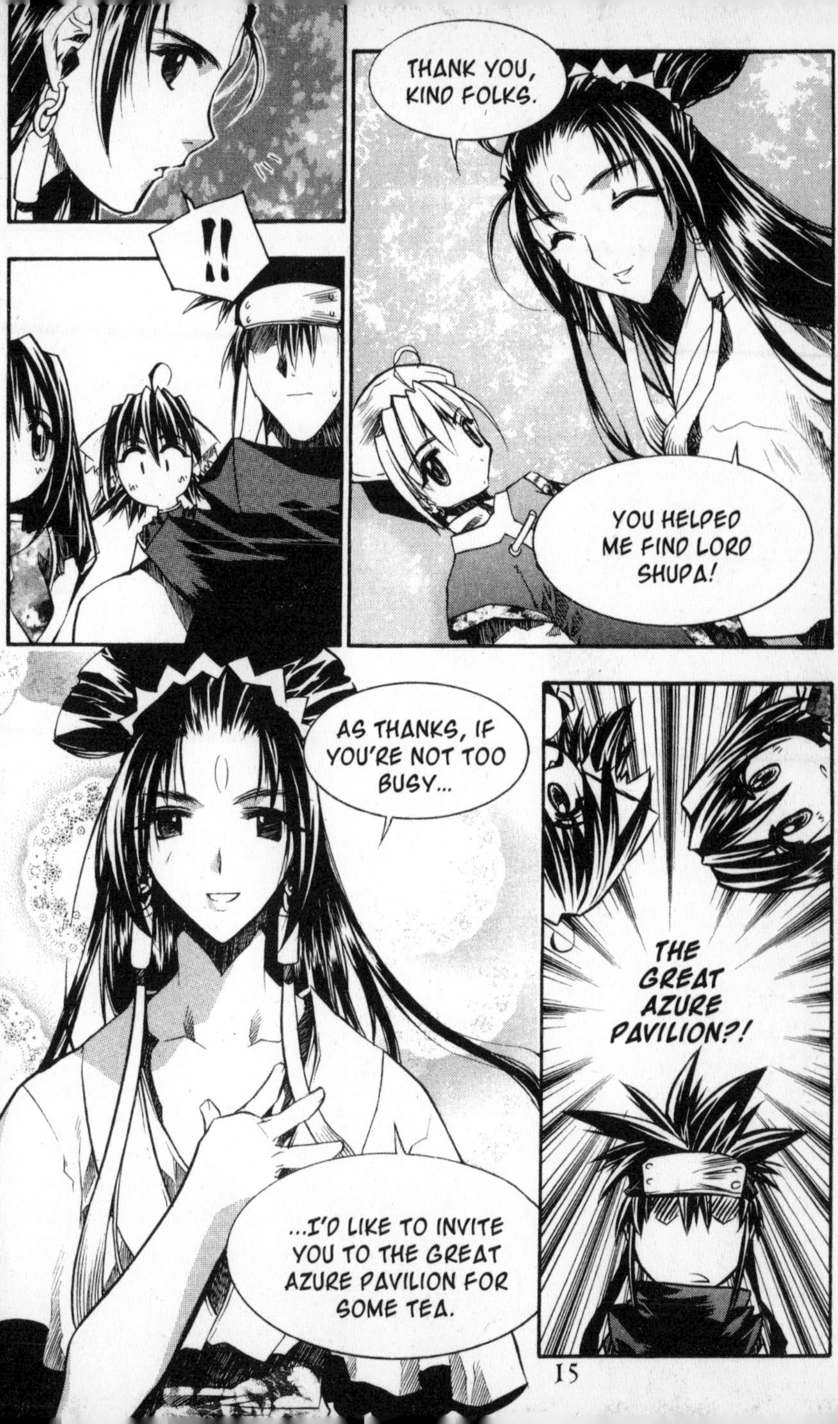
!!
THANK YOU, KIND FOLKS.
YOU HELPED ME FIND LORD SHUPA!
AS THANKS, IF YOU'RE NOT TOO BUSY...
...I'D LIKE TO INVITE YOU TO THE GREAT AZURE PAVILION FOR SOME TEA.
THE GREAT AZURE PAVILION?!

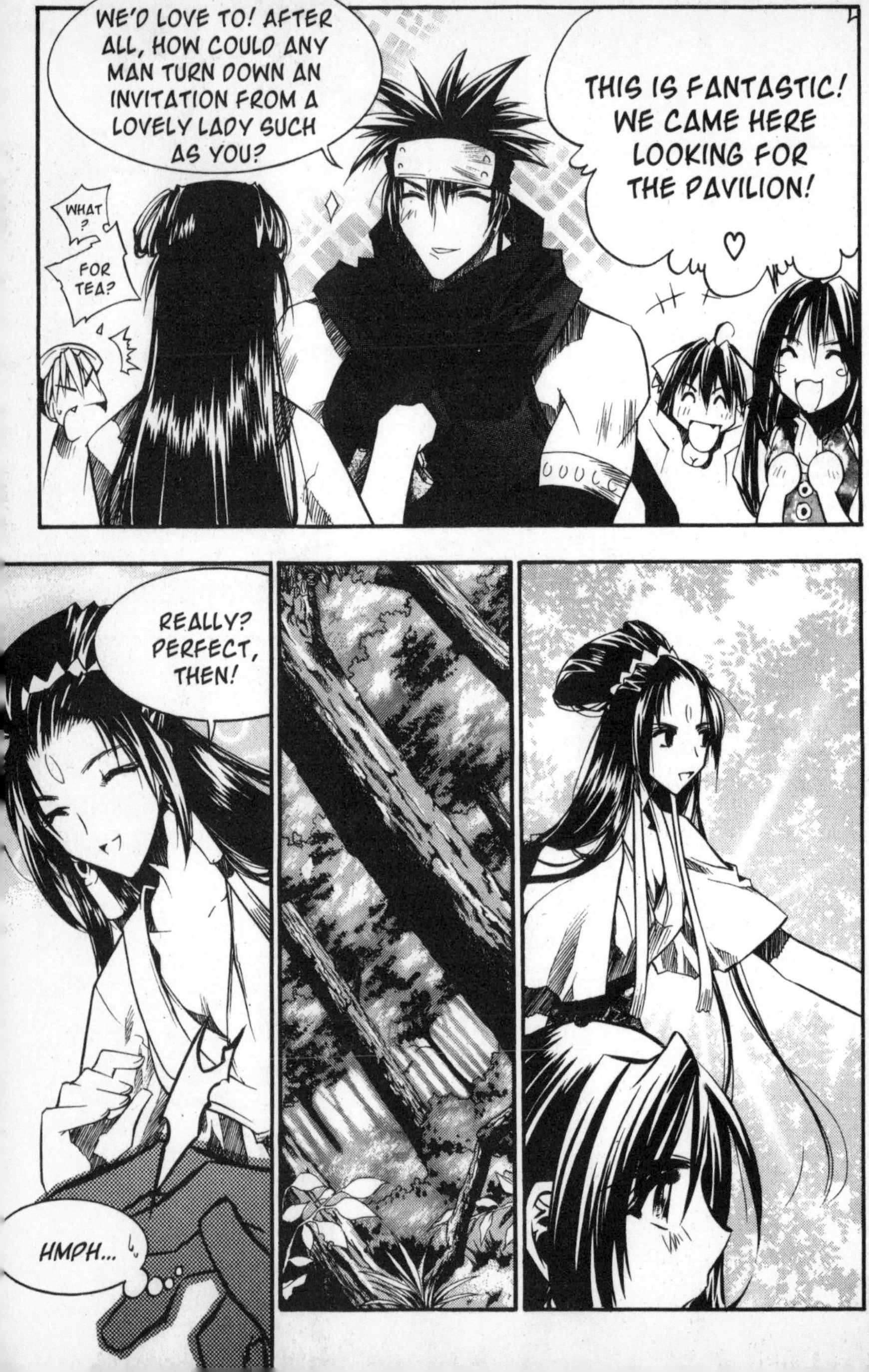
WE'D LOVE TO! AFTER ALL, HOW COULD ANY MAN TURN DOWN AN INVITATION FROM A LOVELY LADY SUCH AS YOU?
WHAT?
FOR TEA?
THIS IS FANTASTIC! WE CAME HERE LOOKING FOR THE PAVILION!
REALLY? PERFECT, THEN!
HMPH...

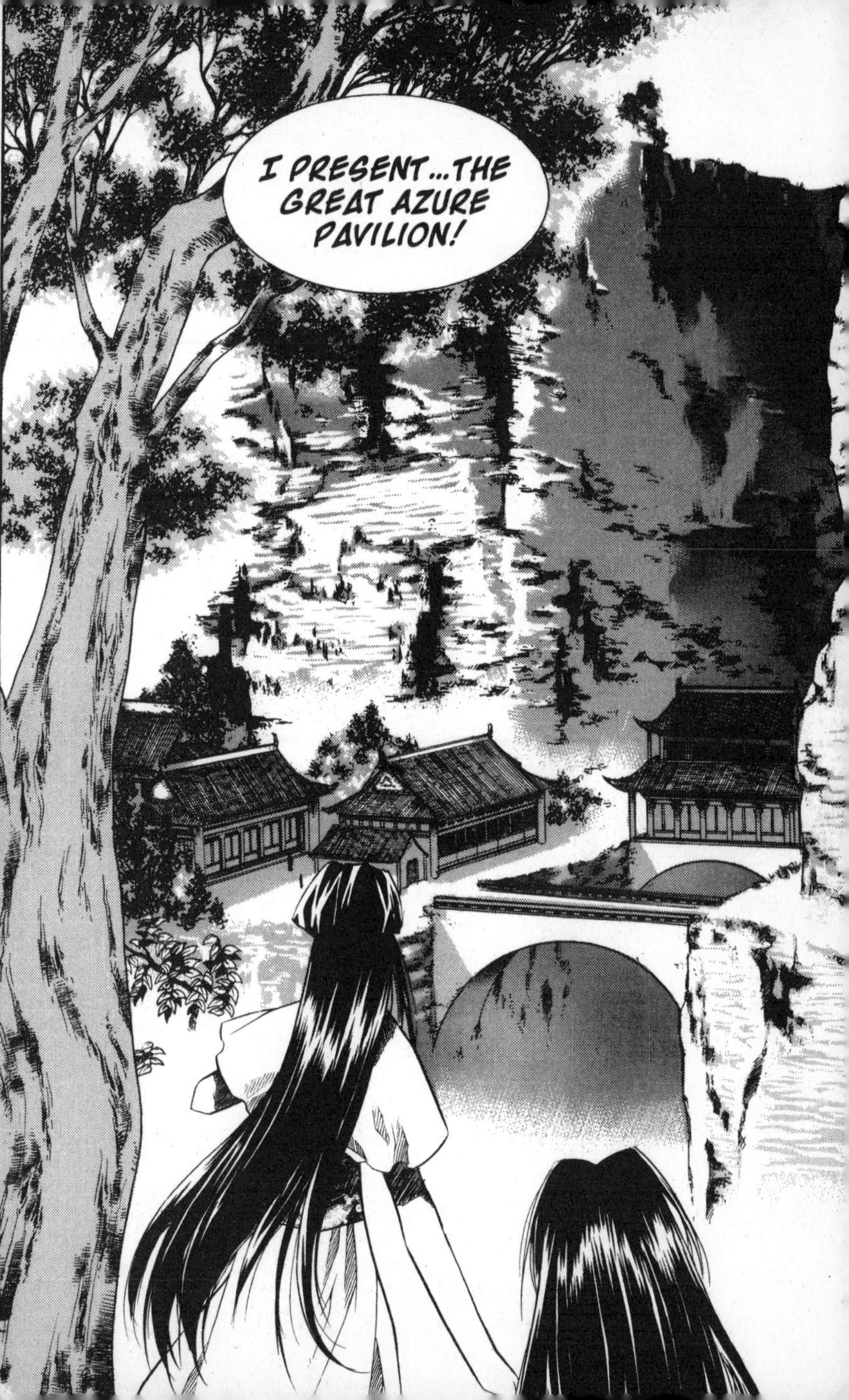
I PRESENT...THE GREAT AZURE PAVILION!

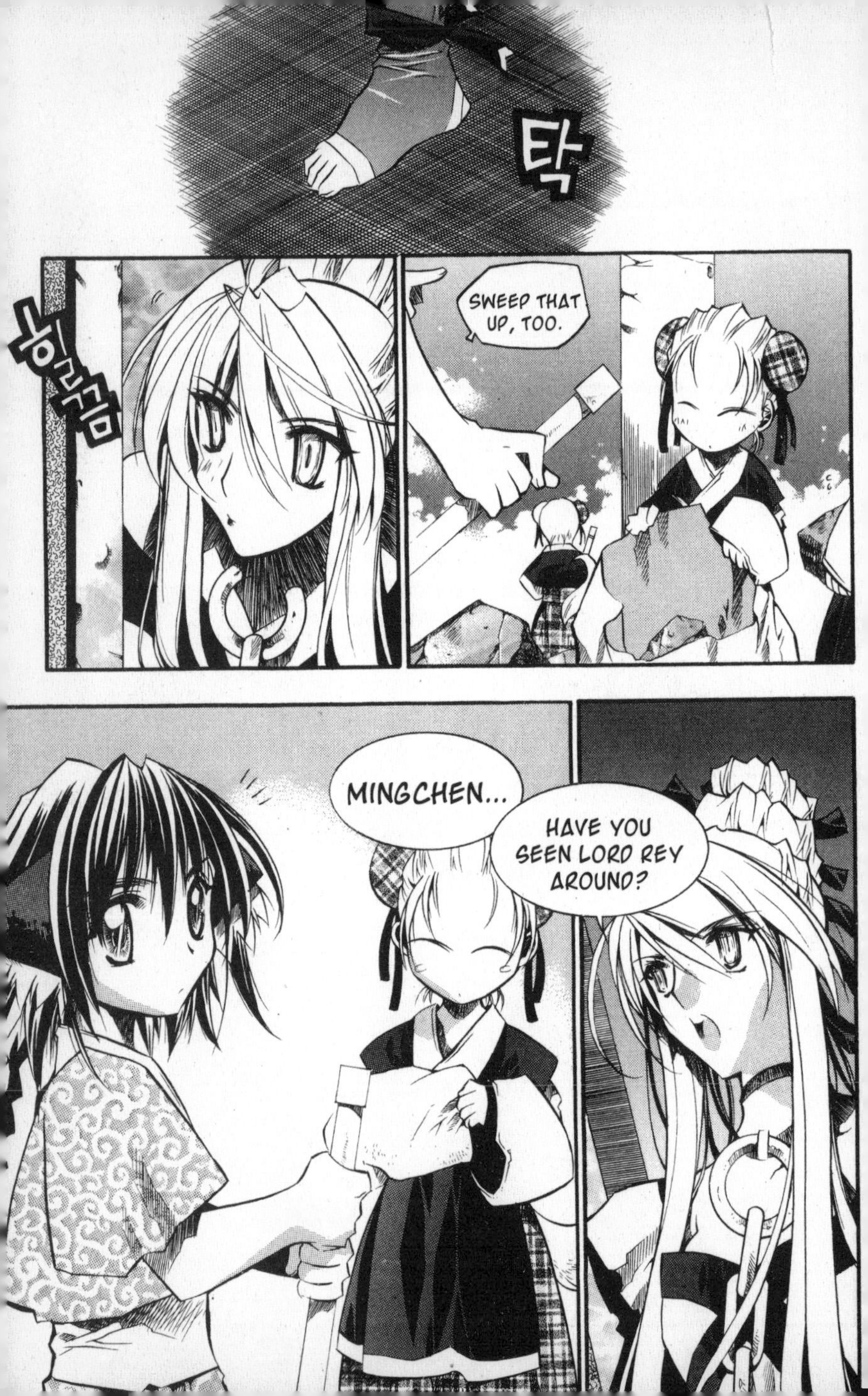
탁
흘끔
SWEEP THAT UP, TOO.
MINGCHEN...
HAVE YOU SEEN LORD REY AROUND?

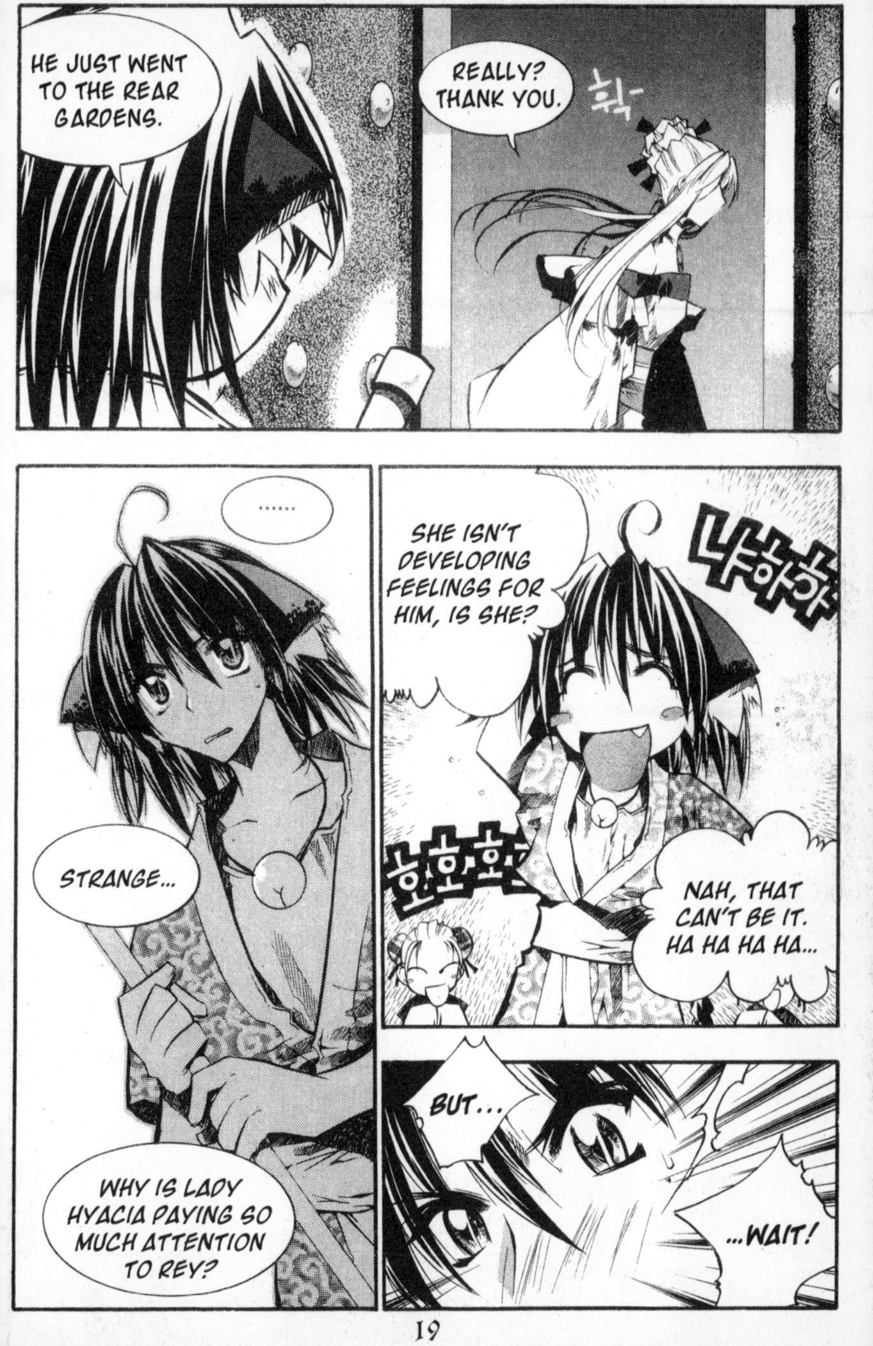
HE JUST WENT TO THE REAR GARDENS.
REALLY? THANK YOU.
휙-
......
STRANGE...
WHY IS LADY HYACIA PAYING SO MUCH ATTENTION TO REY?
SHE ISN'T DEVELOPING FEELINGS FOR HIM, IS SHE?
냐하하
호호호
NAH, THAT CAN'T BE IT. HA HA HA HA...
BUT...
...WAIT!

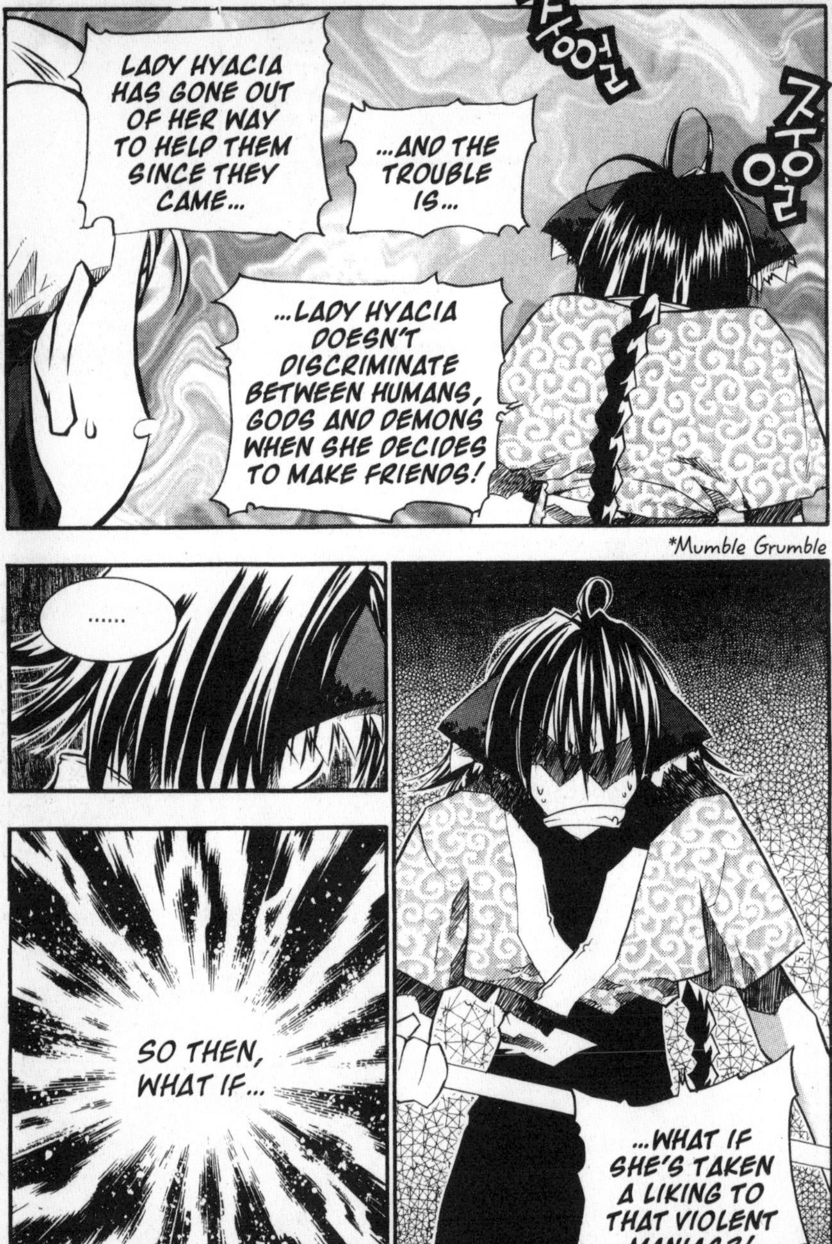
LADY HYACIA HAS GONE OUT OF HER WAY TO HELP THEM SINCE THEY CAME...
...AND THE TROUBLE IS...
중얼
중얼
...LADY HYACIA DOESN'T DISCRIMINATE BETWEEN HUMANS, GODS AND DEMONS WHEN SHE DECIDES TO MAKE FRIENDS!
*Mumble Grumble
......
SO THEN, WHAT IF...
...WHAT IF SHE'S TAKEN A LIKING TO THAT VIOLENT MANIAC?!

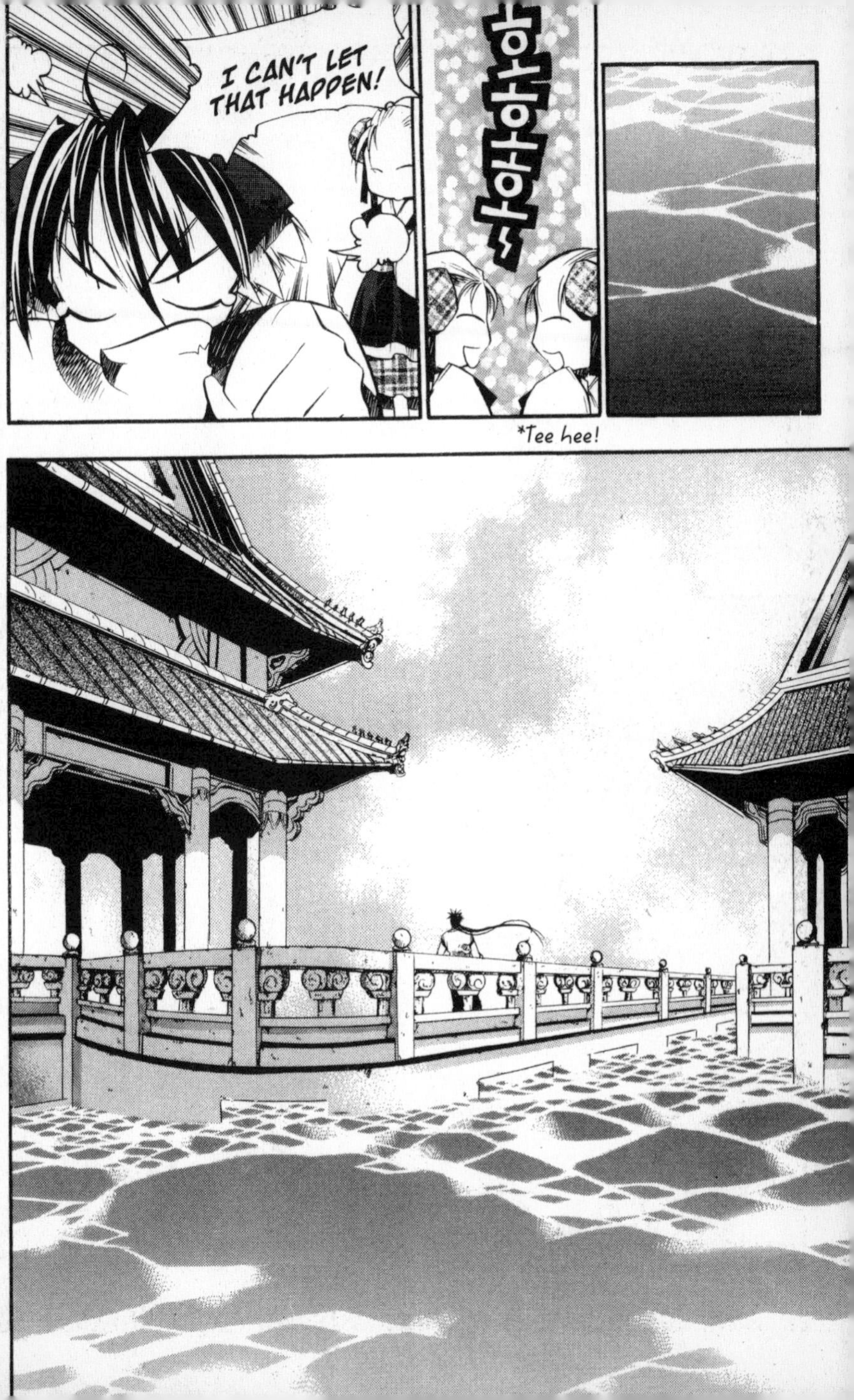
I CAN'T LET THAT HAPPEN!
호호호호
*Tee hee!

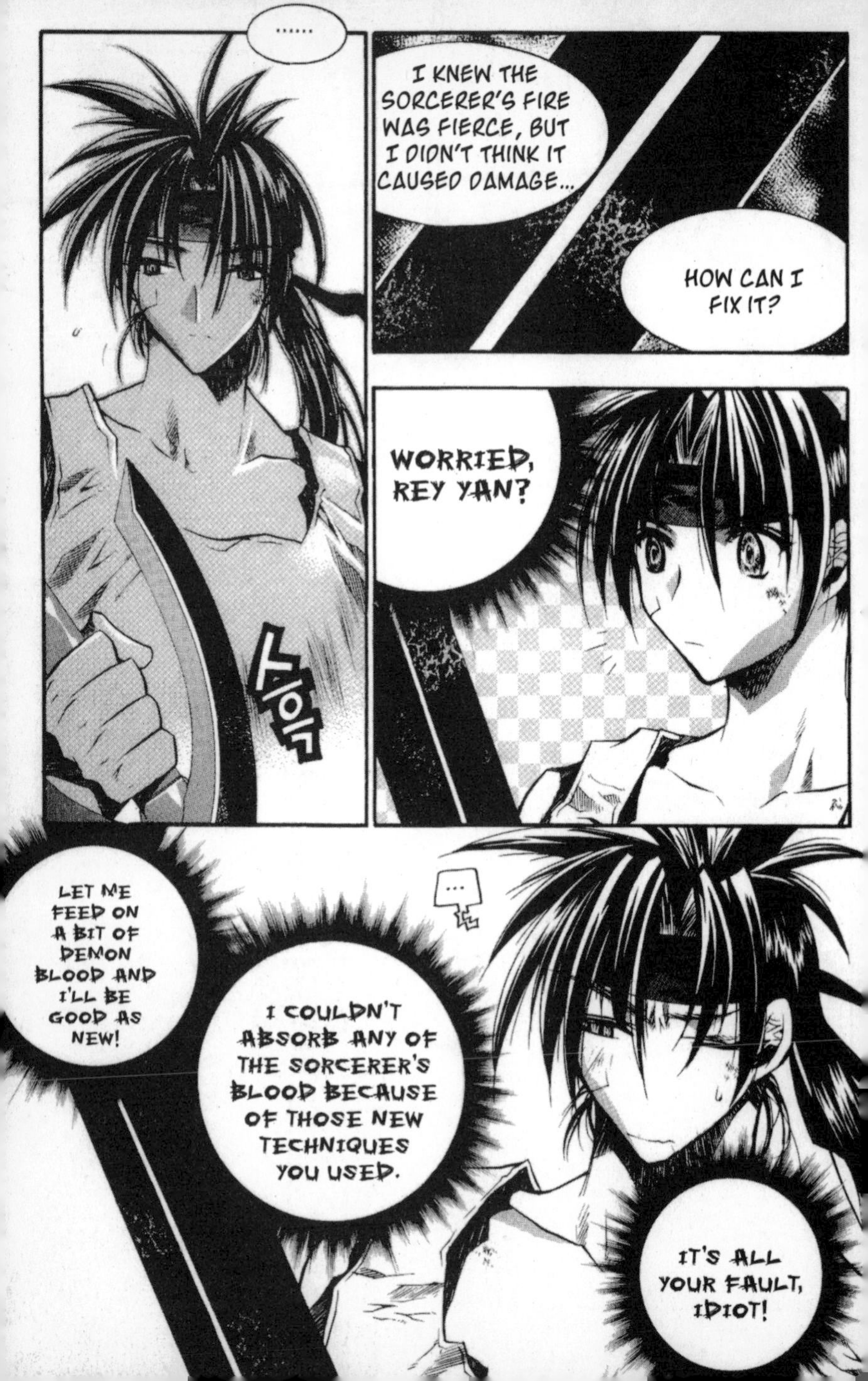
......
I KNEW THE SORCERER'S FIRE WAS FIERCE, BUT I DIDN'T THINK IT CAUSED DAMAGE...
HOW CAN I FIX IT?
WORRIED, REY YAN?
LET ME FEED ON A BIT OF DEMON BLOOD AND I'LL BE GOOD AS NEW!
...
I COULDN'T ABSORB ANY OF THE SORCERER'S BLOOD BECAUSE OF THOSE NEW TECHNIQUES YOU USED.
IT'S ALL YOUR FAULT, IDIOT!

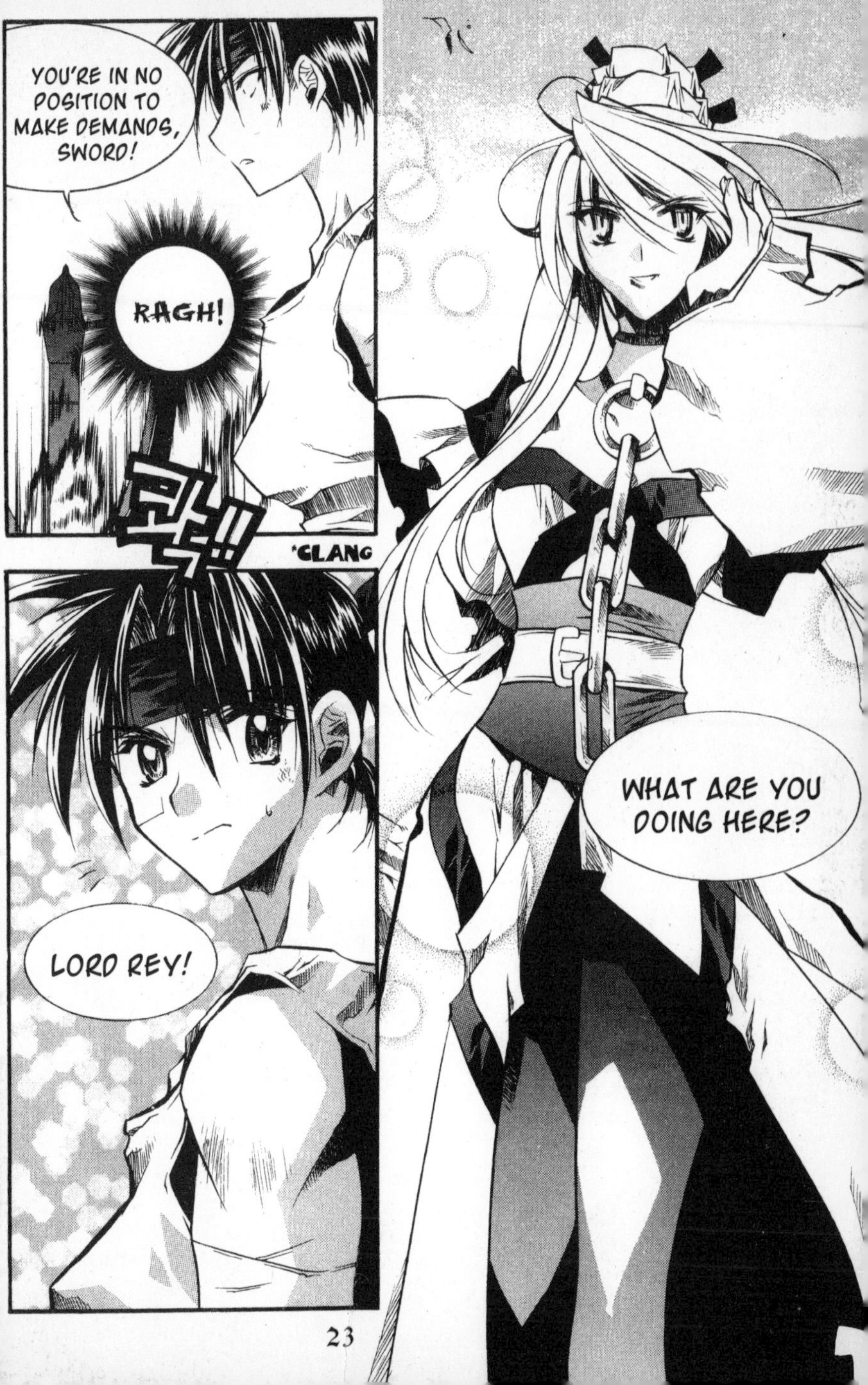
YOU'RE IN NO POSITION TO MAKE DEMANDS, SWORD!
RAGH!
*CLANG
LORD REY!
WHAT ARE YOU DOING HERE?

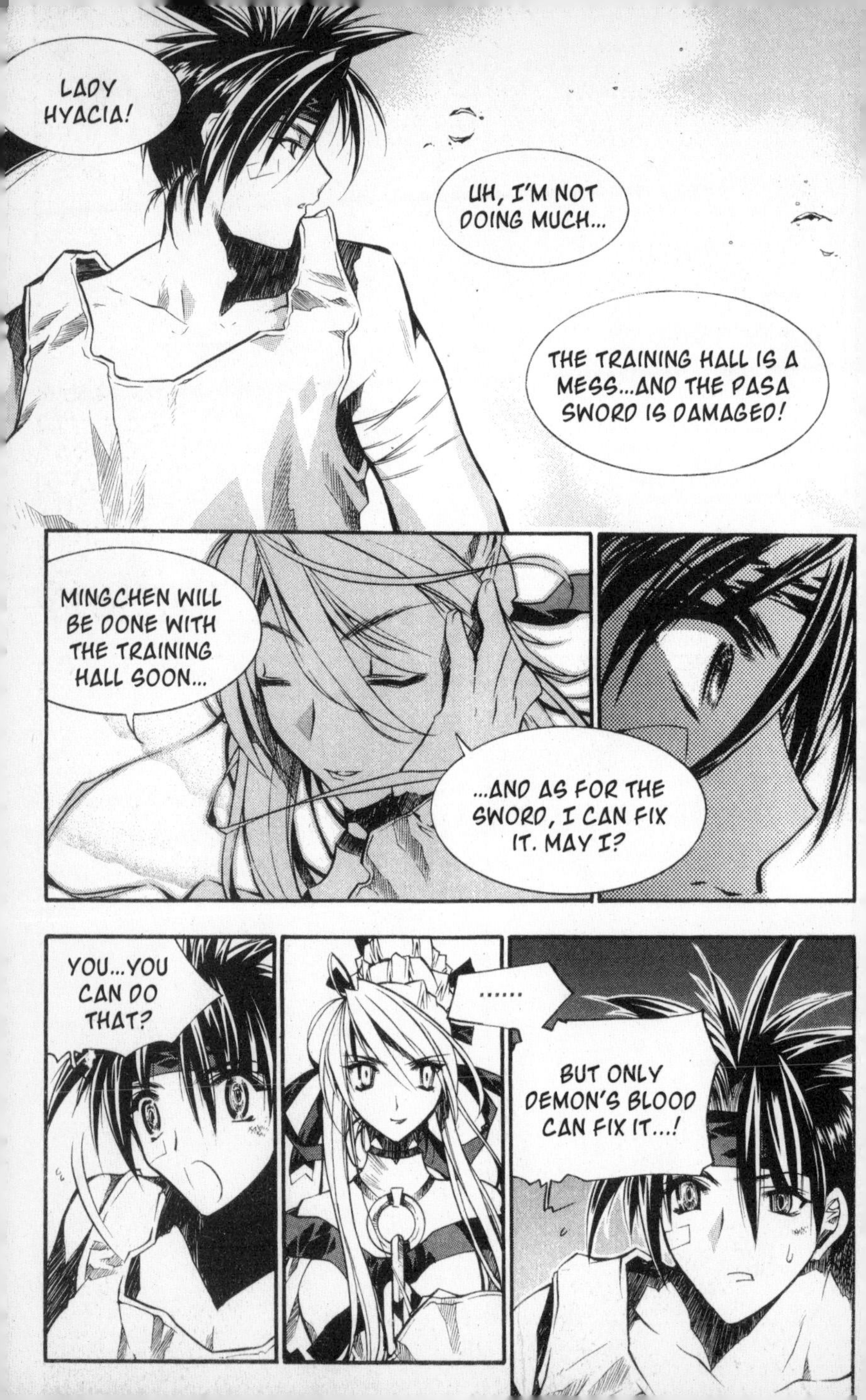
LADY HYACIA!
UH, I'M NOT DOING MUCH...
THE TRAINING HALL IS A MESS...AND THE PASA SWORD IS DAMAGED!
MINGCHEN WILL BE DONE WITH THE TRAINING HALL SOON...
...AND AS FOR THE SWORD, I CAN FIX IT. MAY I?
YOU...YOU CAN DO THAT?
......
BUT ONLY DEMON'S BLOOD CAN FIX IT...!

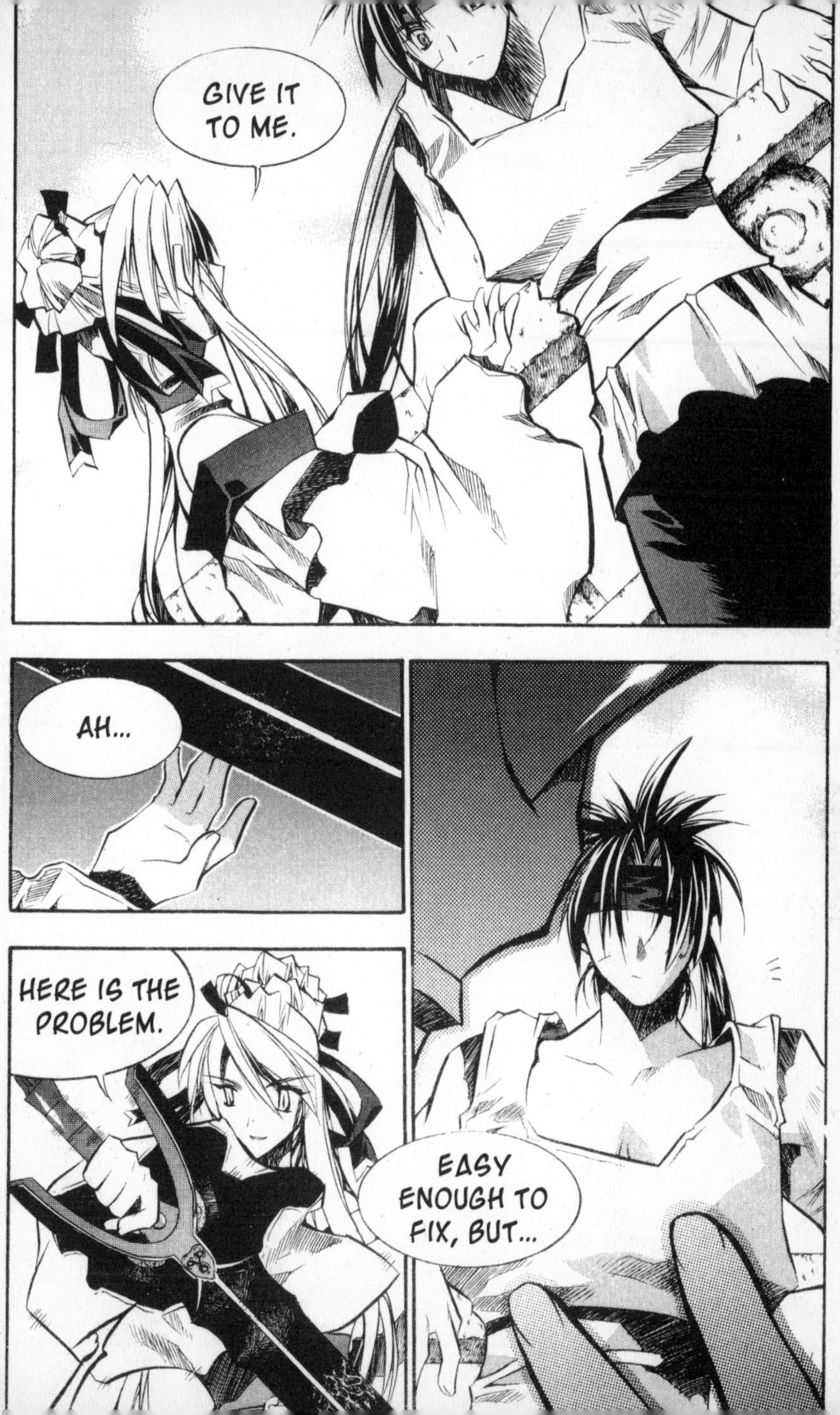
GIVE IT TO ME.
AH...
HERE IS THE PROBLEM.
EASY ENOUGH TO FIX, BUT...

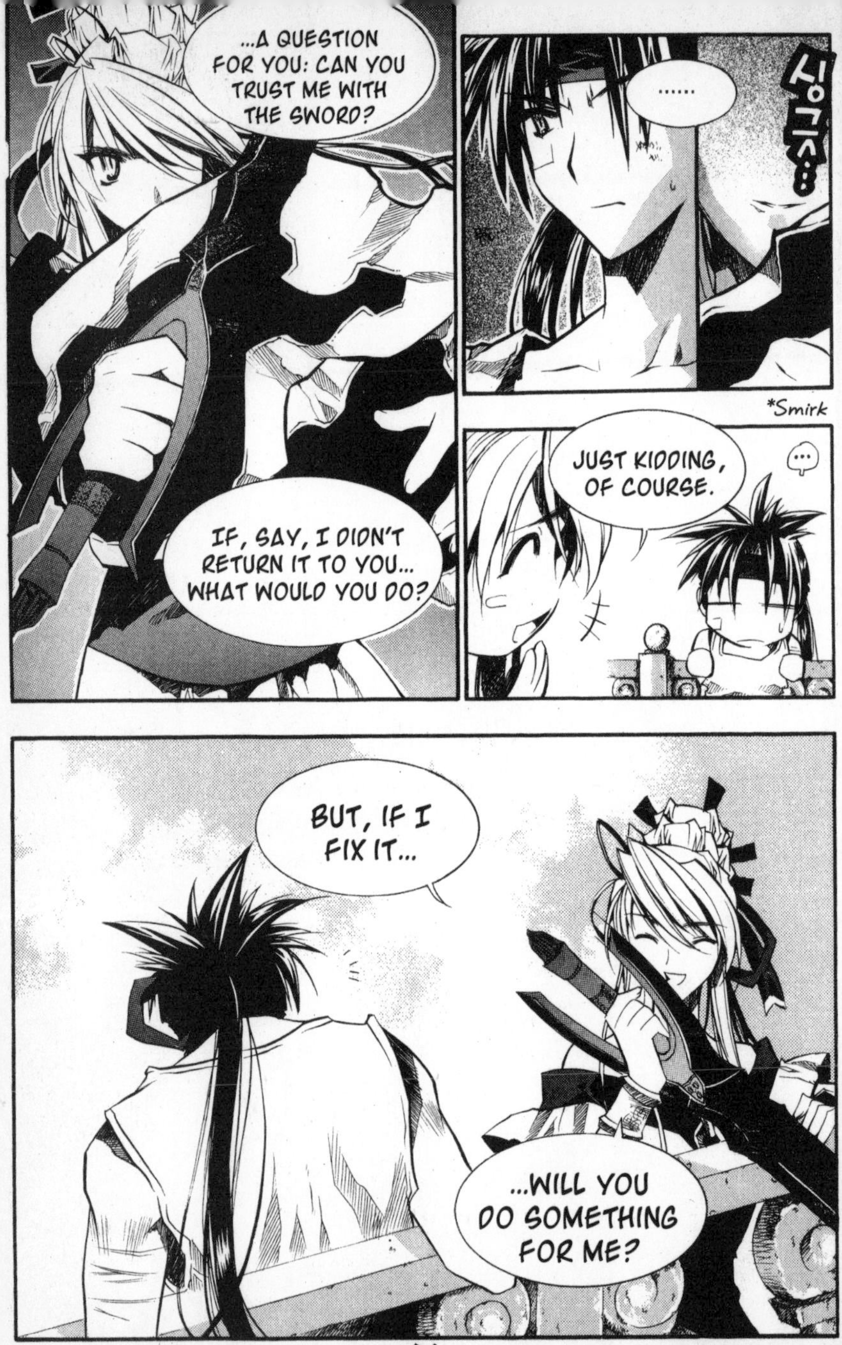
...A QUESTION FOR YOU: CAN YOU TRUST ME WITH THE SWORD?
IF, SAY, I DIDN'T RETURN IT TO YOU... WHAT WOULD YOU DO?
......
*Smirk
JUST KIDDING, OF COURSE.
...
BUT, IF I FIX IT...
...WILL YOU DO SOMETHING FOR ME?

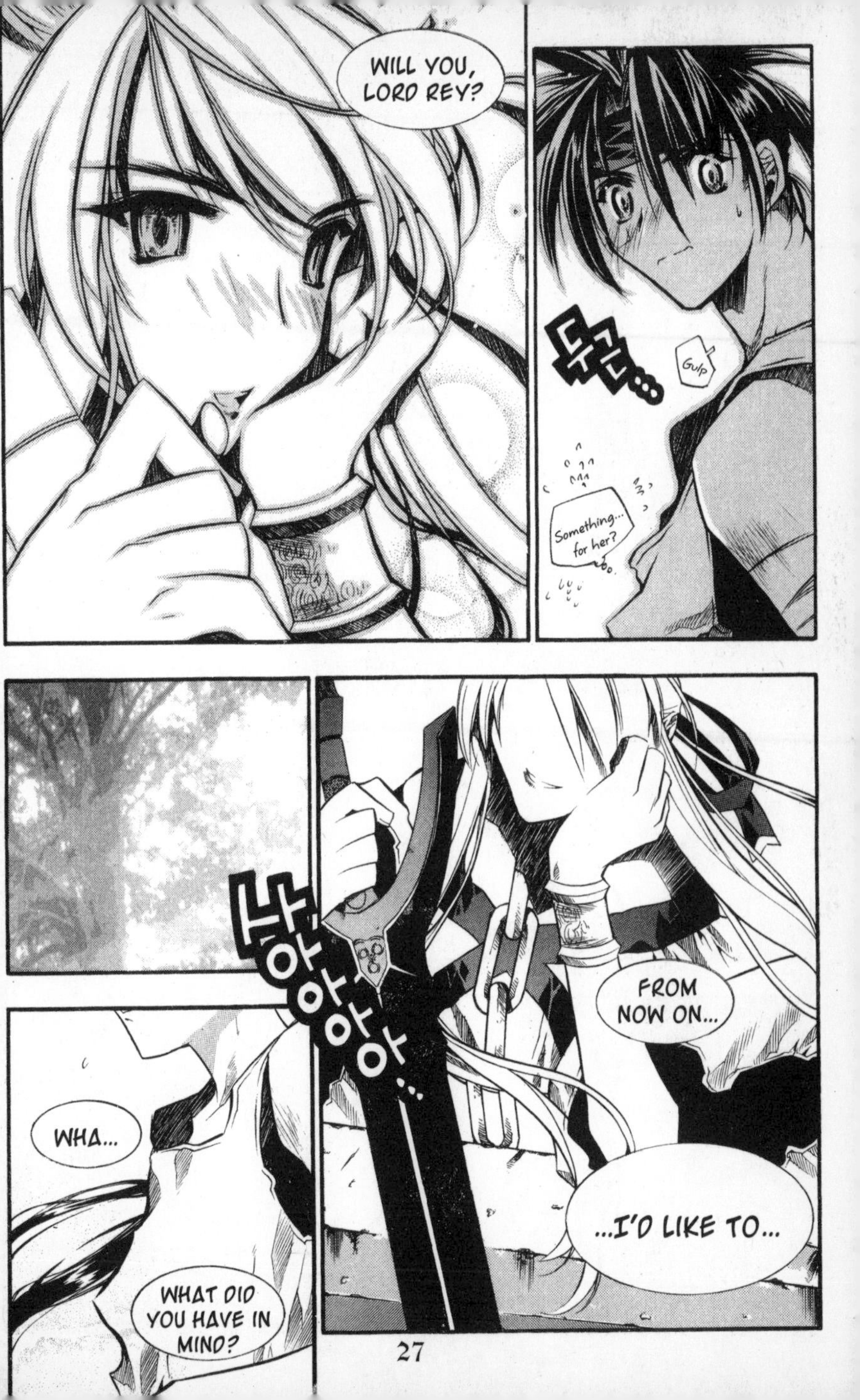

WILL YOU, LORD REY?
Gulp
Something... for her?
WHA...
WHAT DID YOU HAVE IN MIND?
FROM NOW ON...
...I'D LIKE TO...

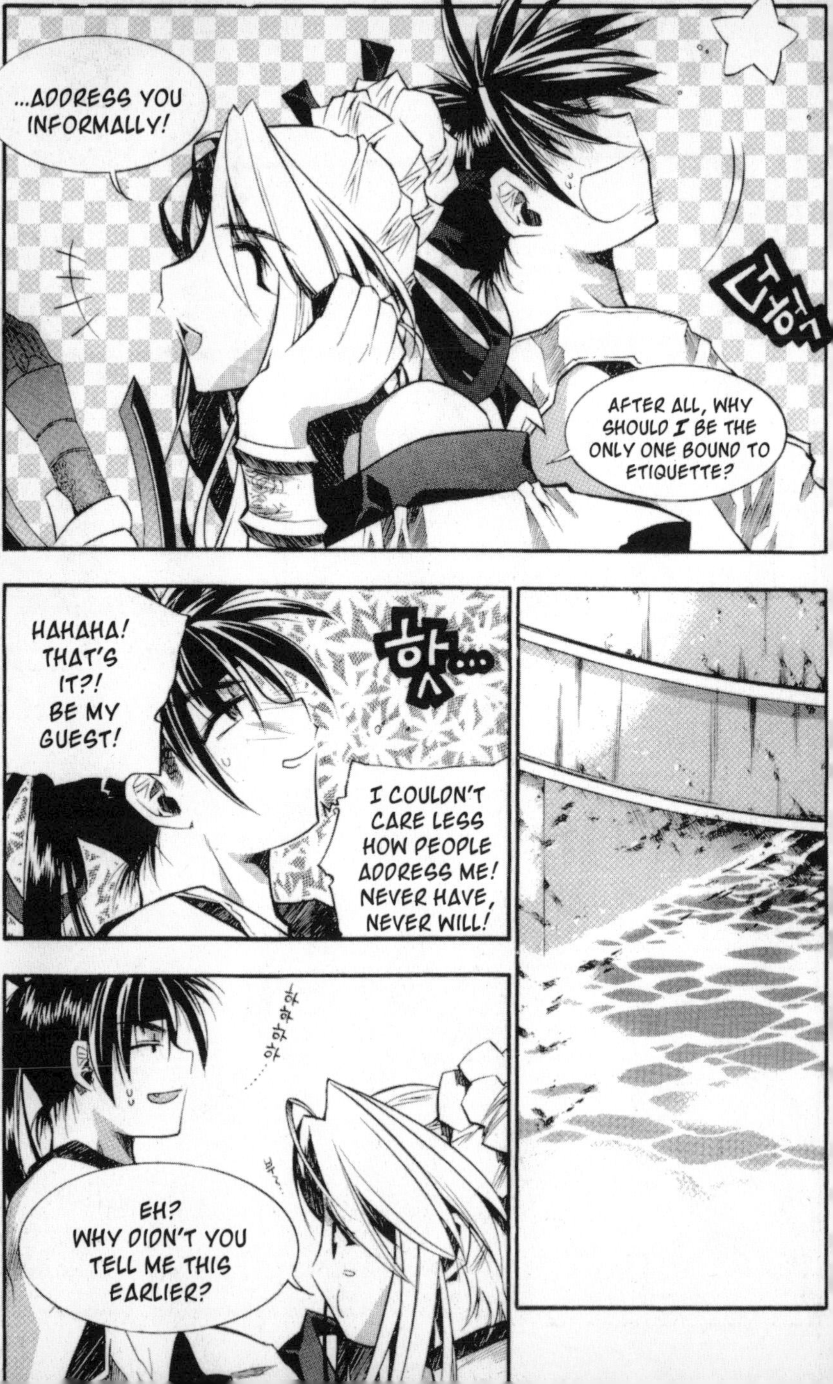
...ADDRESS YOU INFORMALLY!
AFTER ALL, WHY SHOULD I BE THE ONLY ONE BOUND TO ETIQUETTE?
HAHAHA! THAT'S IT?! BE MY GUEST!
핫...
I COULDN'T CARE LESS HOW PEOPLE ADDRESS ME! NEVER HAVE, NEVER WILL!
EH? WHY DIDN'T YOU TELL ME THIS EARLIER?

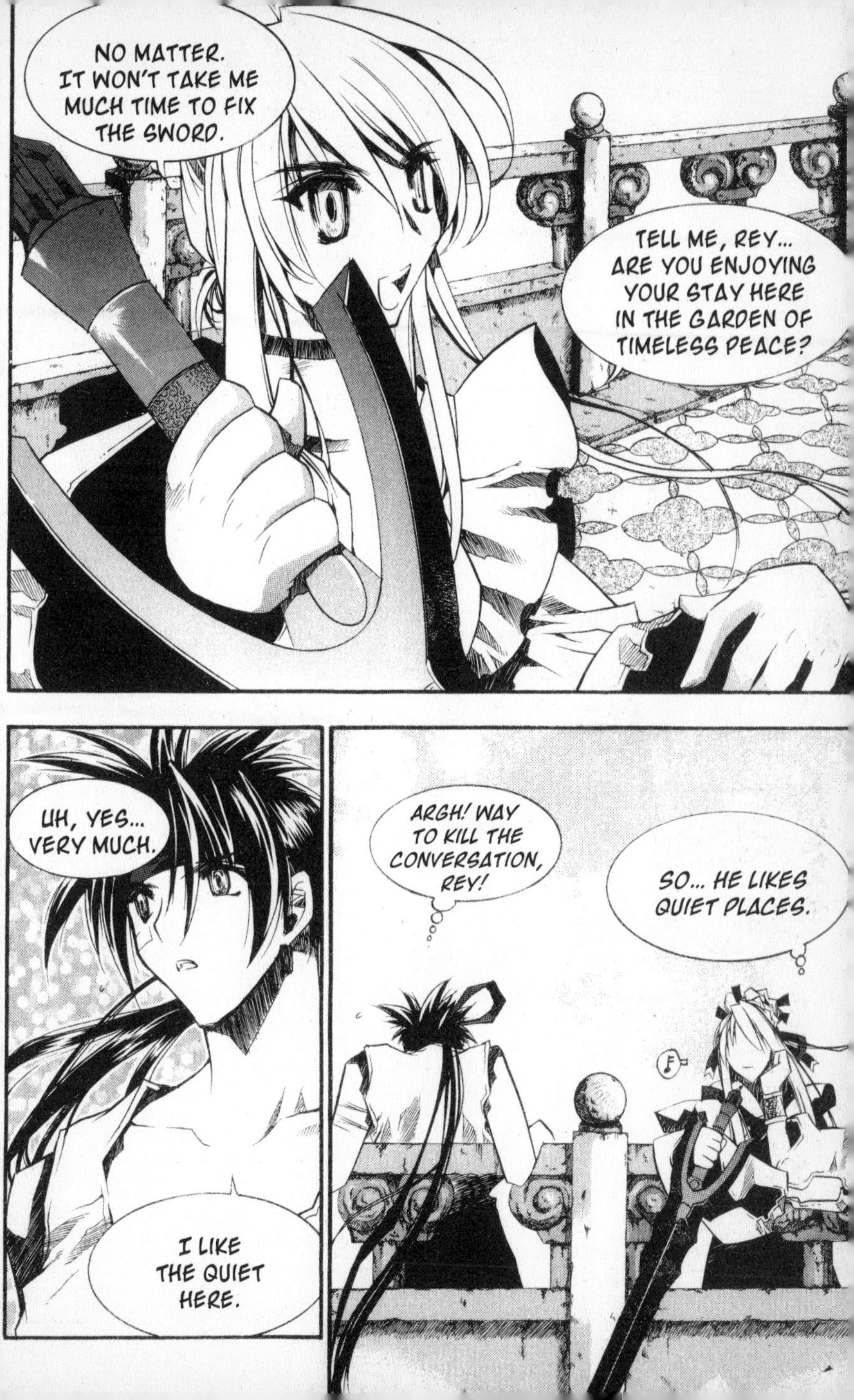
NO MATTER. IT WON'T TAKE ME MUCH TIME TO FIX THE SWORD.
TELL ME, REY... ARE YOU ENJOYING YOUR STAY HERE IN THE GARDEN OF TIMELESS PEACE?
UH, YES... VERY MUCH.
I LIKE THE QUIET HERE.
ARGH! WAY TO KILL THE CONVERSATION, REY!
SO... HE LIKES QUIET PLACES.

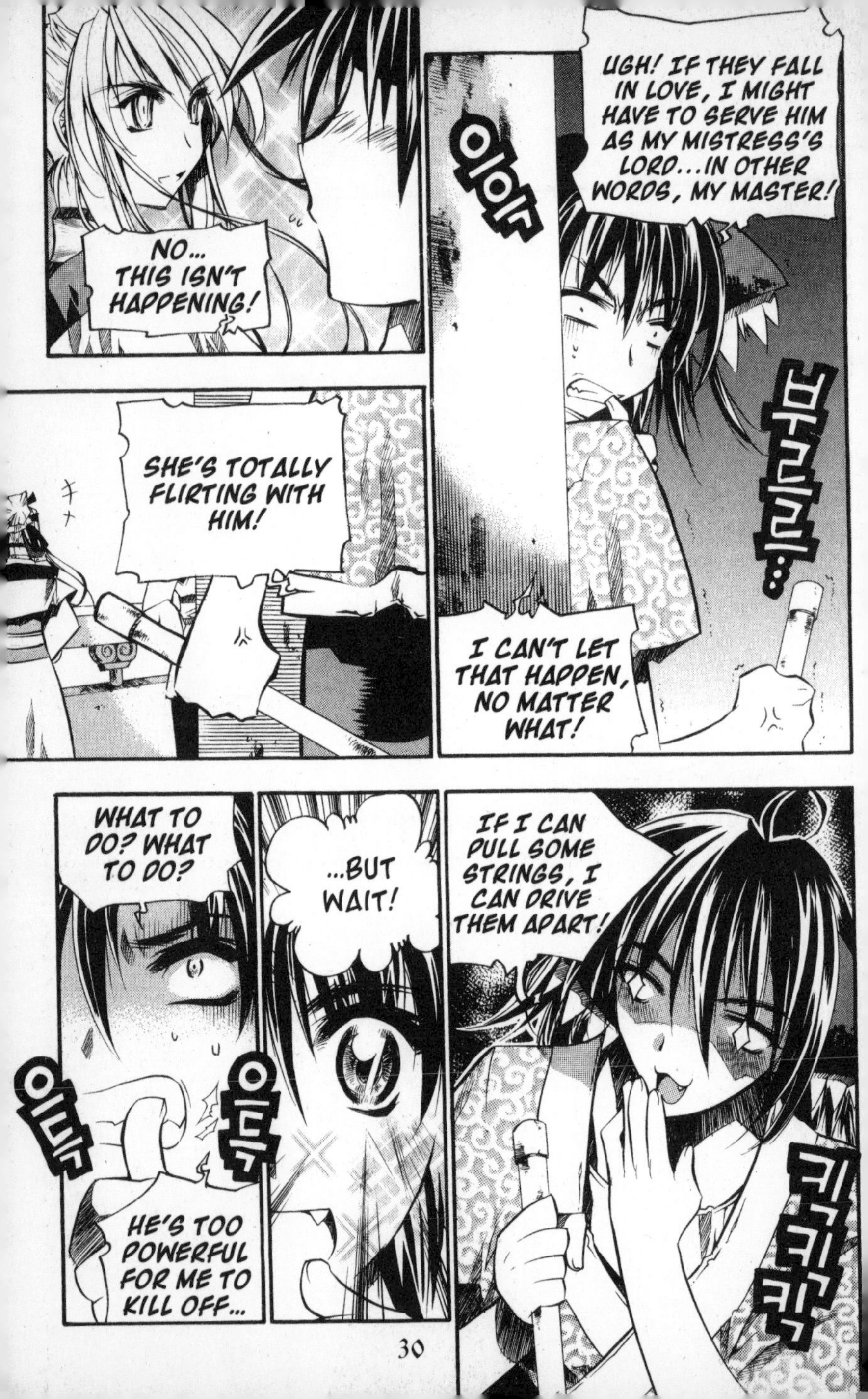
NO... THIS ISN'T HAPPENING!
SHE'S TOTALLY FLIRTING WITH HIM!
UGH! IF THEY FALL IN LOVE, I MIGHT HAVE TO SERVE HIM AS MY MISTRESS'S LORD...IN OTHER WORDS, MY MASTER!
I CAN'T LET THAT HAPPEN, NO MATTER WHAT!
WHAT TO DO? WHAT TO DO?
HE'S TOO POWERFUL FOR ME TO KILL OFF...
...BUT WAIT!
IF I CAN PULL SOME STRINGS, I CAN DRIVE THEM APART!

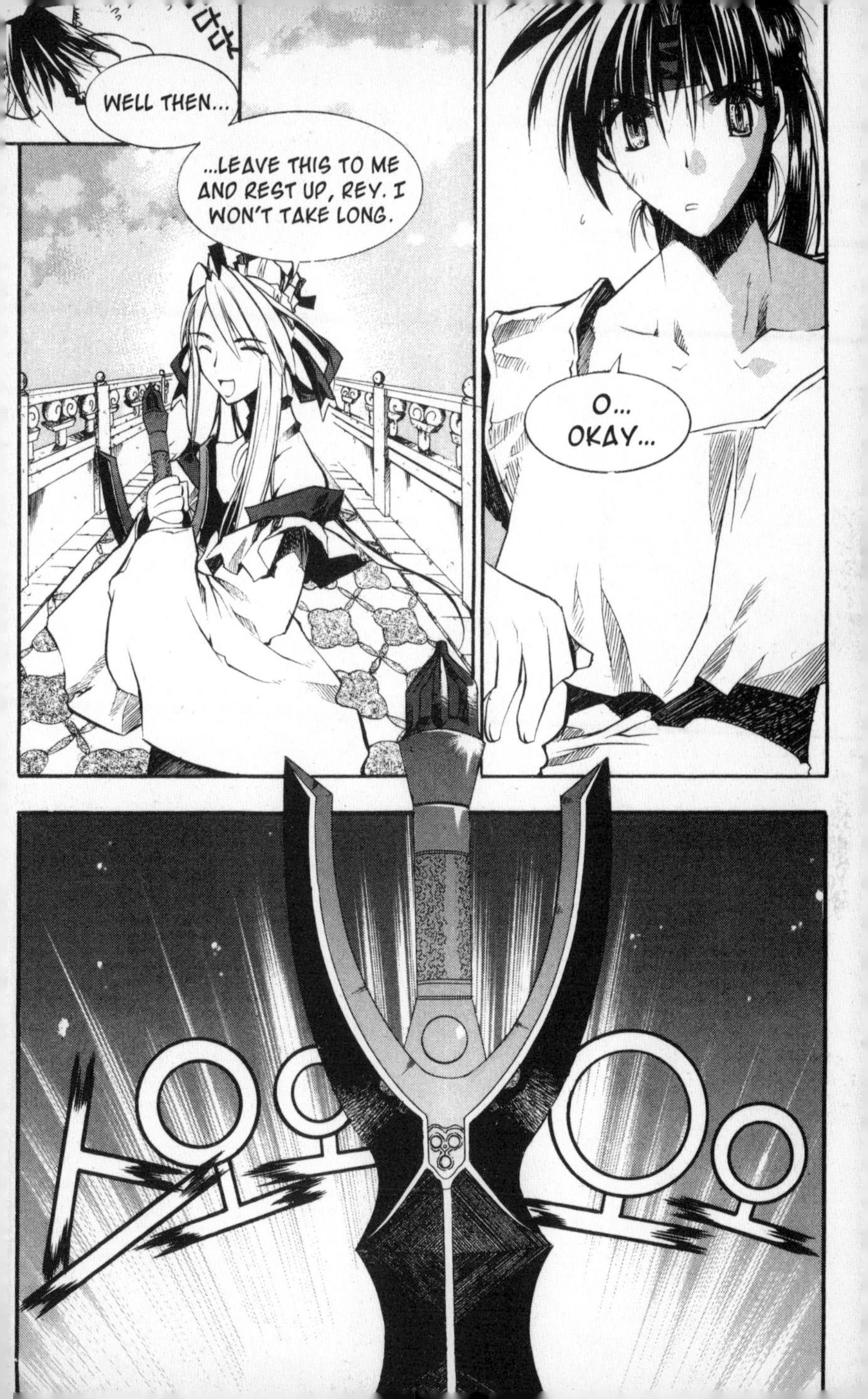
WELL THEN...
...LEAVE THIS TO ME AND REST UP, REY. I WON'T TAKE LONG.
O... OKAY...

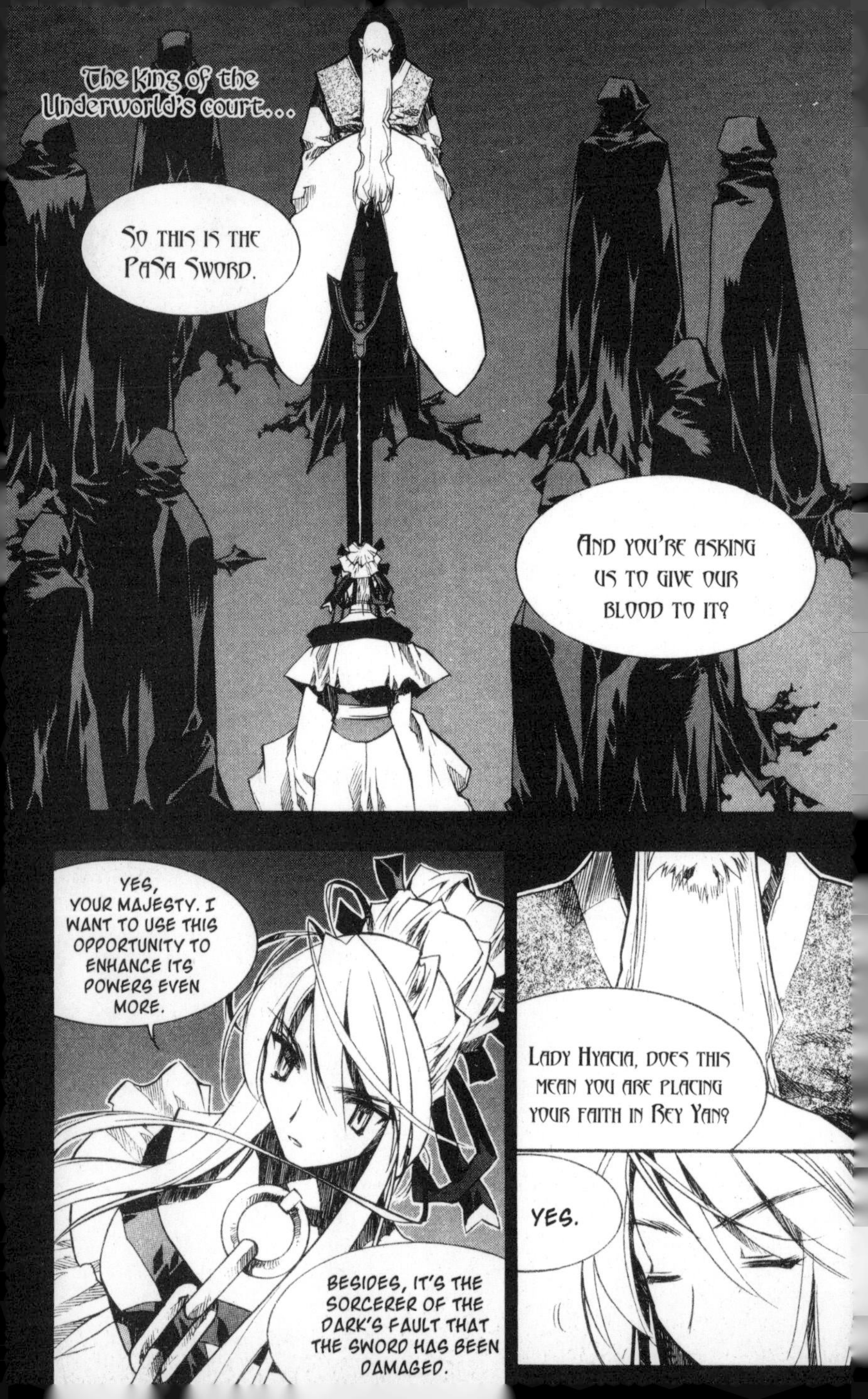
The King of the Underworld's court...
SO THIS IS THE PASA SWORD.
AND YOU'RE ASKING US TO GIVE OUR BLOOD TO IT?
YES, YOUR MAJESTY. I WANT TO USE THIS OPPORTUNITY TO ENHANCE ITS POWERS EVEN MORE.
BESIDES, IT'S THE SORCERER OF THE DARK'S FAULT THAT THE SWORD HAS BEEN DAMAGED.
LADY HYACIA, DOES THIS MEAN YOU ARE PLACING YOUR FAITH IN REY YAN?
YES.

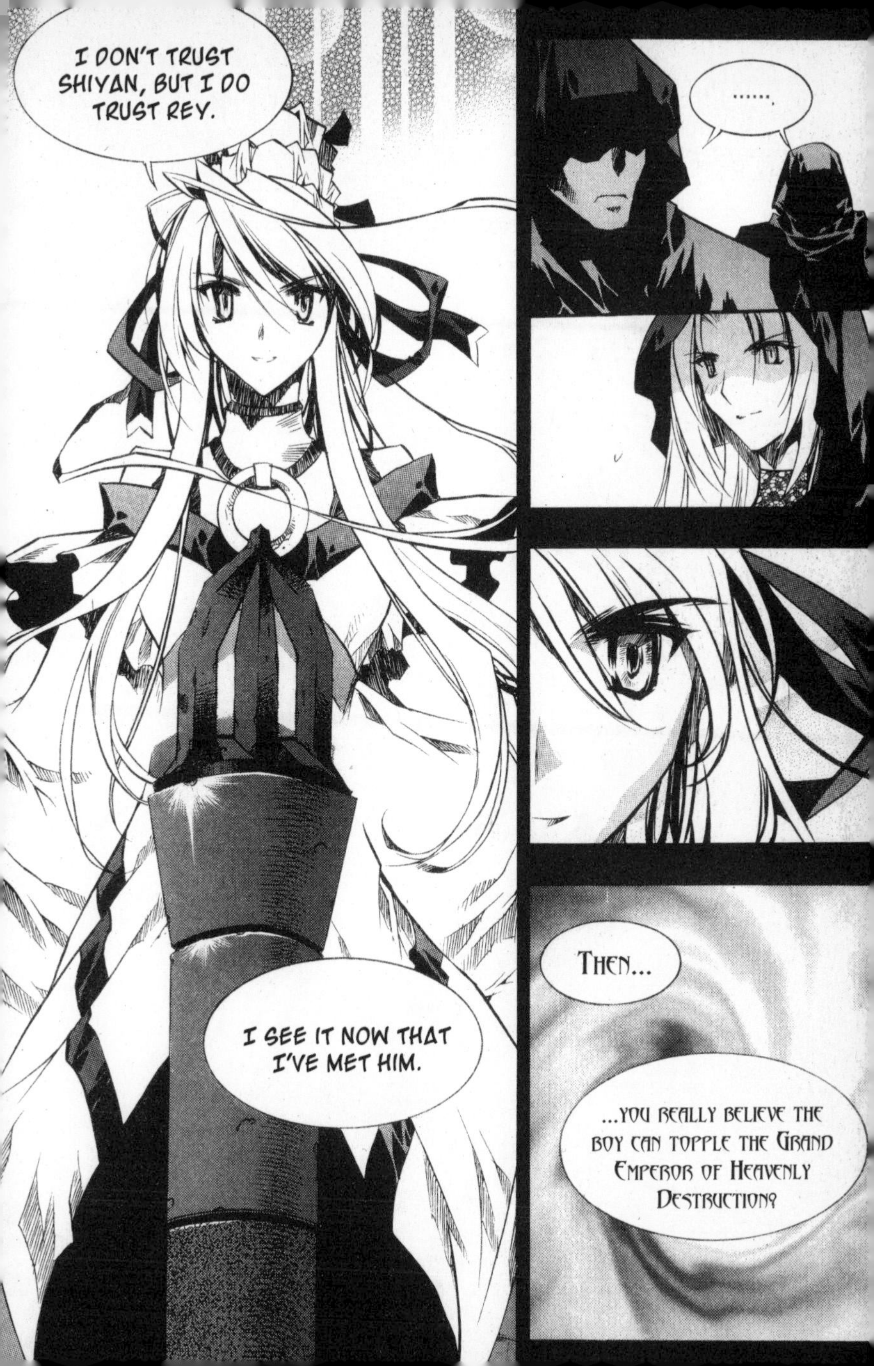
I DON'T TRUST SHIYAN, BUT I DO TRUST REY.
I SEE IT NOW THAT I'VE MET HIM.
......
THEN...
...YOU REALLY BELIEVE THE BOY CAN TOPPLE THE GRAND EMPEROR OF HEAVENLY DESTRUCTION?

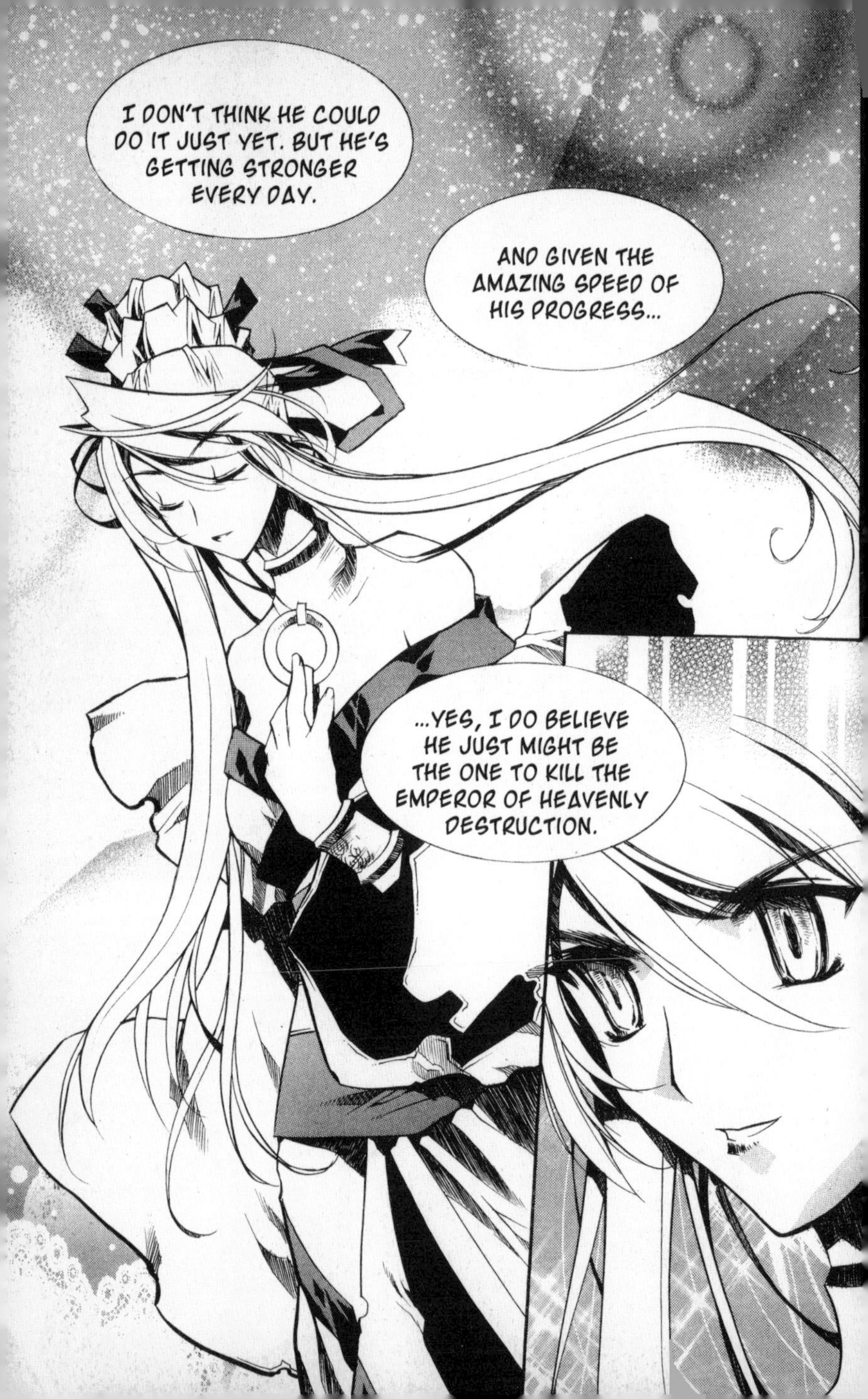
I DON'T THINK HE COULD DO IT JUST YET. BUT HE'S GETTING STRONGER EVERY DAY.
AND GIVEN THE AMAZING SPEED OF HIS PROGRESS...
...YES, I DO BELIEVE HE JUST MIGHT BE THE ONE TO KILL THE EMPEROR OF HEAVENLY DESTRUCTION.

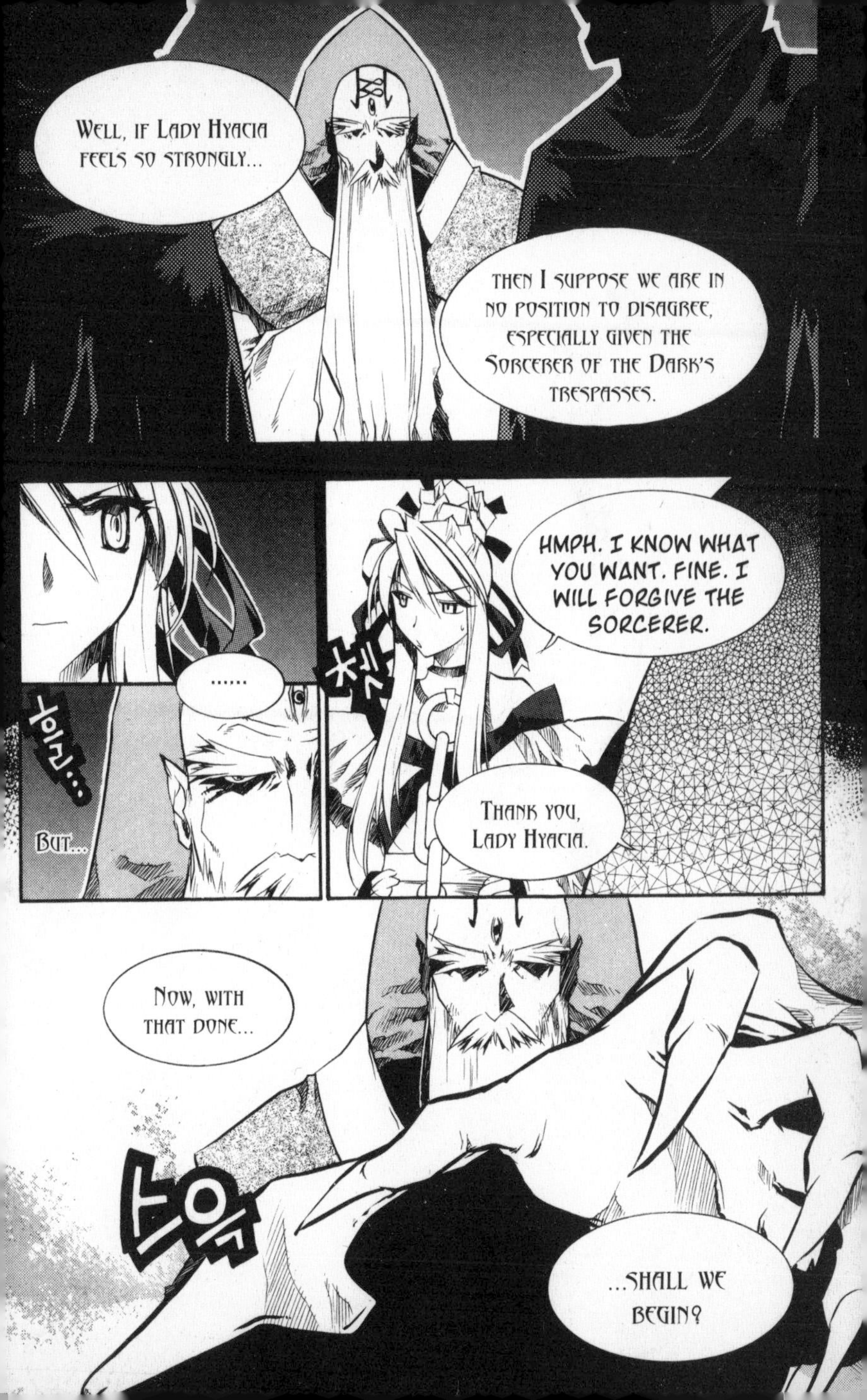
Well, if Lady Hyacia feels so strongly...
then I suppose we are in no position to disagree, especially given the Sorcerer of the Dark's trespasses.
......
But...
Hmph. I know what you want. Fine. I will forgive the sorcerer.
Thank you, Lady Hyacia.
Now, with that done...
...shall we begin?

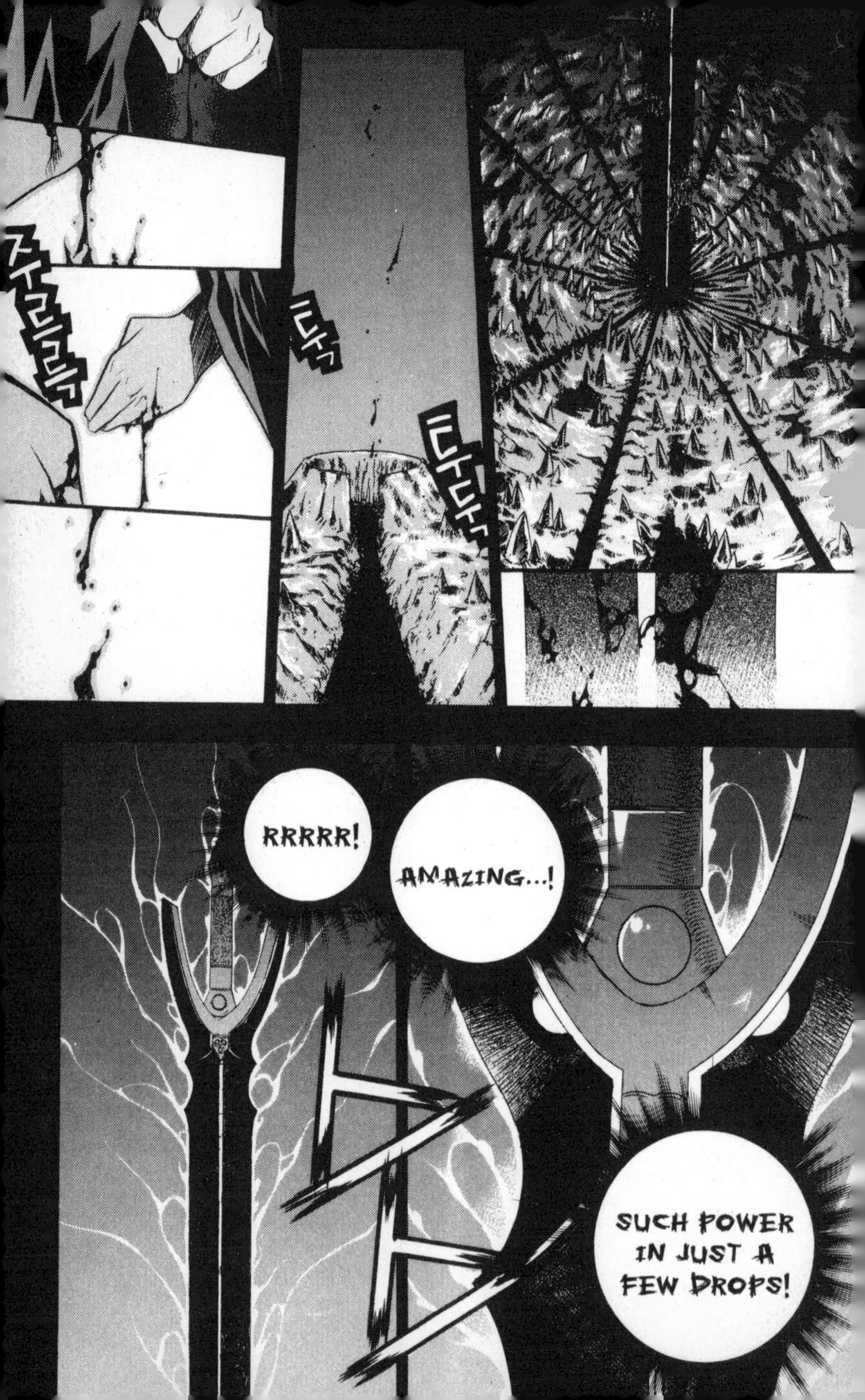
RRRRR!
AMAZING...!
SUCH POWER IN JUST A FEW DROPS!

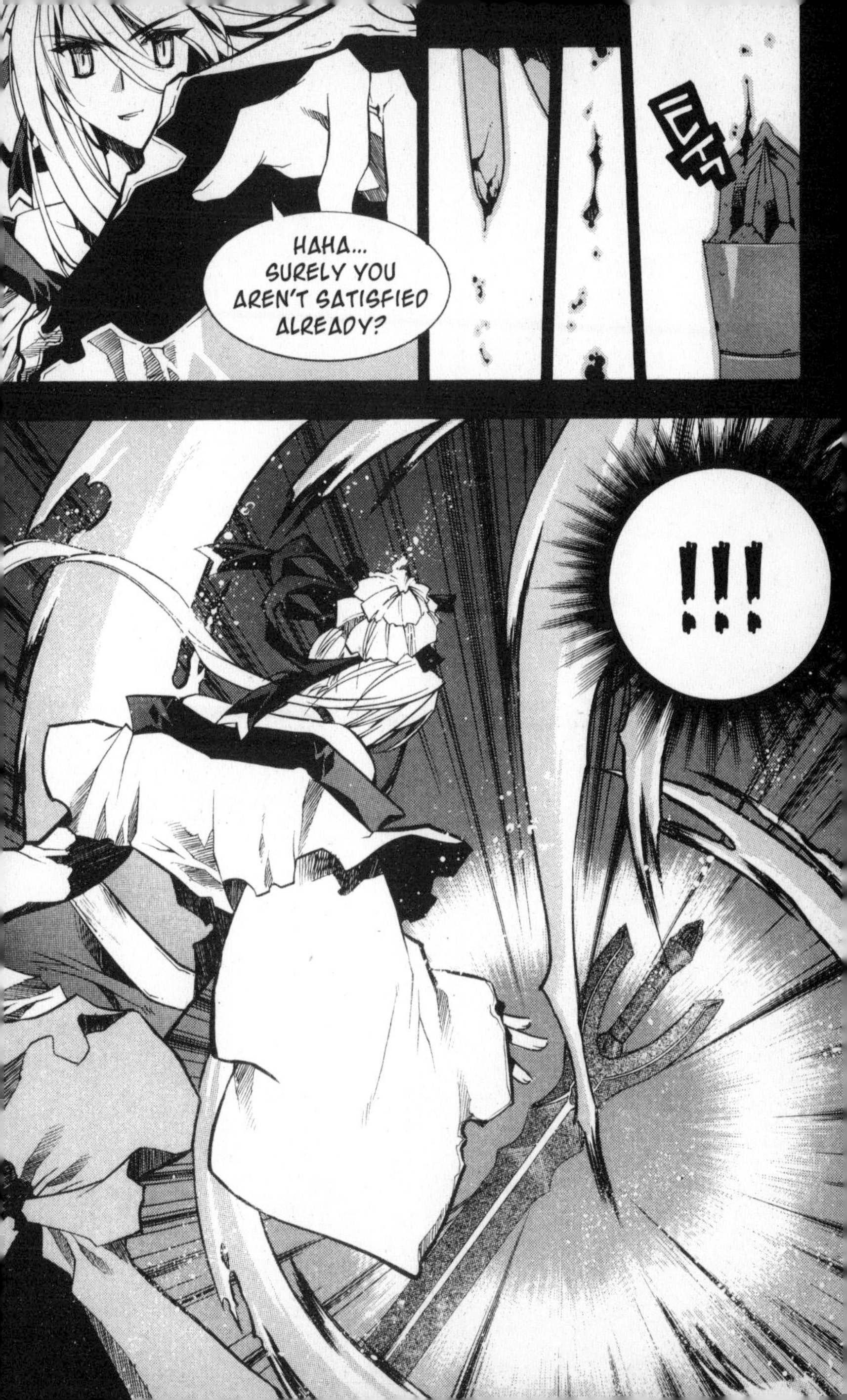
HAHA... SURELY YOU AREN'T SATISFIED ALREADY?
!!!

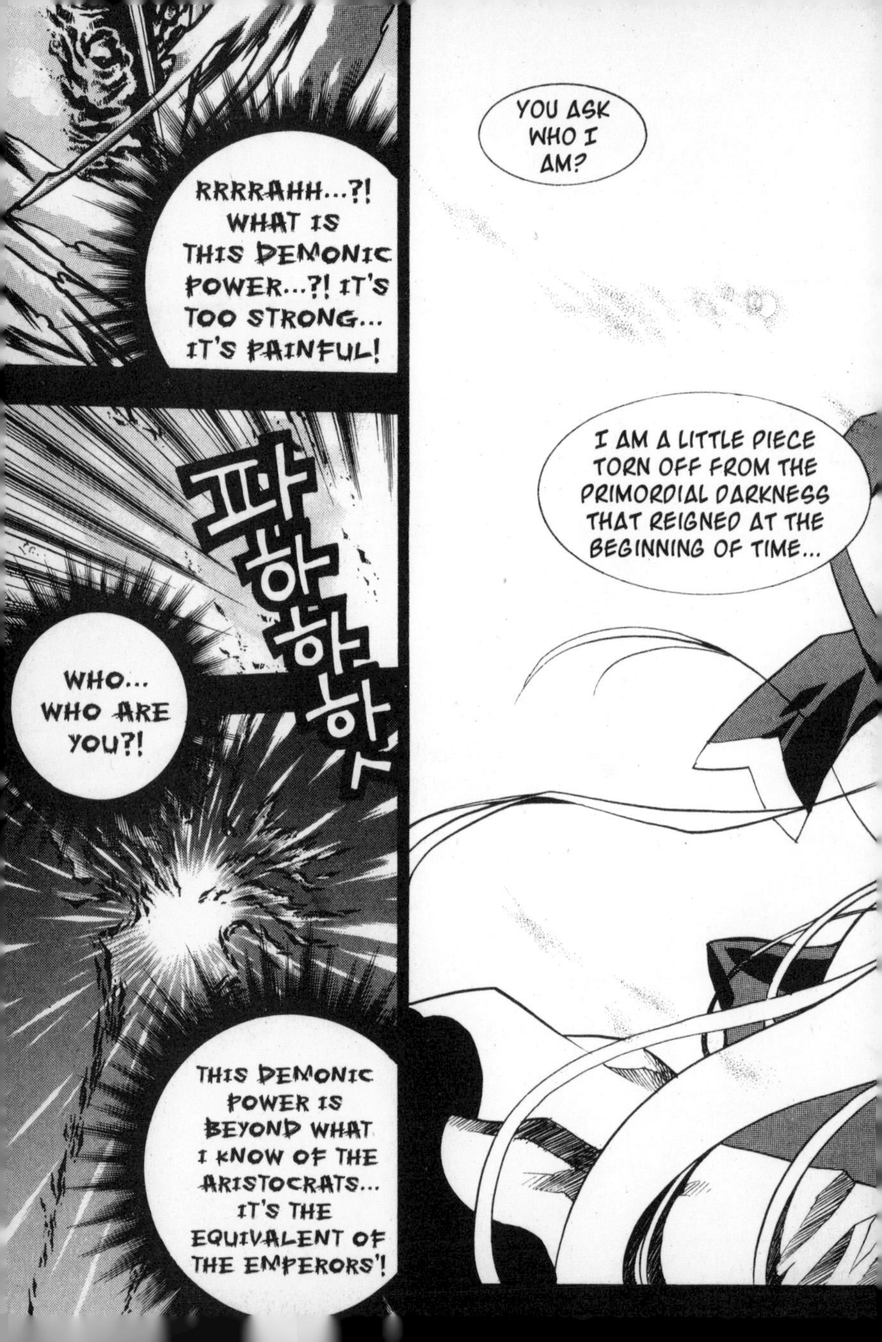
RRRRAHH...?! WHAT IS THIS DEMONIC POWER...?! IT'S TOO STRONG... IT'S PAINFUL!
파하하핫
WHO... WHO ARE YOU?!
THIS DEMONIC POWER IS BEYOND WHAT I KNOW OF THE ARISTOCRATS... IT'S THE EQUIVALENT OF THE EMPERORS'!
YOU ASK WHO I AM?
I AM A LITTLE PIECE TORN OFF FROM THE PRIMORDIAL DARKNESS THAT REIGNED AT THE BEGINNING OF TIME...

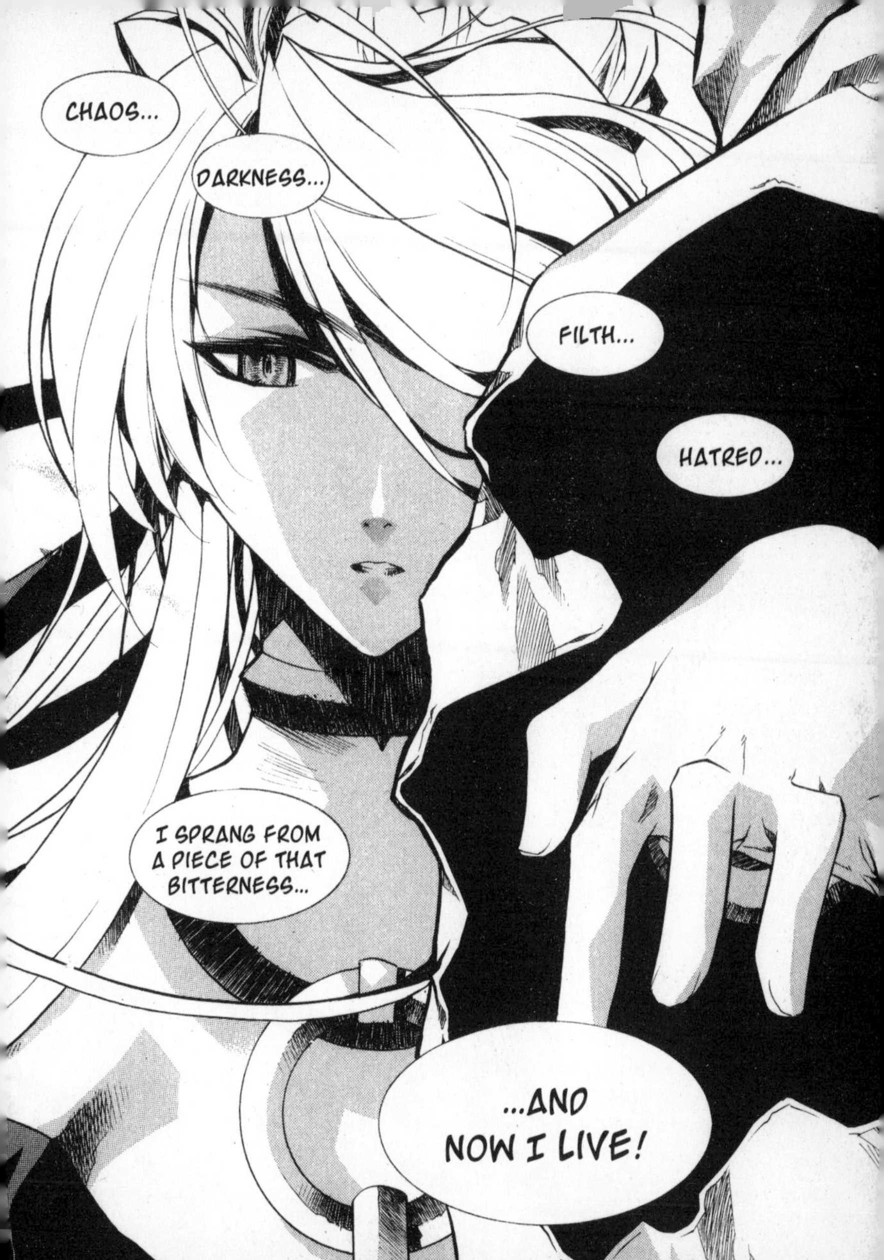
CHAOS...
DARKNESS...
FILTH...
HATRED...
I SPRANG FROM A PIECE OF THAT BITTERNESS...
...AND NOW I LIVE!

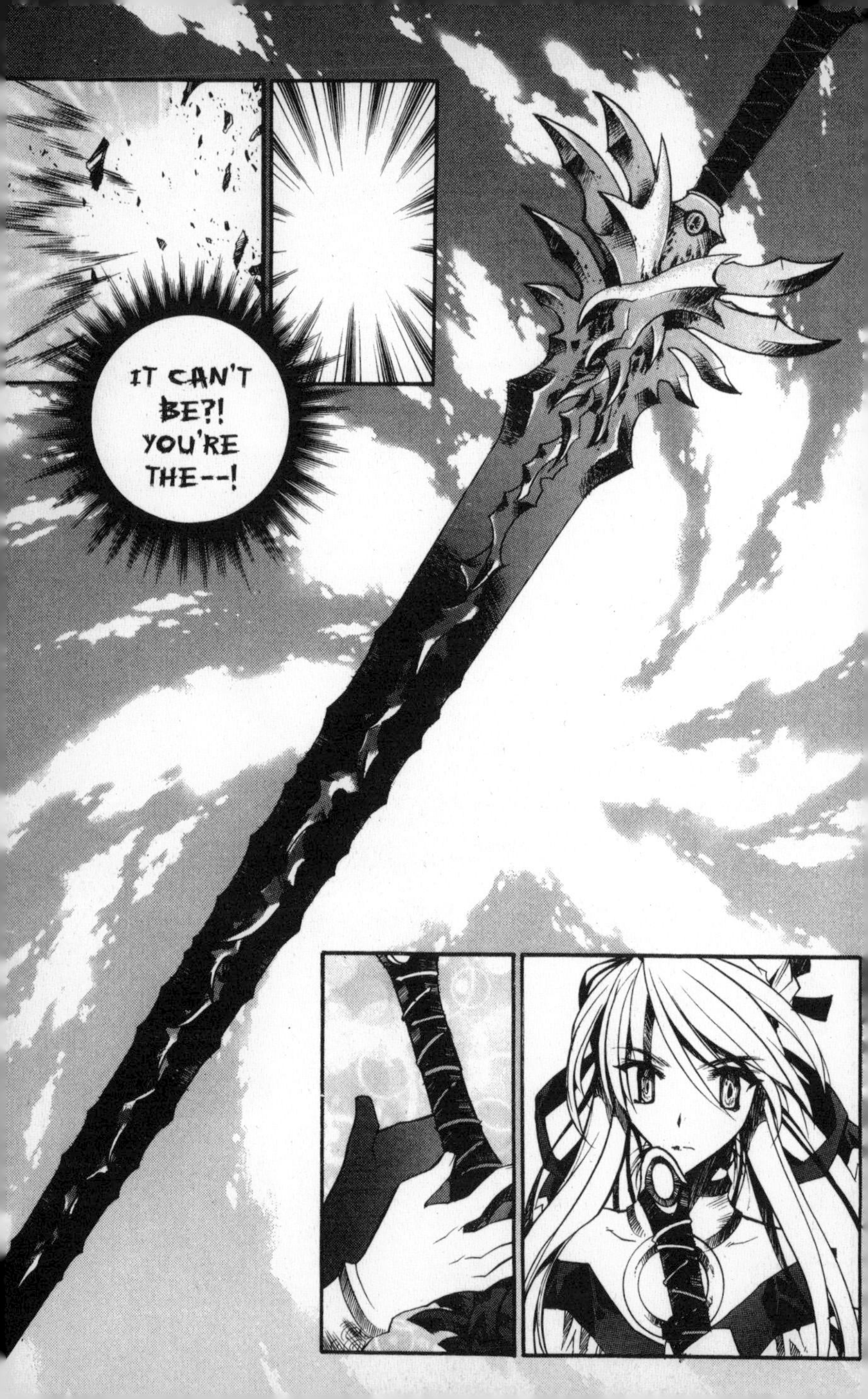
IT CAN'T BE?! YOU'RE THE--!

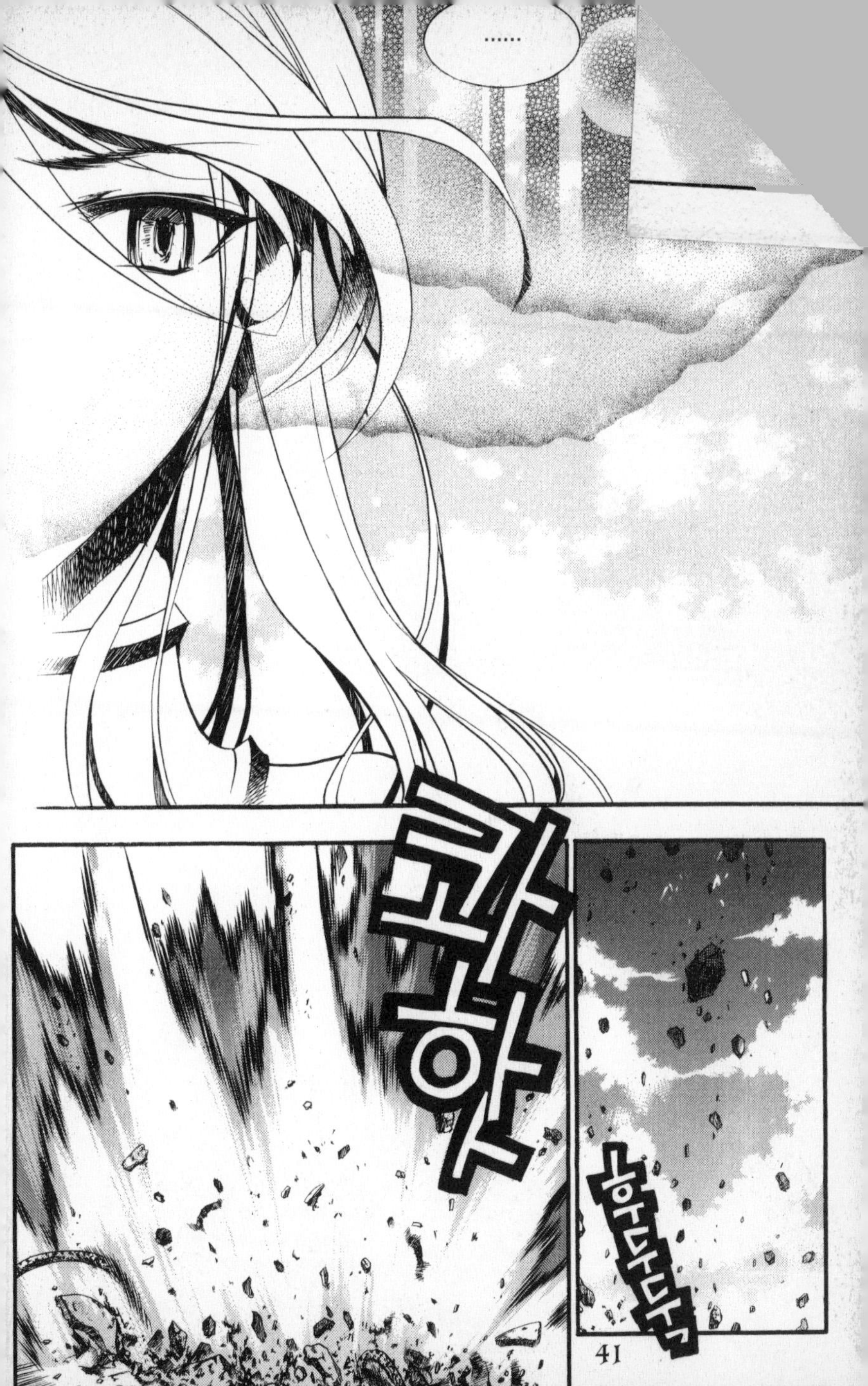
......
콰앙
후ㄷㄷㄷ

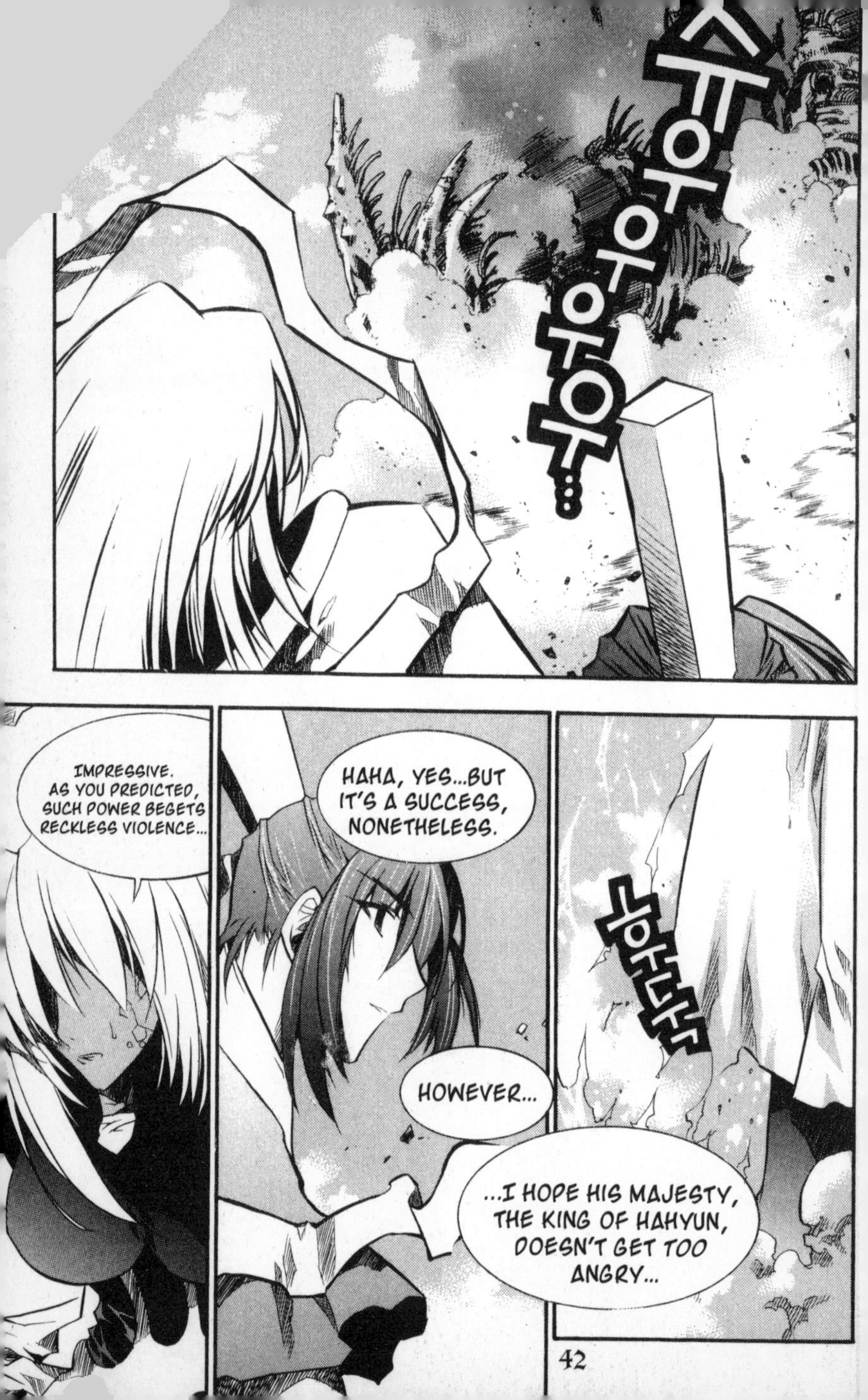
IMPRESSIVE. AS YOU PREDICTED, SUCH POWER BEGETS RECKLESS VIOLENCE...
HAHA, YES...BUT IT'S A SUCCESS, NONETHELESS.
HOWEVER...
...I HOPE HIS MAJESTY, THE KING OF HAHYUN, DOESN'T GET TOO ANGRY...

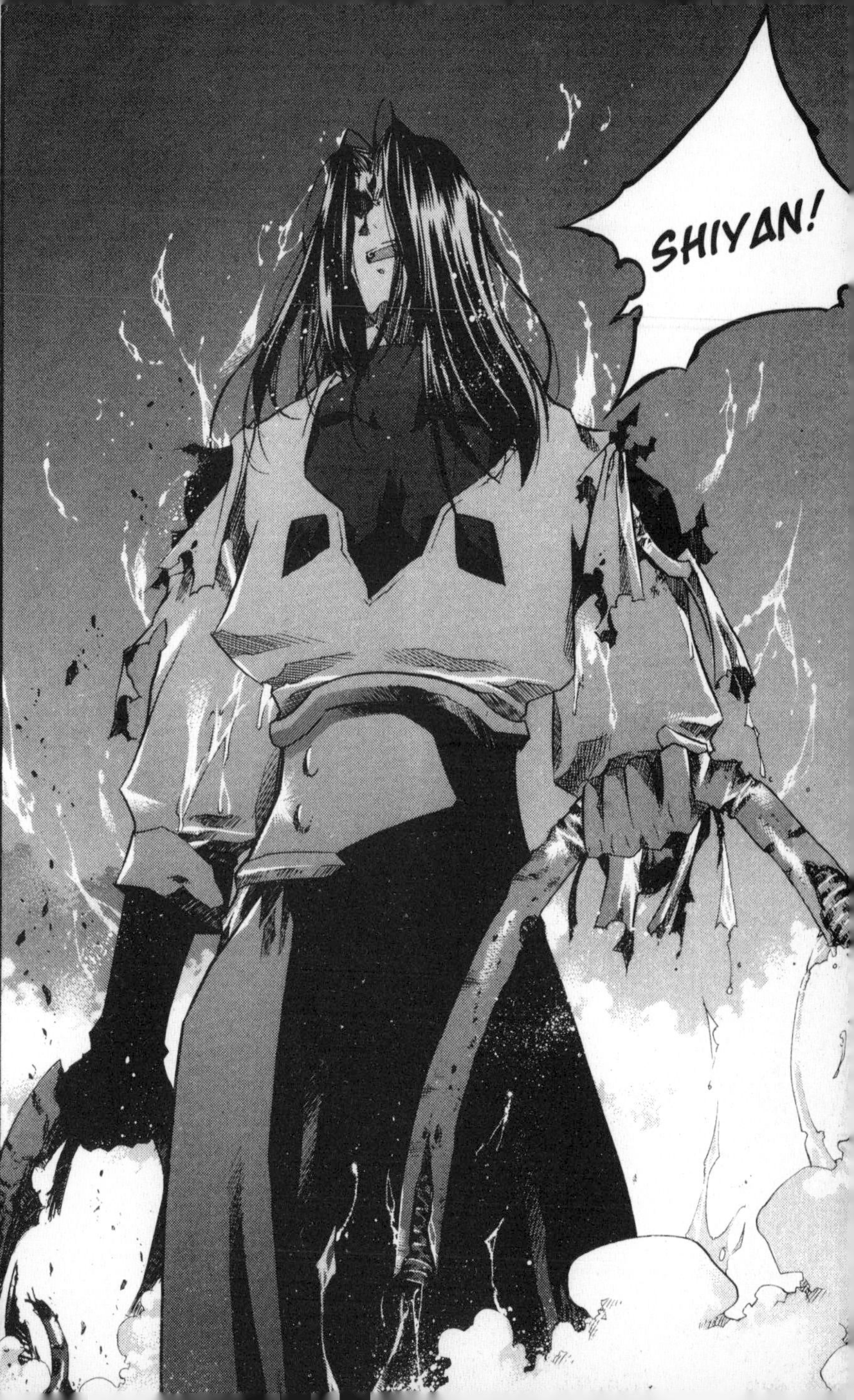
SHIYAN!

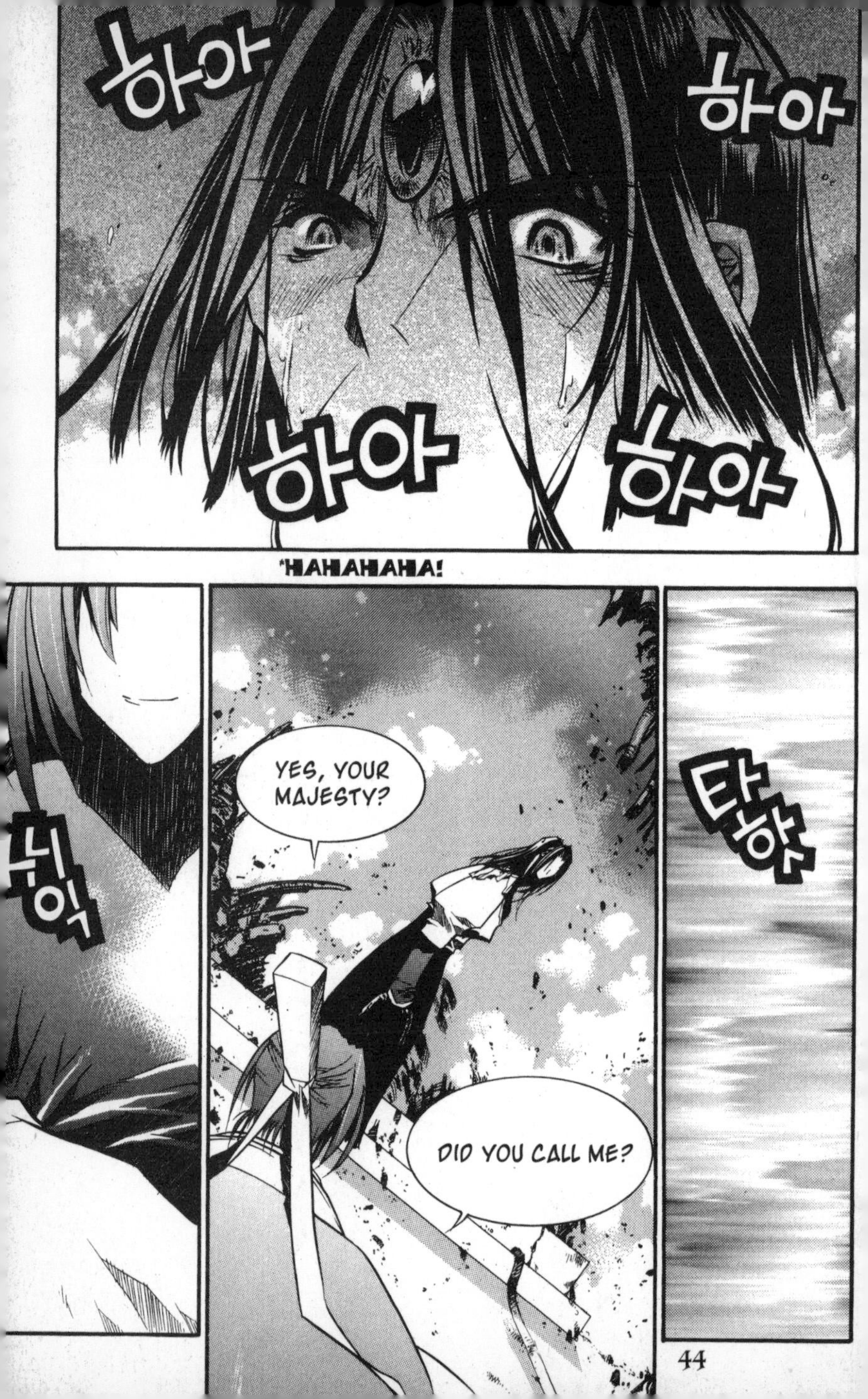
하아
하아
하아
하아
*HAHAHAHA!
YES, YOUR MAJESTY?
DID YOU CALL ME?
타앗

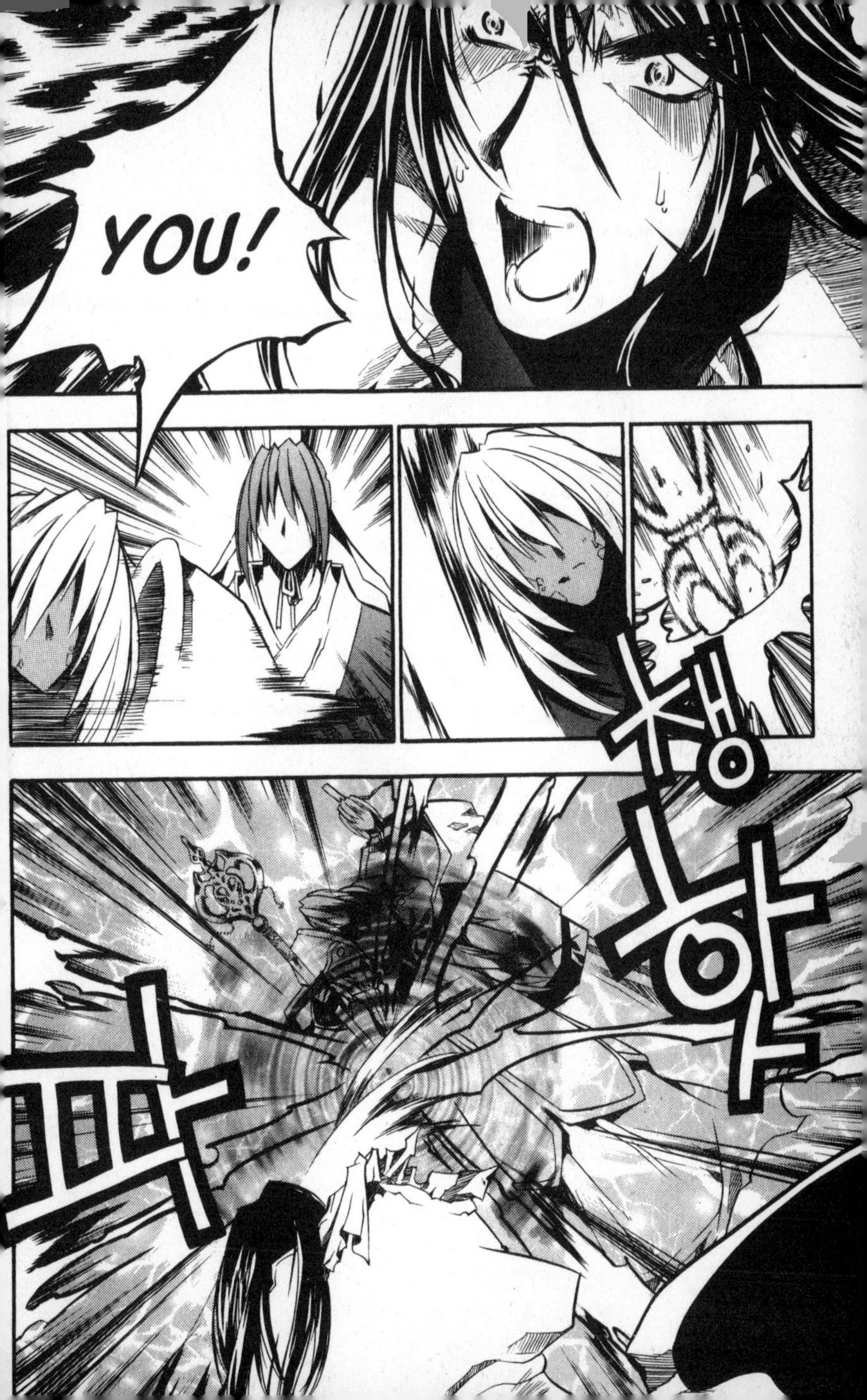
YOU!

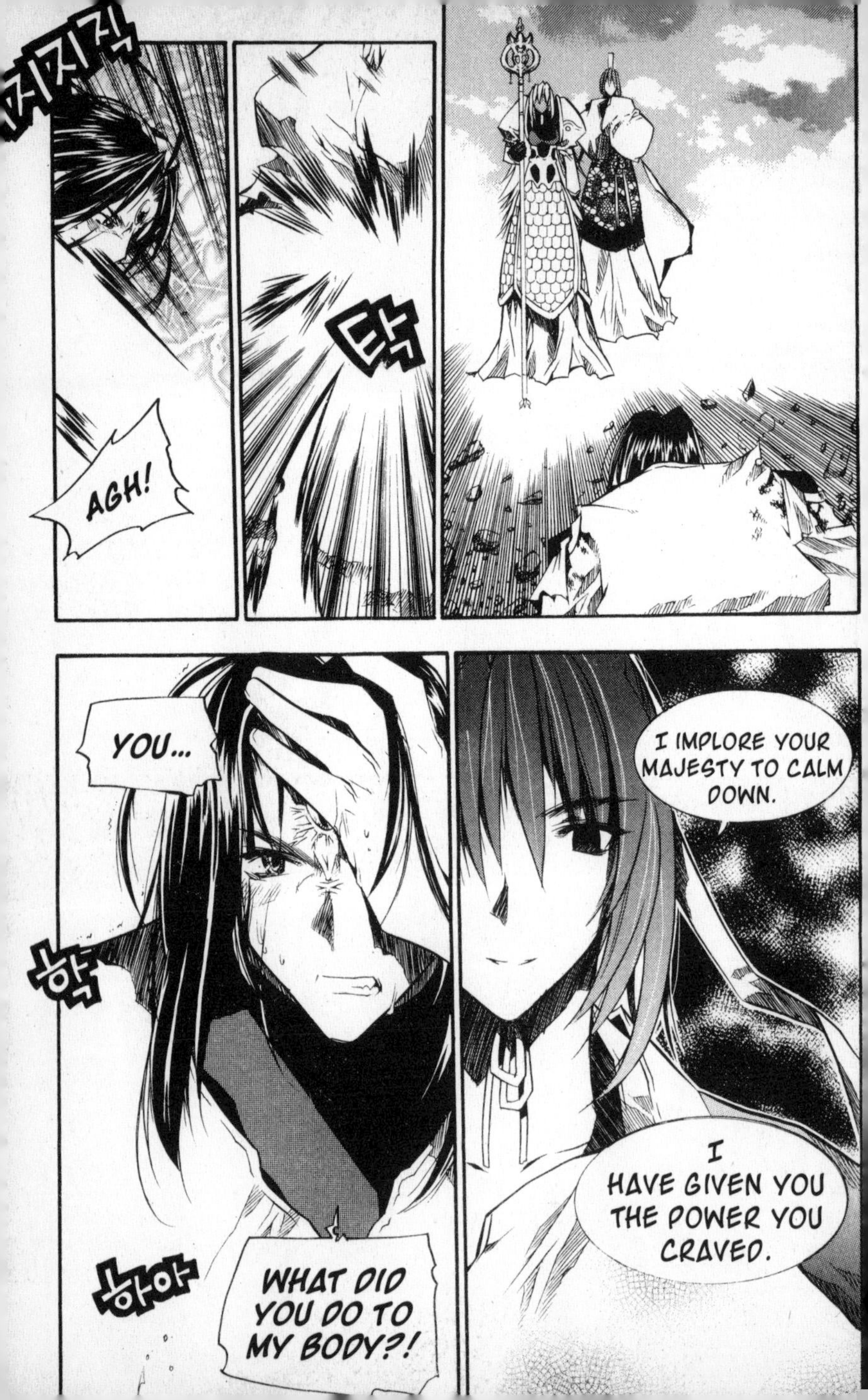
찌지직
AGH!
탁
YOU...
학
하아
WHAT DID YOU DO TO MY BODY?!
I IMPLORE YOUR MAJESTY TO CALM DOWN.
I HAVE GIVEN YOU THE POWER YOU CRAVED.

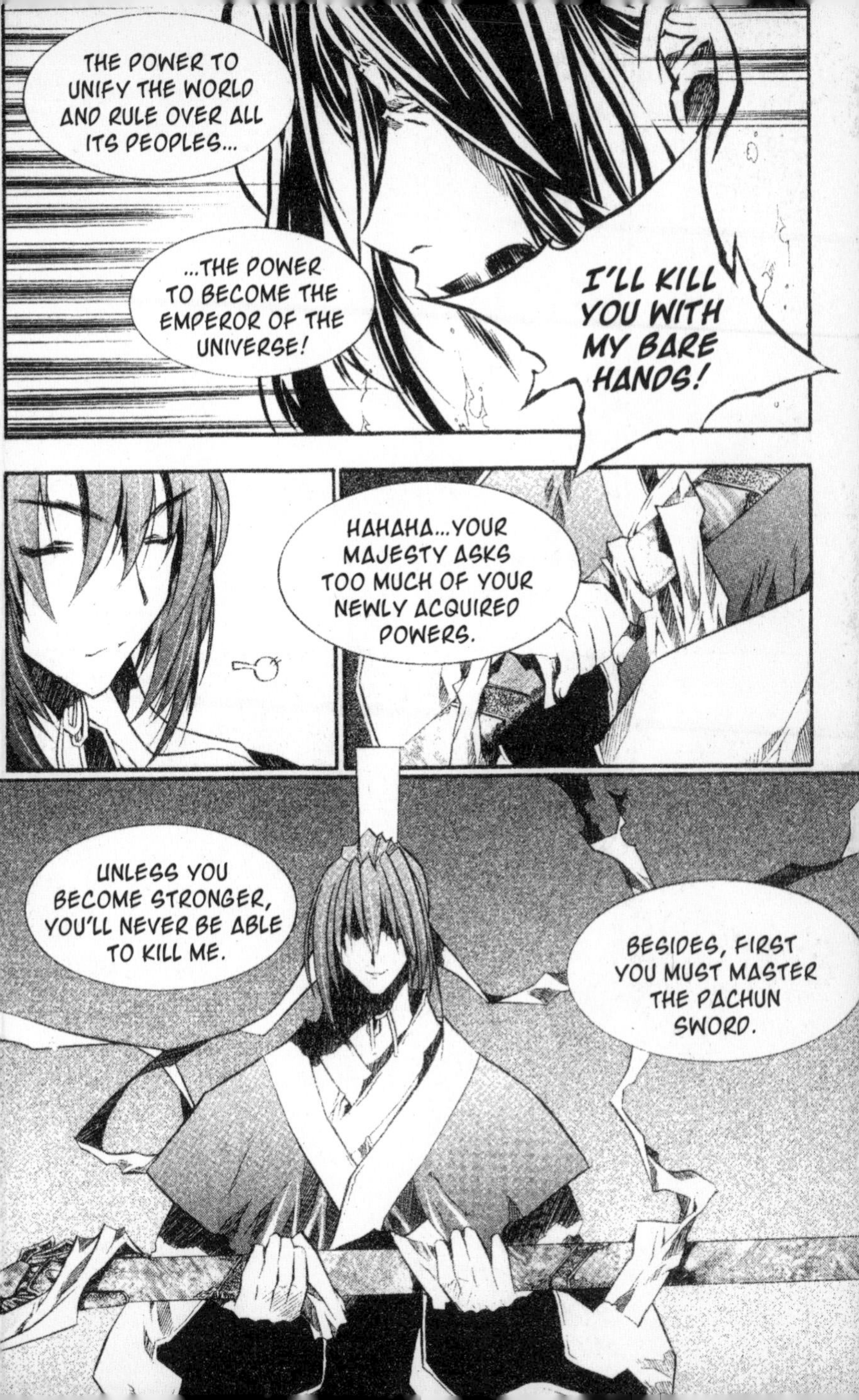
THE POWER TO UNIFY THE WORLD AND RULE OVER ALL ITS PEOPLES...
...THE POWER TO BECOME THE EMPEROR OF THE UNIVERSE!
I'LL KILL YOU WITH MY BARE HANDS!
HAHAHA...YOUR MAJESTY ASKS TOO MUCH OF YOUR NEWLY ACQUIRED POWERS.
UNLESS YOU BECOME STRONGER, YOU'LL NEVER BE ABLE TO KILL ME.
BESIDES, FIRST YOU MUST MASTER THE PACHUN SWORD.

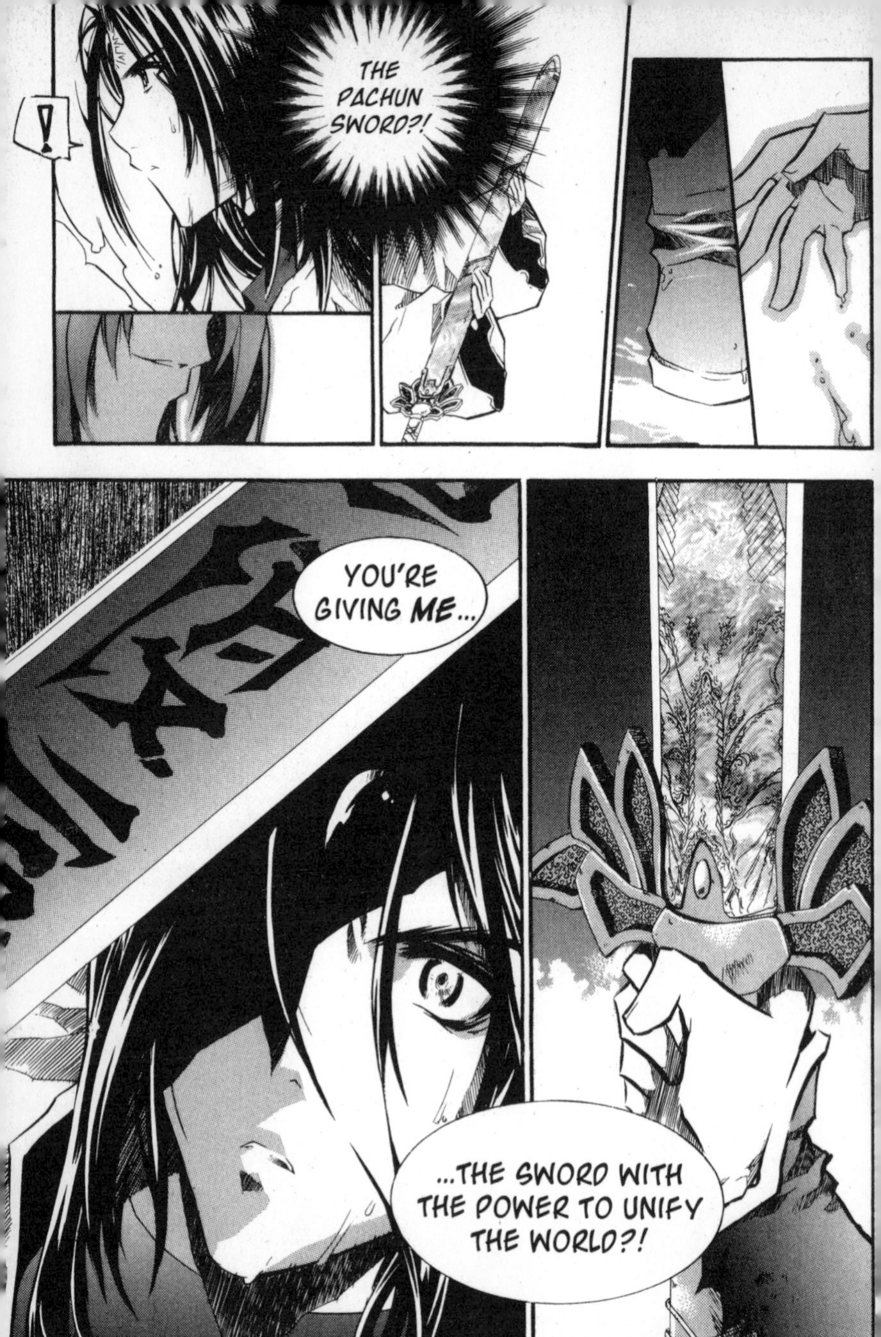
!
THE PACHUN SWORD?!
YOU'RE GIVING **ME**...
...THE SWORD WITH THE POWER TO UNIFY THE WORLD?!

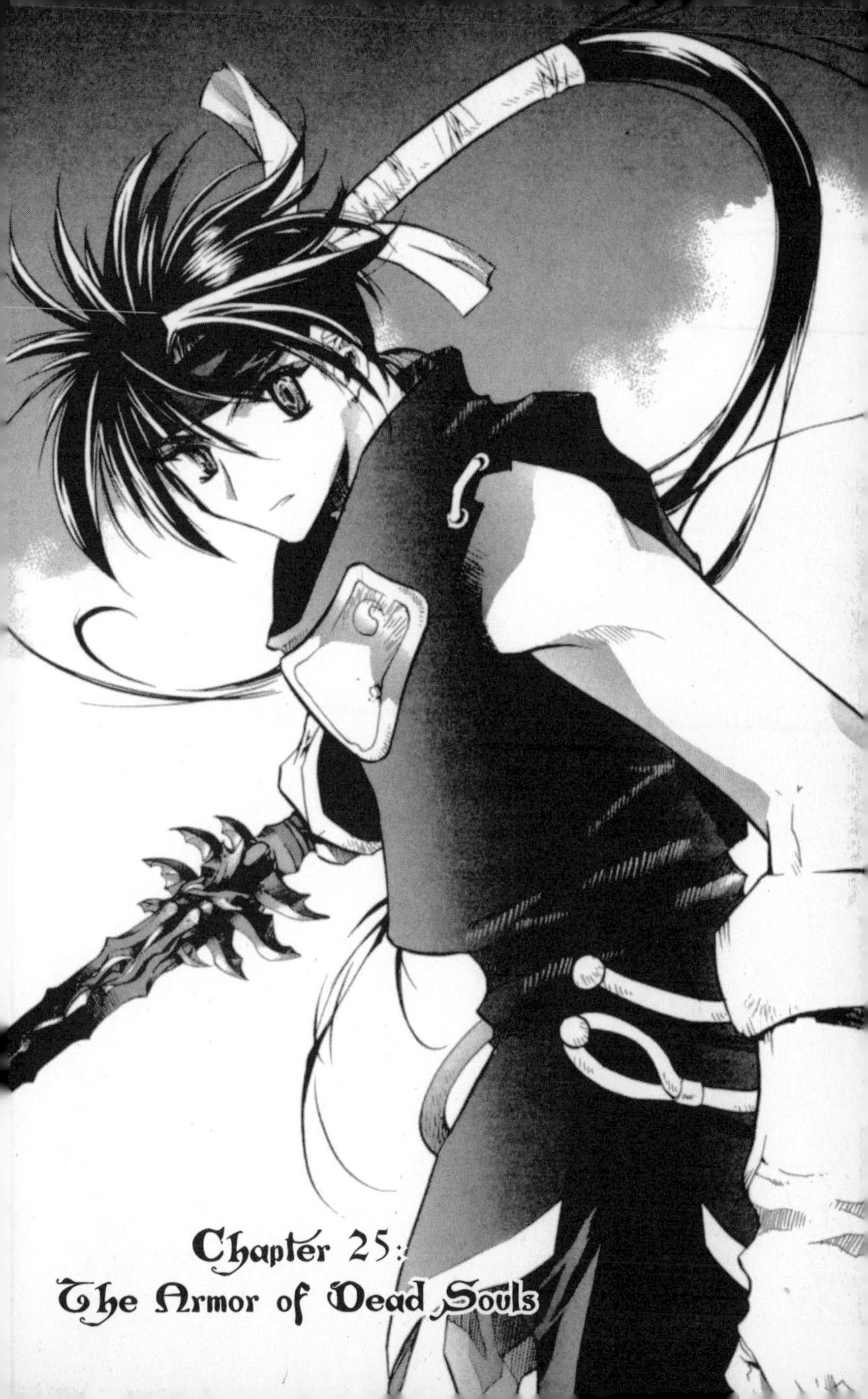

Chapter 25:
The Armor of Dead Souls

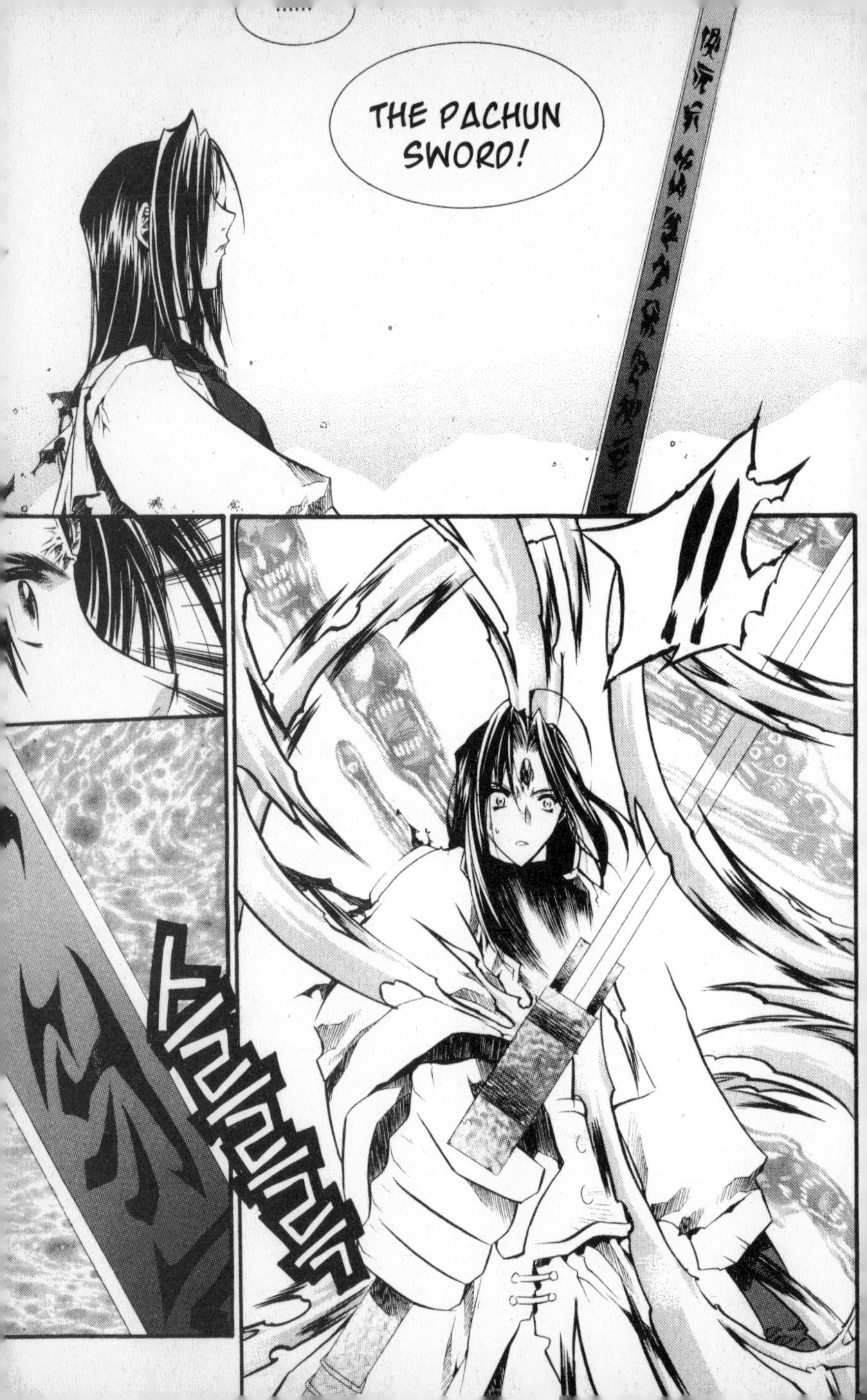
THE PACHUN SWORD!

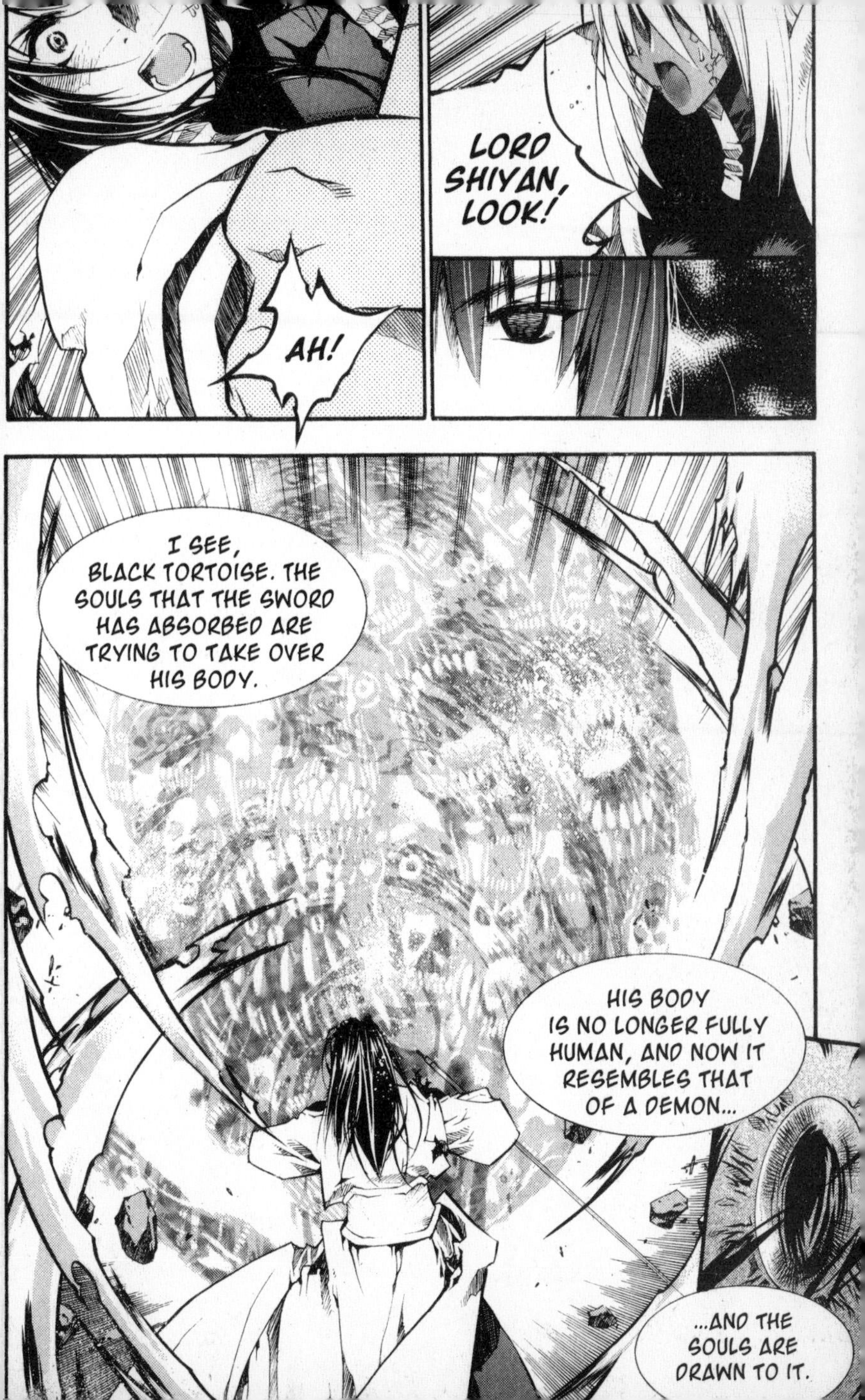
LORD SHIYAN, LOOK!
AH!
I SEE, BLACK TORTOISE. THE SOULS THAT THE SWORD HAS ABSORBED ARE TRYING TO TAKE OVER HIS BODY.
HIS BODY IS NO LONGER FULLY HUMAN, AND NOW IT RESEMBLES THAT OF A DEMON...
...AND THE SOULS ARE DRAWN TO IT.

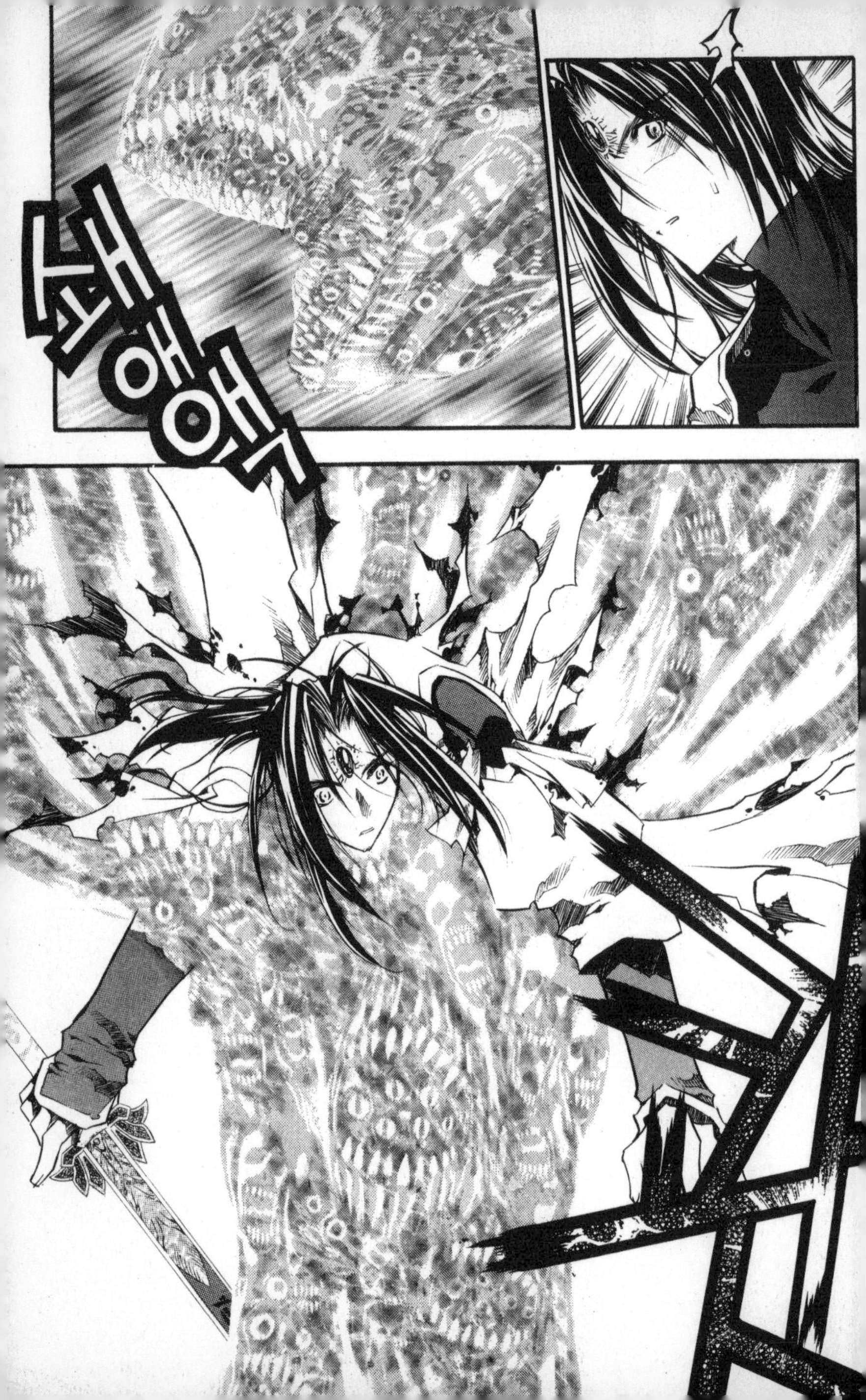
새애애액

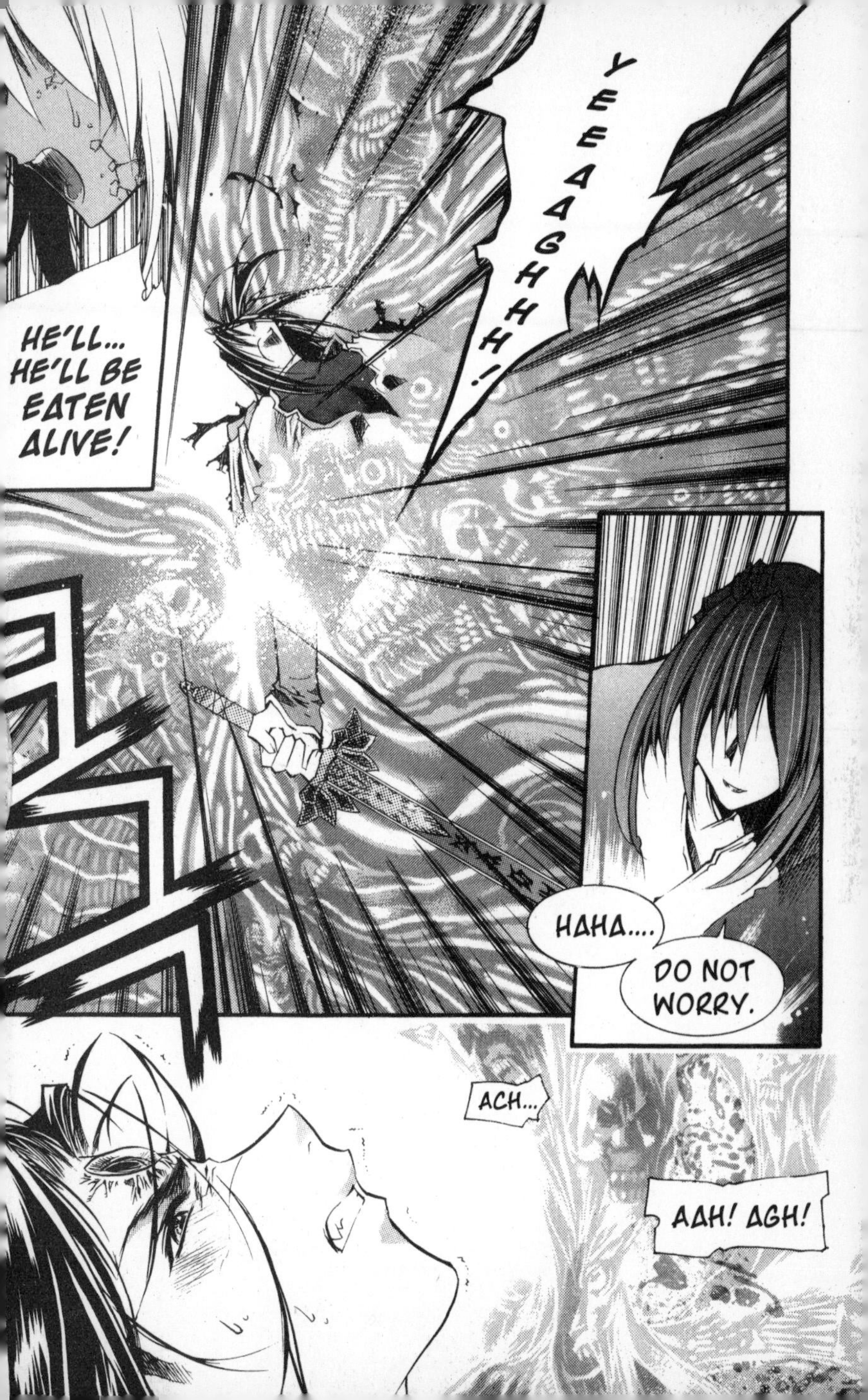
HE'LL... HE'LL BE EATEN ALIVE!
YEEAAGHHHH!
HAHA....
DO NOT WORRY.
ACH...
AAH! AGH!

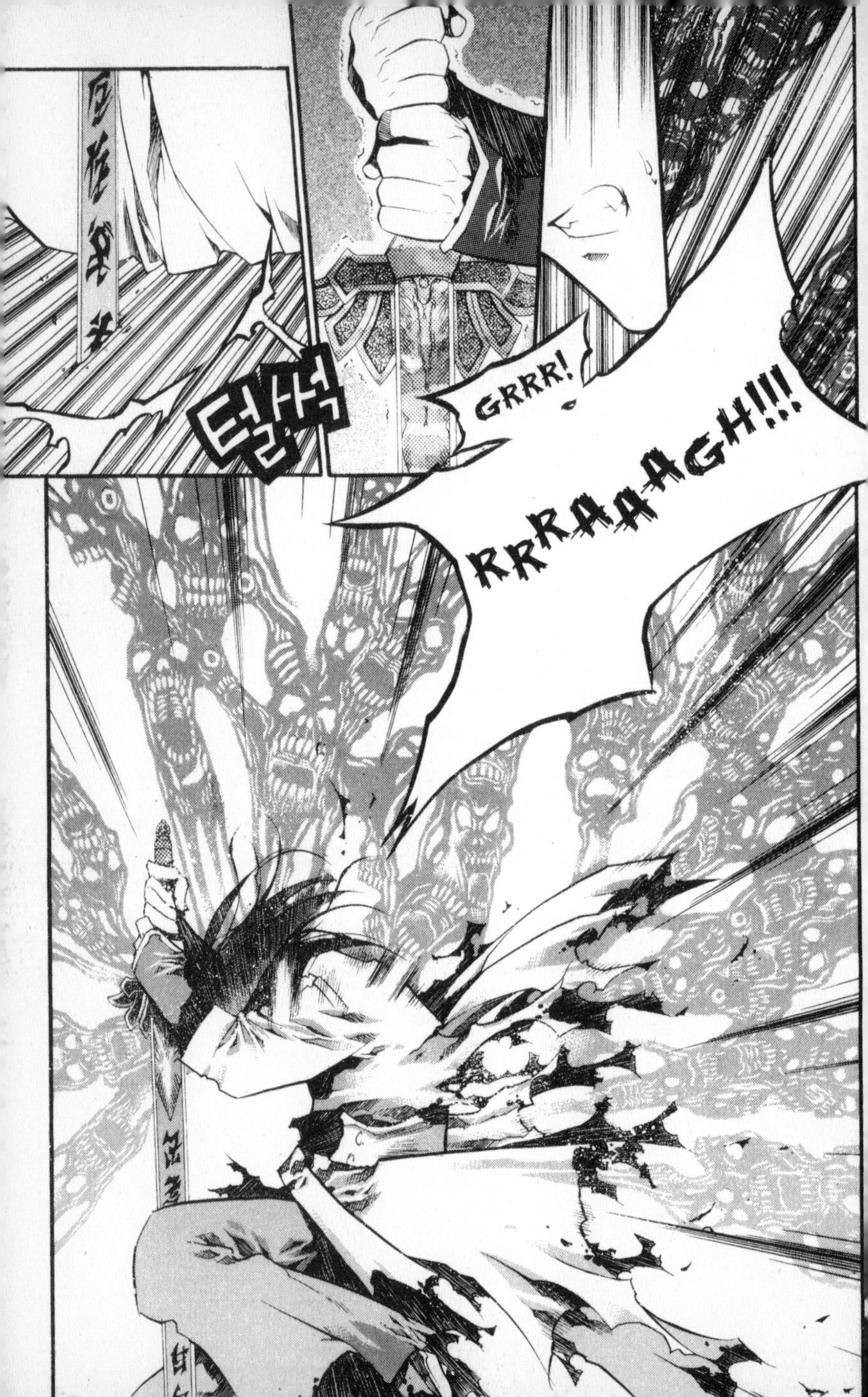
덥석
GRRR!
RRRAAAGH!!!

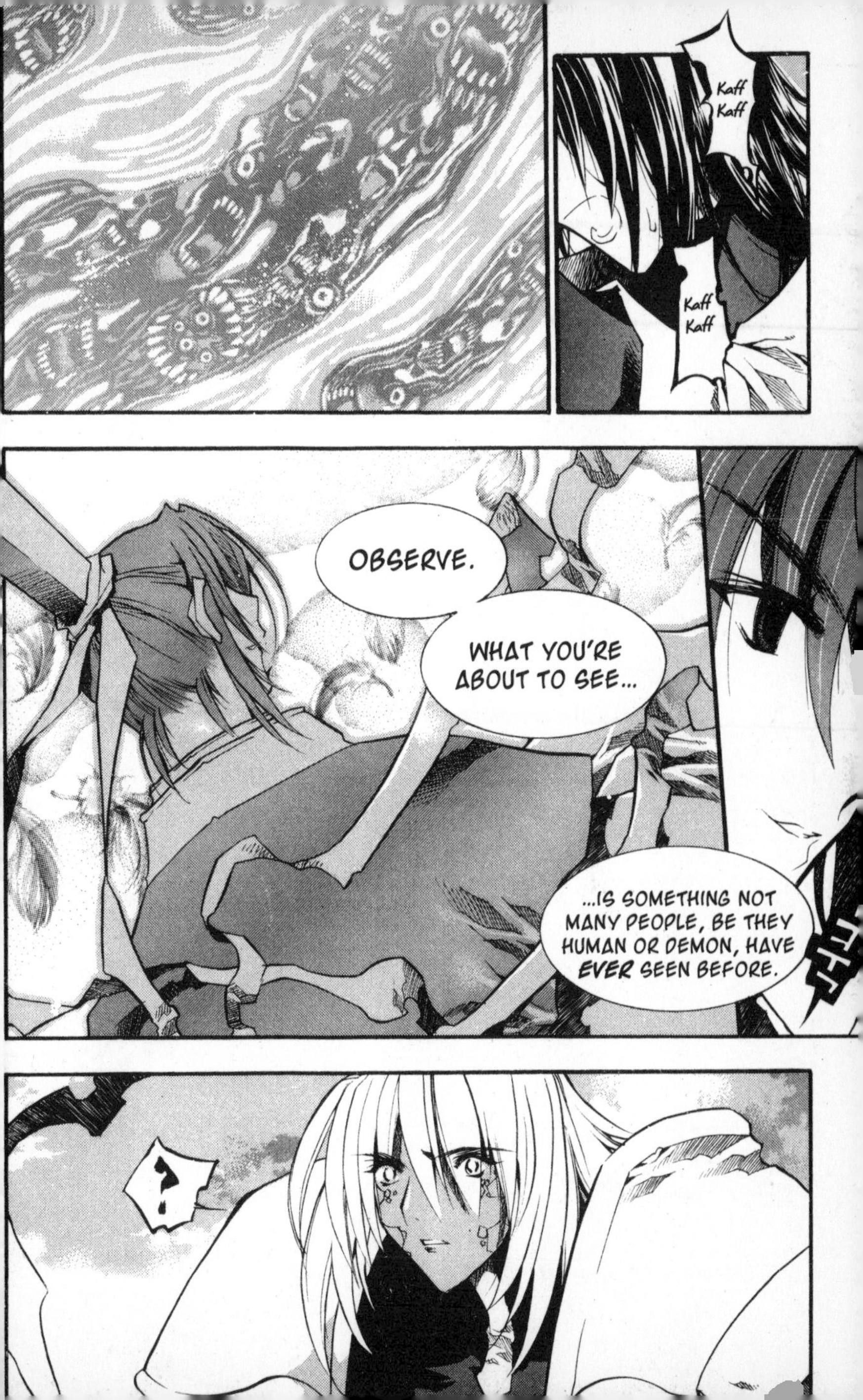
Kaff
Kaff
Kaff
Kaff
OBSERVE.
WHAT YOU'RE ABOUT TO SEE...
...IS SOMETHING NOT MANY PEOPLE, BE THEY HUMAN OR DEMON, HAVE EVER SEEN BEFORE.
?

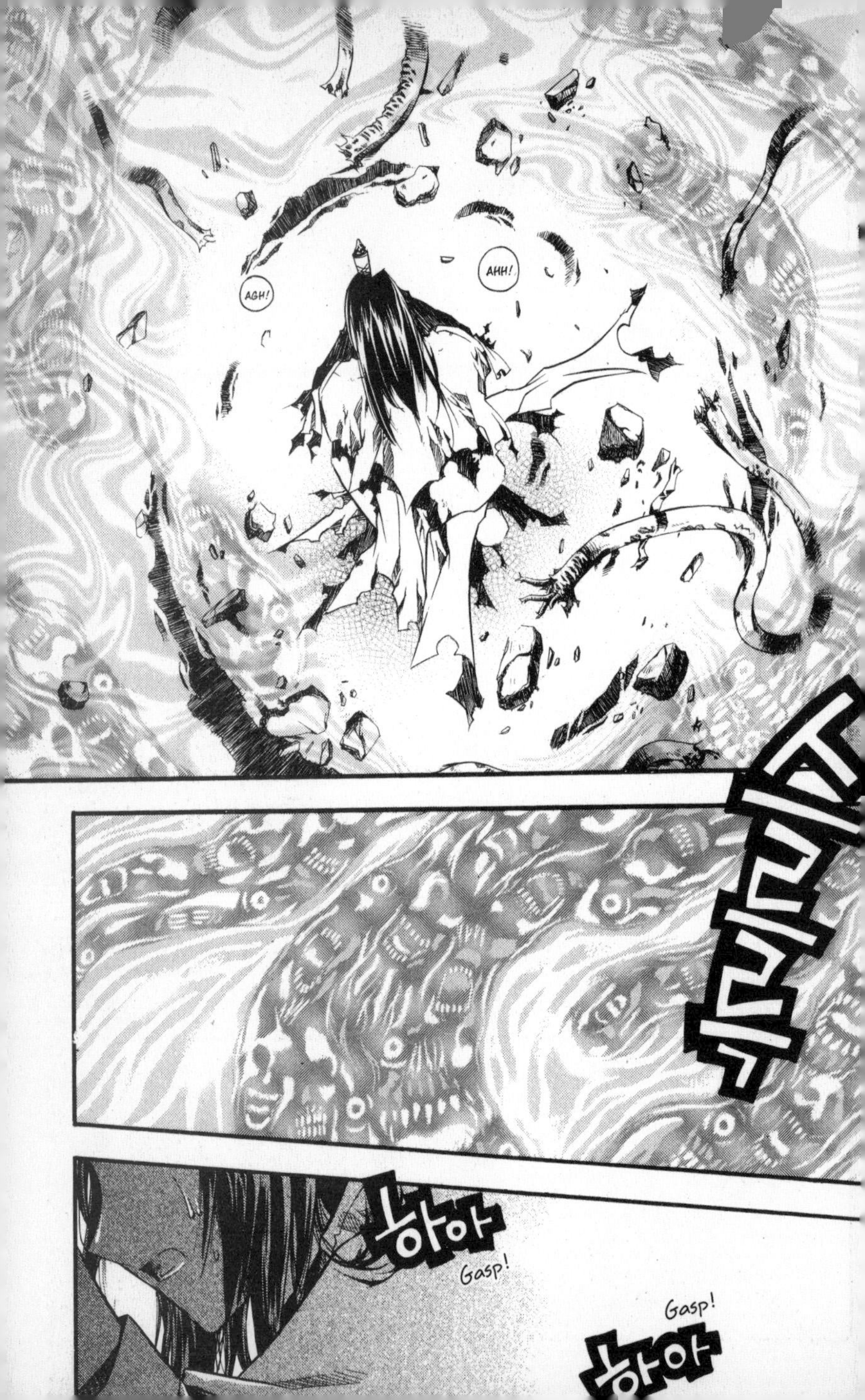
AGH!
AHH!
하아
Gasp!
Gasp!
하아

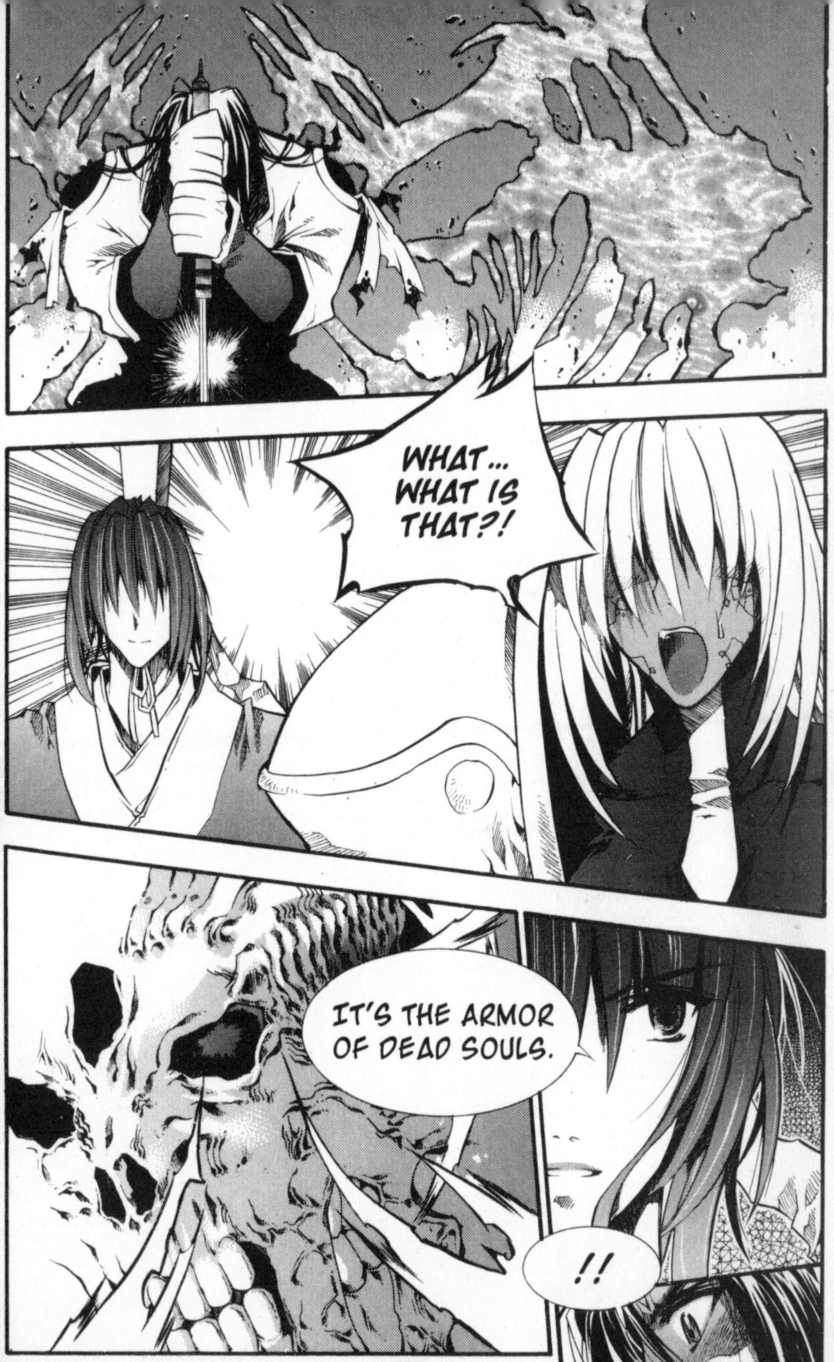
WHAT... WHAT IS THAT?!
IT'S THE ARMOR OF DEAD SOULS.
!!

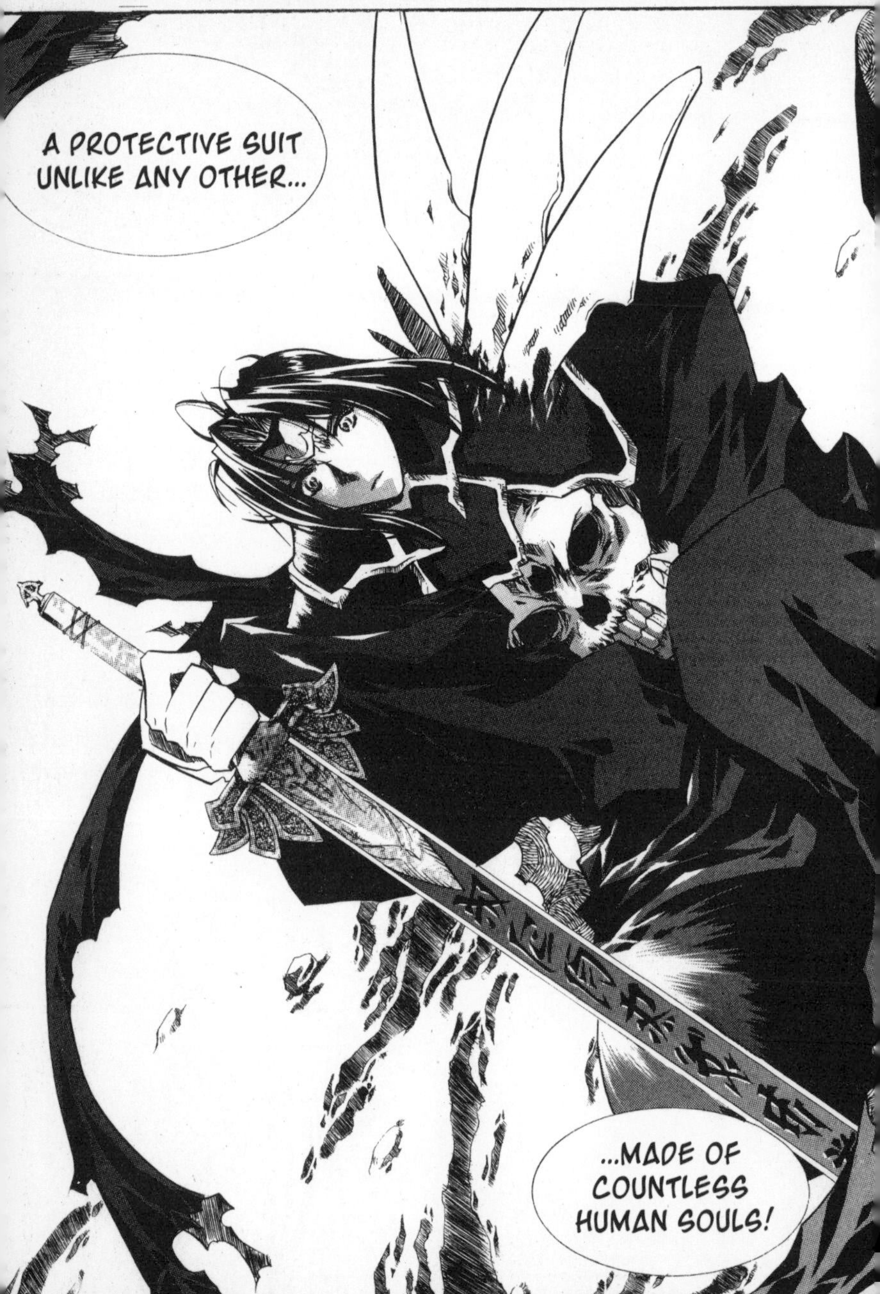
A PROTECTIVE SUIT UNLIKE ANY OTHER...
...MADE OF COUNTLESS HUMAN SOULS!

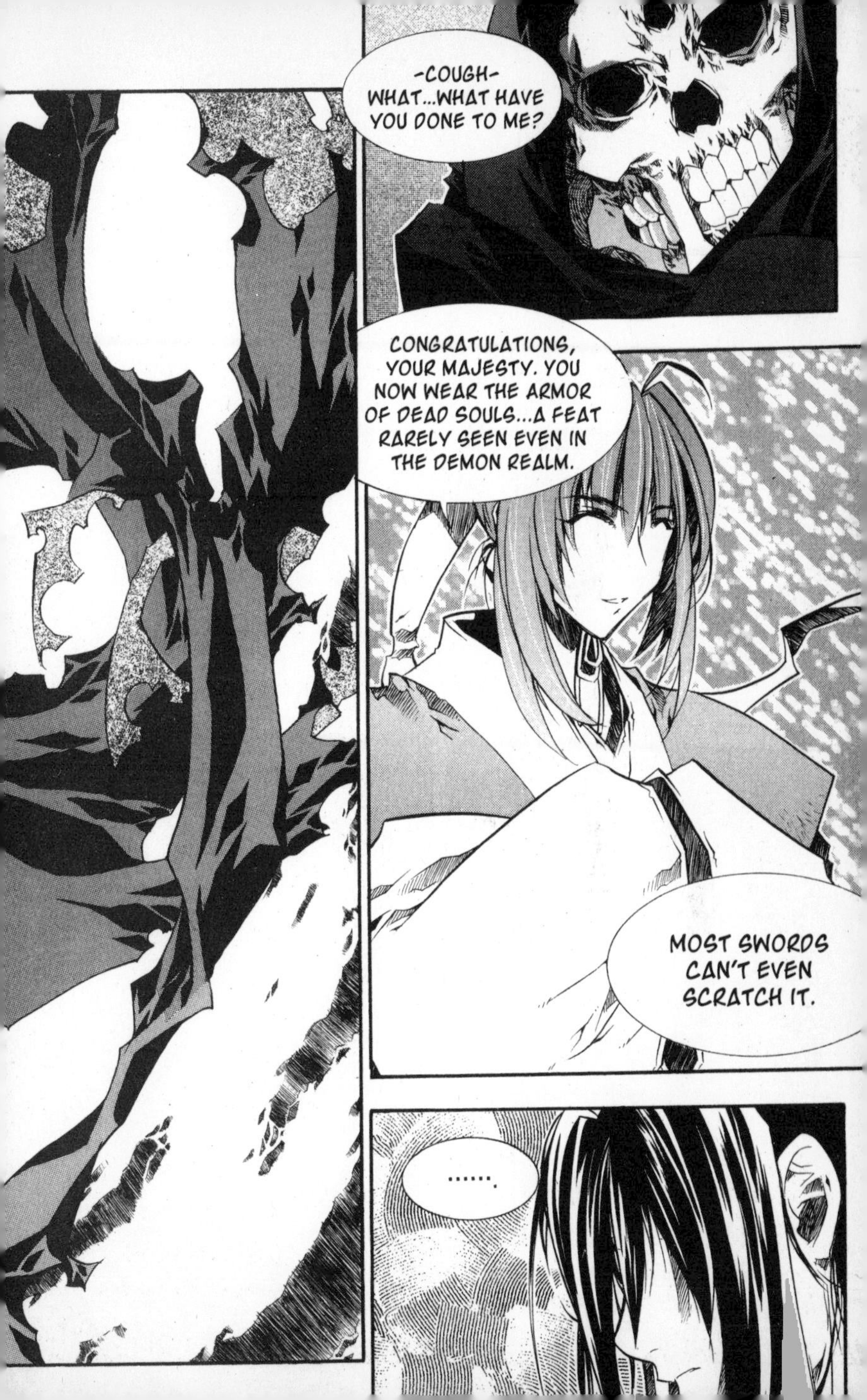
-COUGH-
WHAT...WHAT HAVE YOU DONE TO ME?
CONGRATULATIONS, YOUR MAJESTY. YOU NOW WEAR THE ARMOR OF DEAD SOULS...A FEAT RARELY SEEN EVEN IN THE DEMON REALM.
MOST SWORDS CAN'T EVEN SCRATCH IT.
......

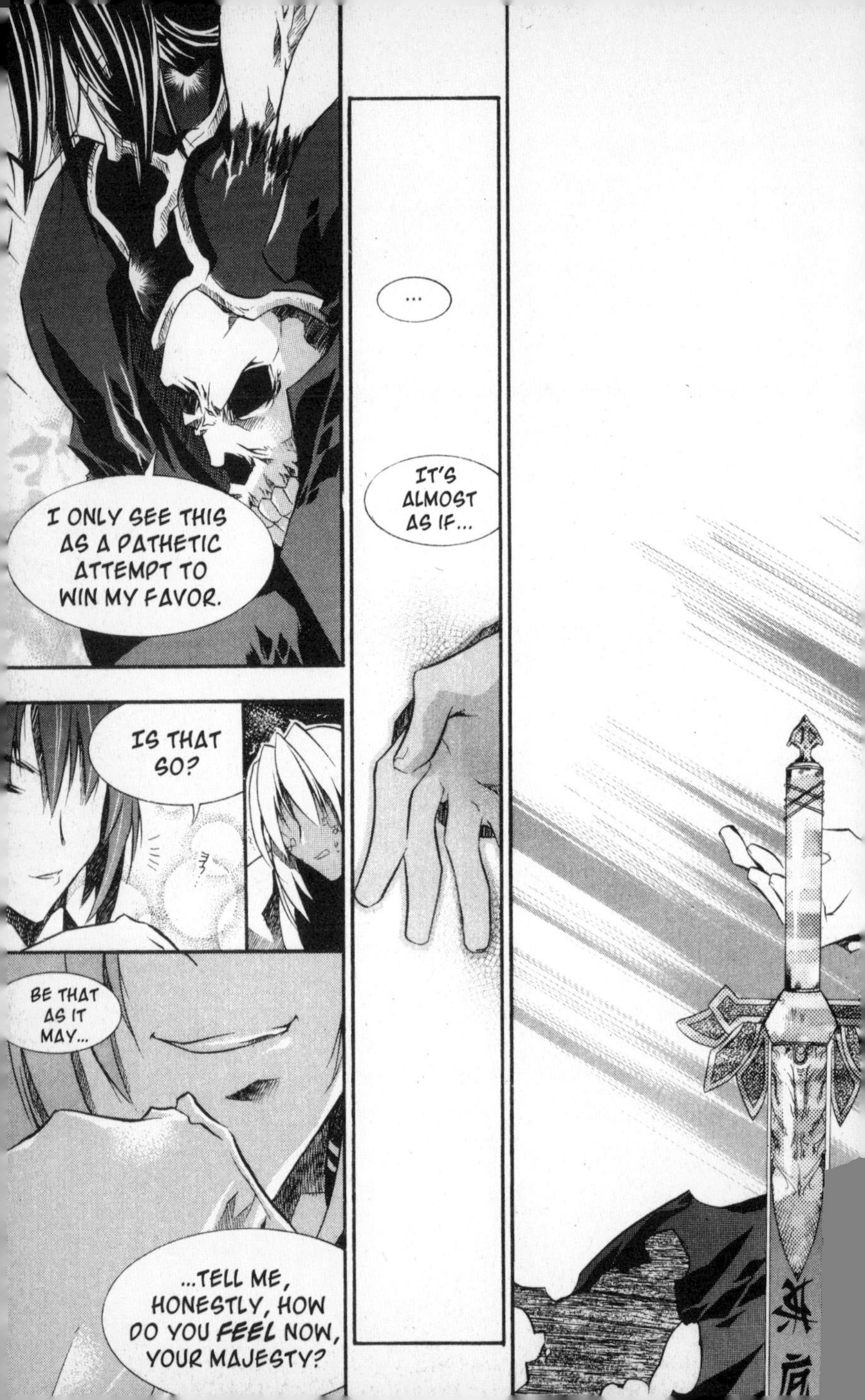
I ONLY SEE THIS AS A PATHETIC ATTEMPT TO WIN MY FAVOR.
IS THAT SO?
BE THAT AS IT MAY...
...TELL ME, HONESTLY, HOW DO YOU *FEEL* NOW, YOUR MAJESTY?
...
IT'S ALMOST AS IF...

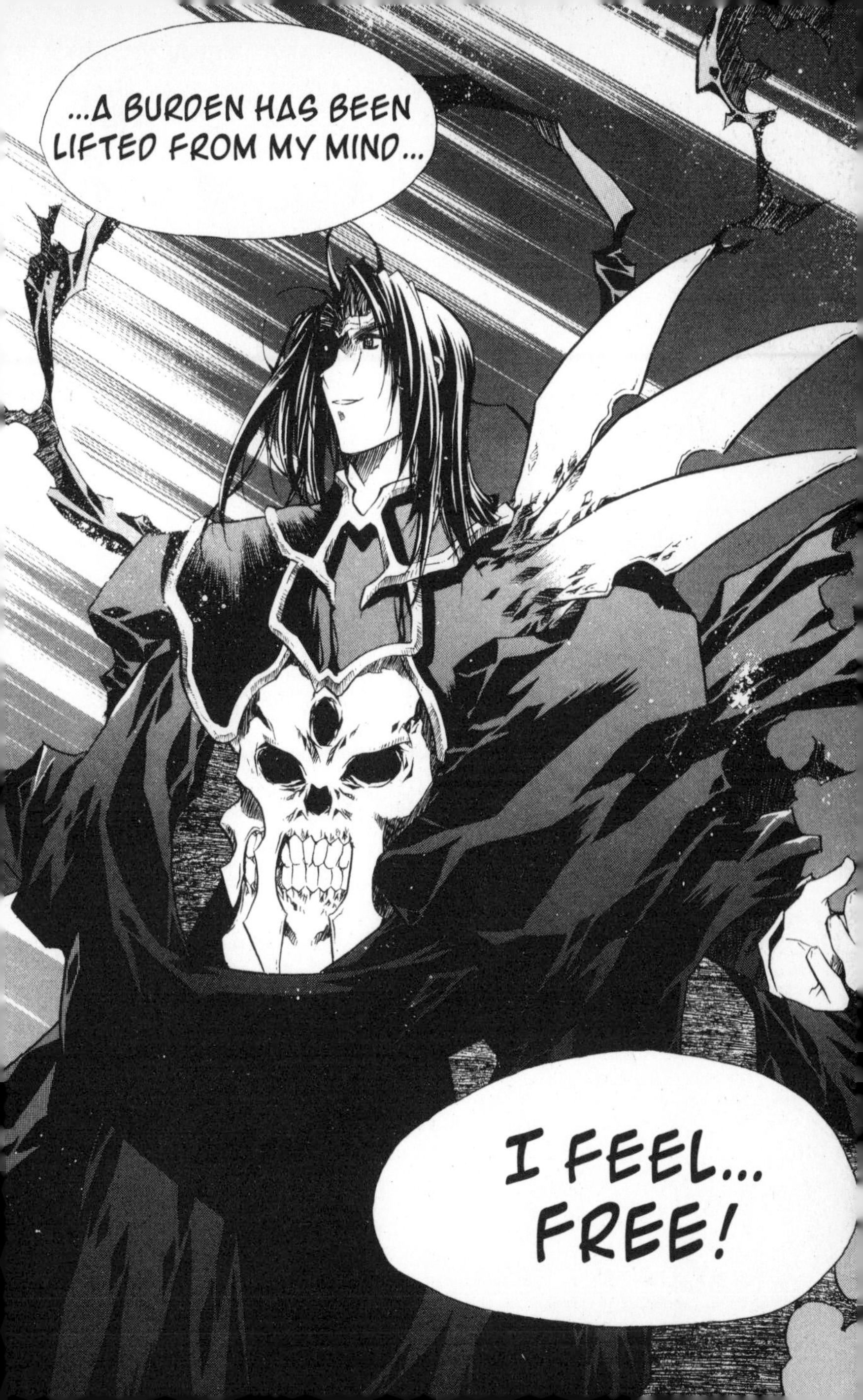
...A BURDEN HAS BEEN LIFTED FROM MY MIND...
I FEEL... FREE!

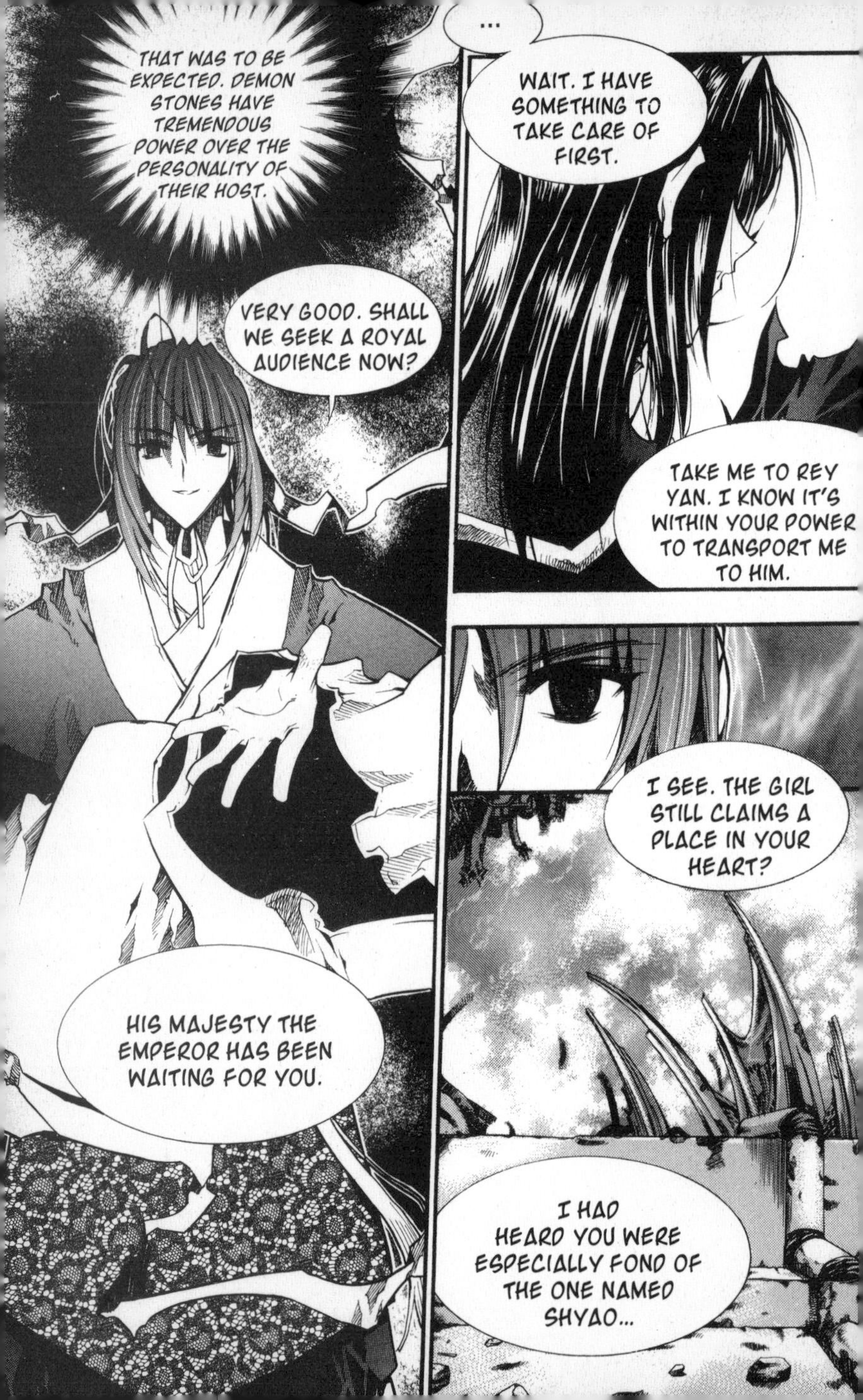
THAT WAS TO BE EXPECTED. DEMON STONES HAVE TREMENDOUS POWER OVER THE PERSONALITY OF THEIR HOST.
VERY GOOD. SHALL WE SEEK A ROYAL AUDIENCE NOW?
HIS MAJESTY THE EMPEROR HAS BEEN WAITING FOR YOU.
...
WAIT. I HAVE SOMETHING TO TAKE CARE OF FIRST.
TAKE ME TO REY YAN. I KNOW IT'S WITHIN YOUR POWER TO TRANSPORT ME TO HIM.
I SEE. THE GIRL STILL CLAIMS A PLACE IN YOUR HEART?
I HAD HEARD YOU WERE ESPECIALLY FOND OF THE ONE NAMED SHYAO...

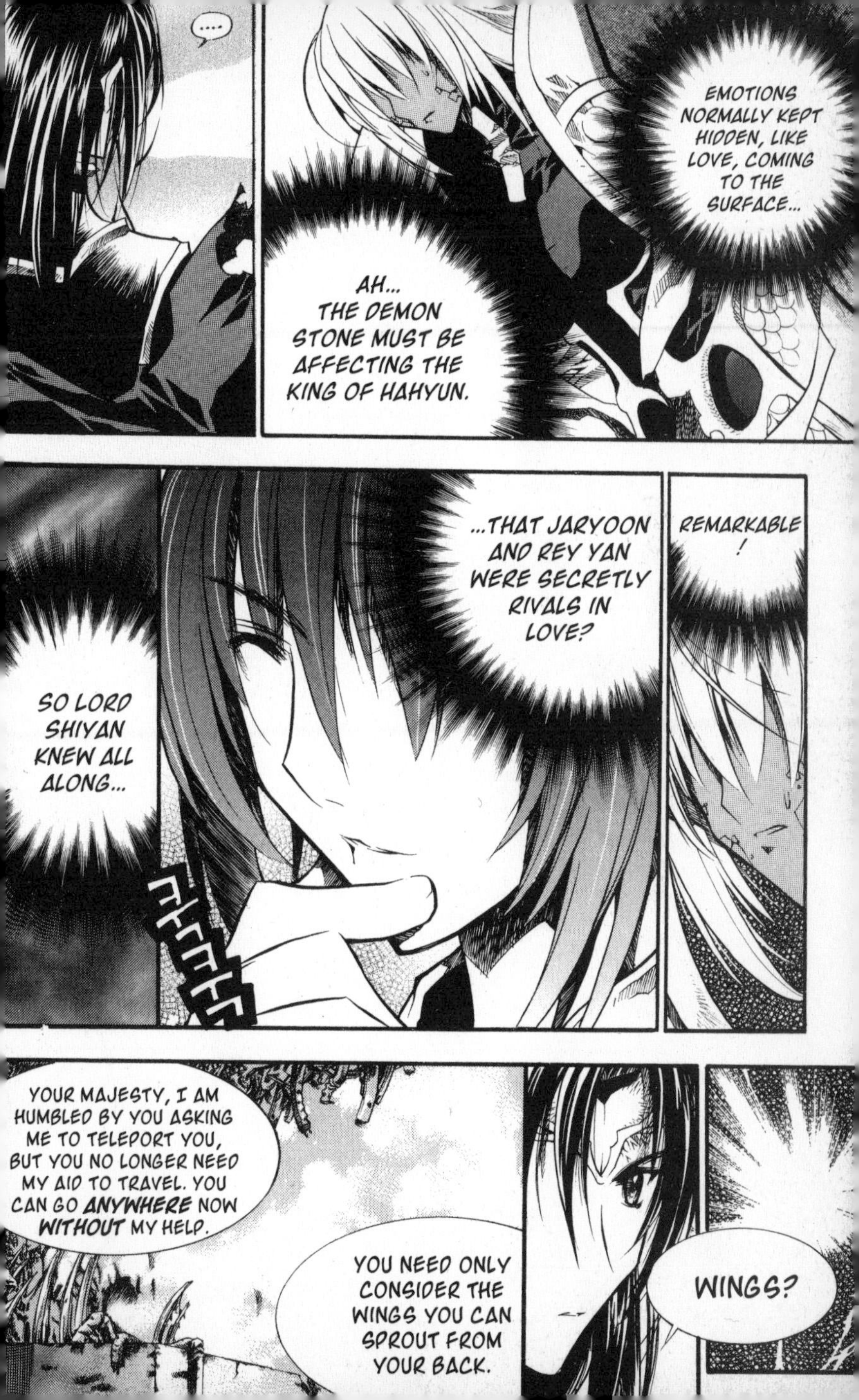
....
AH... THE DEMON STONE MUST BE AFFECTING THE KING OF HAHYUN.
EMOTIONS NORMALLY KEPT HIDDEN, LIKE LOVE, COMING TO THE SURFACE...
SO LORD SHIYAN KNEW ALL ALONG...
...THAT JARYOON AND REY YAN WERE SECRETLY RIVALS IN LOVE?
REMARKABLE!
YOUR MAJESTY, I AM HUMBLED BY YOU ASKING ME TO TELEPORT YOU, BUT YOU NO LONGER NEED MY AID TO TRAVEL. YOU CAN GO **ANYWHERE** NOW **WITHOUT** MY HELP.
YOU NEED ONLY CONSIDER THE WINGS YOU CAN SPROUT FROM YOUR BACK.
WINGS?

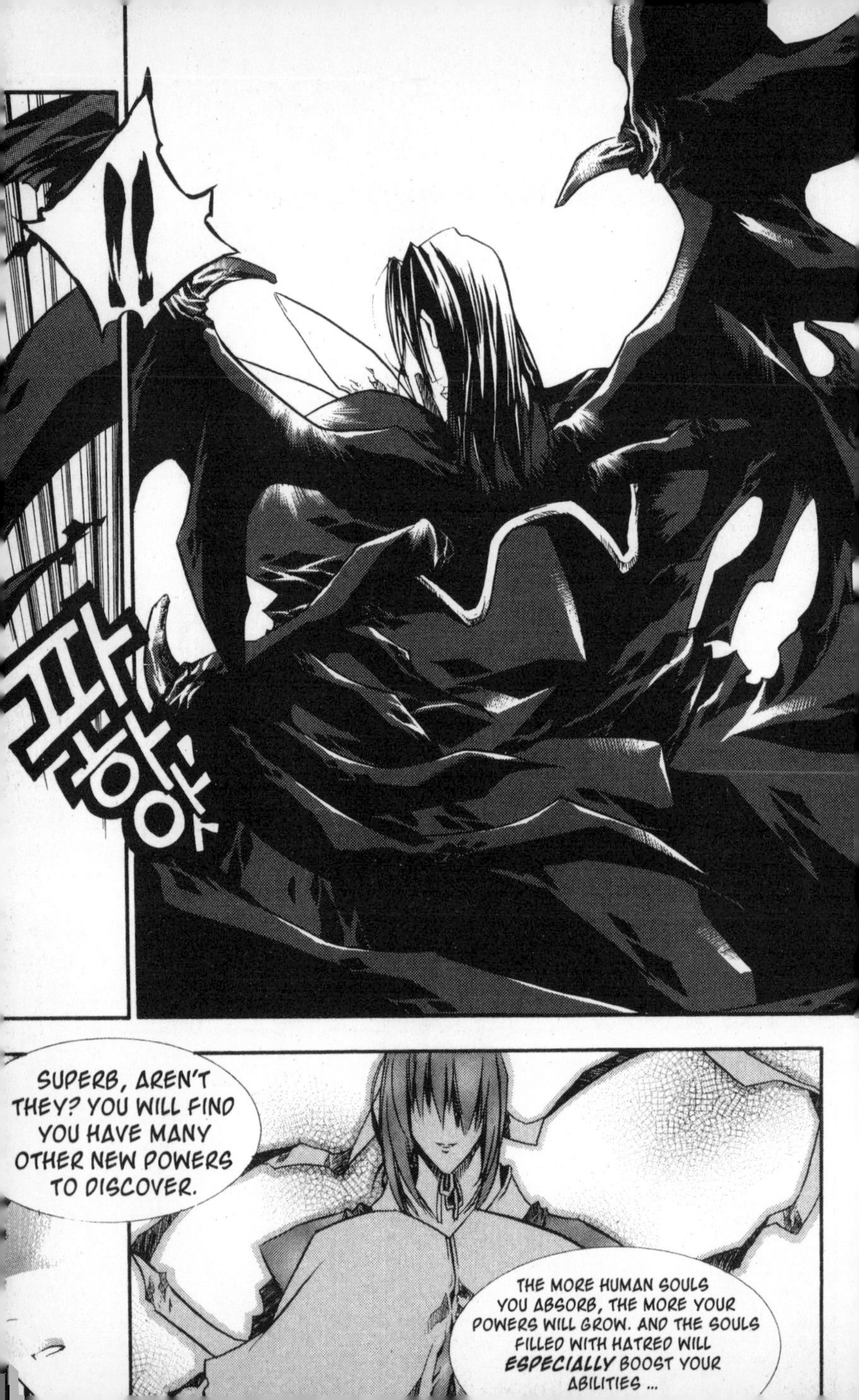
SUPERB, AREN'T THEY? YOU WILL FIND YOU HAVE MANY OTHER NEW POWERS TO DISCOVER.
THE MORE HUMAN SOULS YOU ABSORB, THE MORE YOUR POWERS WILL GROW. AND THE SOULS FILLED WITH HATRED WILL *ESPECIALLY* BOOST YOUR ABILITIES ...

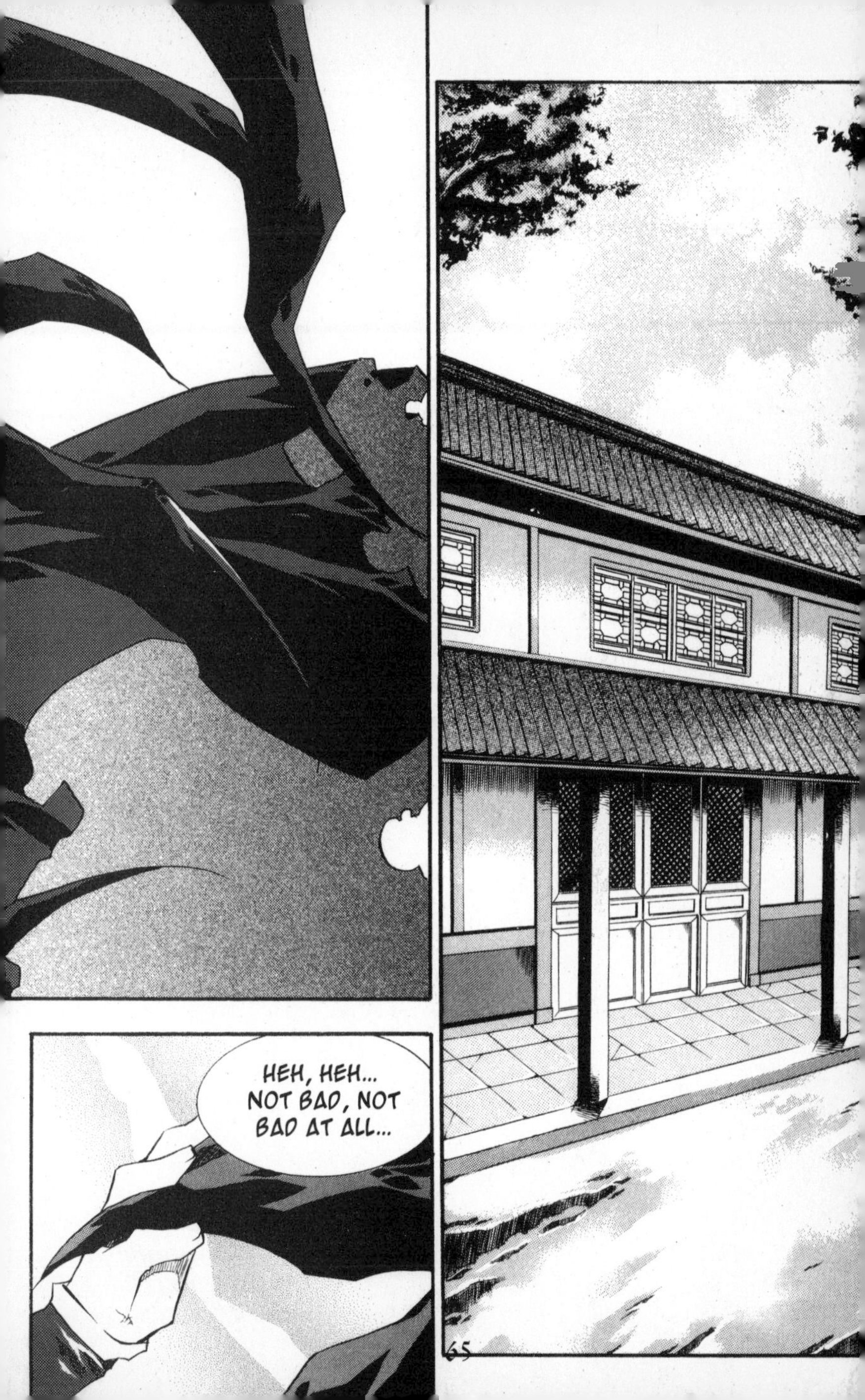
HEH, HEH... NOT BAD, NOT BAD AT ALL...

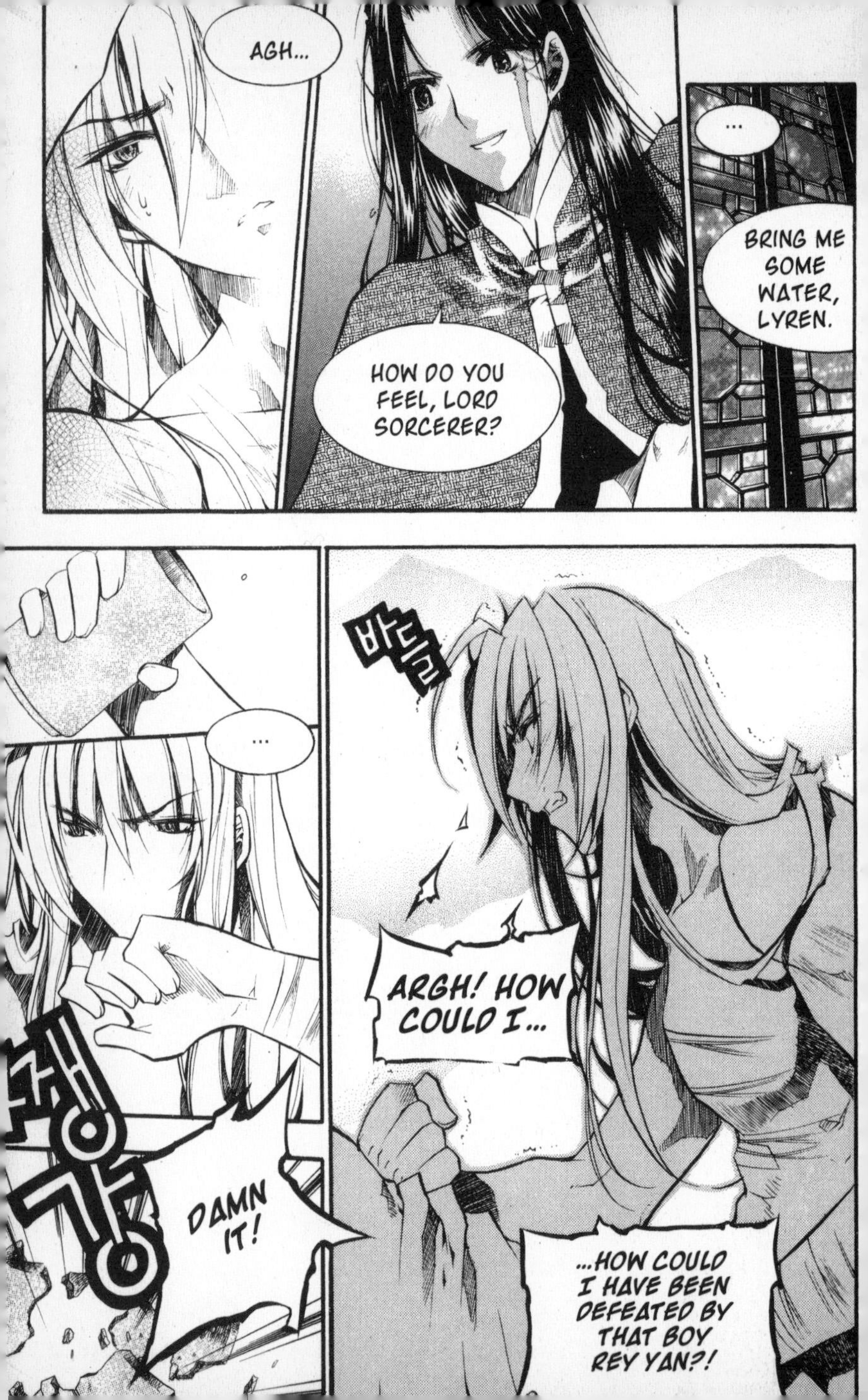
AGH...
HOW DO YOU FEEL, LORD SORCERER?
...
BRING ME SOME WATER, LYREN.
...
DAMN IT!
바득
ARGH! HOW COULD I...
...HOW COULD I HAVE BEEN DEFEATED BY THAT BOY REY YAN?!

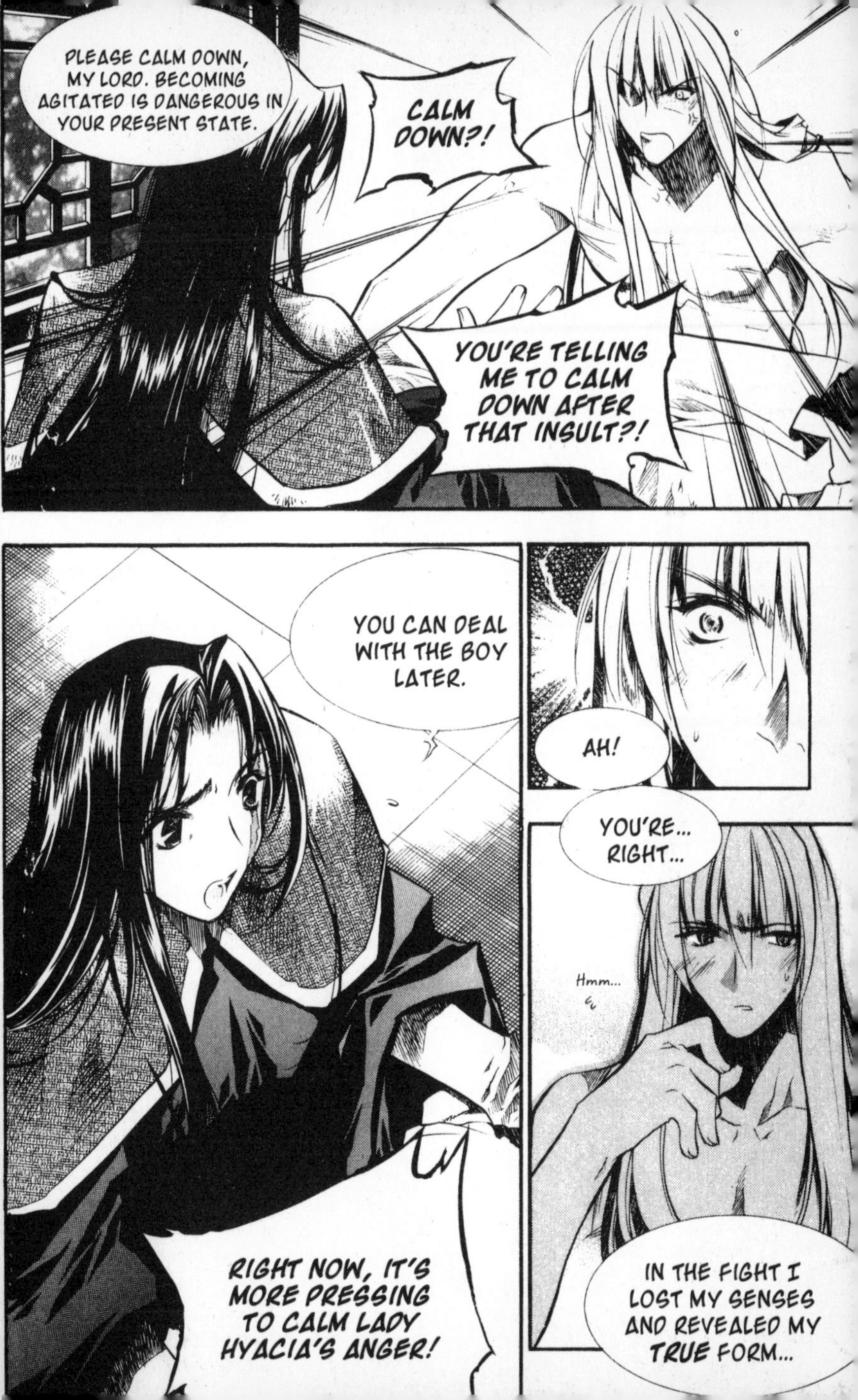
PLEASE CALM DOWN, MY LORD. BECOMING AGITATED IS DANGEROUS IN YOUR PRESENT STATE.
CALM DOWN?!
YOU'RE TELLING ME TO CALM DOWN AFTER THAT INSULT?!
YOU CAN DEAL WITH THE BOY LATER.
RIGHT NOW, IT'S MORE PRESSING TO CALM LADY HYACIA'S ANGER!
AH!
YOU'RE... RIGHT...
Hmm...
IN THE FIGHT I LOST MY SENSES AND REVEALED MY TRUE FORM...

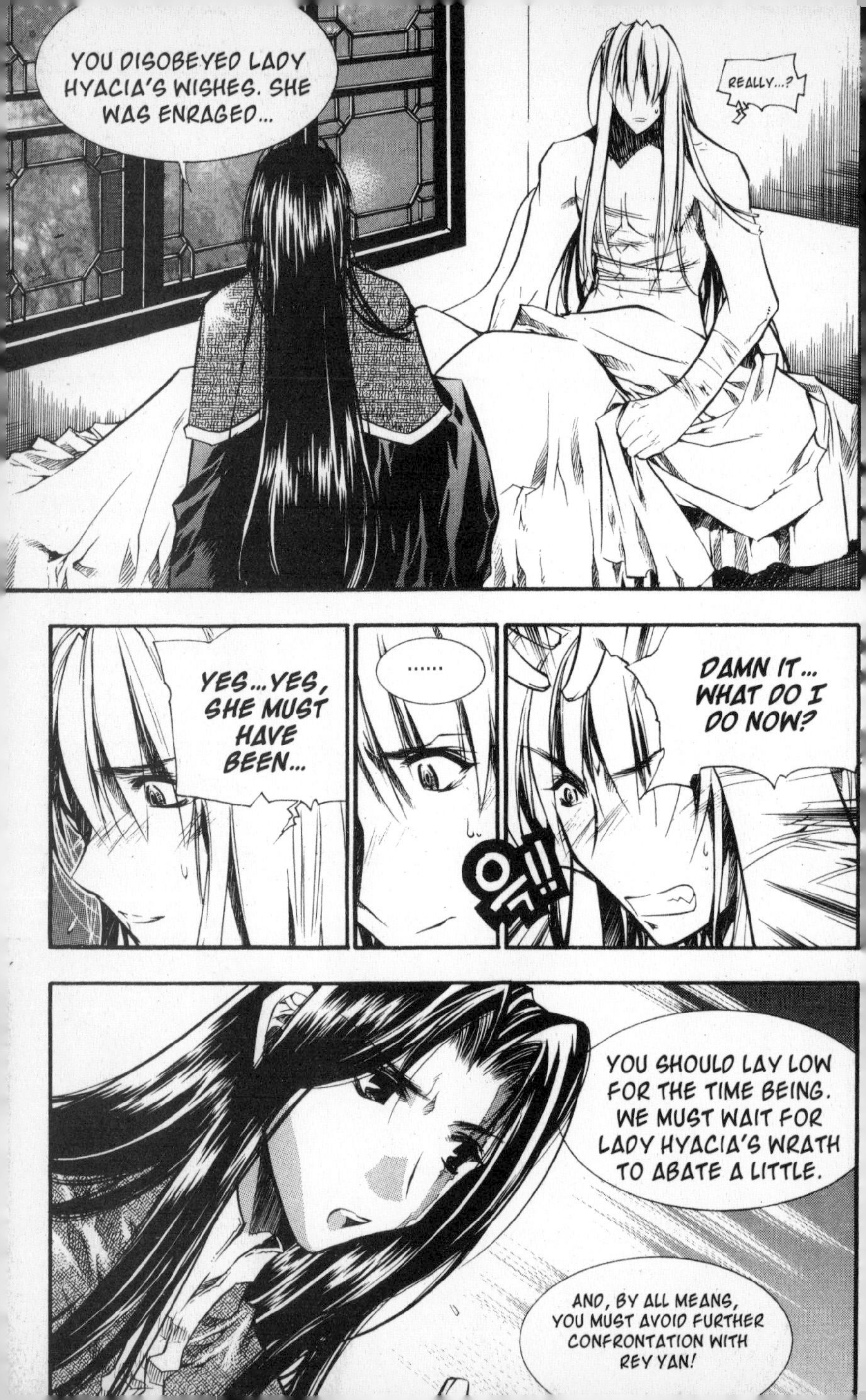
YOU DISOBEYED LADY HYACIA'S WISHES. SHE WAS ENRAGED...
REALLY...?
YES...YES, SHE MUST HAVE BEEN...
......
DAMN IT... WHAT DO I DO NOW?
YOU SHOULD LAY LOW FOR THE TIME BEING. WE MUST WAIT FOR LADY HYACIA'S WRATH TO ABATE A LITTLE.
AND, BY ALL MEANS, YOU MUST AVOID FURTHER CONFRONTATION WITH REY YAN!

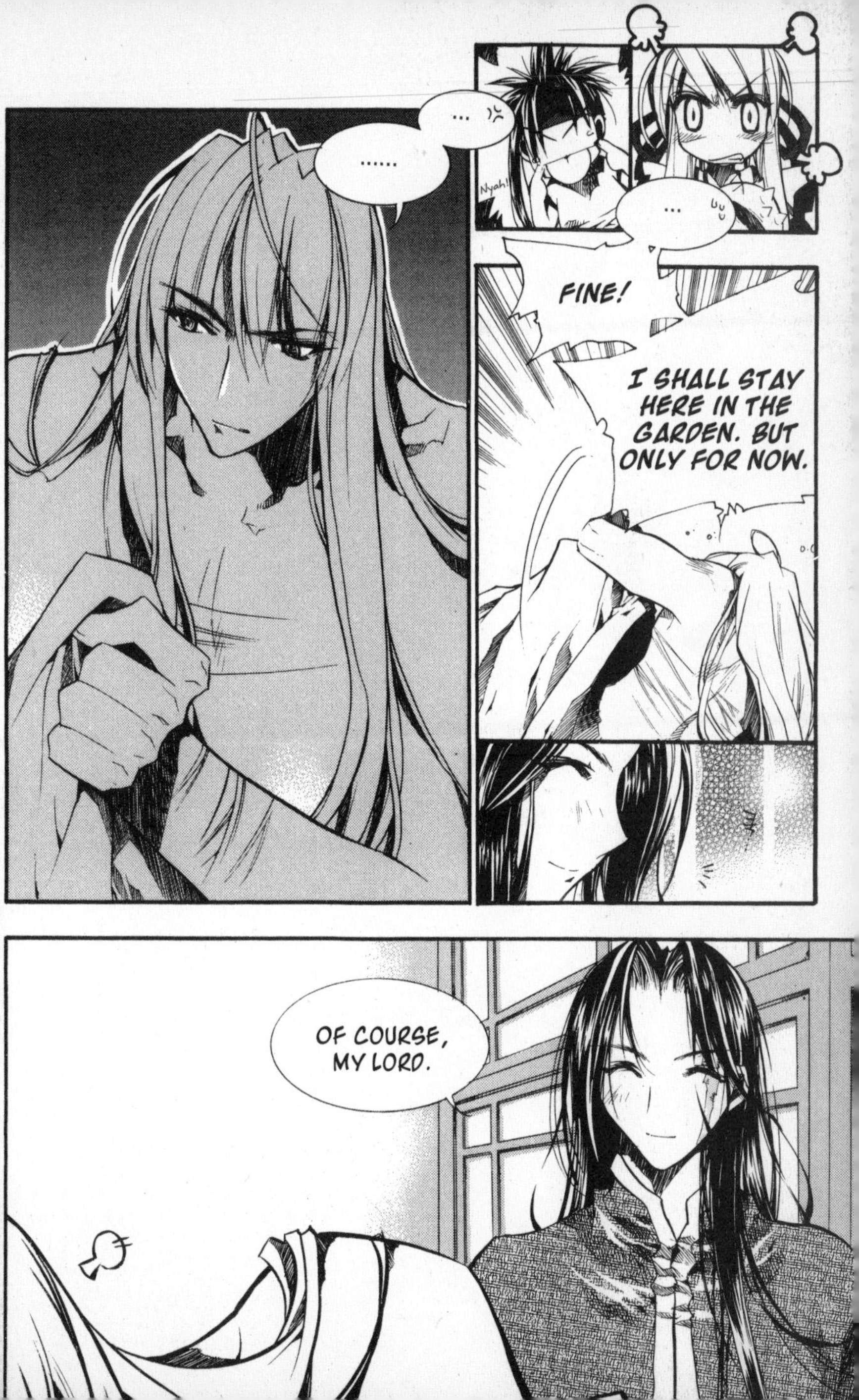
......
...
Nyah!
...
FINE!
I SHALL STAY HERE IN THE GARDEN. BUT ONLY FOR NOW.
OF COURSE, MY LORD.

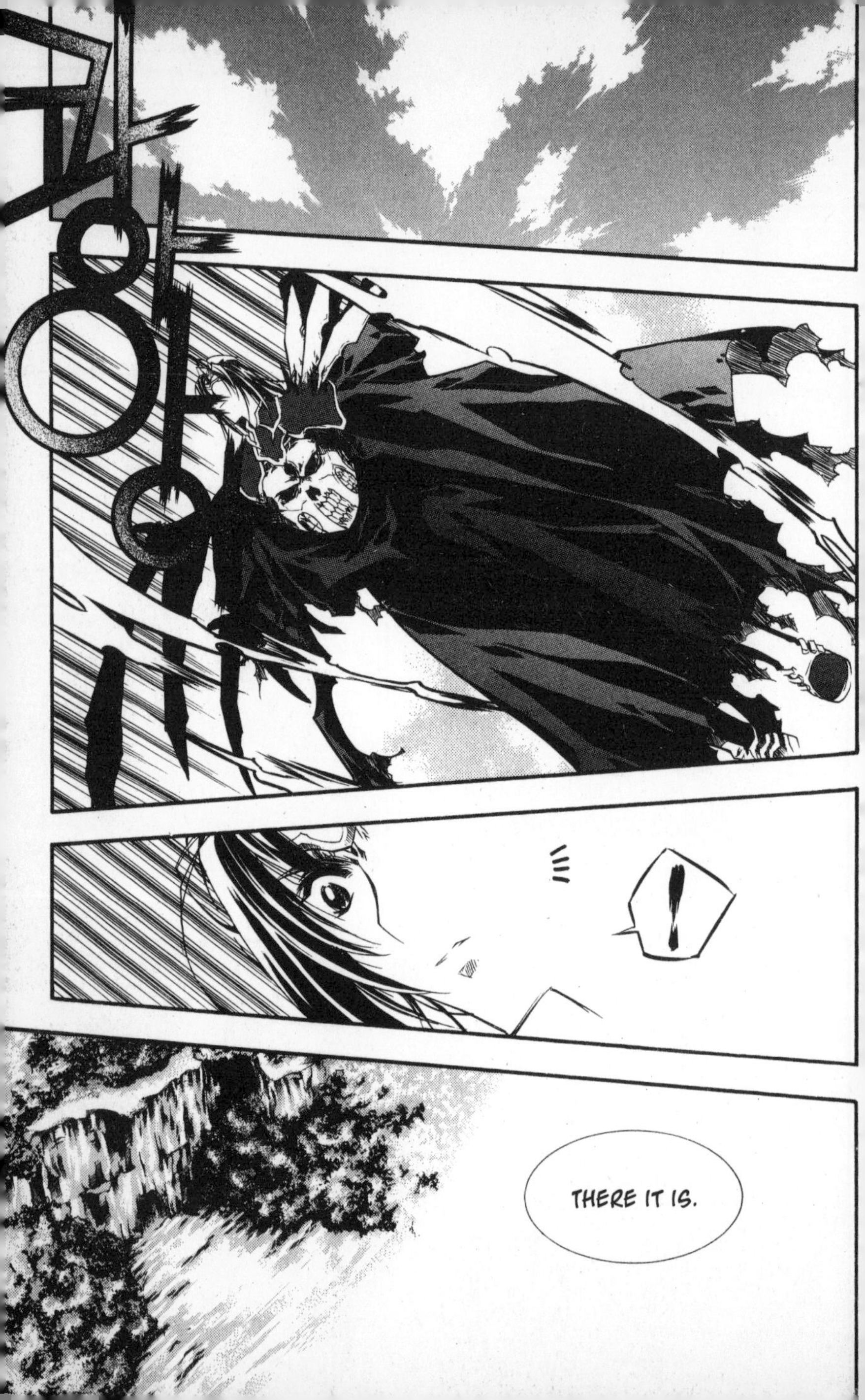
!
THERE IT IS.

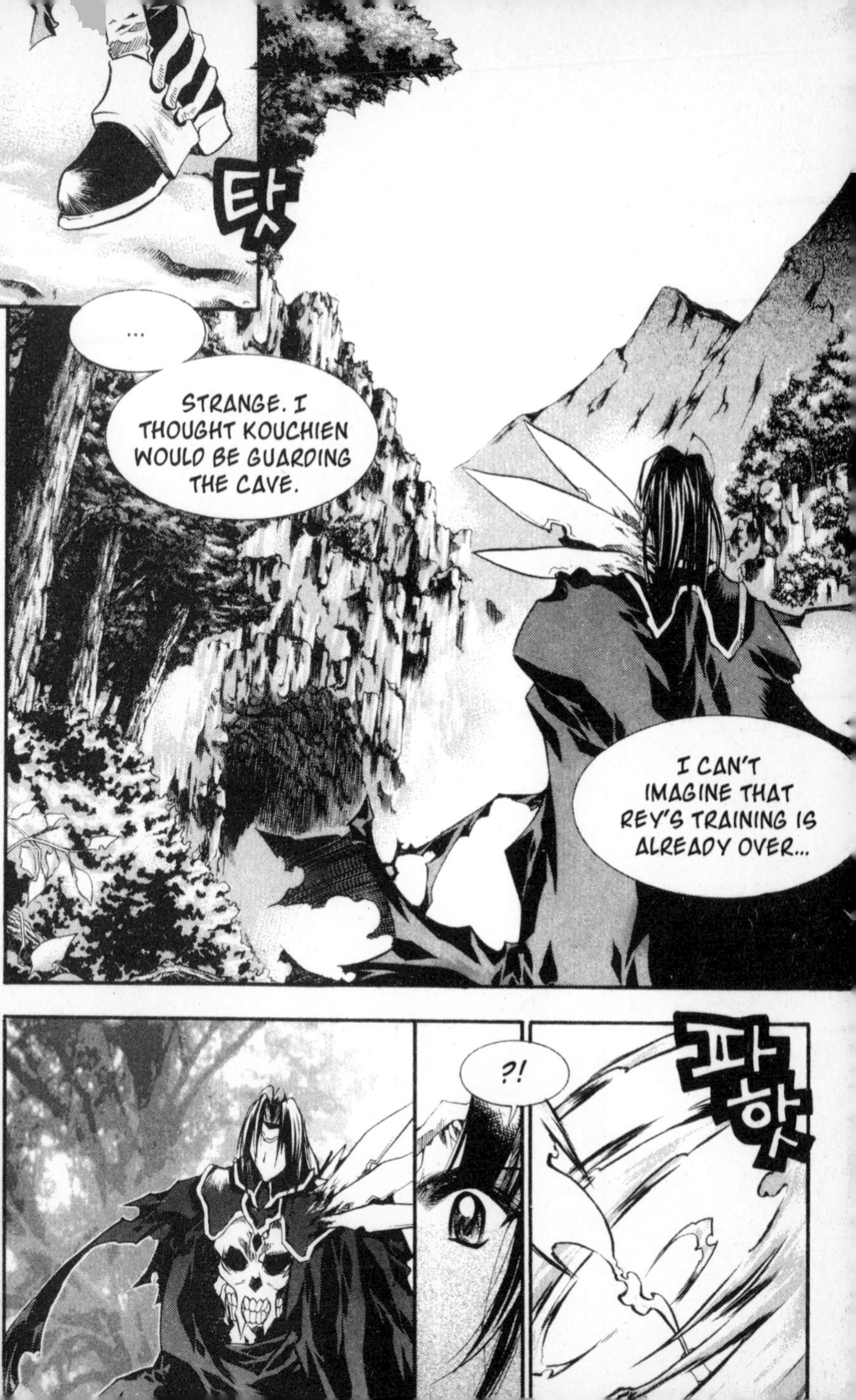
탓
...
STRANGE. I THOUGHT KOUCHIEN WOULD BE GUARDING THE CAVE.
I CAN'T IMAGINE THAT REY'S TRAINING IS ALREADY OVER...
?!
파핫

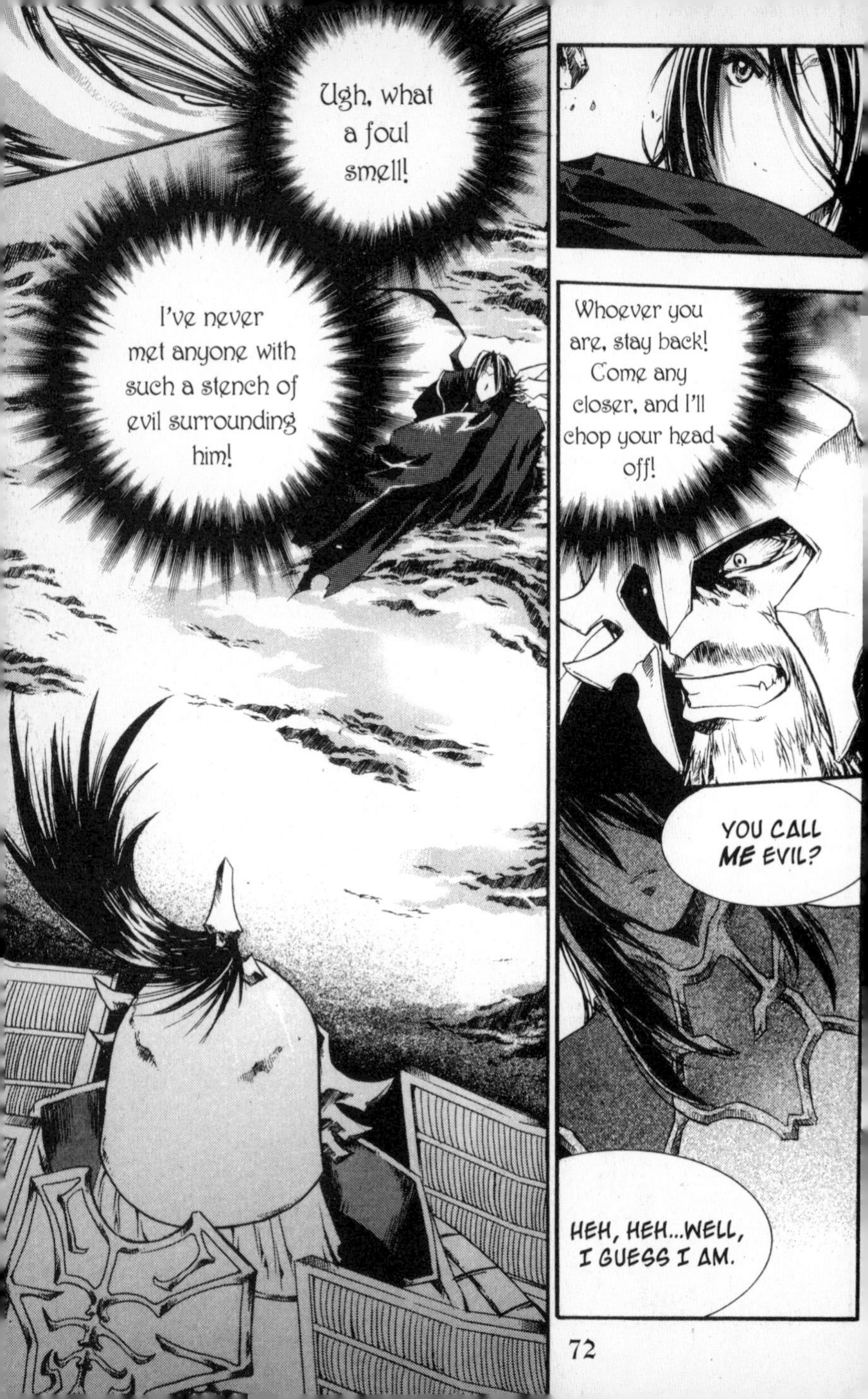
Ugh, what a foul smell!
I've never met anyone with such a stench of evil surrounding him!
Whoever you are, stay back! Come any closer, and I'll chop your head off!
YOU CALL ME EVIL?
HEH, HEH...WELL, I GUESS I AM.

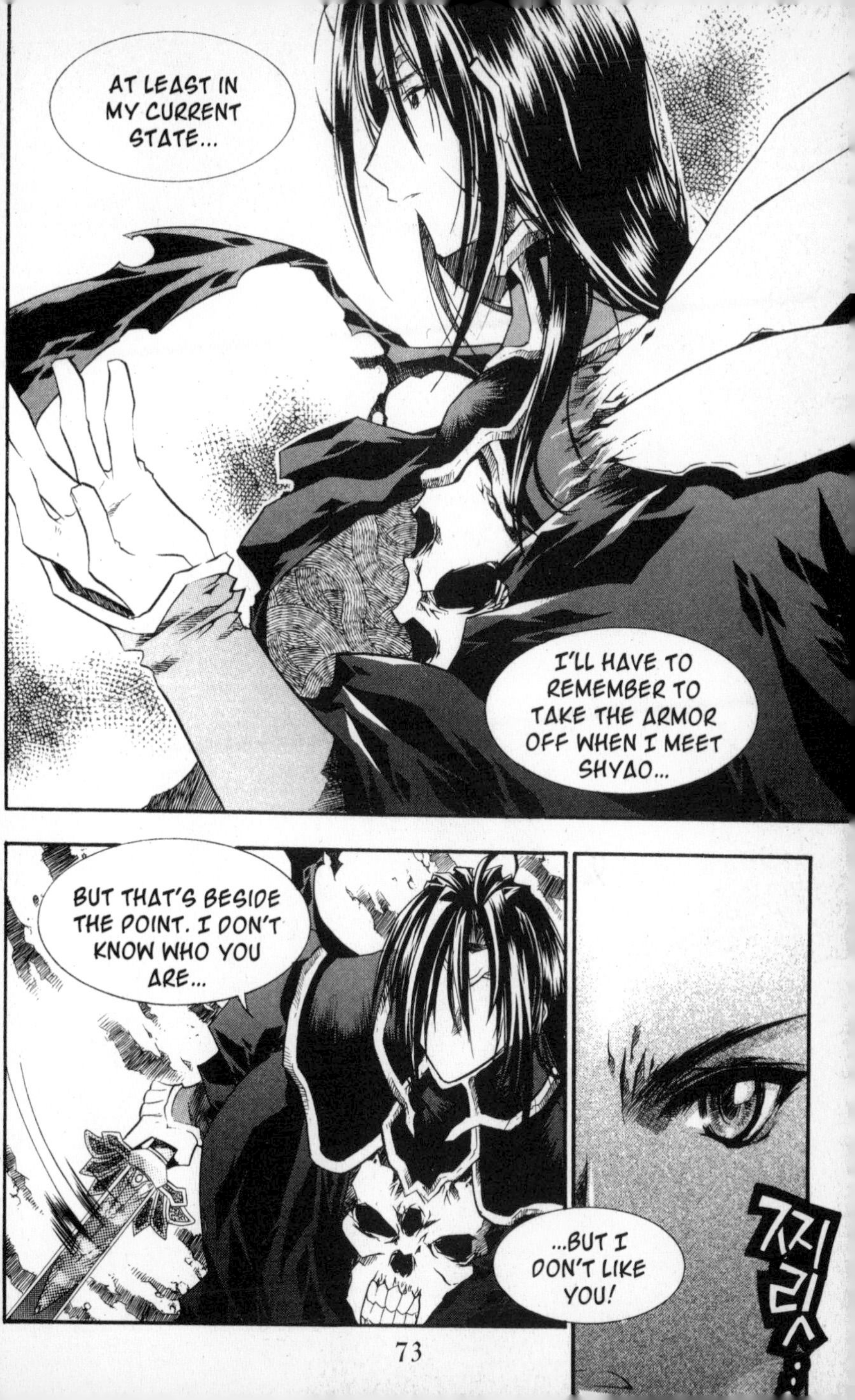
AT LEAST IN MY CURRENT STATE...
I'LL HAVE TO REMEMBER TO TAKE THE ARMOR OFF WHEN I MEET SHYAO...
BUT THAT'S BESIDE THE POINT. I DON'T KNOW WHO YOU ARE...
...BUT I DON'T LIKE YOU!

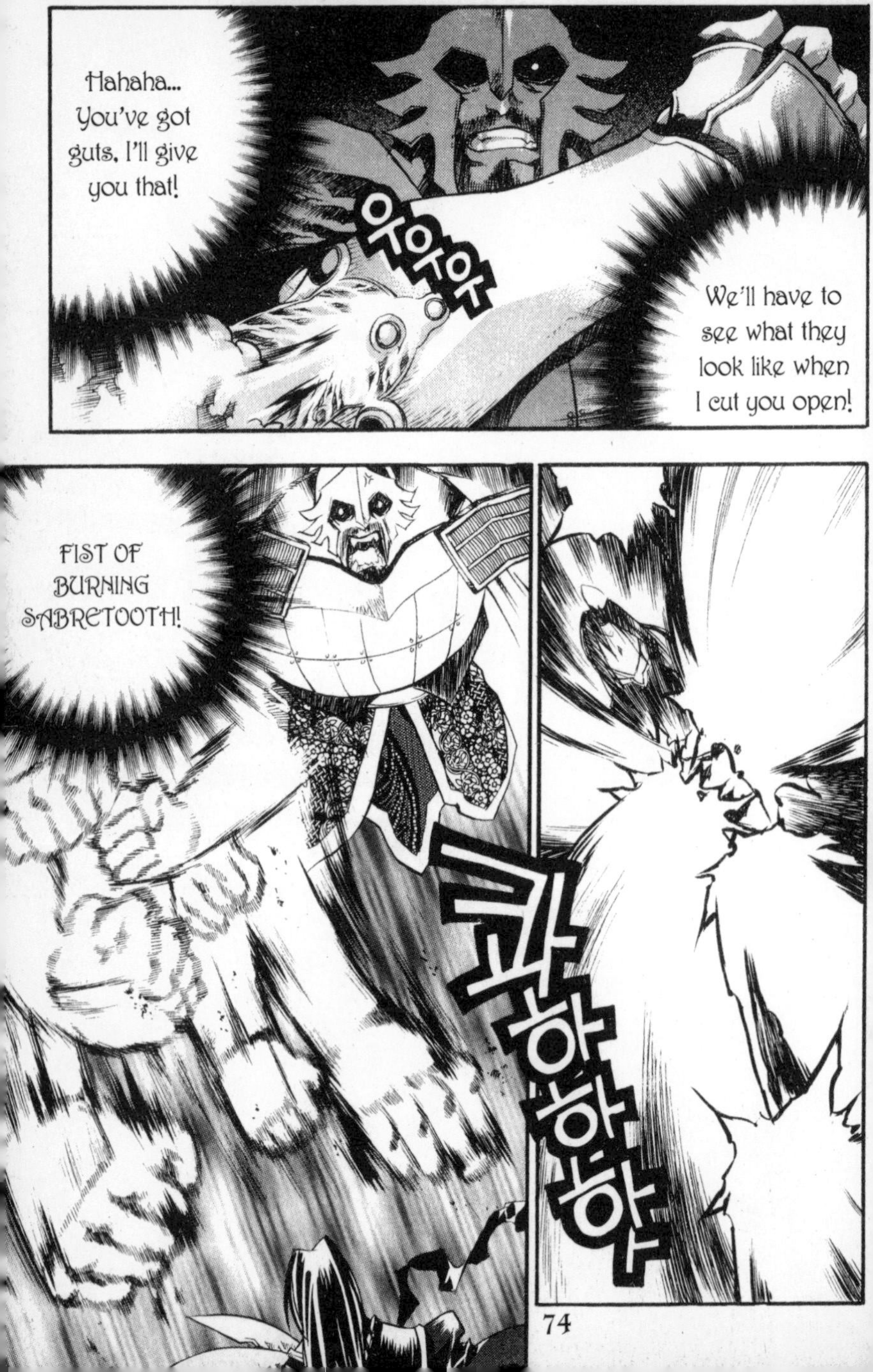
Hahaha...
You've got guts, I'll give you that!
아아아악
We'll have to see what they look like when I cut you open!
FIST OF BURNING SABRETOOTH!
콰하하하

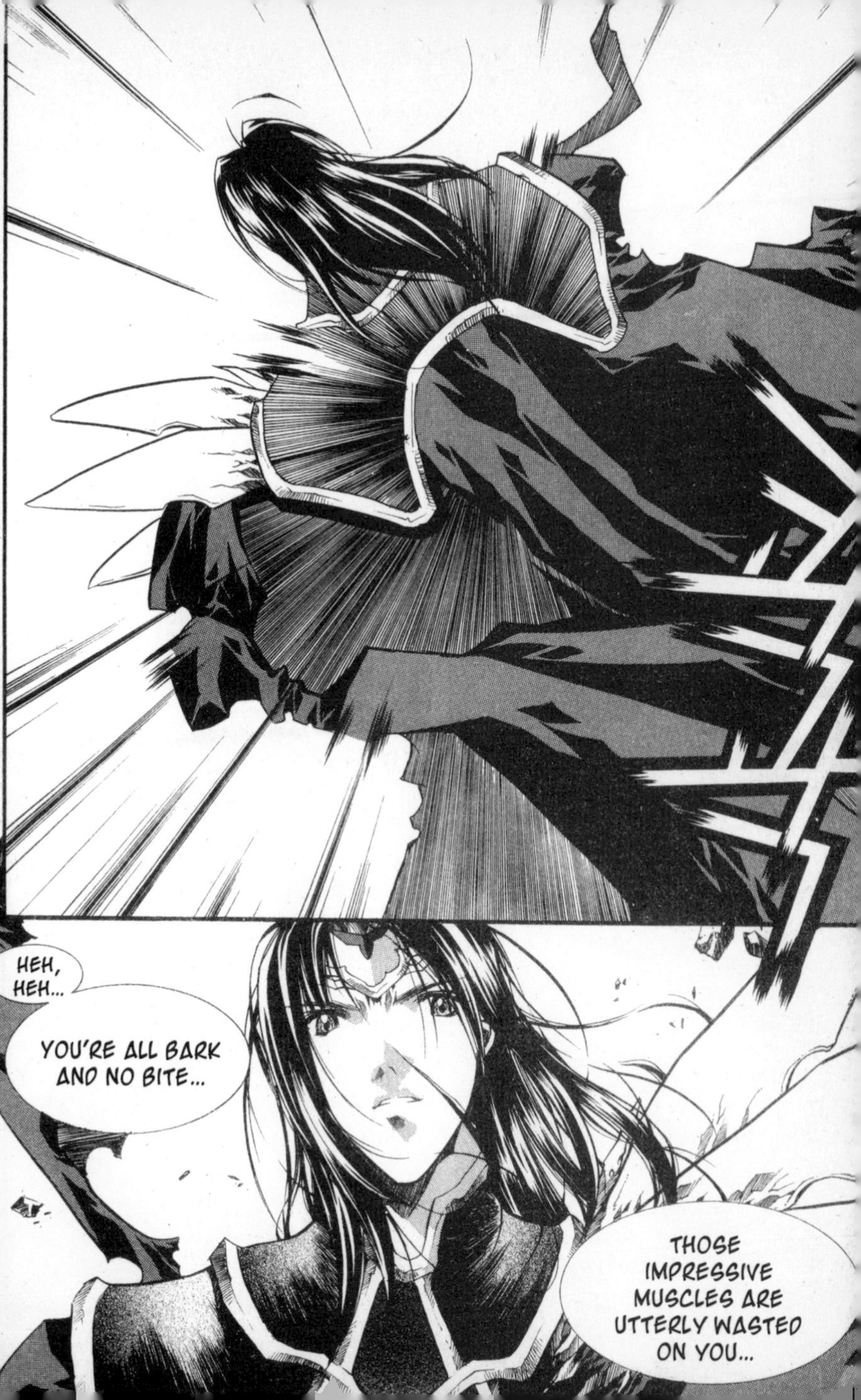
HEH, HEH...
YOU'RE ALL BARK AND NO BITE...
THOSE IMPRESSIVE MUSCLES ARE UTTERLY WASTED ON YOU...

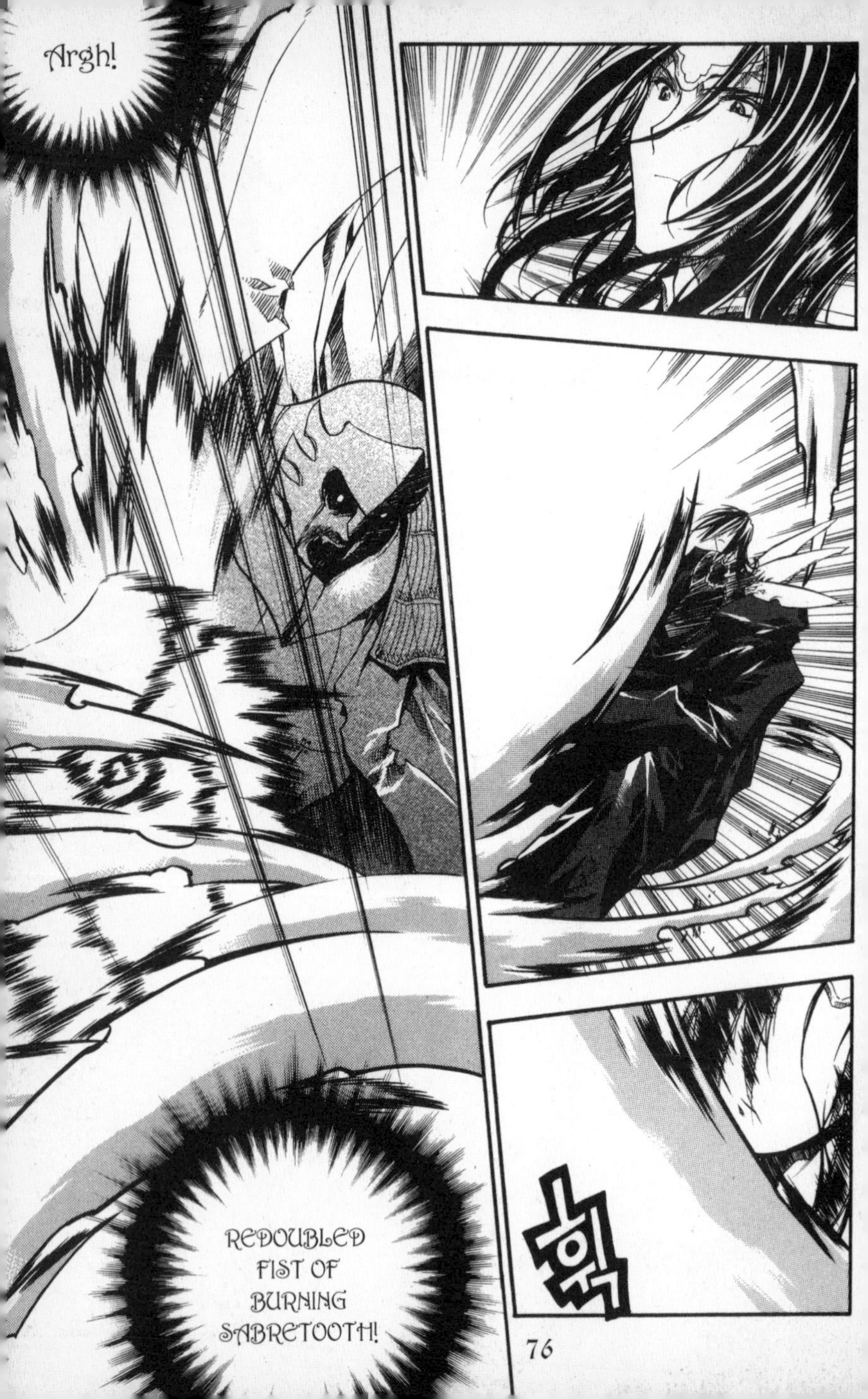
Argh!
REDOUBLED FIST OF BURNING SABRETOOTH!
휙

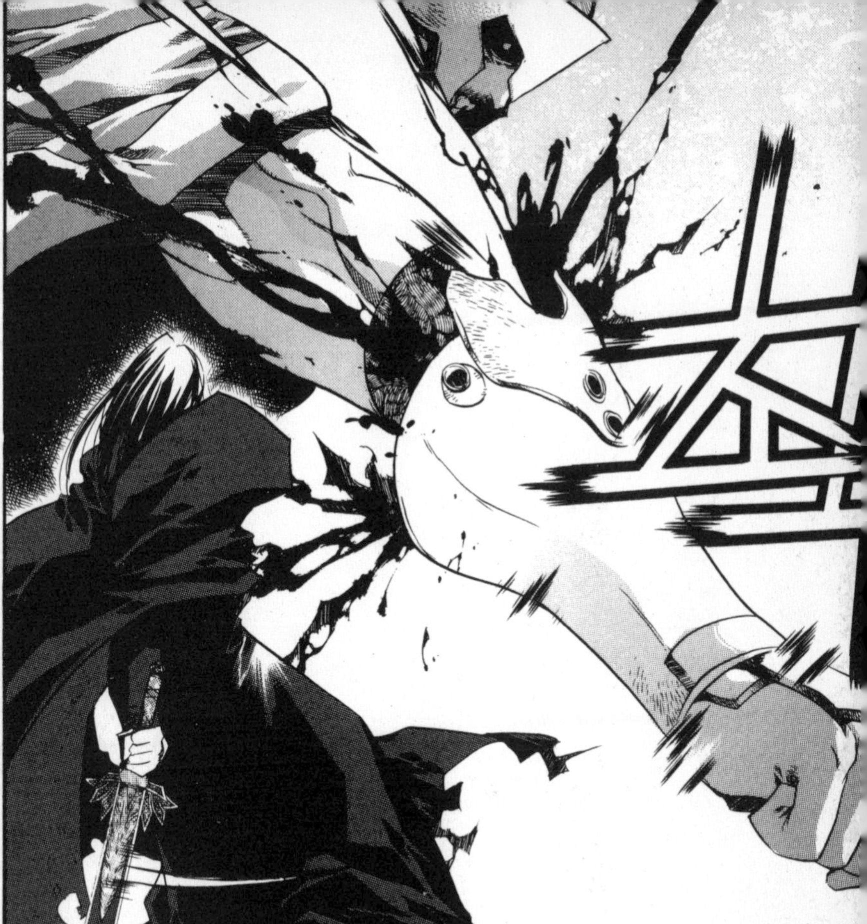

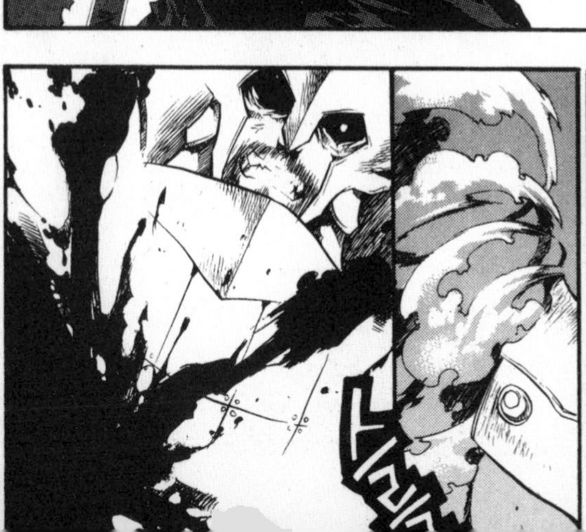

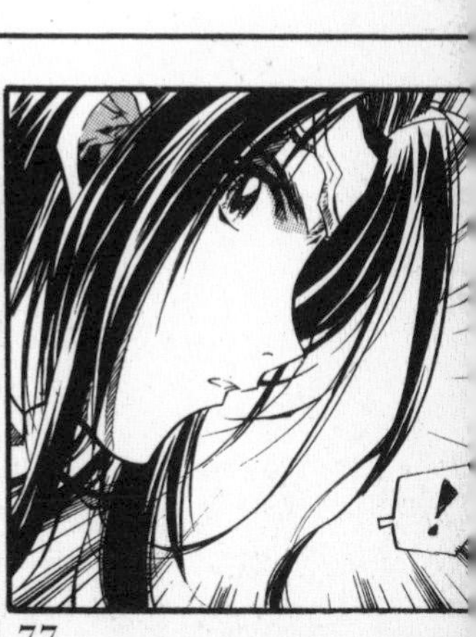
!

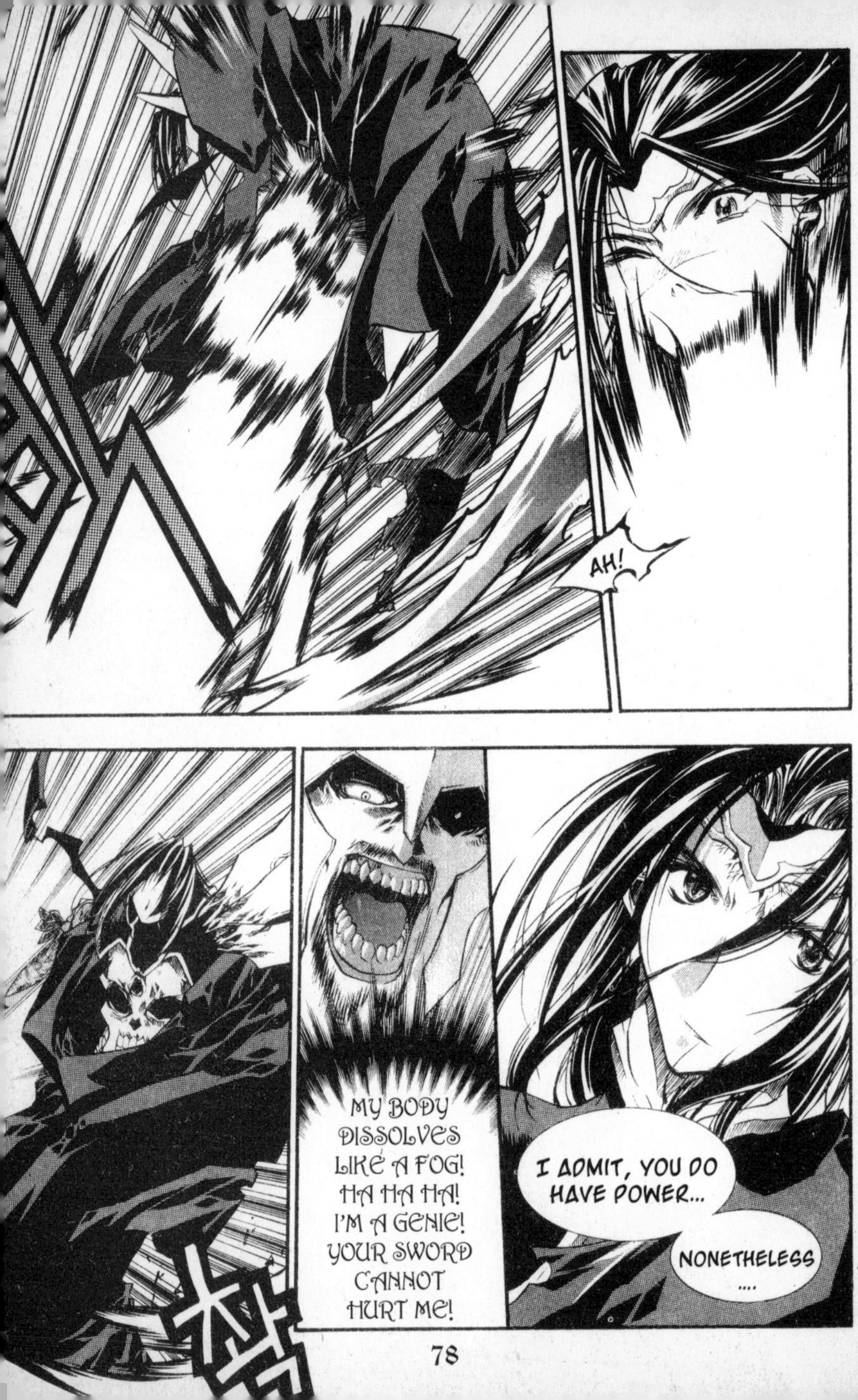
AH!
MY BODY DISSOLVES LIKE A FOG! HA HA HA! I'M A GENIE! YOUR SWORD CANNOT HURT ME!
I ADMIT, YOU DO HAVE POWER...
NONETHELESS ....

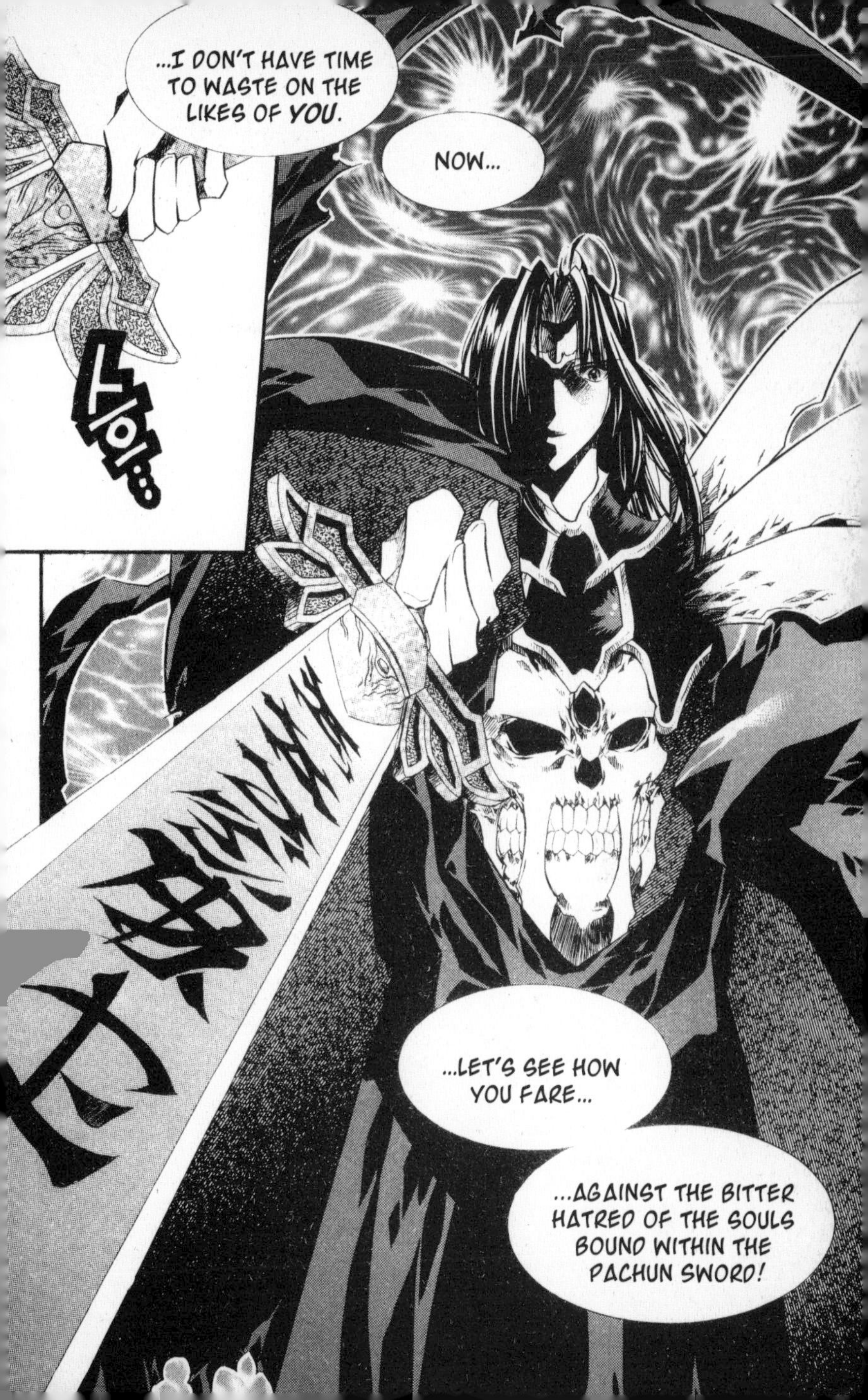
...I DON'T HAVE TIME TO WASTE ON THE LIKES OF YOU.
NOW...
...LET'S SEE HOW YOU FARE...
...AGAINST THE BITTER HATRED OF THE SOULS BOUND WITHIN THE PACHUN SWORD!

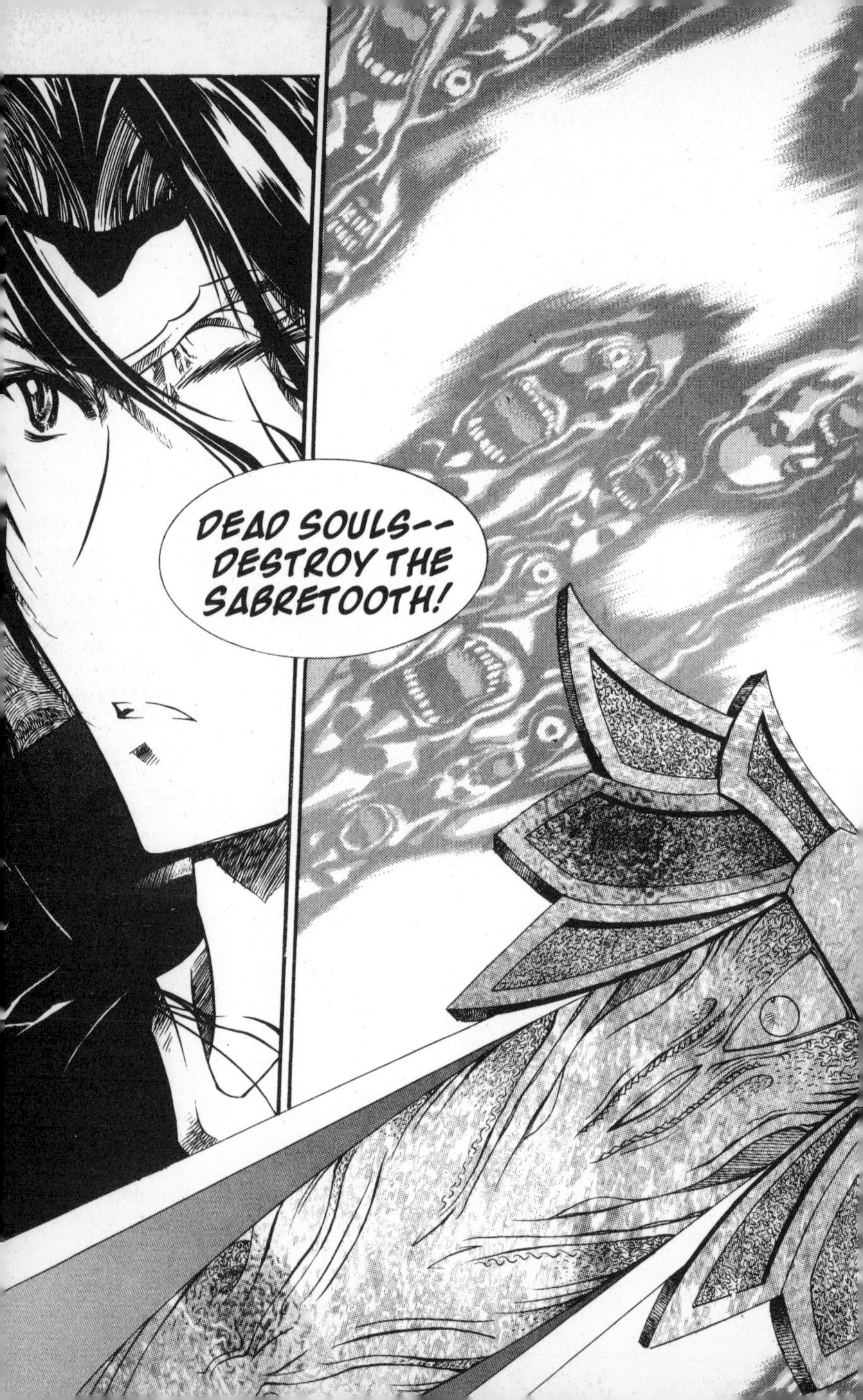
DEAD SOULS--
DESTROY THE
SABRETOOTH!

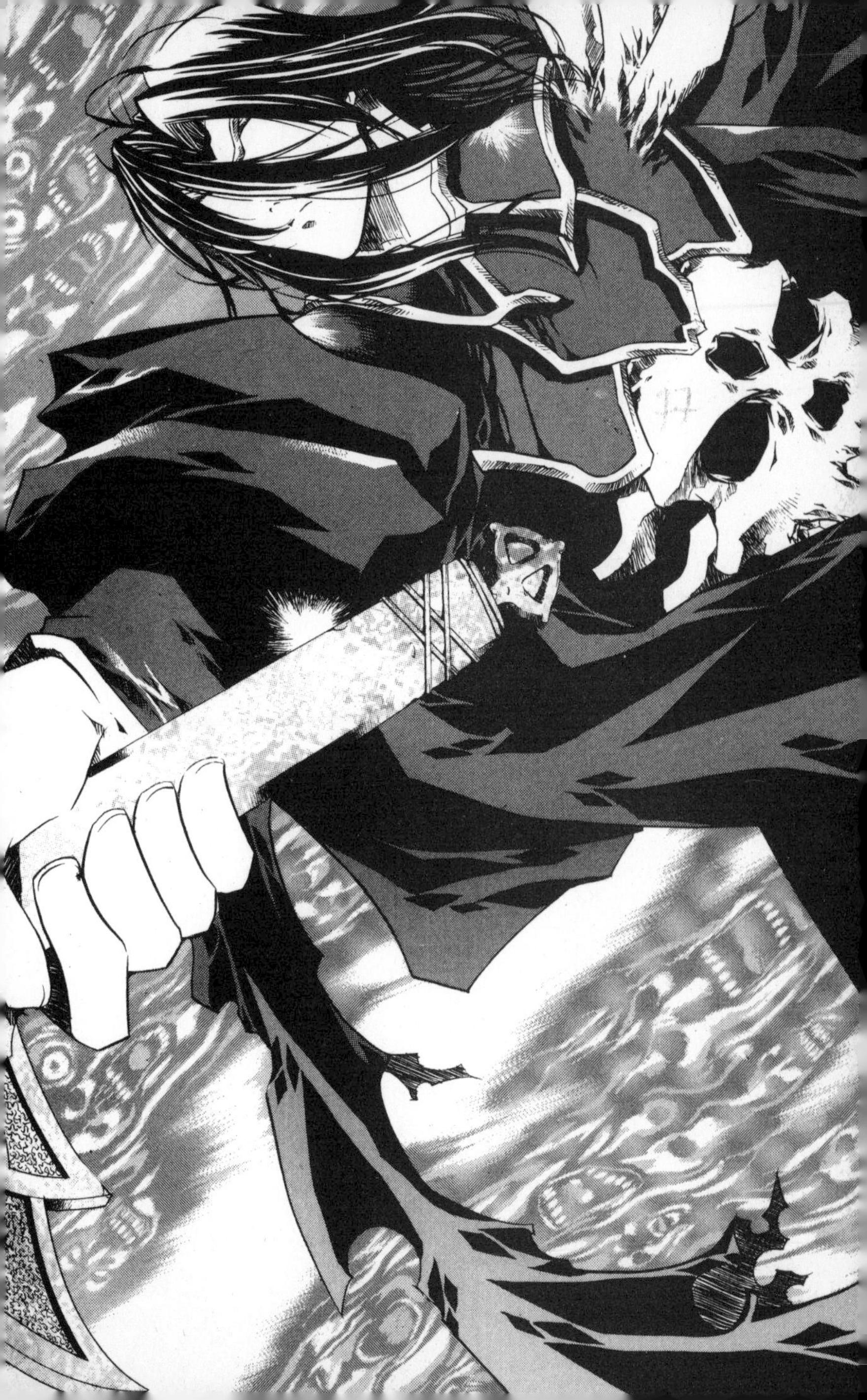

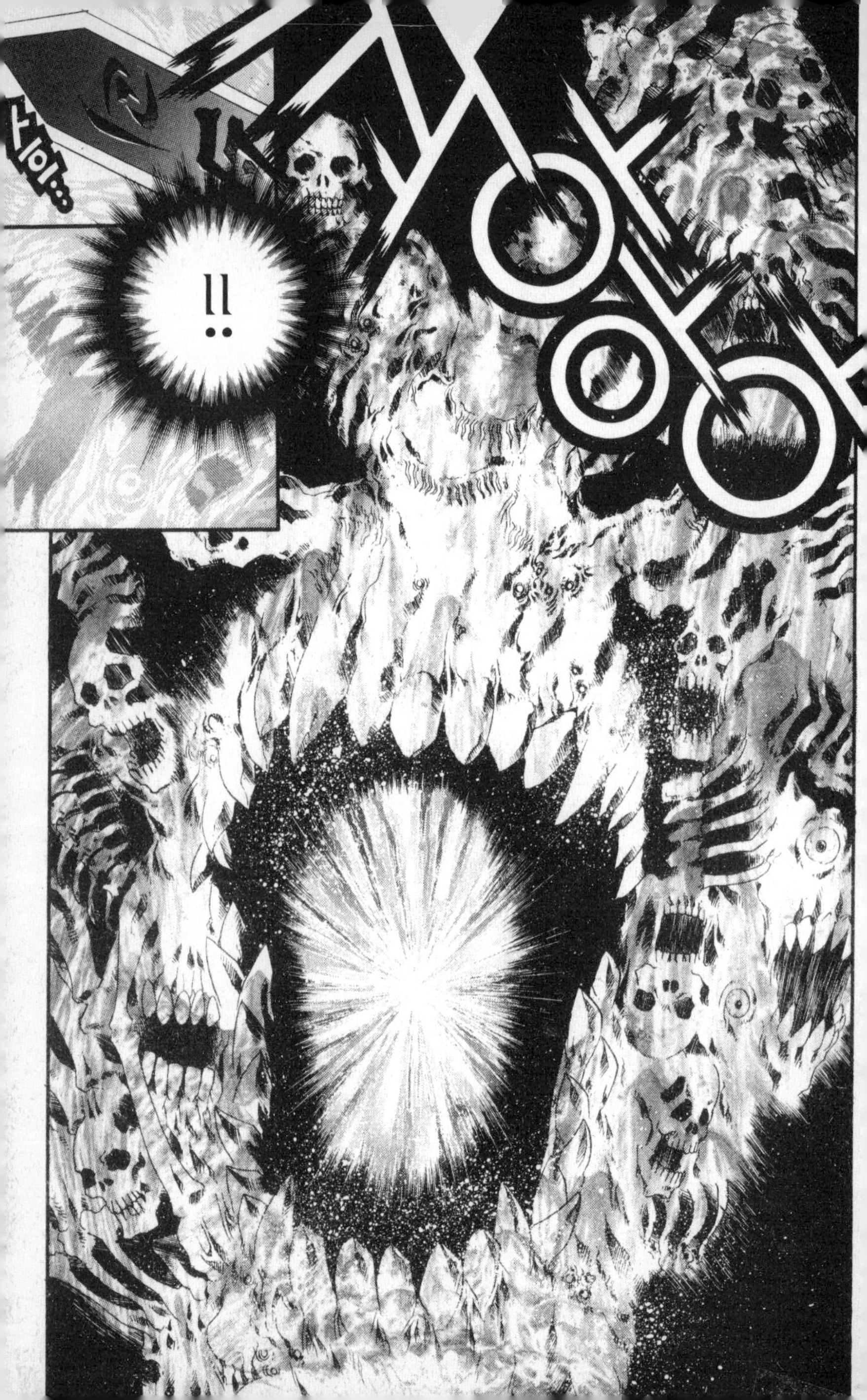
시이…
!!

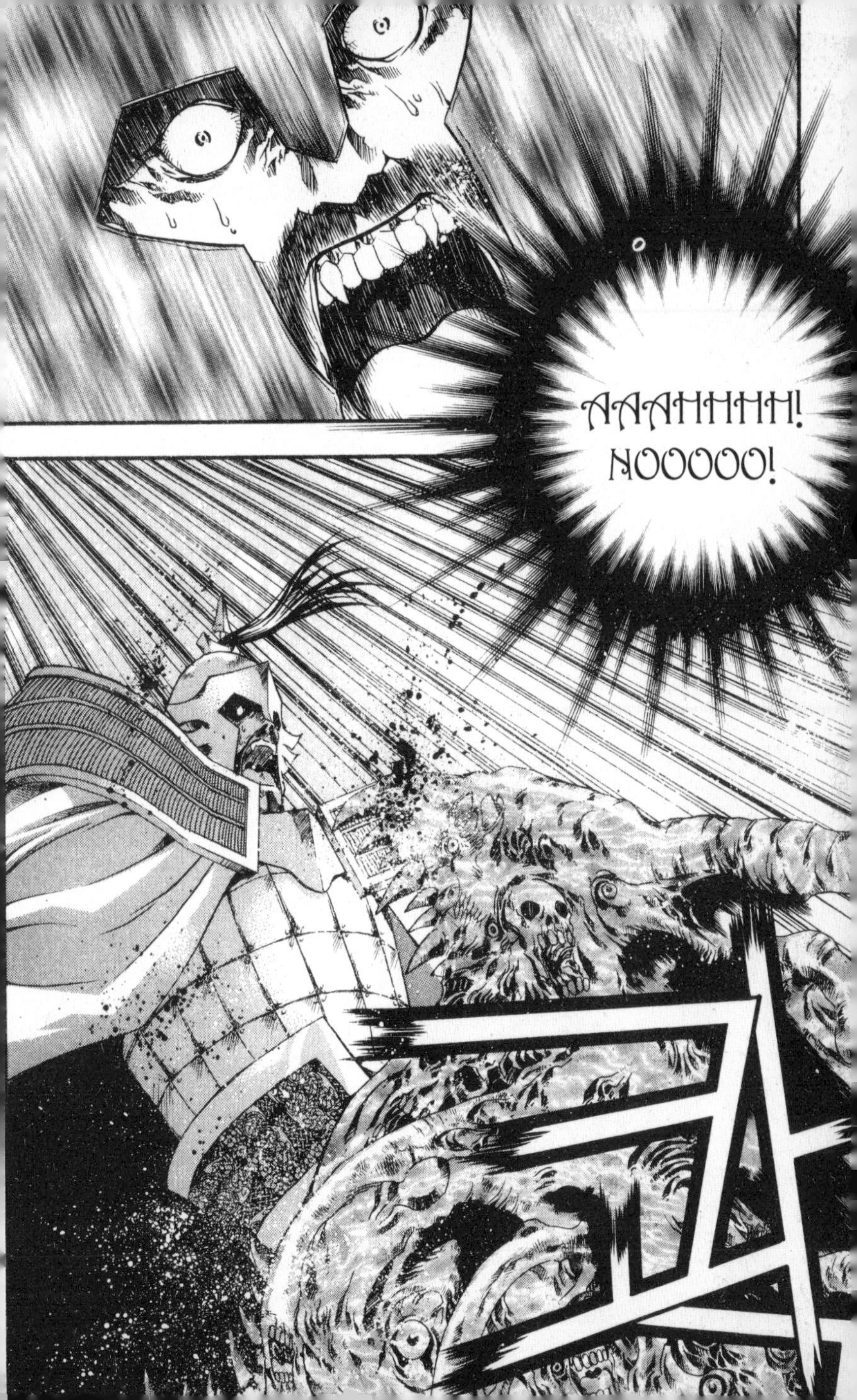
AAAHHHH! NOOOOO!

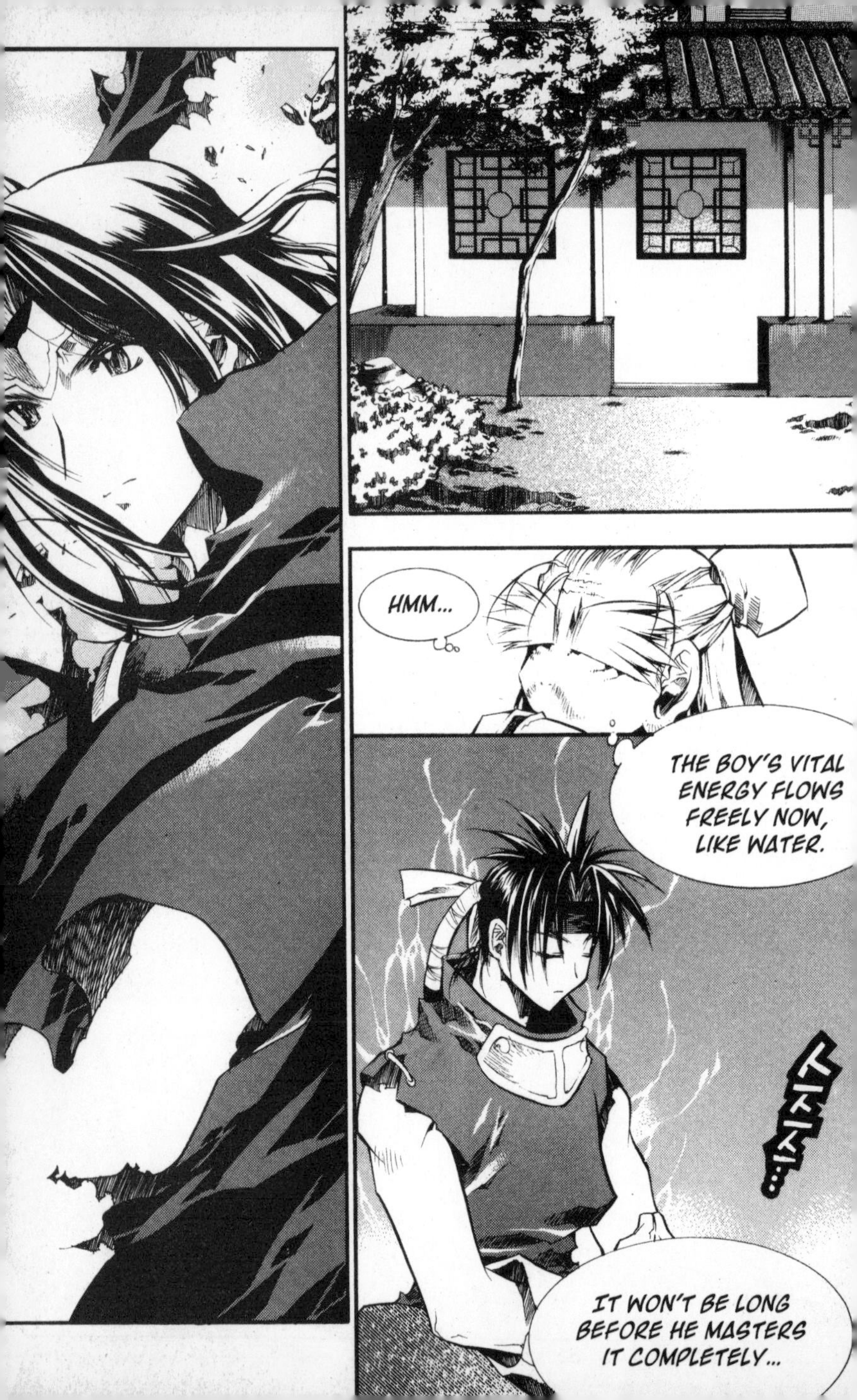
HMM...
THE BOY'S VITAL ENERGY FLOWS FREELY NOW, LIKE WATER.
IT WON'T BE LONG BEFORE HE MASTERS IT COMPLETELY...

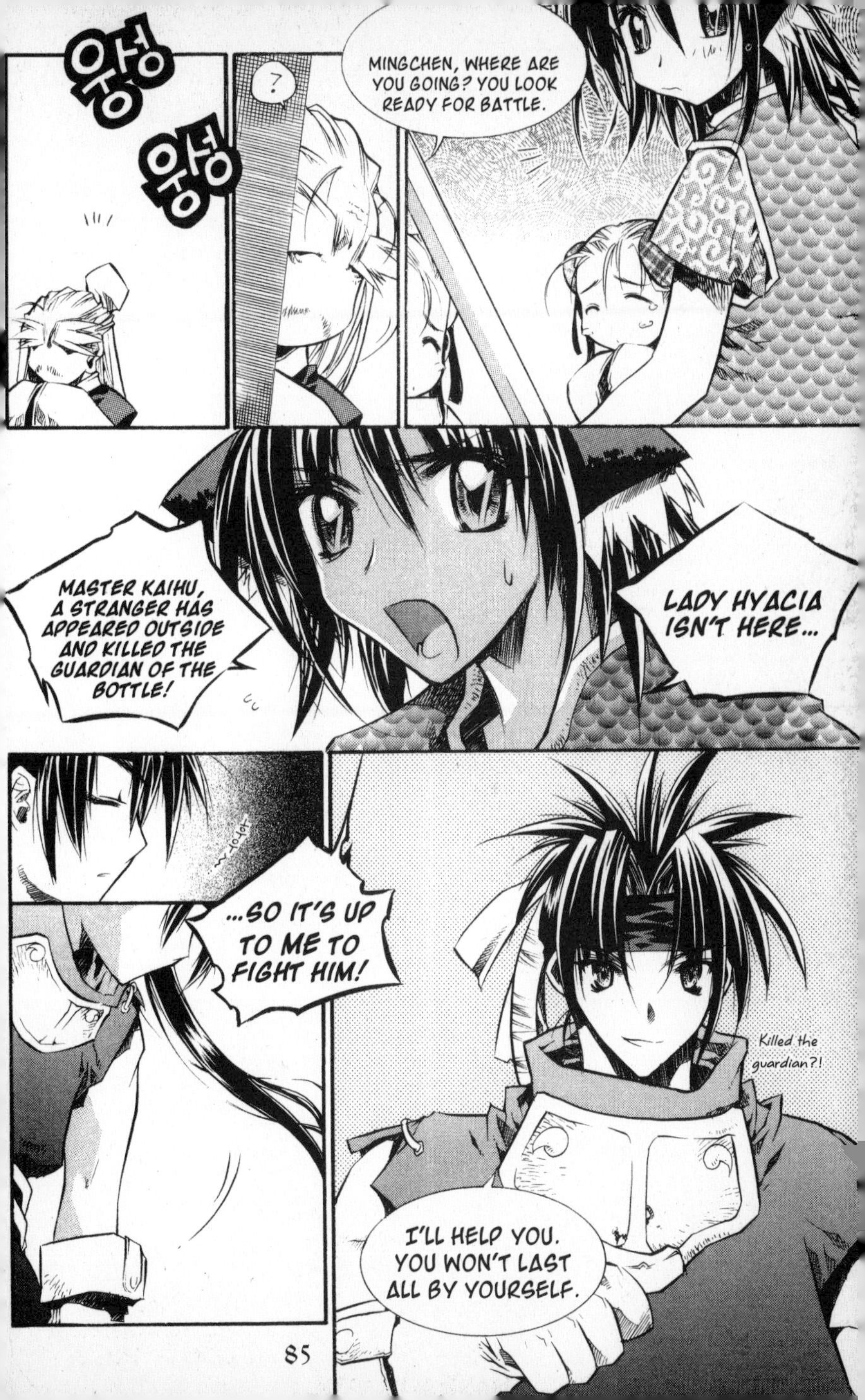
웅성
웅성
?
MINGCHEN, WHERE ARE YOU GOING? YOU LOOK READY FOR BATTLE.
MASTER KAIHU, A STRANGER HAS APPEARED OUTSIDE AND KILLED THE GUARDIAN OF THE BOTTLE!
LADY HYACIA ISN'T HERE...
...SO IT'S UP TO ME TO FIGHT HIM!
Killed the guardian?!
I'LL HELP YOU. YOU WON'T LAST ALL BY YOURSELF.

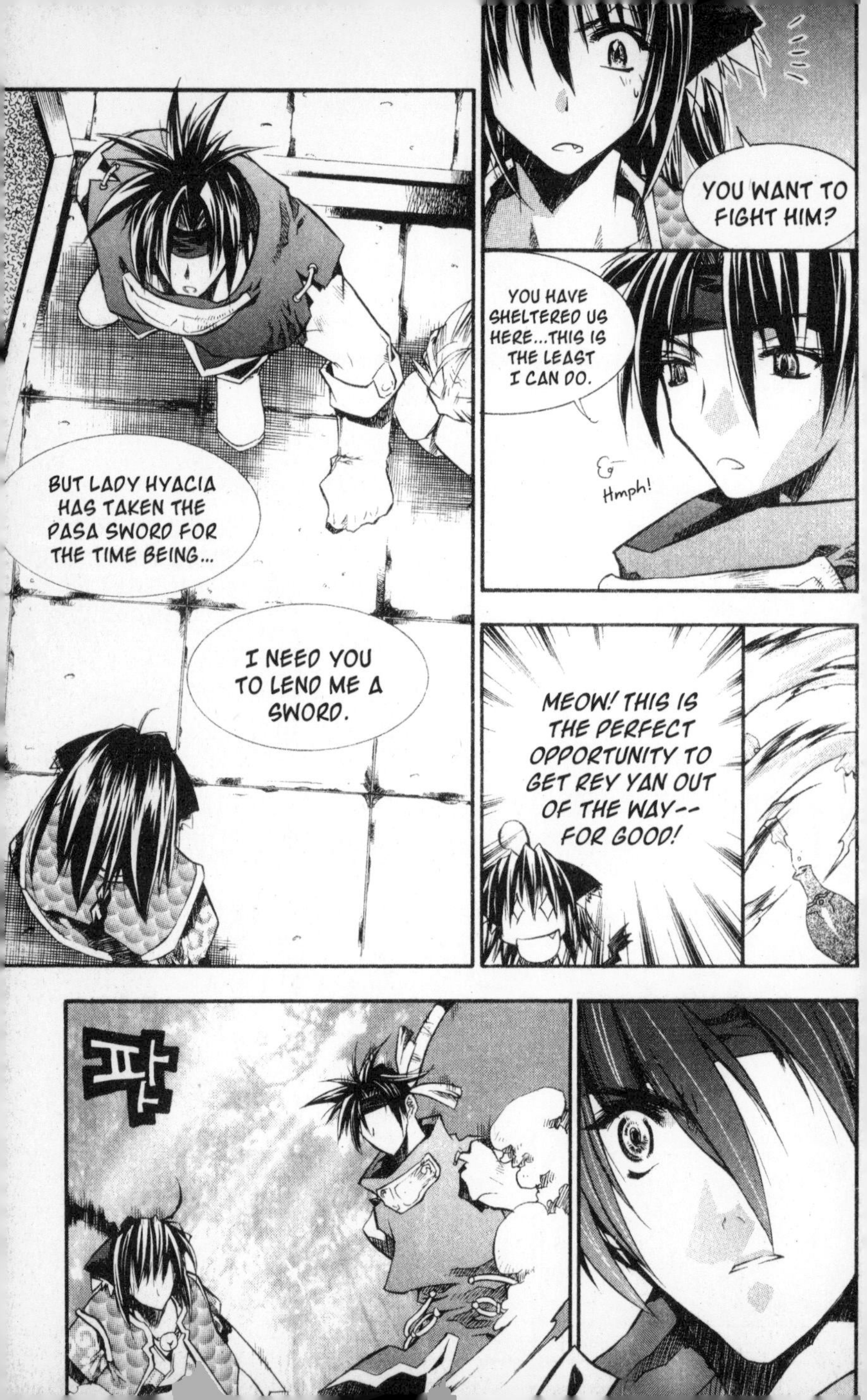
BUT LADY HYACIA HAS TAKEN THE PASA SWORD FOR THE TIME BEING...
I NEED YOU TO LEND ME A SWORD.
YOU WANT TO FIGHT HIM?
YOU HAVE SHELTERED US HERE...THIS IS THE LEAST I CAN DO.
Hmph!
MEOW! THIS IS THE PERFECT OPPORTUNITY TO GET REY YAN OUT OF THE WAY--FOR GOOD!
팍

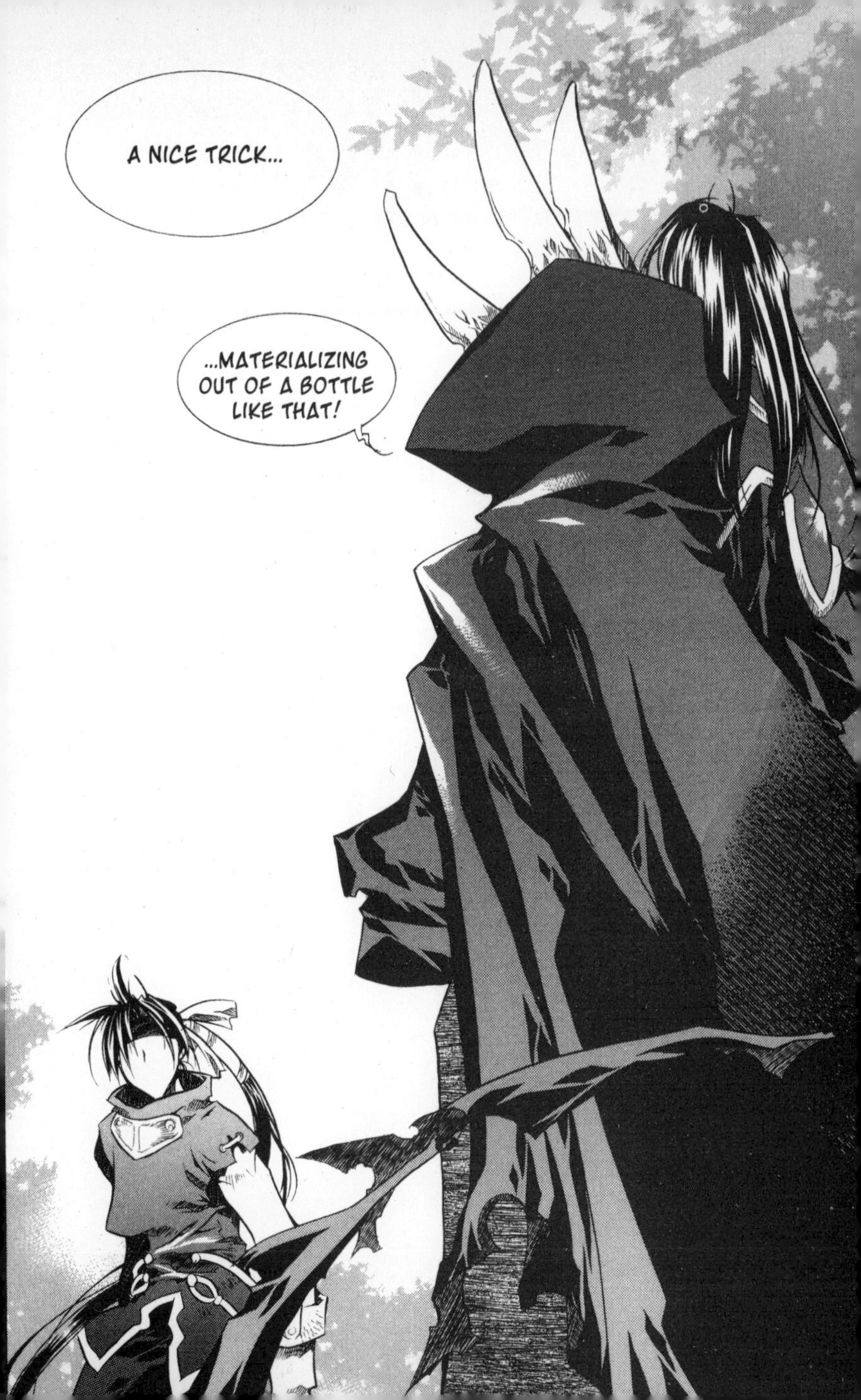
A NICE TRICK...
...MATERIALIZING OUT OF A BOTTLE LIKE THAT!

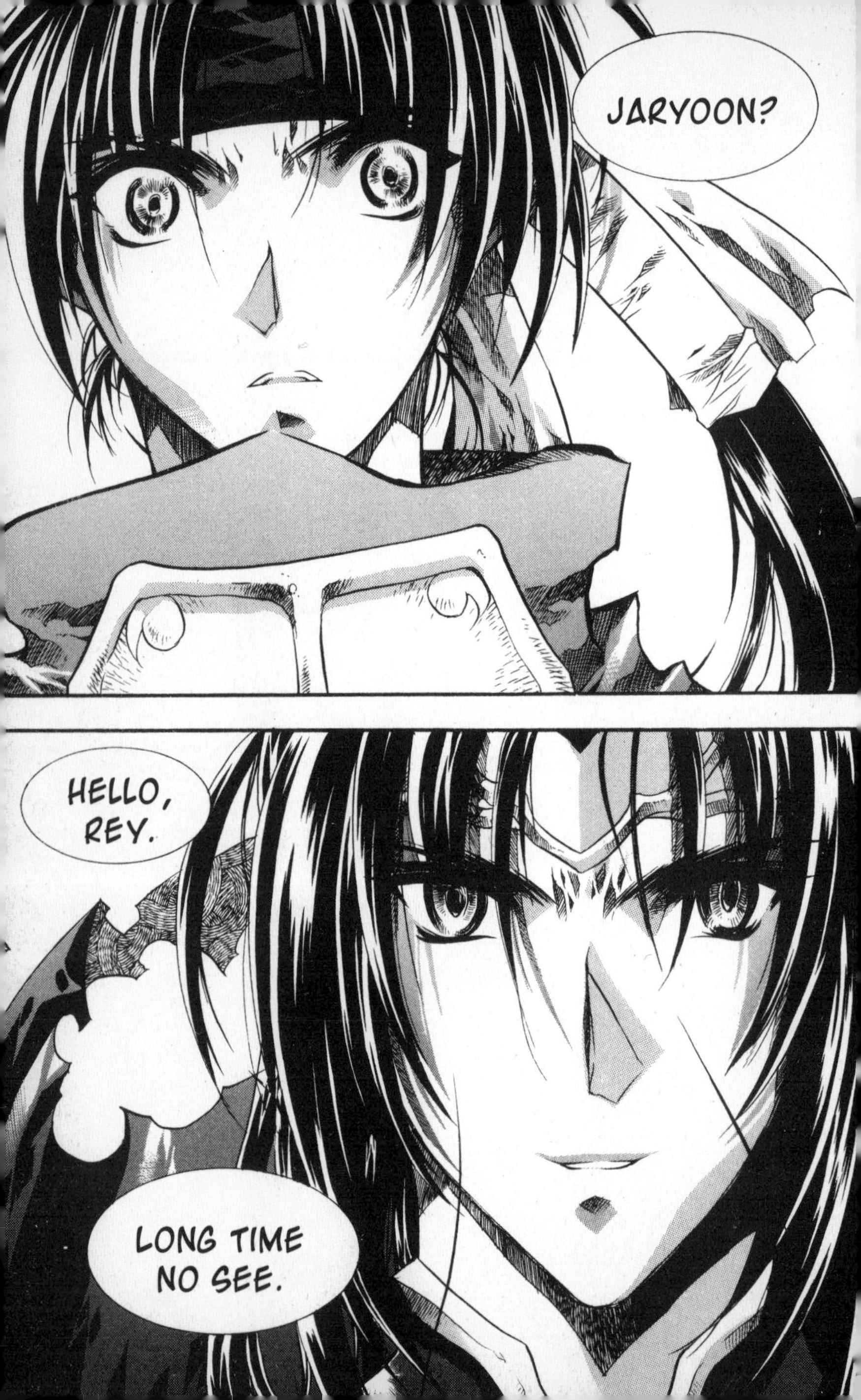
JARYOON?
HELLO, REY.
LONG TIME NO SEE.

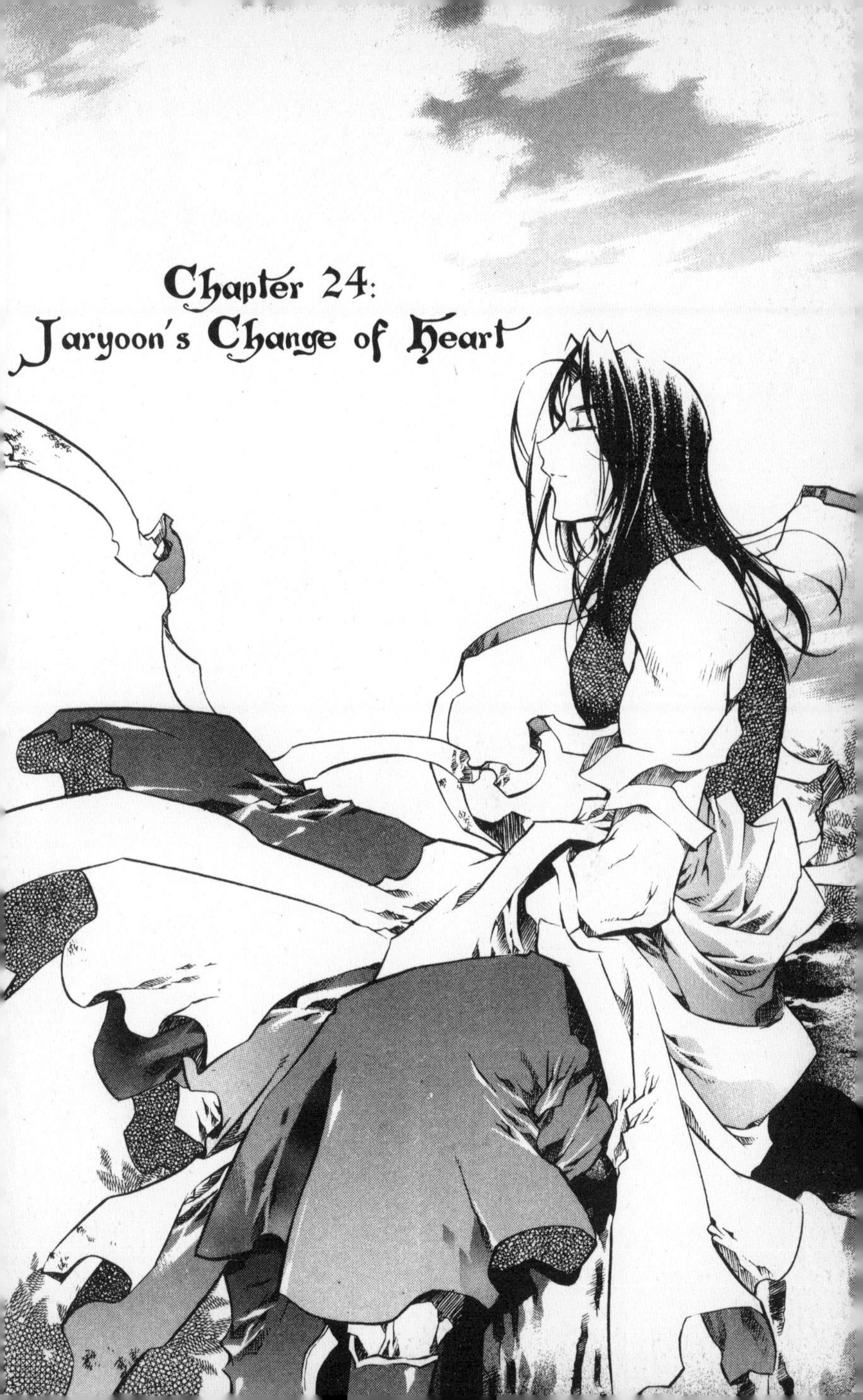
Chapter 24:
Jaryoon's Change of Heart

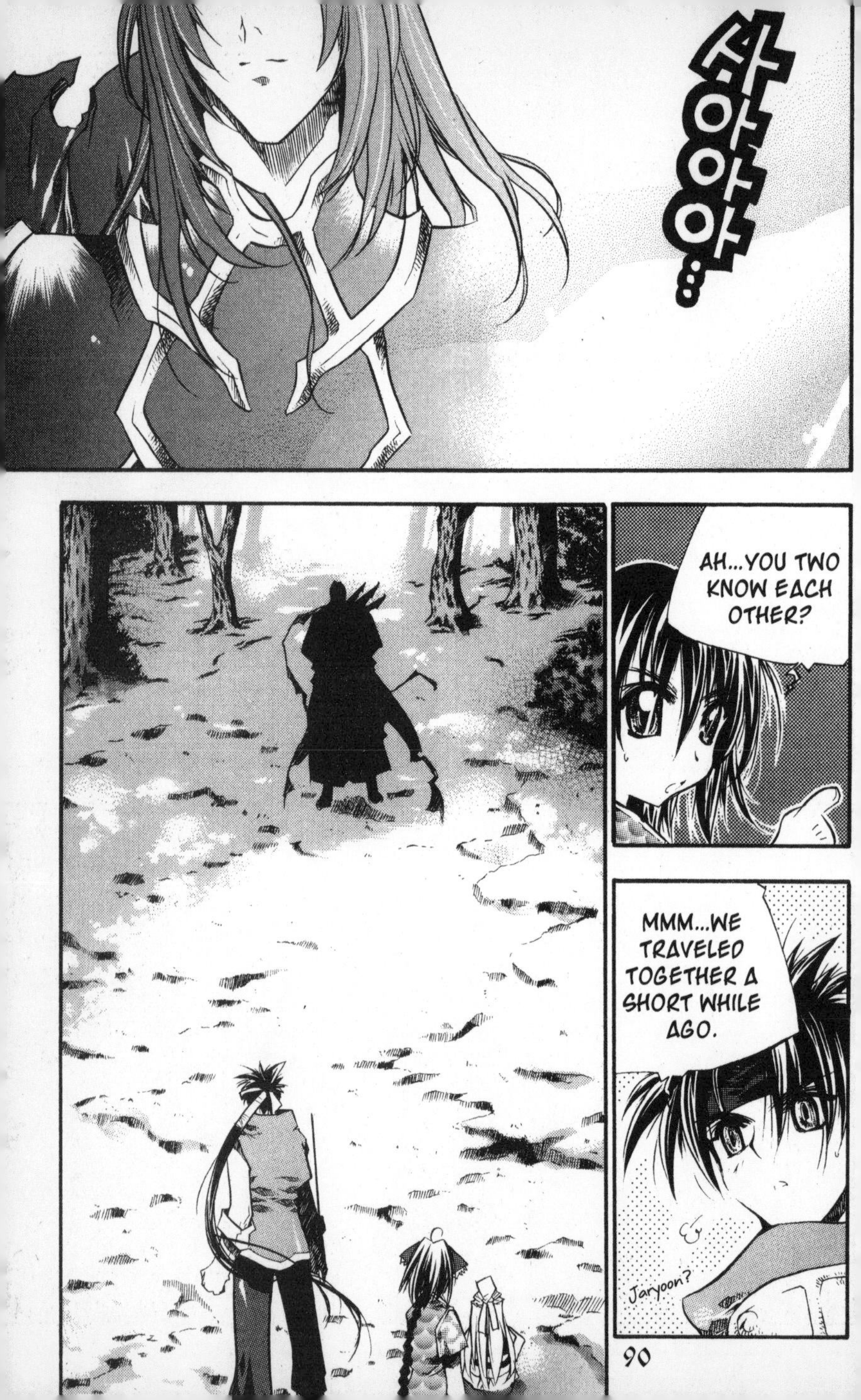
사아아아...
AH...YOU TWO KNOW EACH OTHER?
MMM...WE TRAVELED TOGETHER A SHORT WHILE AGO.
Jaryoon?

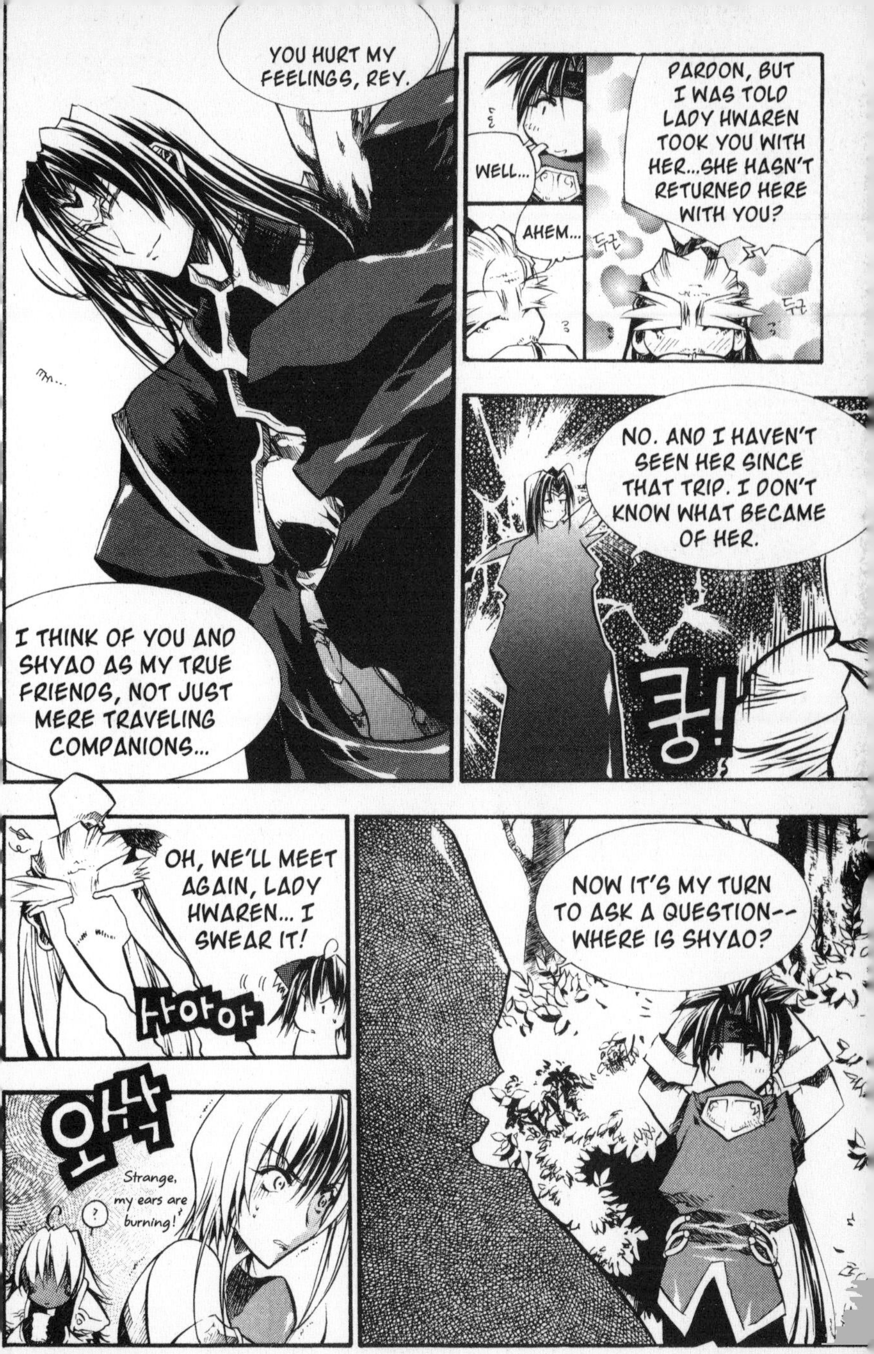
YOU HURT MY FEELINGS, REY.
I THINK OF YOU AND SHYAO AS MY TRUE FRIENDS, NOT JUST MERE TRAVELING COMPANIONS...
WELL...
PARDON, BUT I WAS TOLD LADY HWAREN TOOK YOU WITH HER...SHE HASN'T RETURNED HERE WITH YOU?
AHEM...
NO. AND I HAVEN'T SEEN HER SINCE THAT TRIP. I DON'T KNOW WHAT BECAME OF HER.
쿵!
OH, WE'LL MEET AGAIN, LADY HWAREN... I SWEAR IT!
오싹
Strange, my ears are burning!
?
NOW IT'S MY TURN TO ASK A QUESTION-- WHERE IS SHYAO?

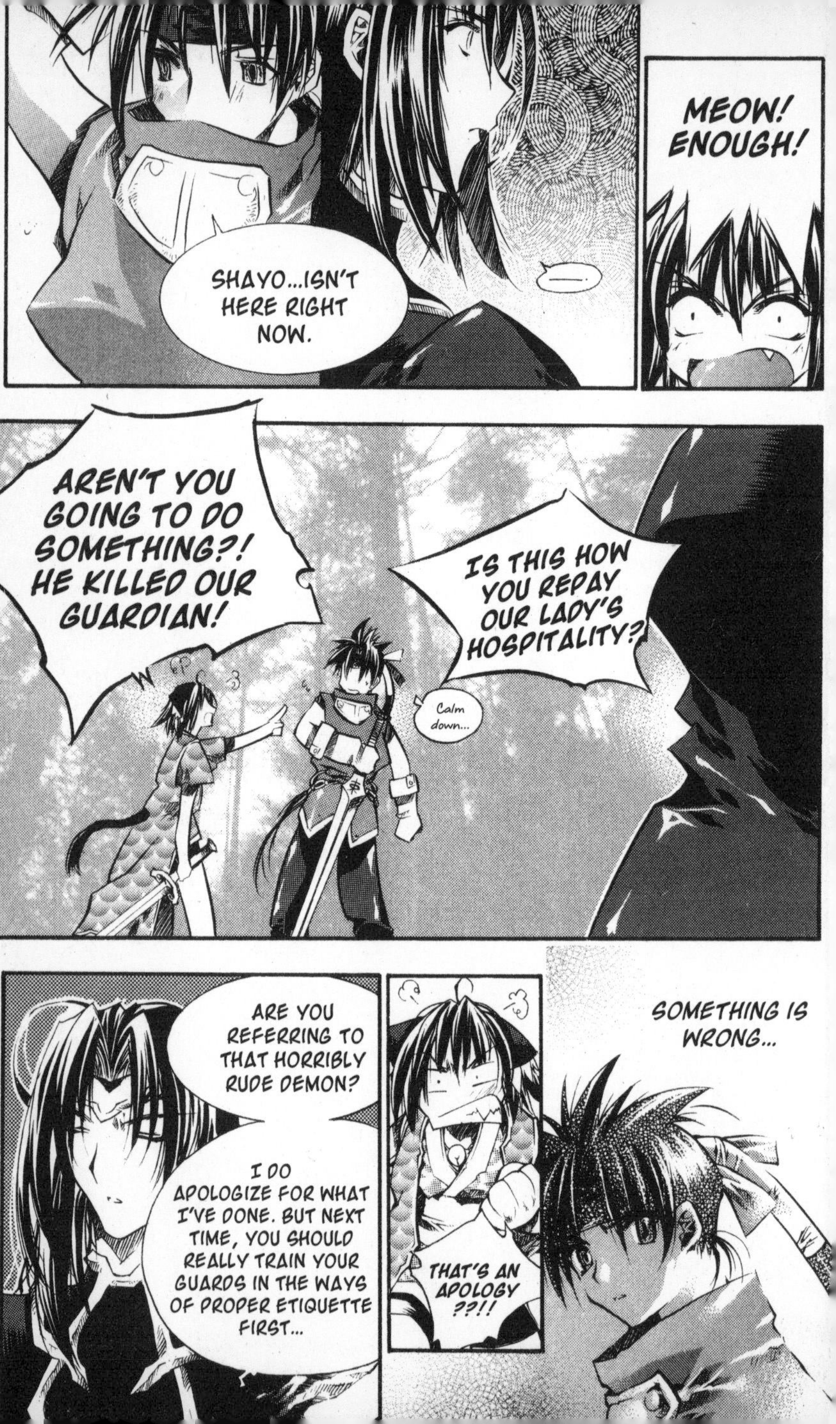
SHAYO...ISN'T HERE RIGHT NOW.
—.
MEOW! ENOUGH!
AREN'T YOU GOING TO DO SOMETHING?! HE KILLED OUR GUARDIAN!
IS THIS HOW YOU REPAY OUR LADY'S HOSPITALITY?!
Calm down...
ARE YOU REFERRING TO THAT HORRIBLY RUDE DEMON?
I DO APOLOGIZE FOR WHAT I'VE DONE. BUT NEXT TIME, YOU SHOULD REALLY TRAIN YOUR GUARDS IN THE WAYS OF PROPER ETIQUETTE FIRST...
THAT'S AN APOLOGY ??!!
SOMETHING IS WRONG...

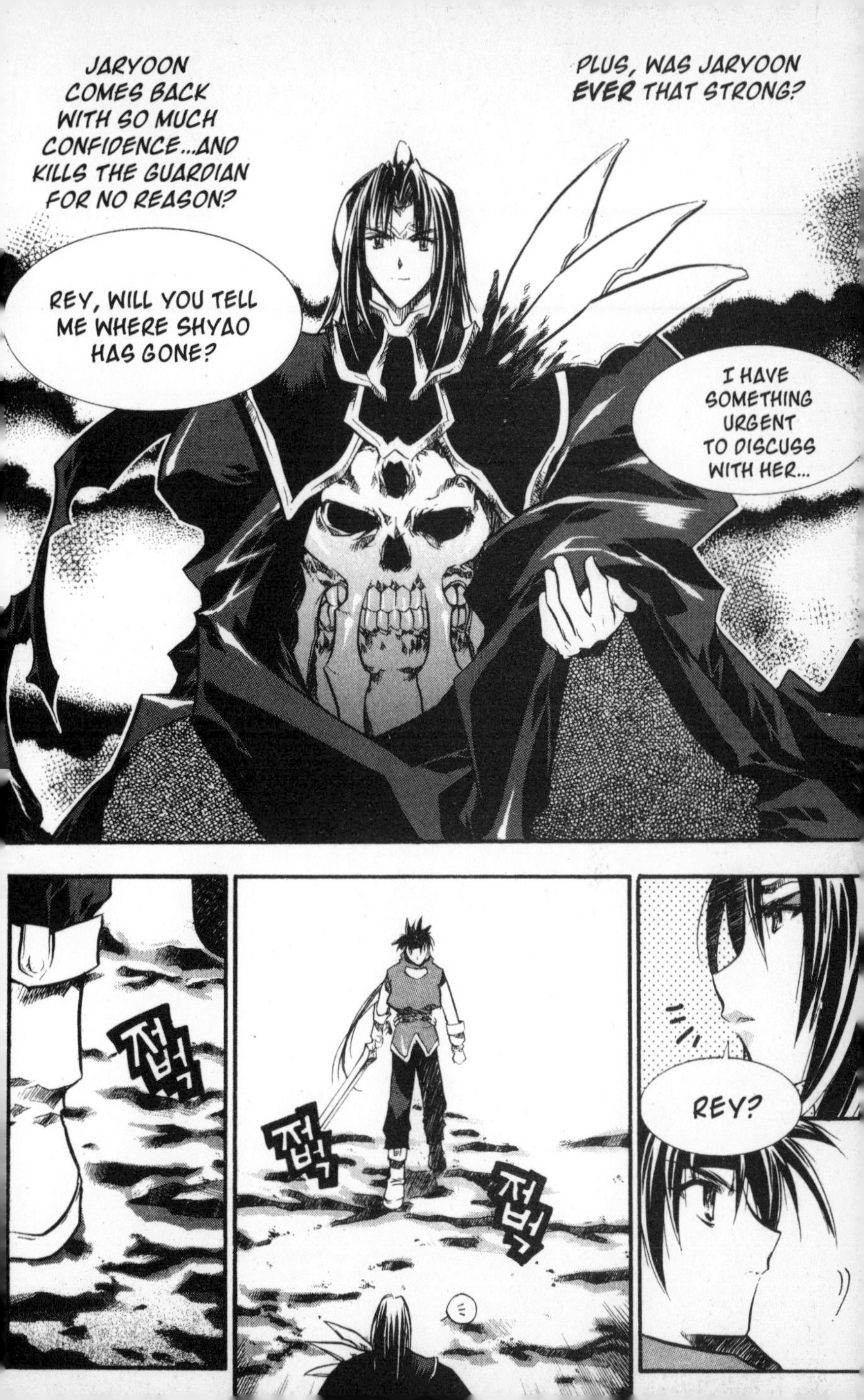
JARYOON COMES BACK WITH SO MUCH CONFIDENCE...AND KILLS THE GUARDIAN FOR NO REASON?
PLUS, WAS JARYOON EVER THAT STRONG?
REY, WILL YOU TELL ME WHERE SHYAO HAS GONE?
I HAVE SOMETHING URGENT TO DISCUSS WITH HER...
저벅
저벅
저벅
REY?

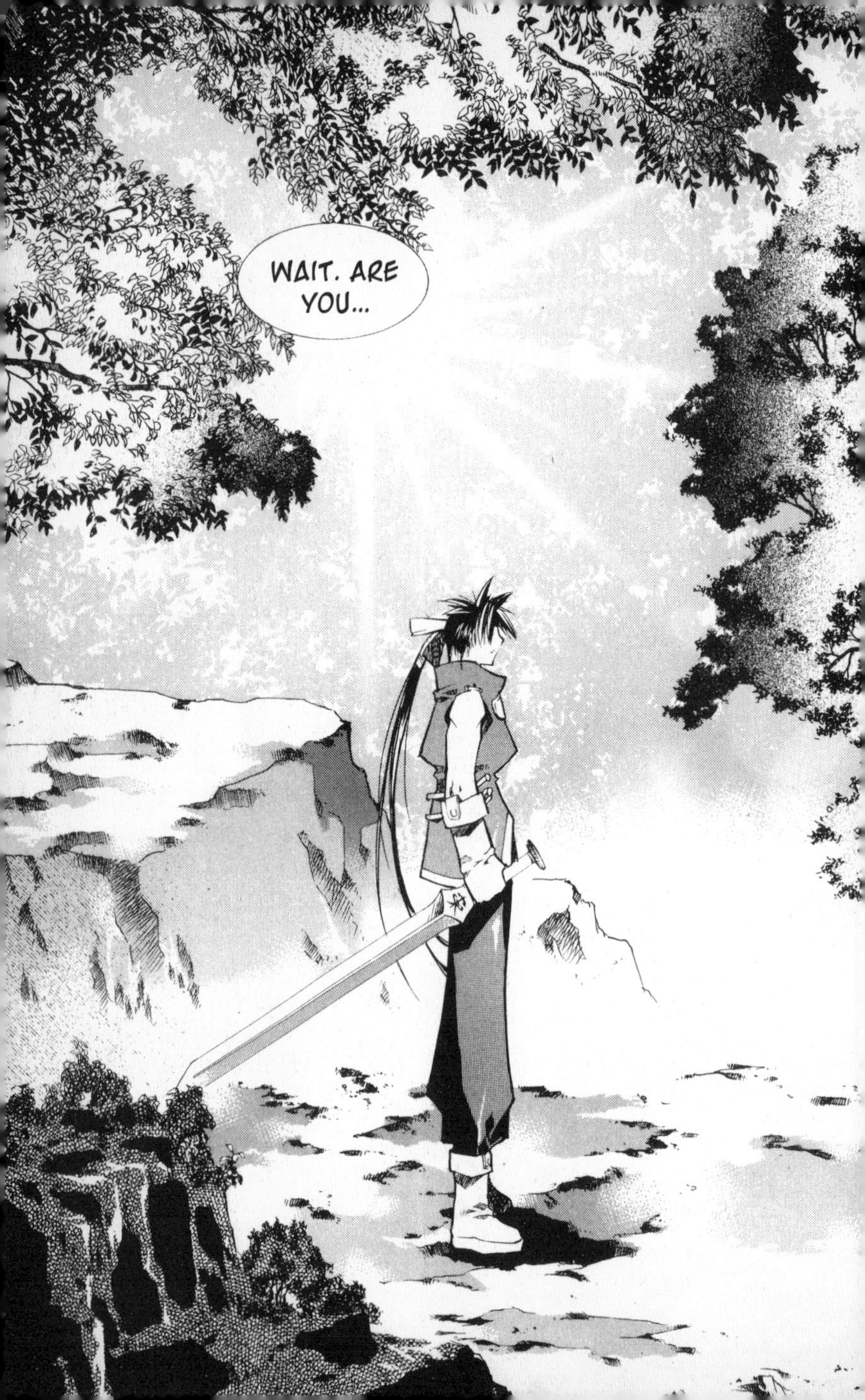
WAIT. ARE YOU...

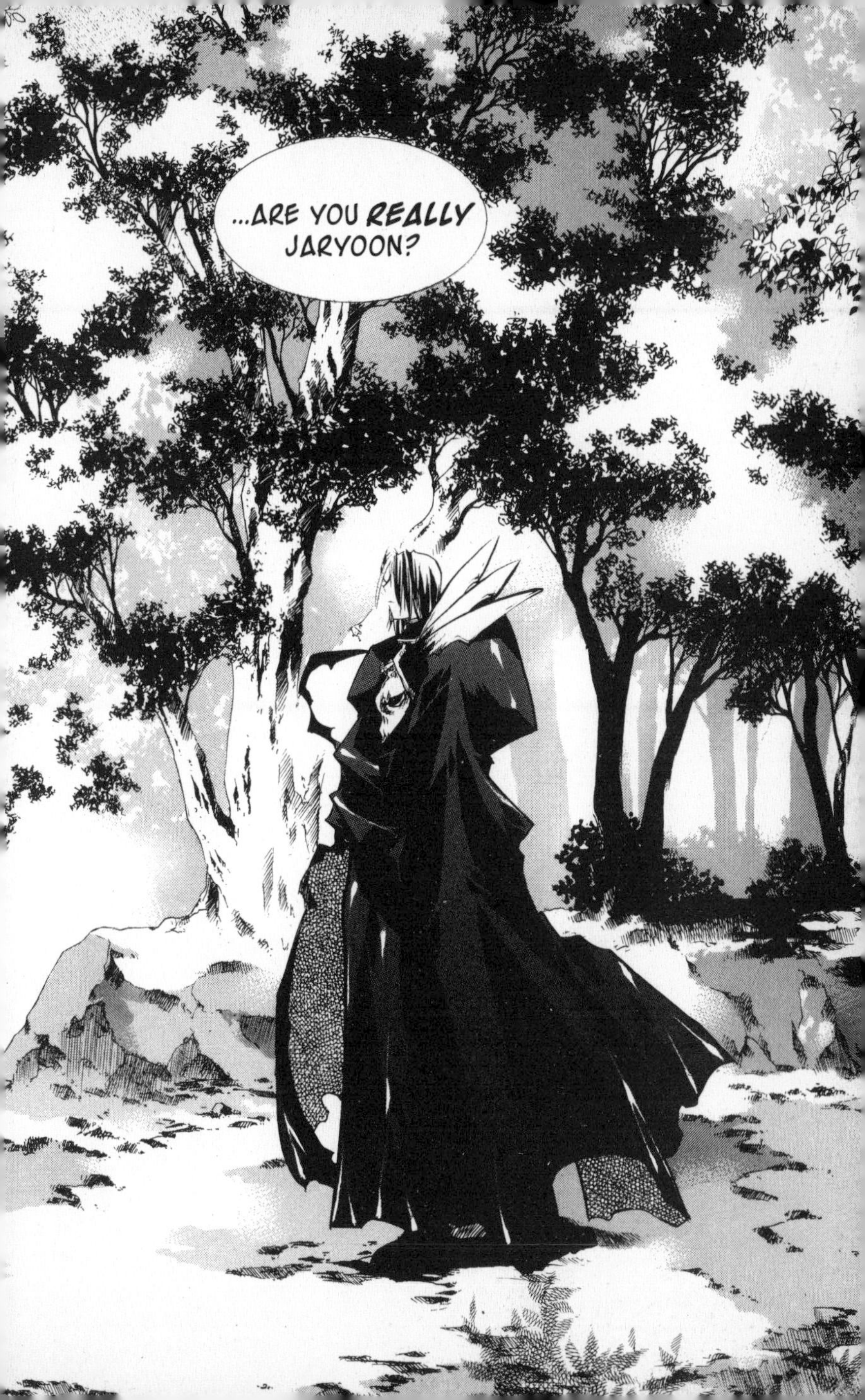
...ARE YOU REALLY JARYOON?

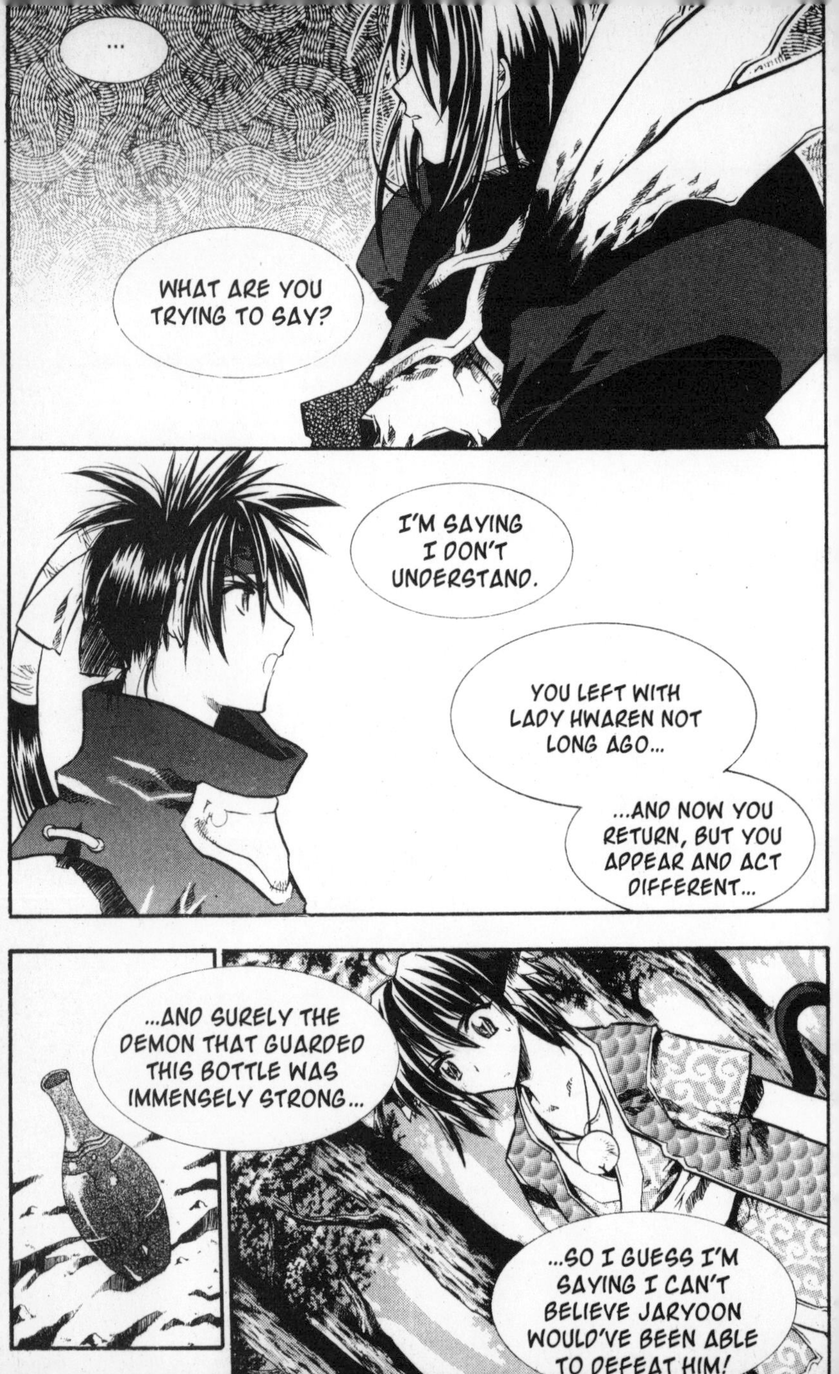
...
WHAT ARE YOU TRYING TO SAY?
I'M SAYING I DON'T UNDERSTAND.
YOU LEFT WITH LADY HWAREN NOT LONG AGO...
...AND NOW YOU RETURN, BUT YOU APPEAR AND ACT DIFFERENT...
...AND SURELY THE DEMON THAT GUARDED THIS BOTTLE WAS IMMENSELY STRONG...
...SO I GUESS I'M SAYING I CAN'T BELIEVE JARYOON WOULD'VE BEEN ABLE TO DEFEAT HIM!

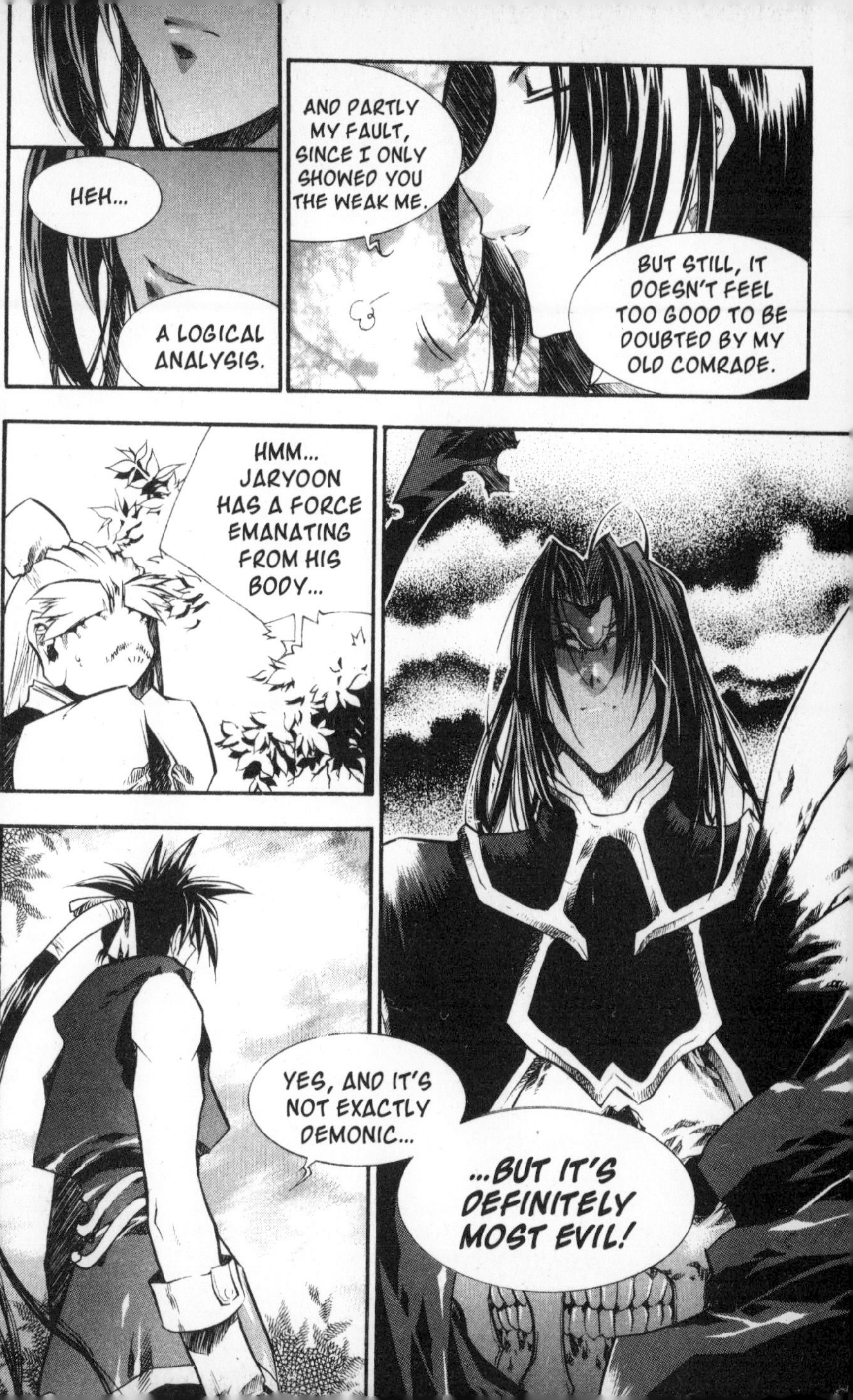
HEH...
A LOGICAL ANALYSIS.
AND PARTLY MY FAULT, SINCE I ONLY SHOWED YOU THE WEAK ME.
BUT STILL, IT DOESN'T FEEL TOO GOOD TO BE DOUBTED BY MY OLD COMRADE.
HMM... JARYOON HAS A FORCE EMANATING FROM HIS BODY...
YES, AND IT'S NOT EXACTLY DEMONIC...
...BUT IT'S DEFINITELY MOST EVIL!

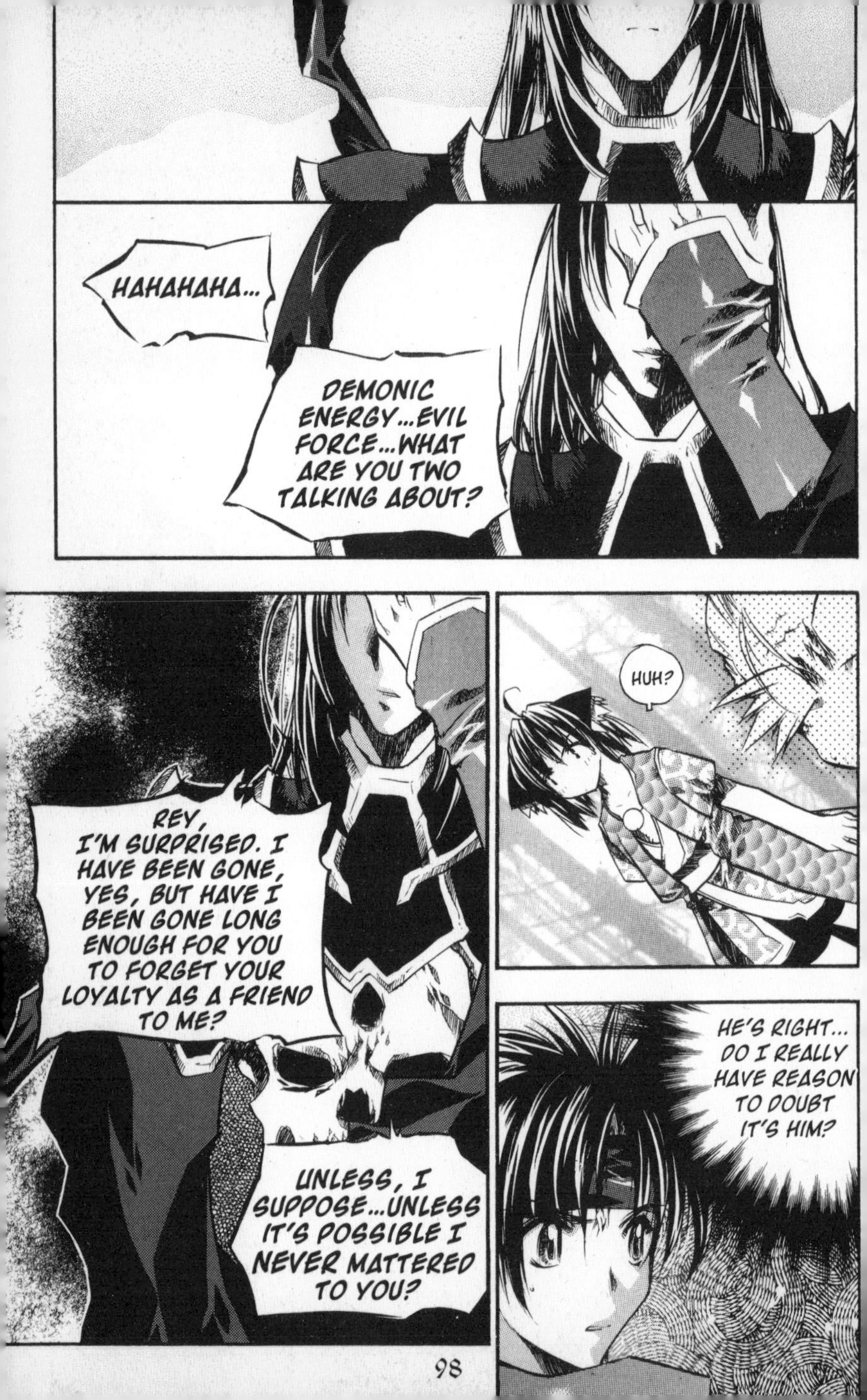
HAHAHAHA...
DEMONIC ENERGY...EVIL FORCE...WHAT ARE YOU TWO TALKING ABOUT?
REY, I'M SURPRISED. I HAVE BEEN GONE, YES, BUT HAVE I BEEN GONE LONG ENOUGH FOR YOU TO FORGET YOUR LOYALTY AS A FRIEND TO ME?
UNLESS, I SUPPOSE...UNLESS IT'S POSSIBLE I NEVER MATTERED TO YOU?
HUH?
HE'S RIGHT... DO I REALLY HAVE REASON TO DOUBT IT'S HIM?

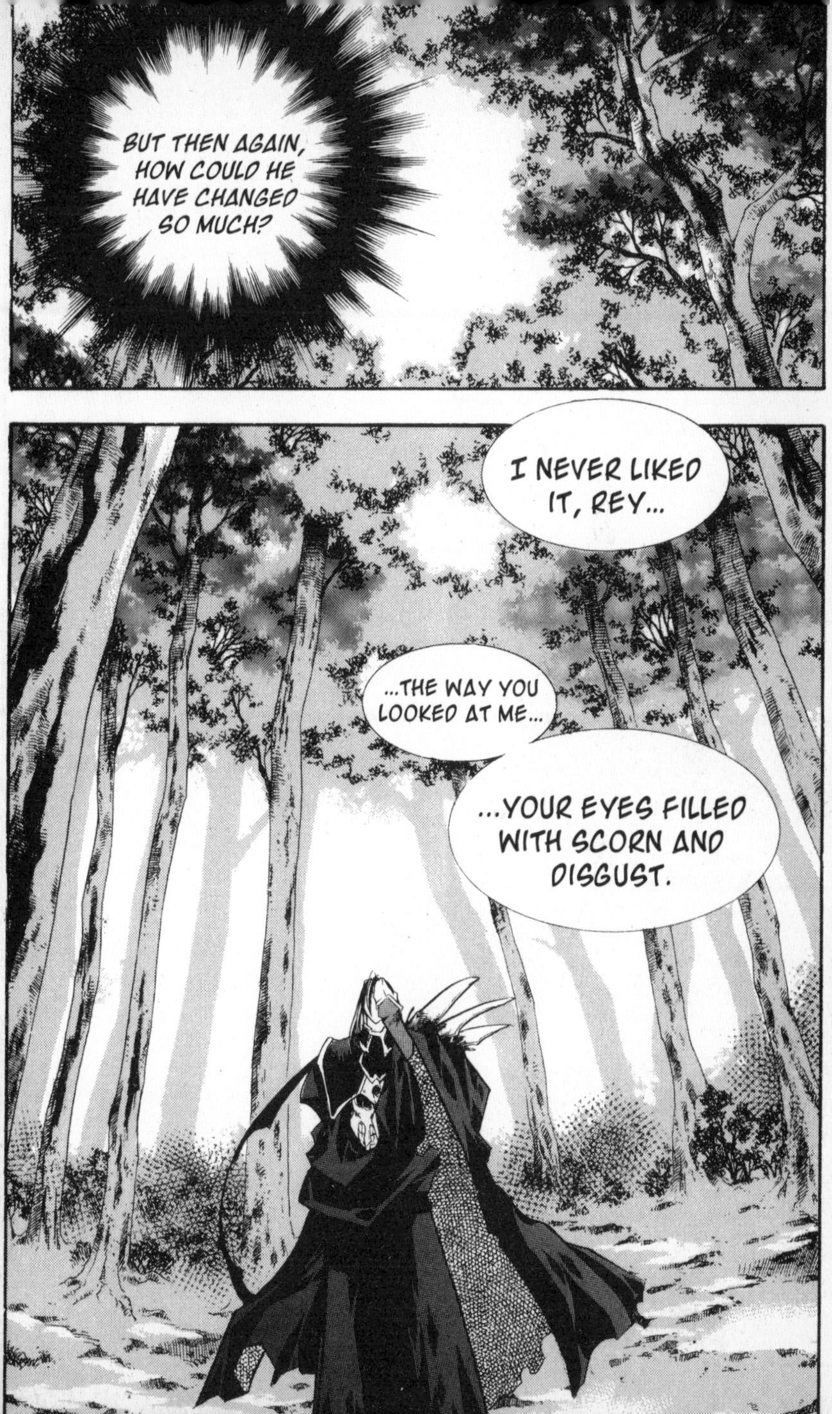
BUT THEN AGAIN, HOW COULD HE HAVE CHANGED SO MUCH?
I NEVER LIKED IT, REY...
...THE WAY YOU LOOKED AT ME...
...YOUR EYES FILLED WITH SCORN AND DISGUST.

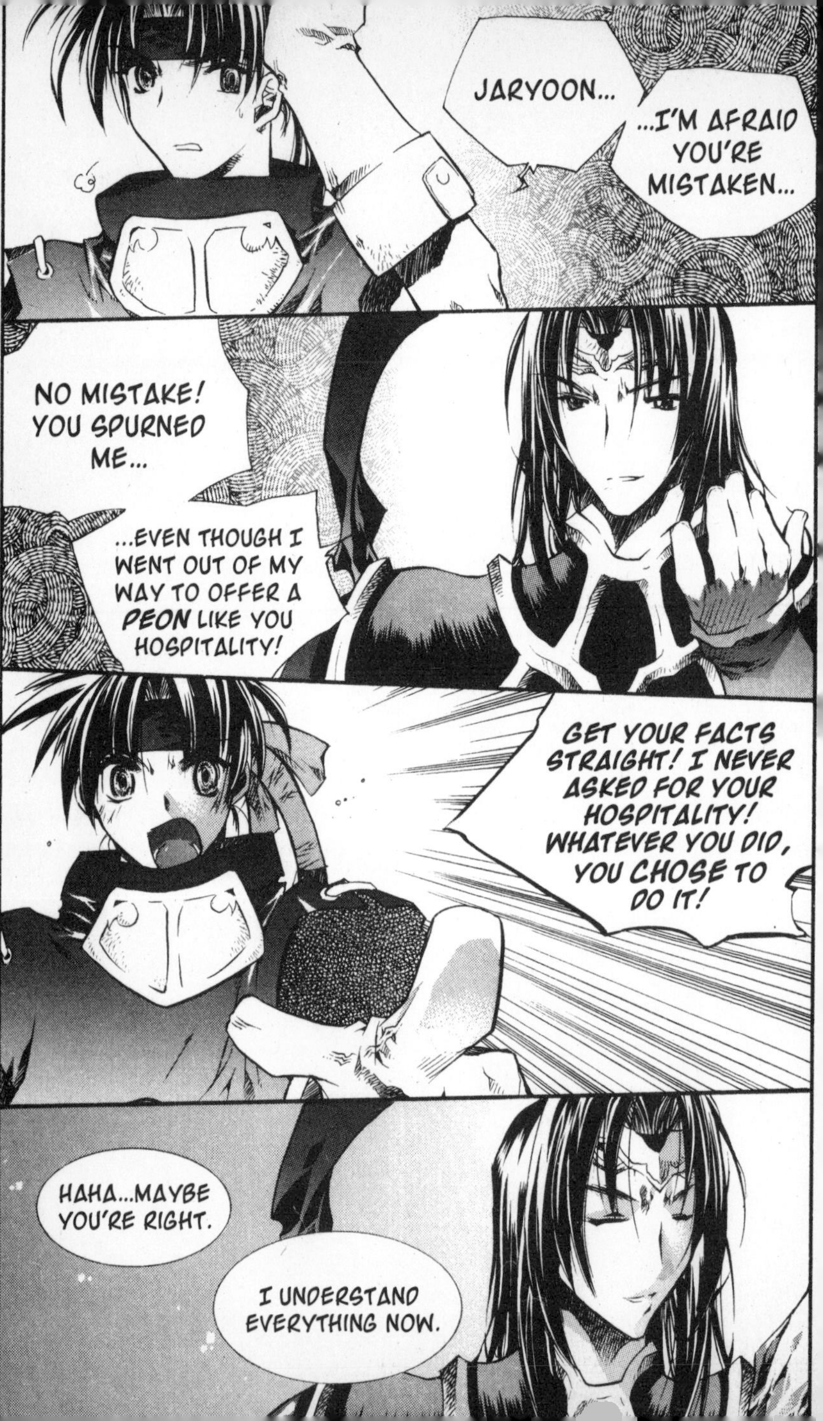
JARYOON...
...I'M AFRAID YOU'RE MISTAKEN...
NO MISTAKE! YOU SPURNED ME...
...EVEN THOUGH I WENT OUT OF MY WAY TO OFFER A *PEON* LIKE YOU HOSPITALITY!
GET YOUR FACTS STRAIGHT! I NEVER ASKED FOR YOUR HOSPITALITY! WHATEVER YOU DID, YOU CHOSE TO DO IT!
HAHA...MAYBE YOU'RE RIGHT.
I UNDERSTAND EVERYTHING NOW.

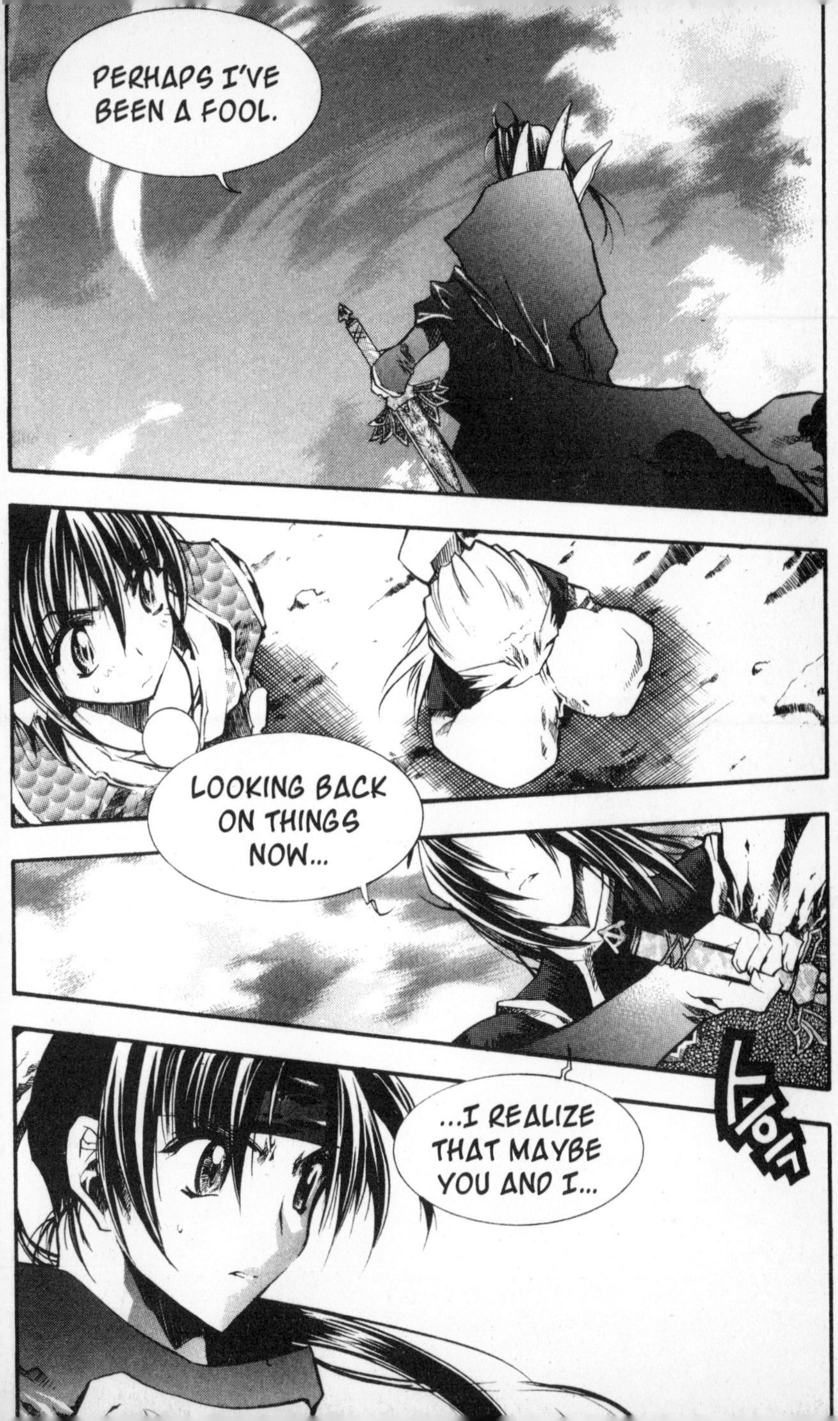
PERHAPS I'VE BEEN A FOOL.
LOOKING BACK ON THINGS NOW...
...I REALIZE THAT MAYBE YOU AND I...

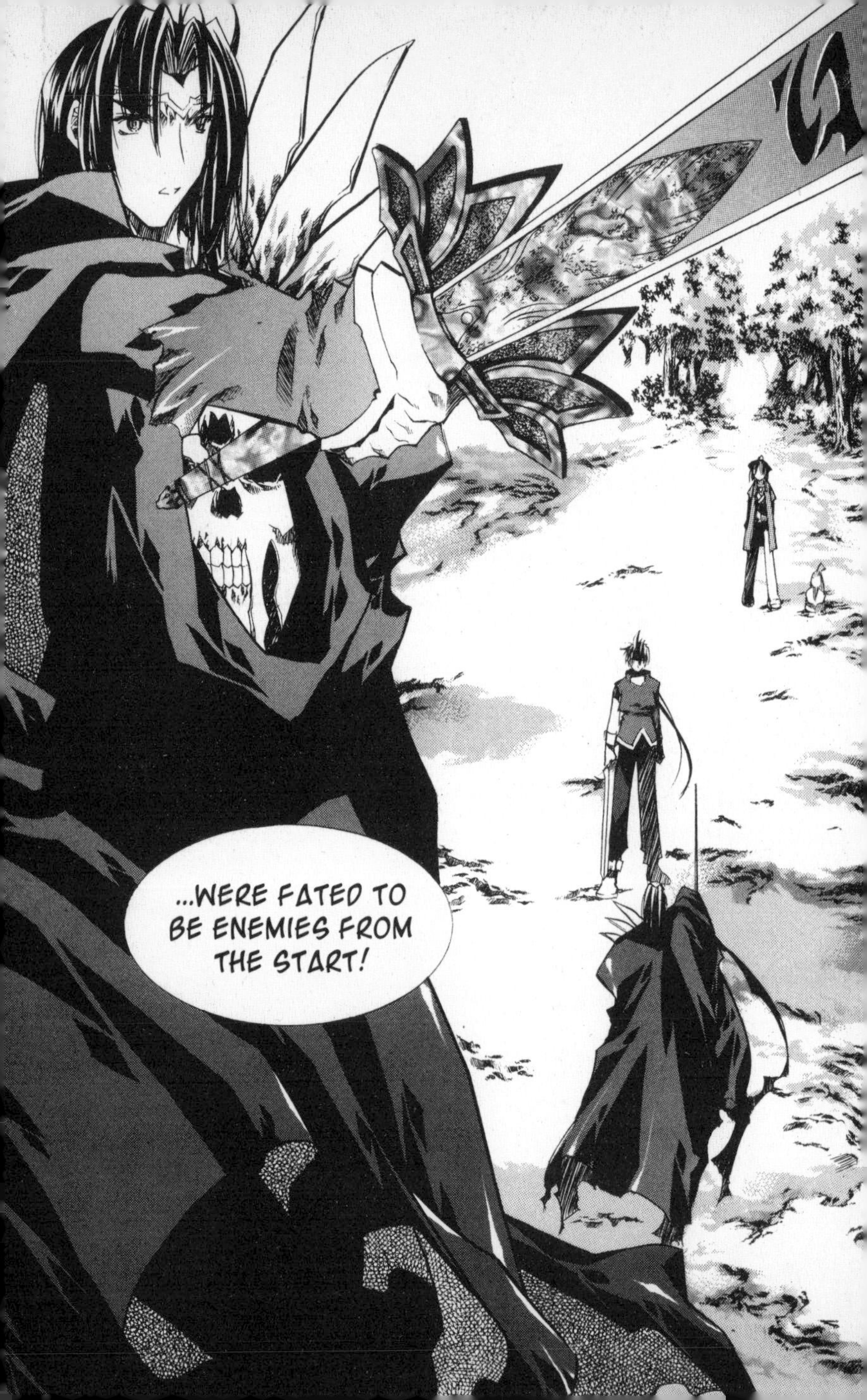
...WERE FATED TO BE ENEMIES FROM THE START!

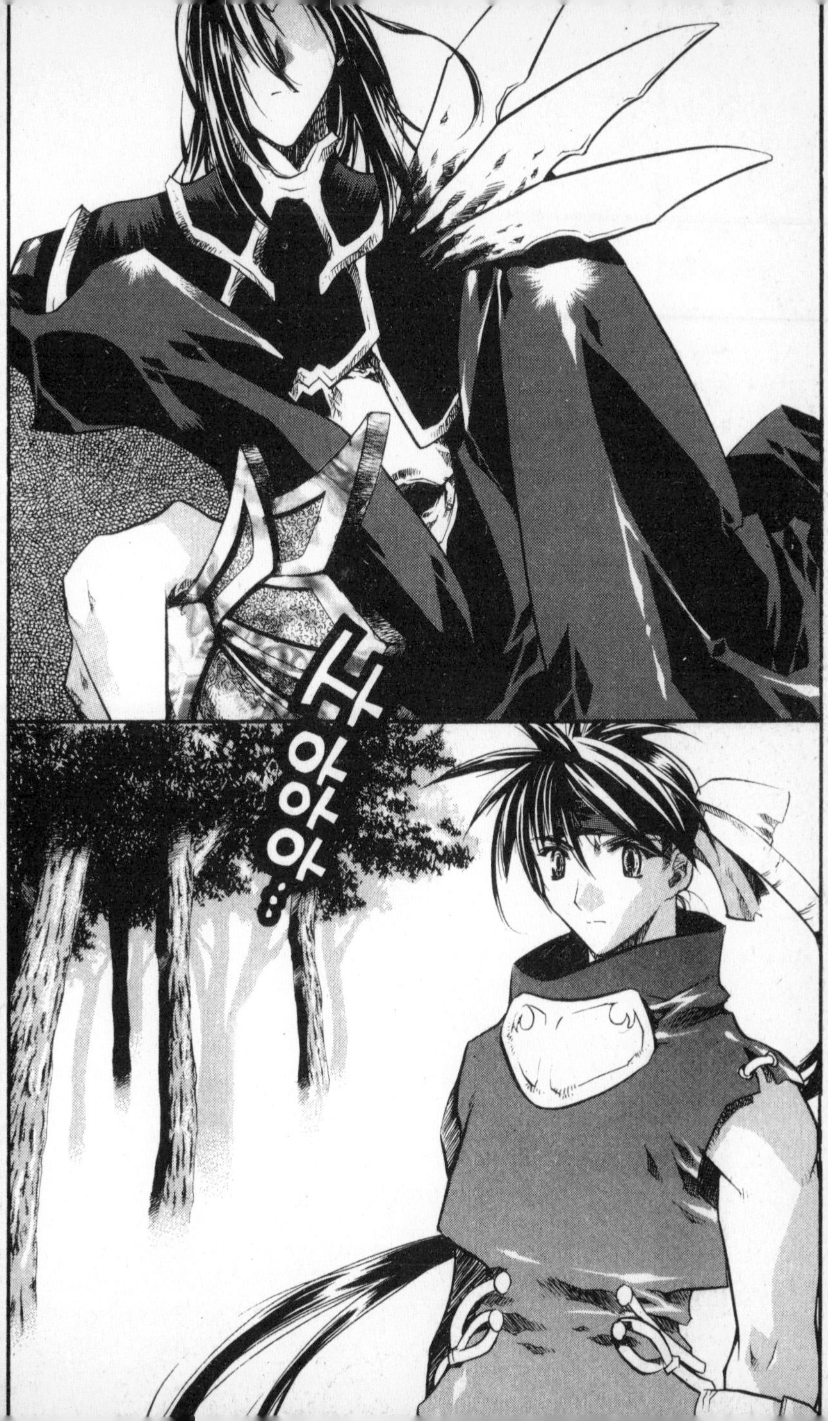
다아아아...

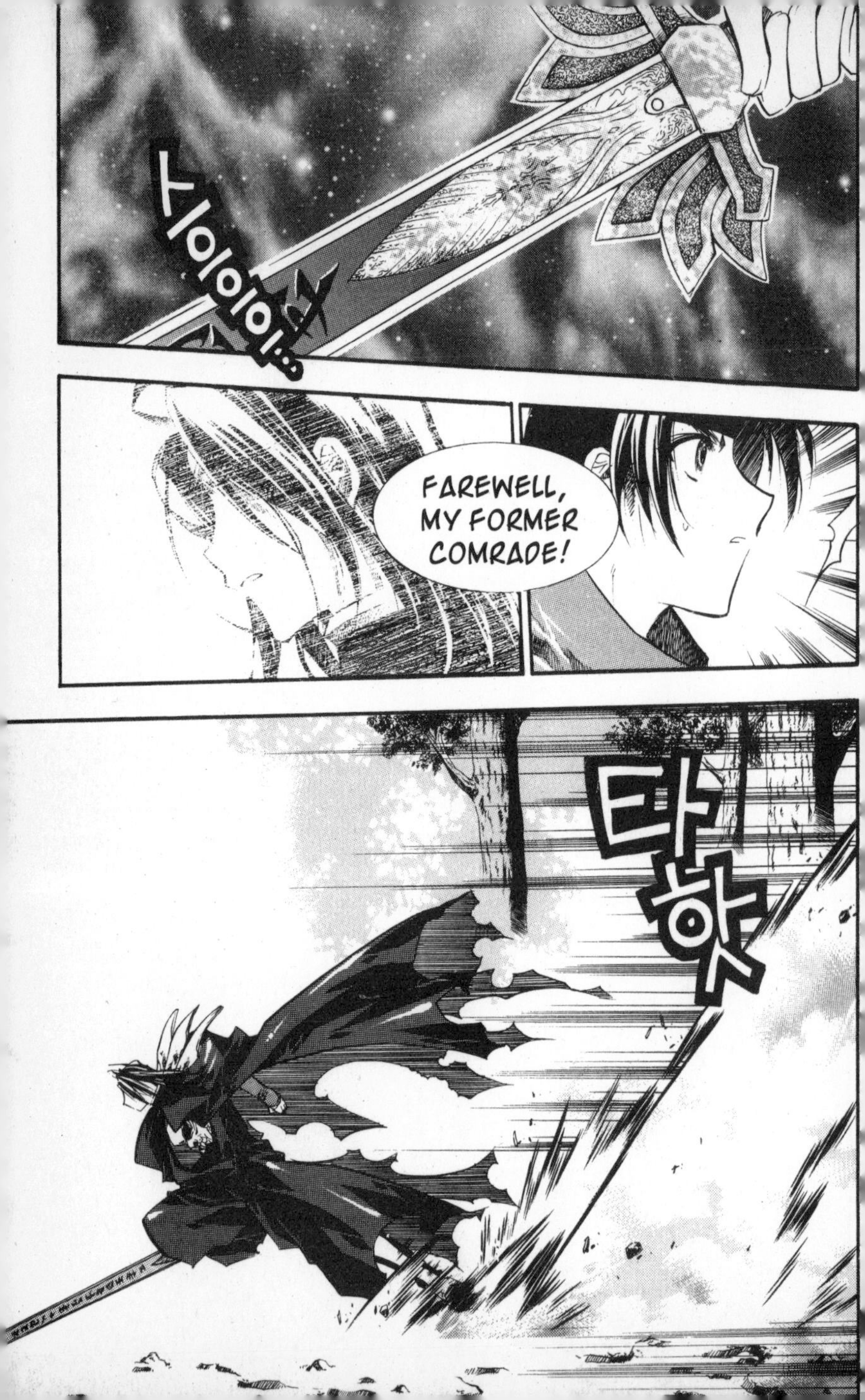
FAREWELL, MY FORMER COMRADE!
타핫

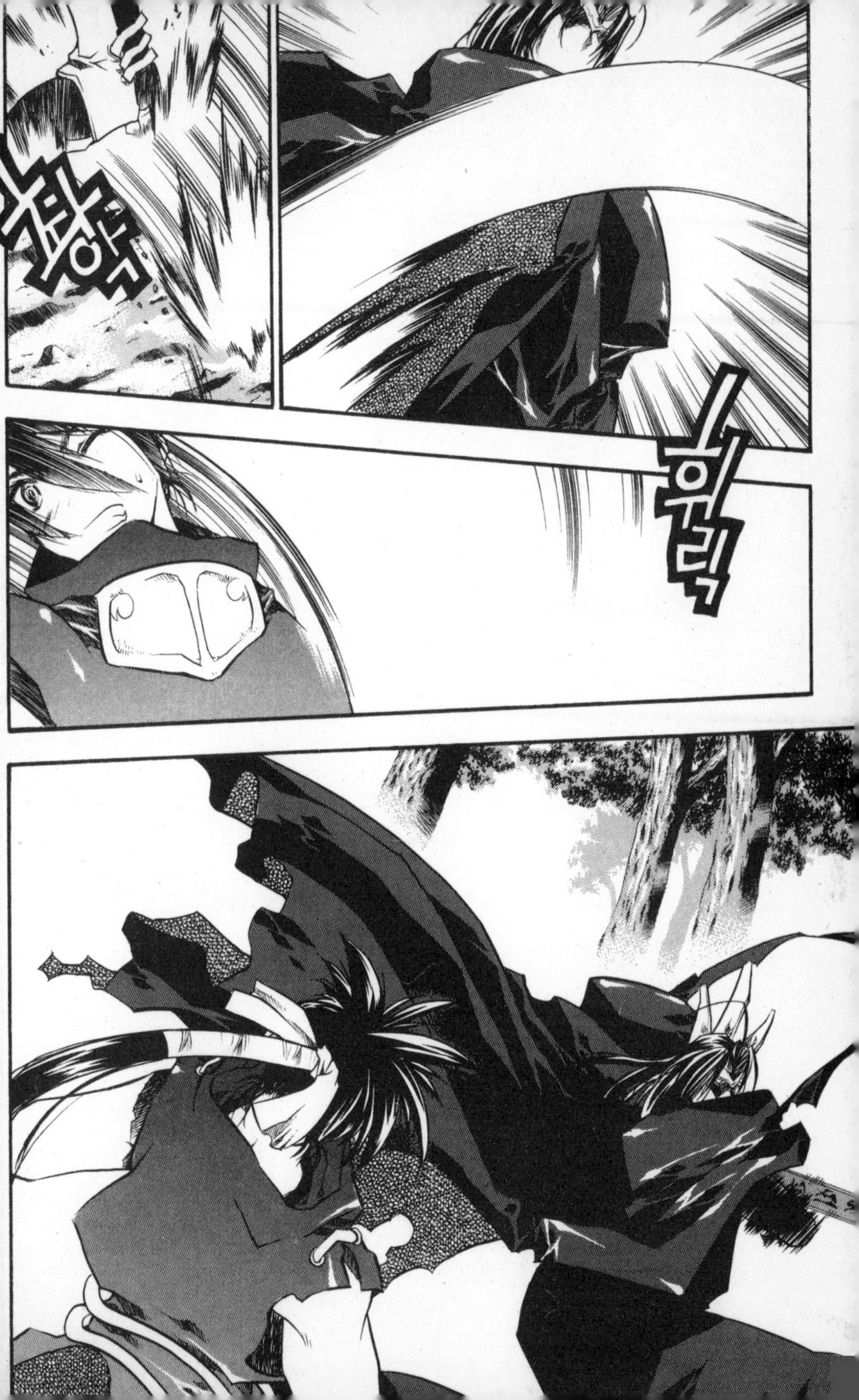
콰악
휘릭

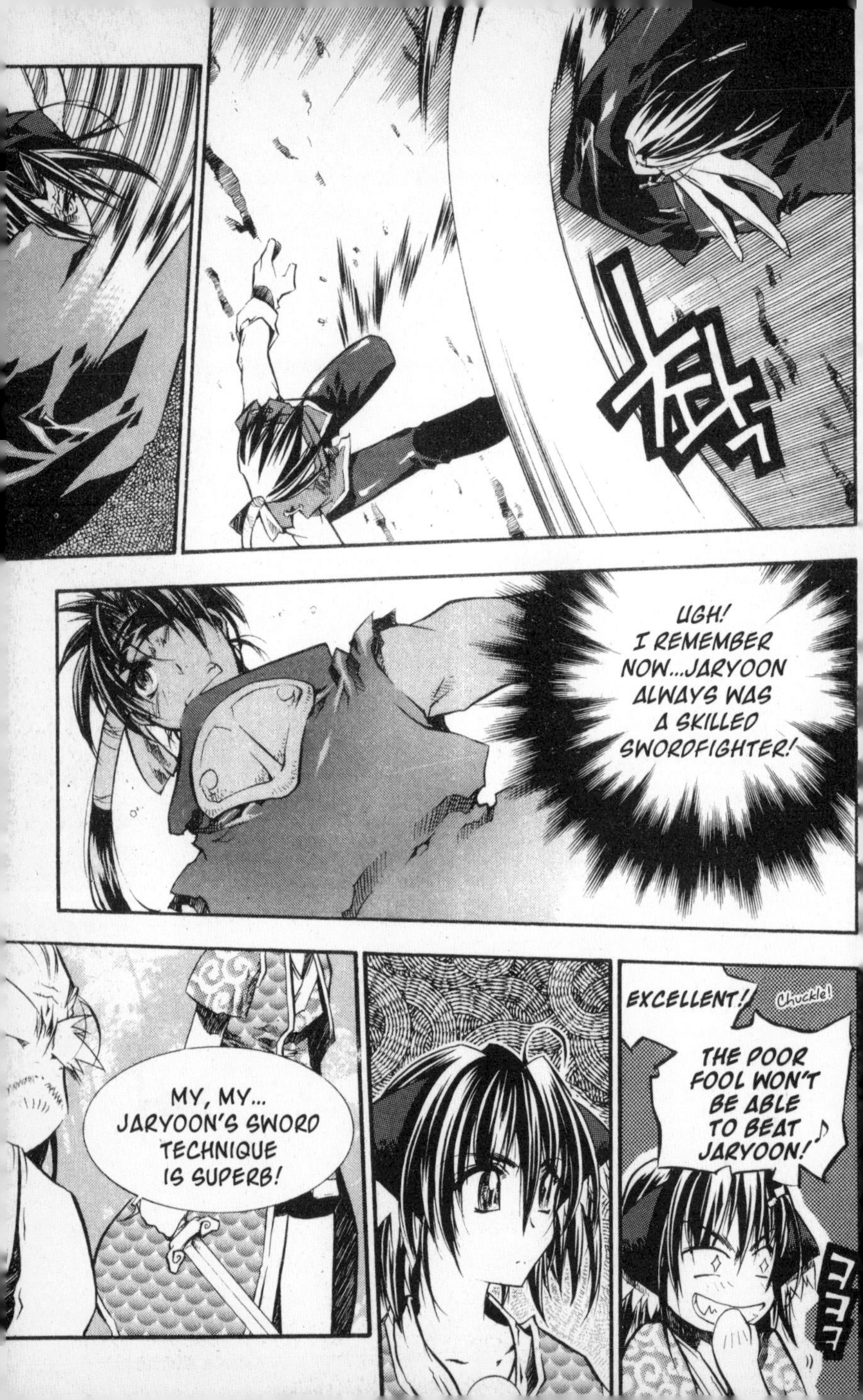
UGH! I REMEMBER NOW...JARYOON ALWAYS WAS A SKILLED SWORDFIGHTER!
MY, MY... JARYOON'S SWORD TECHNIQUE IS SUPERB!
EXCELLENT!
Chuckle!
THE POOR FOOL WON'T BE ABLE TO BEAT JARYOON!♪

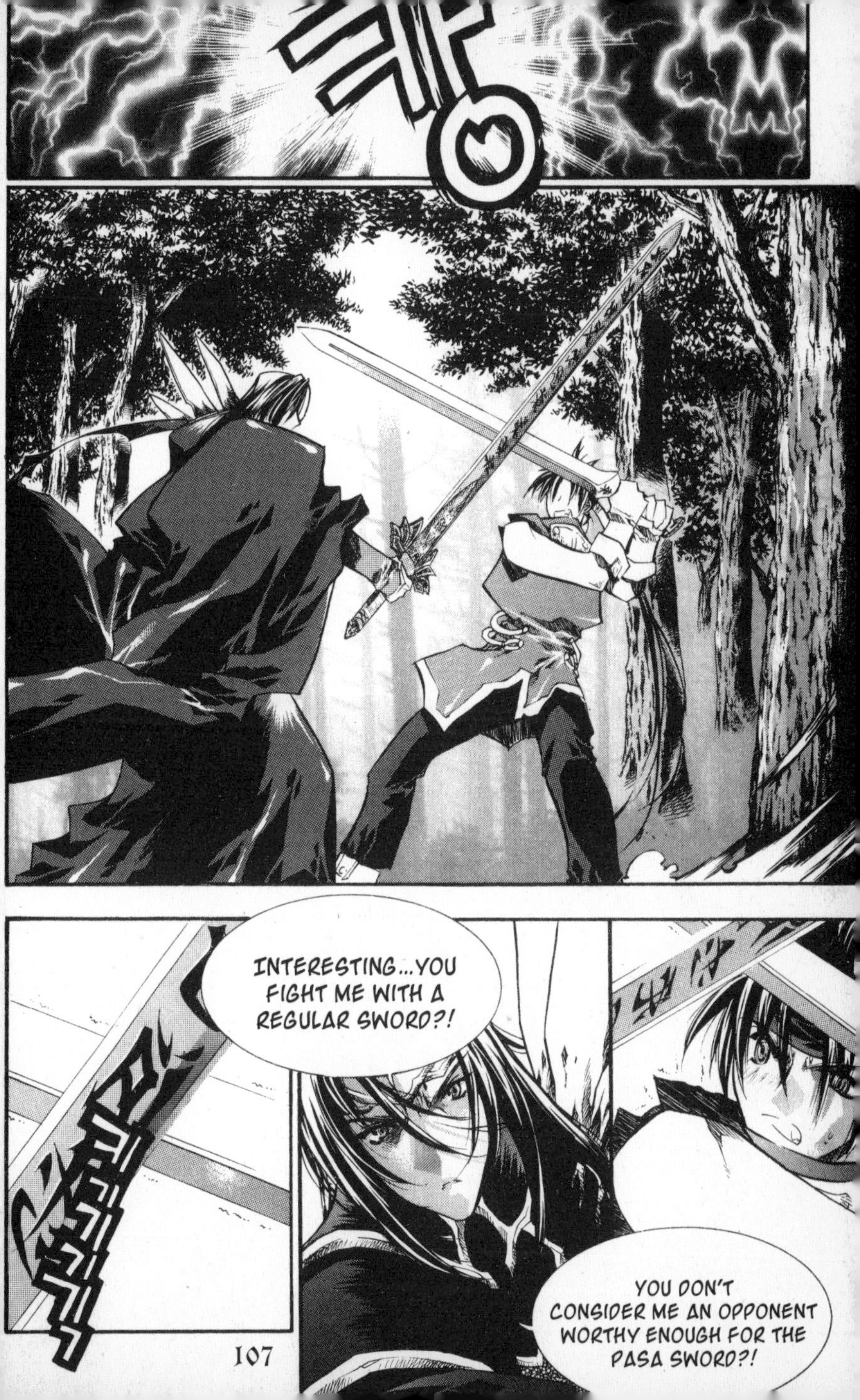
INTERESTING...YOU FIGHT ME WITH A REGULAR SWORD?!
YOU DON'T CONSIDER ME AN OPPONENT WORTHY ENOUGH FOR THE PASA SWORD?!

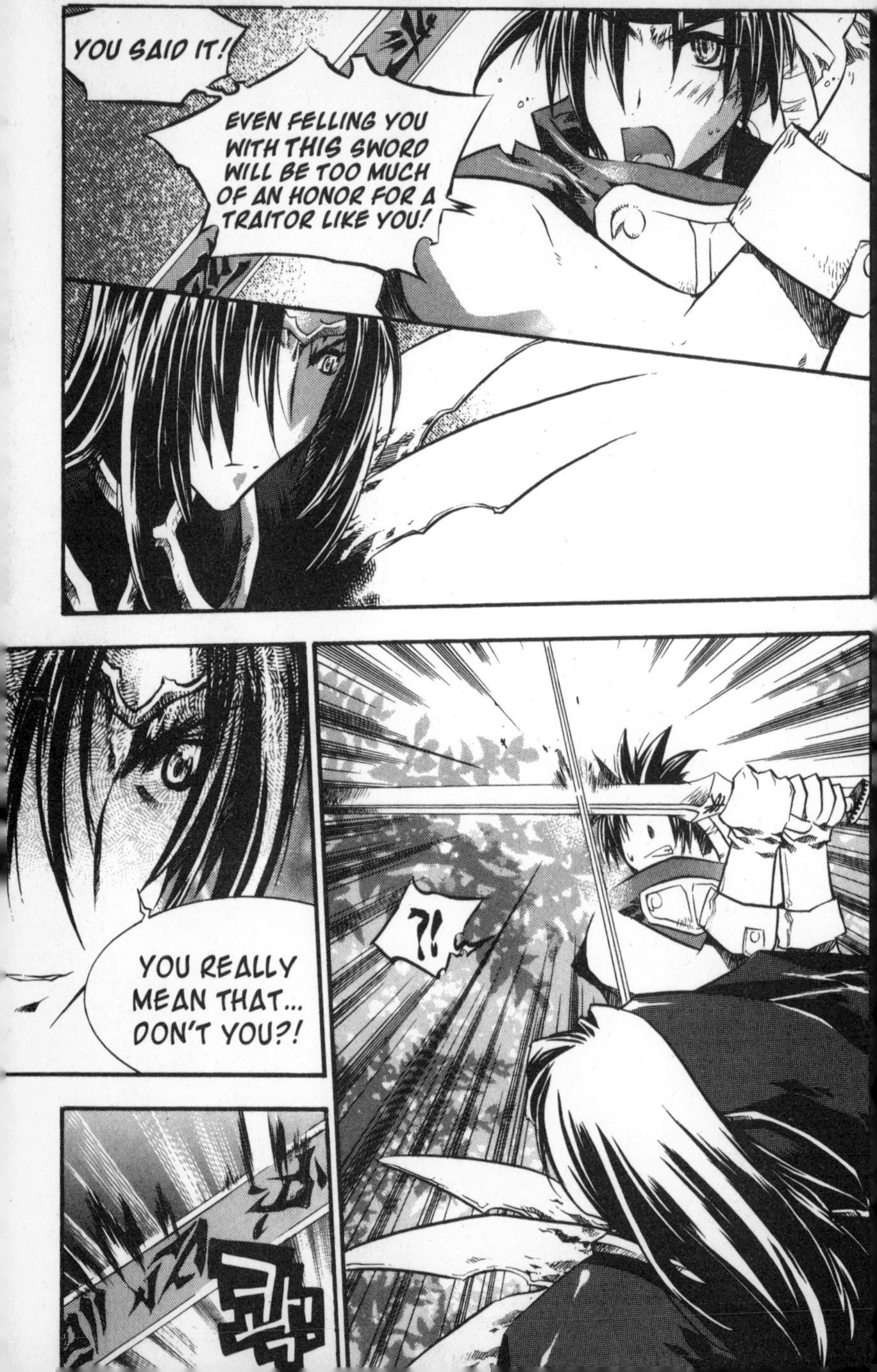
YOU SAID IT!
EVEN FELLING YOU WITH THIS SWORD WILL BE TOO MUCH OF AN HONOR FOR A TRAITOR LIKE YOU!
YOU REALLY MEAN THAT... DON'T YOU?!
?!

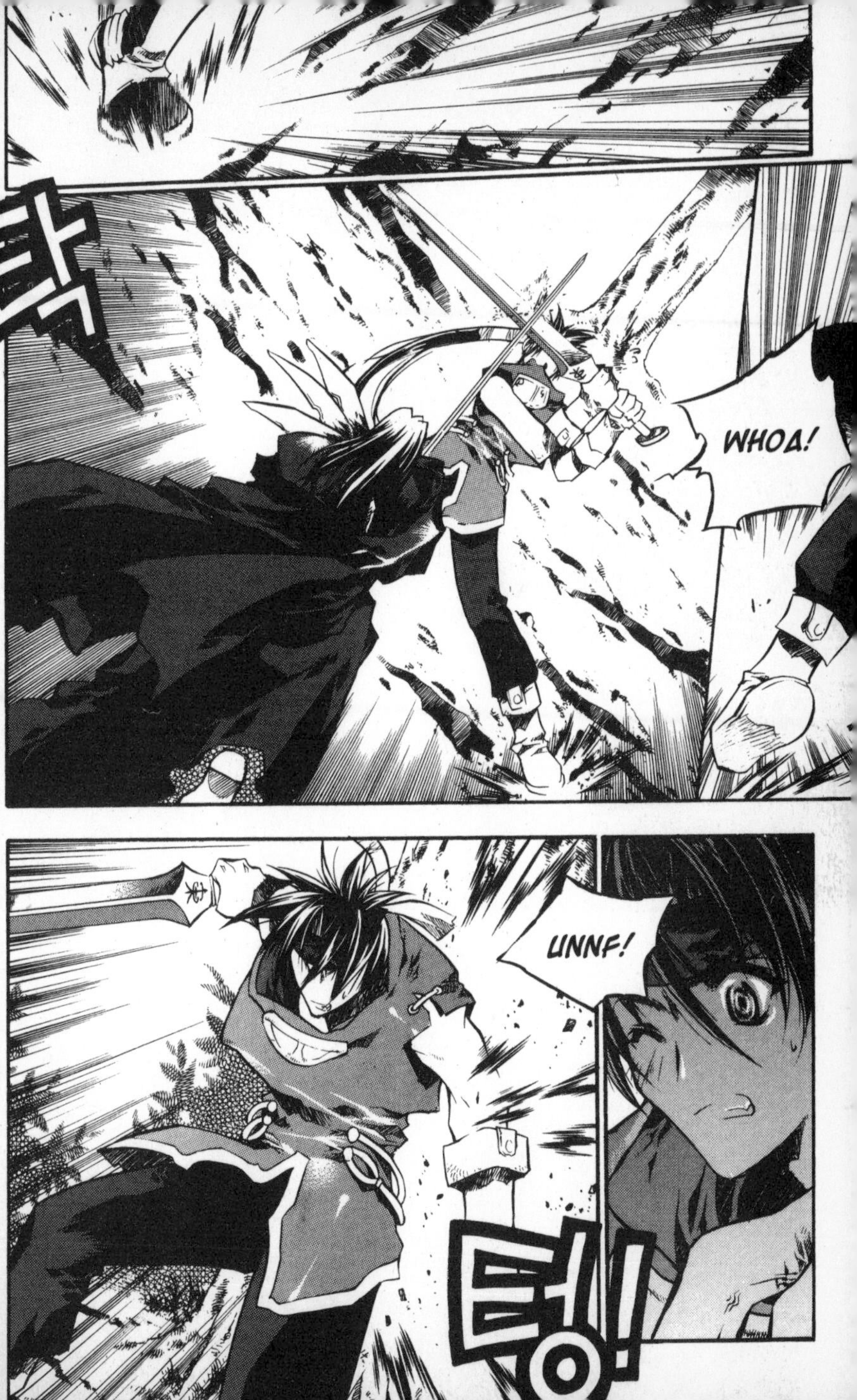
콱
WHOA!
UNNF!
텅!

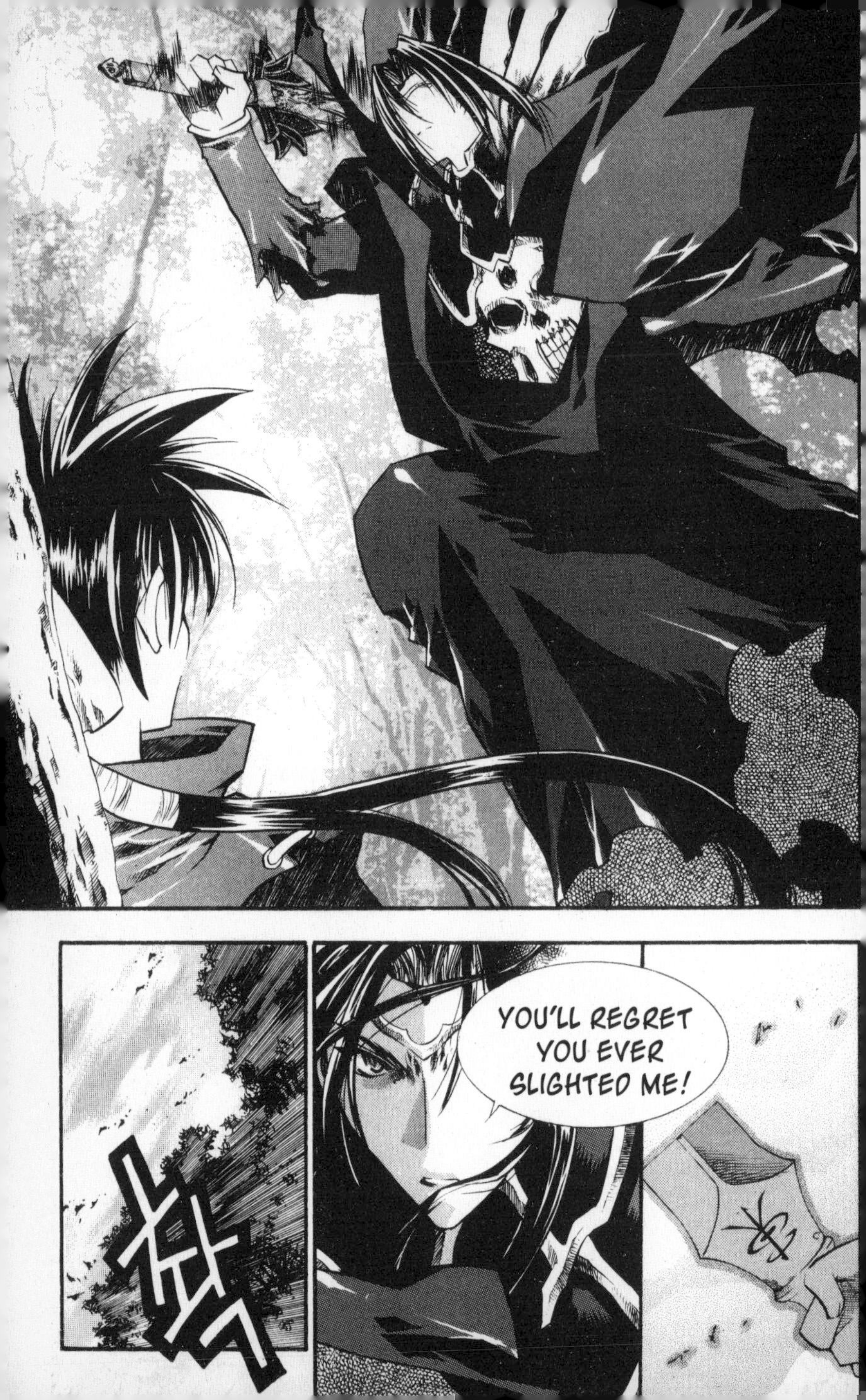
YOU'LL REGRET YOU EVER SLIGHTED ME!

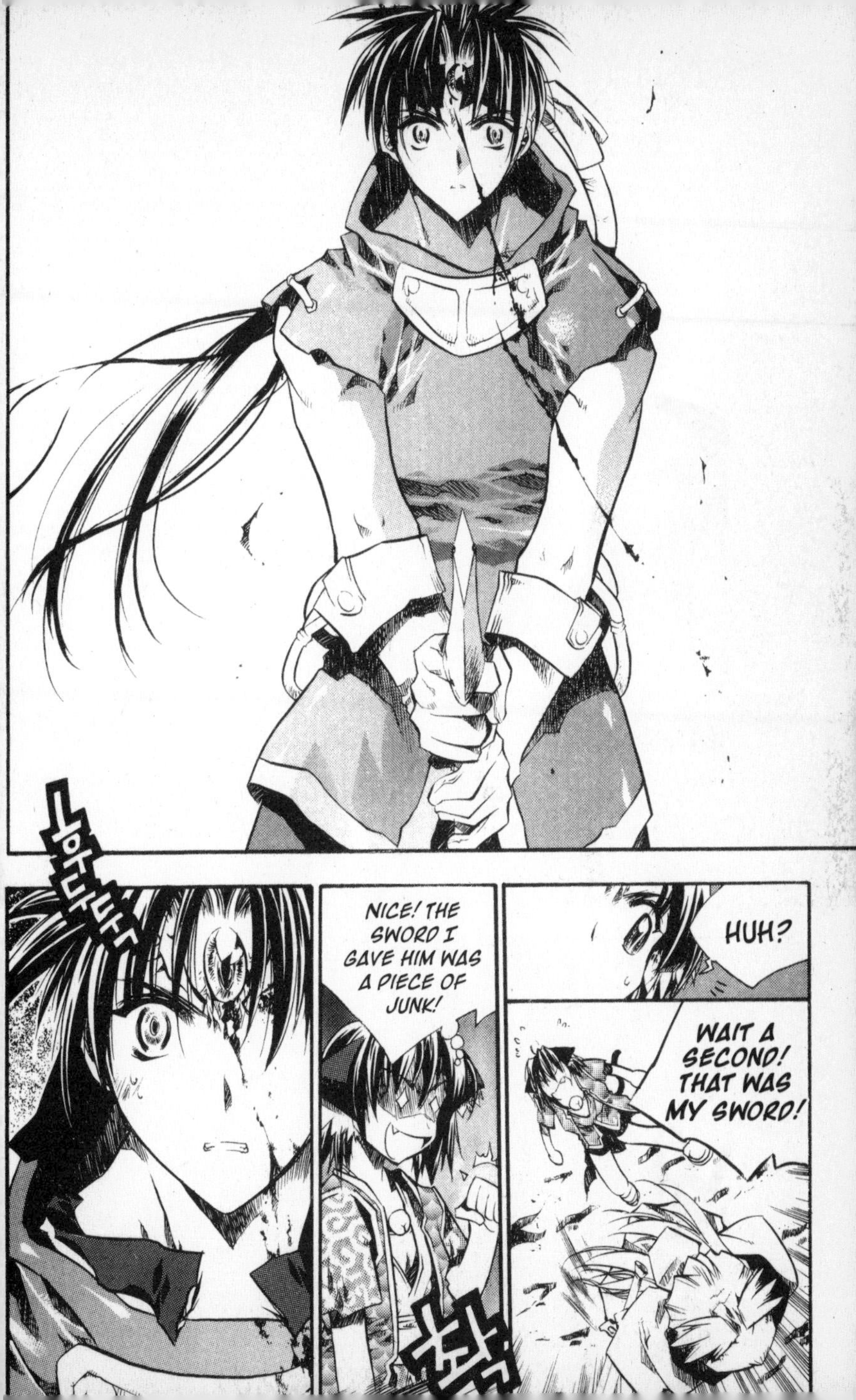
NICE! THE SWORD I GAVE HIM WAS A PIECE OF JUNK!
HUH?
WAIT A SECOND! THAT WAS MY SWORD!

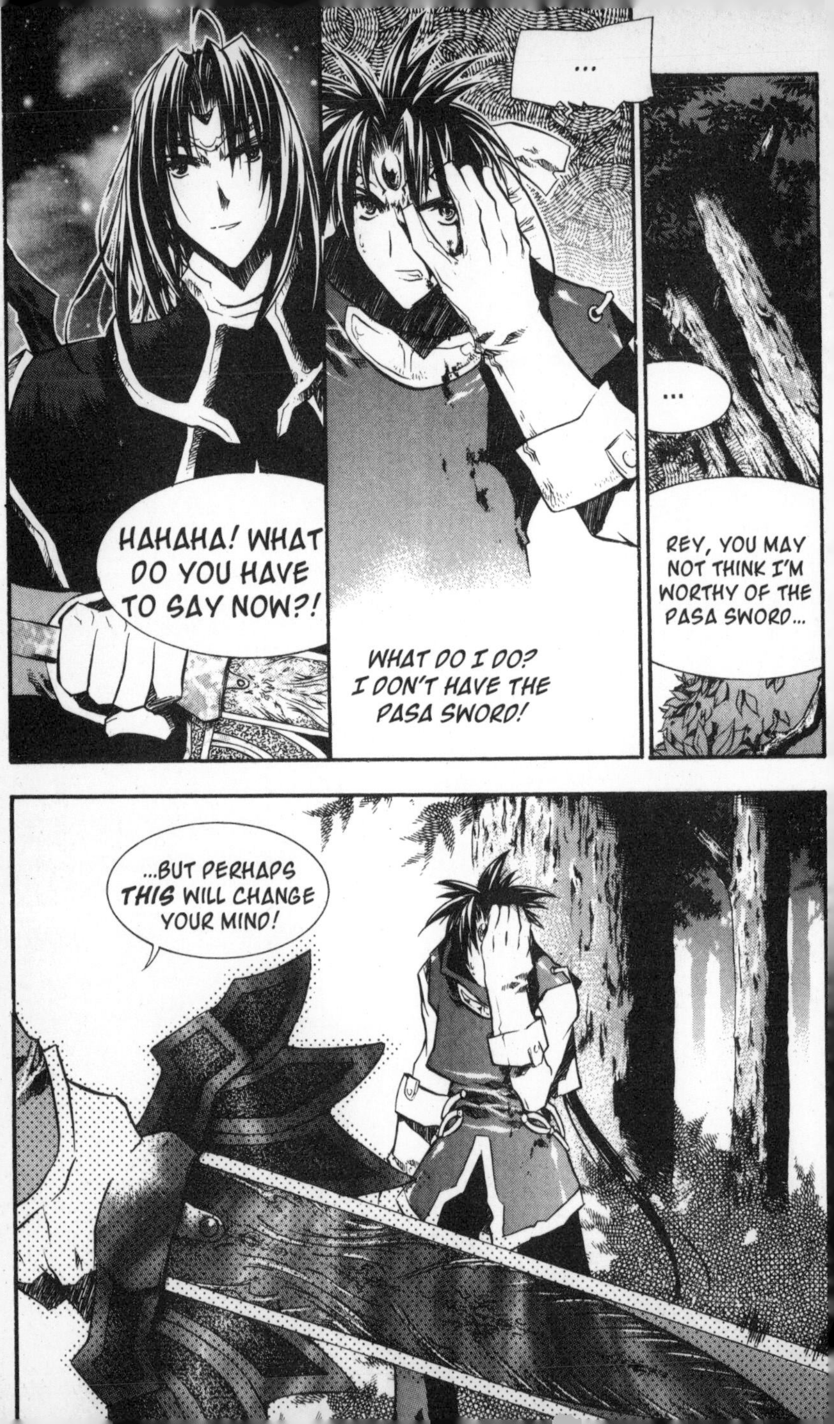
HAHAHA! WHAT DO YOU HAVE TO SAY NOW?!
...
WHAT DO I DO? I DON'T HAVE THE PASA SWORD!
...
REY, YOU MAY NOT THINK I'M WORTHY OF THE PASA SWORD...
...BUT PERHAPS THIS WILL CHANGE YOUR MIND!

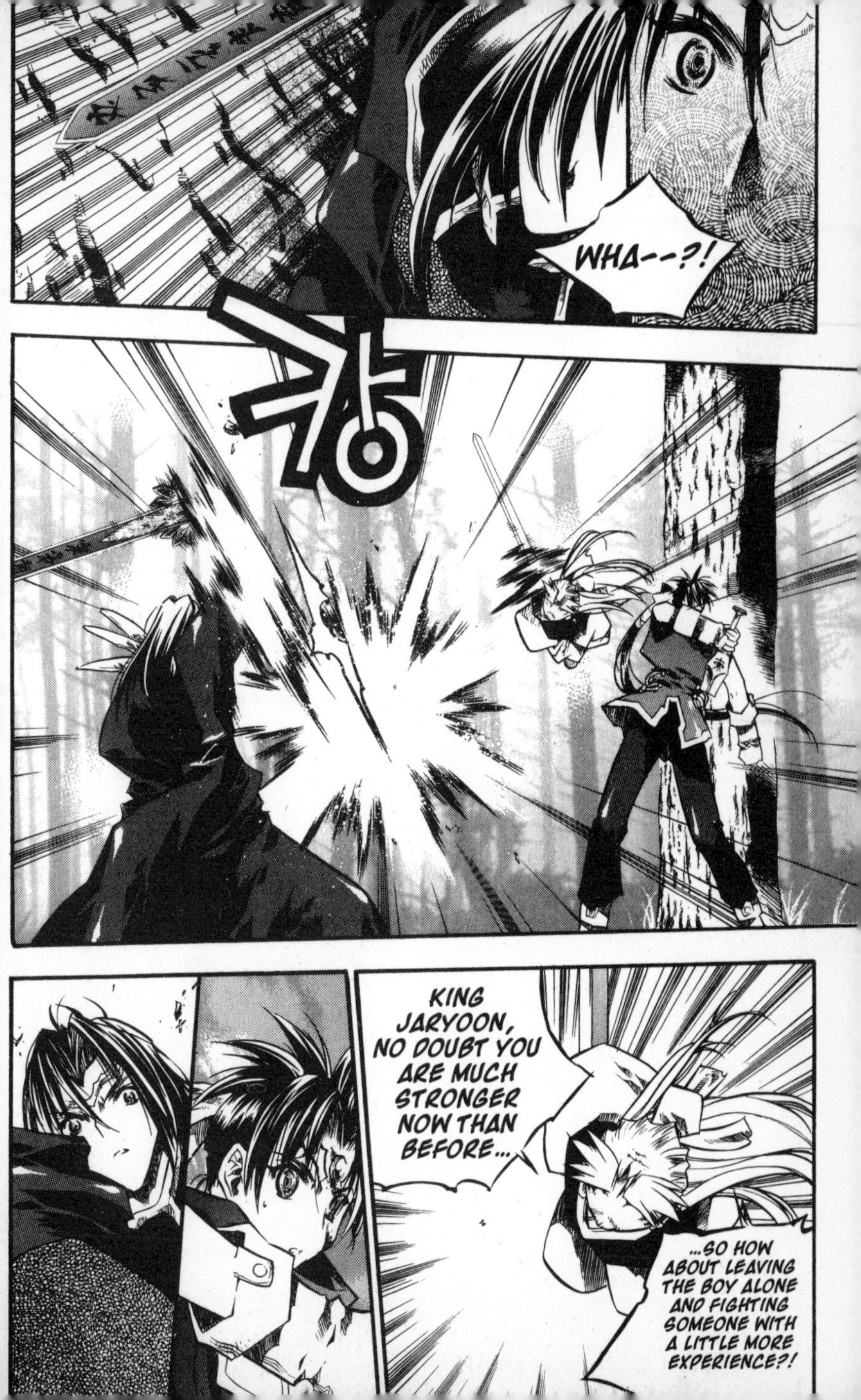
WHA--?!
KING JARYOON, NO DOUBT YOU ARE MUCH STRONGER NOW THAN BEFORE...
...SO HOW ABOUT LEAVING THE BOY ALONE AND FIGHTING SOMEONE WITH A LITTLE MORE EXPERIENCE?!

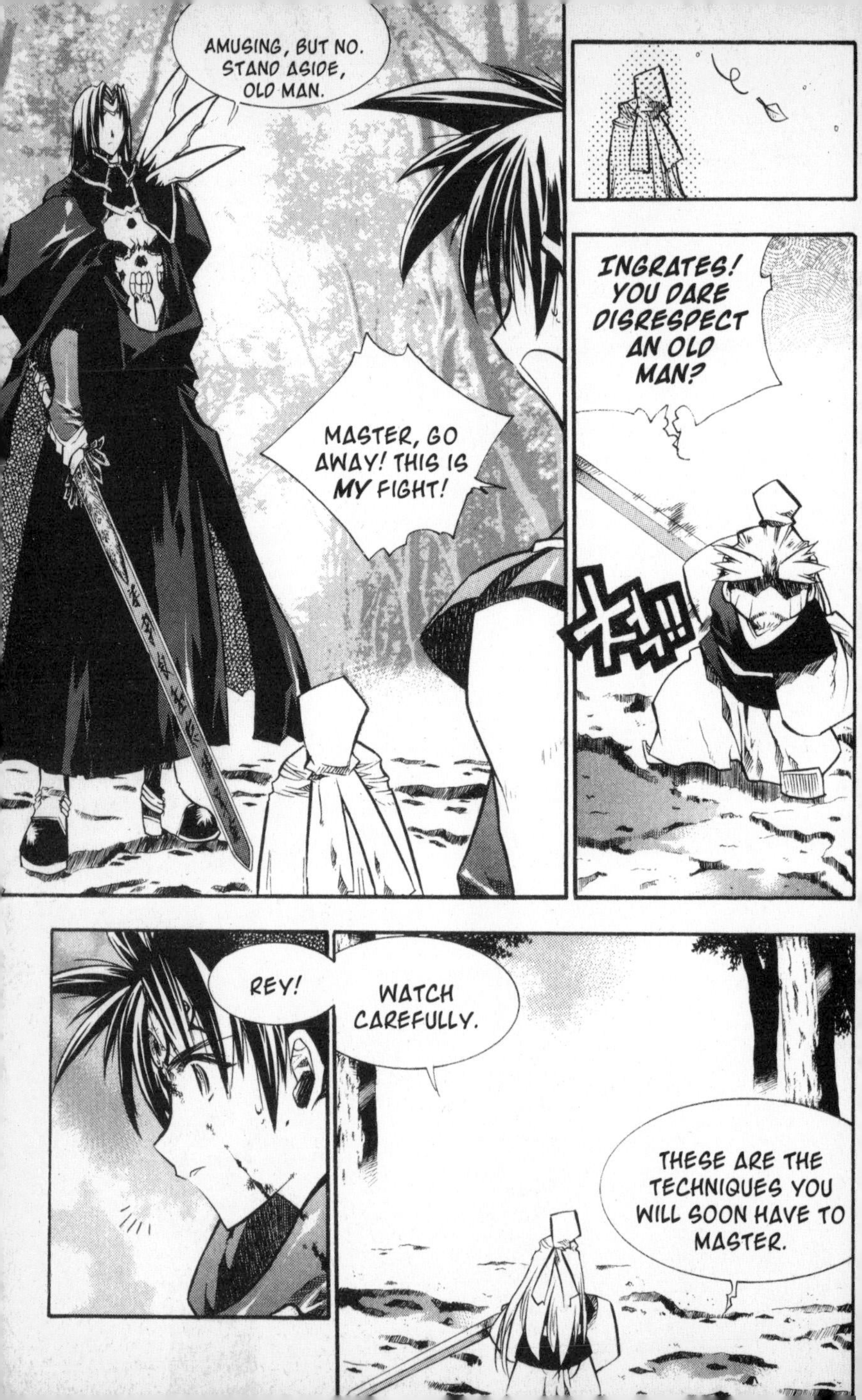
AMUSING, BUT NO. STAND ASIDE, OLD MAN.
MASTER, GO AWAY! THIS IS MY FIGHT!
INGRATES! YOU DARE DISRESPECT AN OLD MAN?
REY!
WATCH CAREFULLY.
THESE ARE THE TECHNIQUES YOU WILL SOON HAVE TO MASTER.

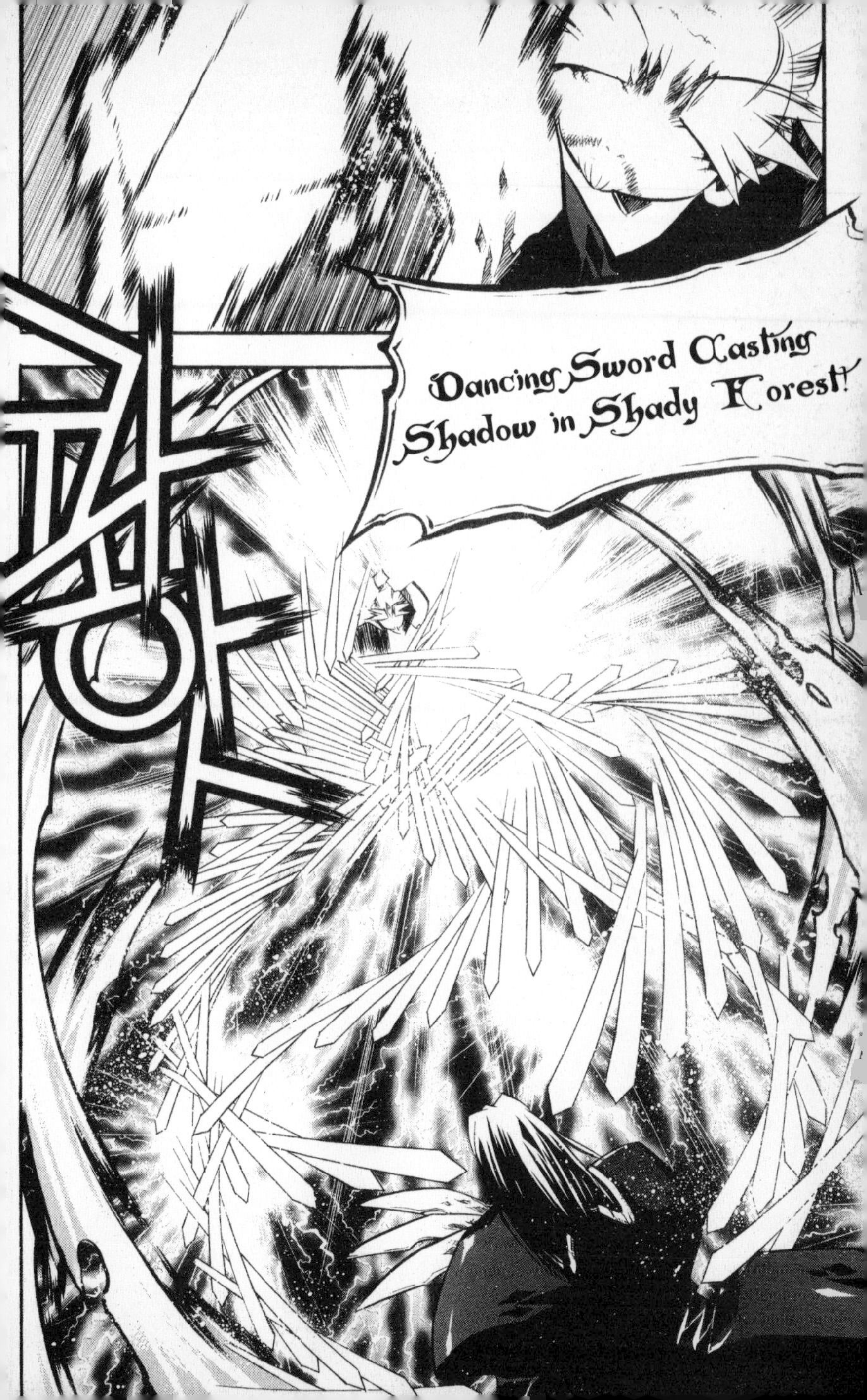
Dancing Sword Casting Shadow in Shady Forest!

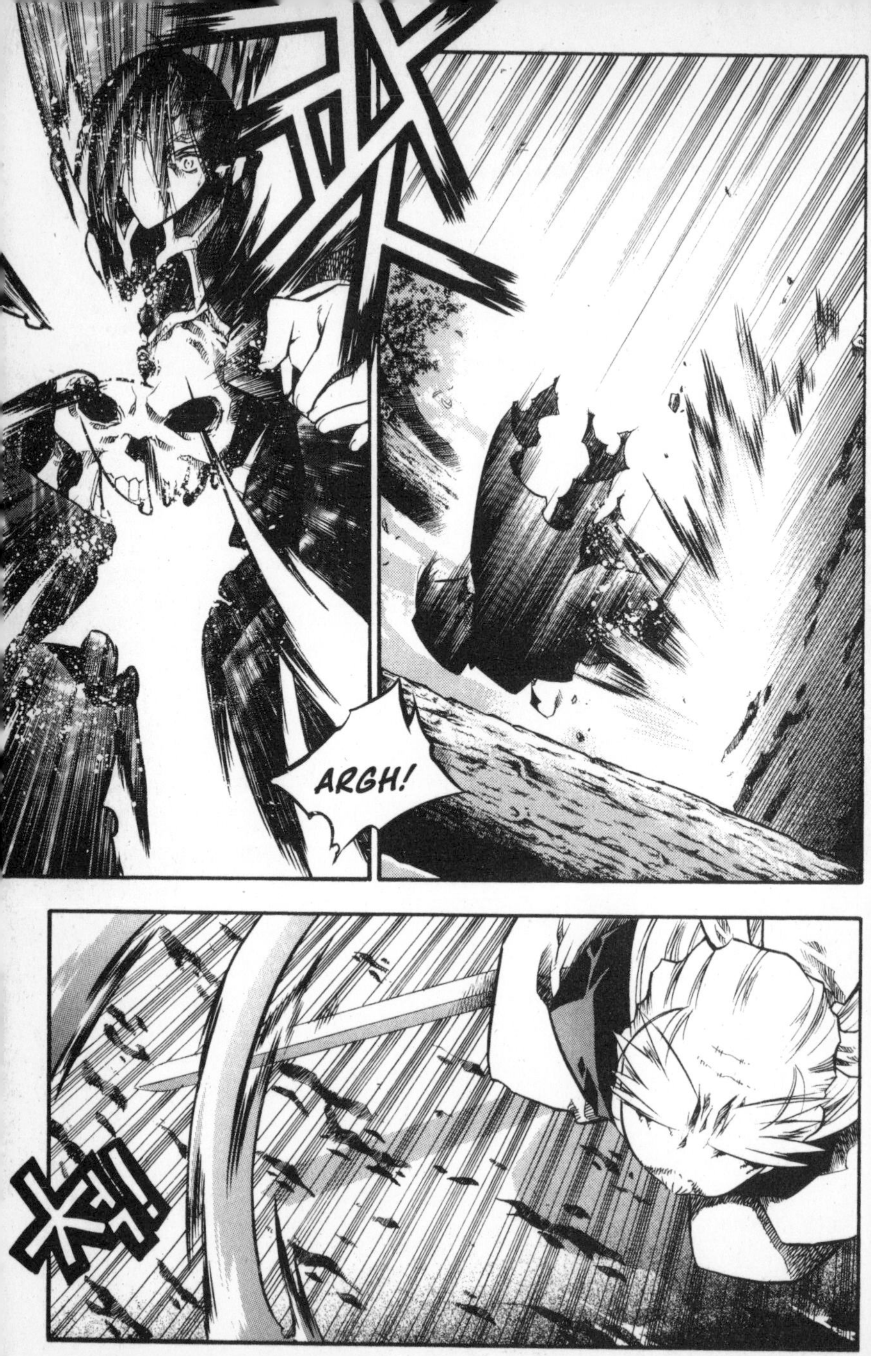
ARGH!

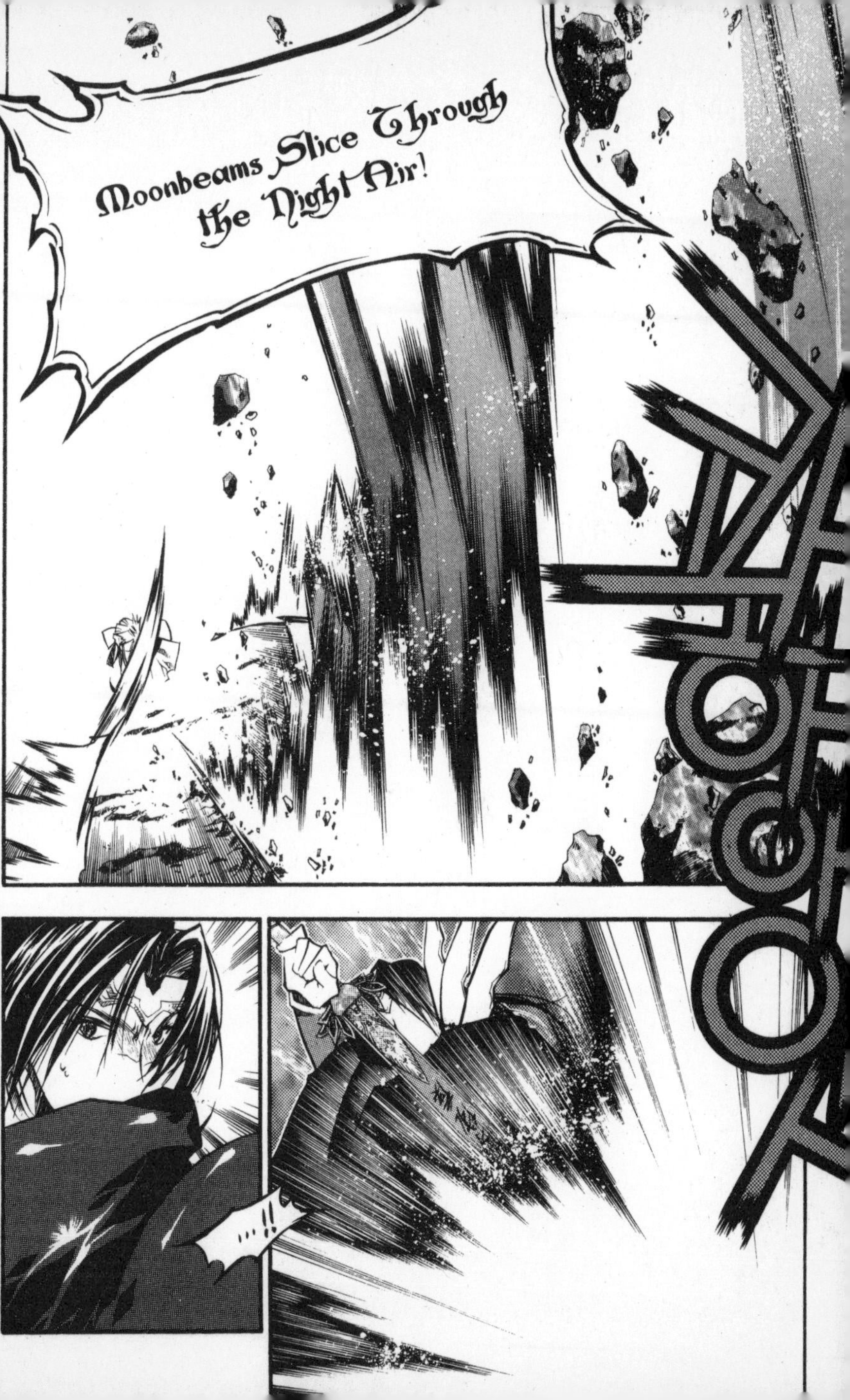
Moonbeams Slice Through the Night Air!
...!!

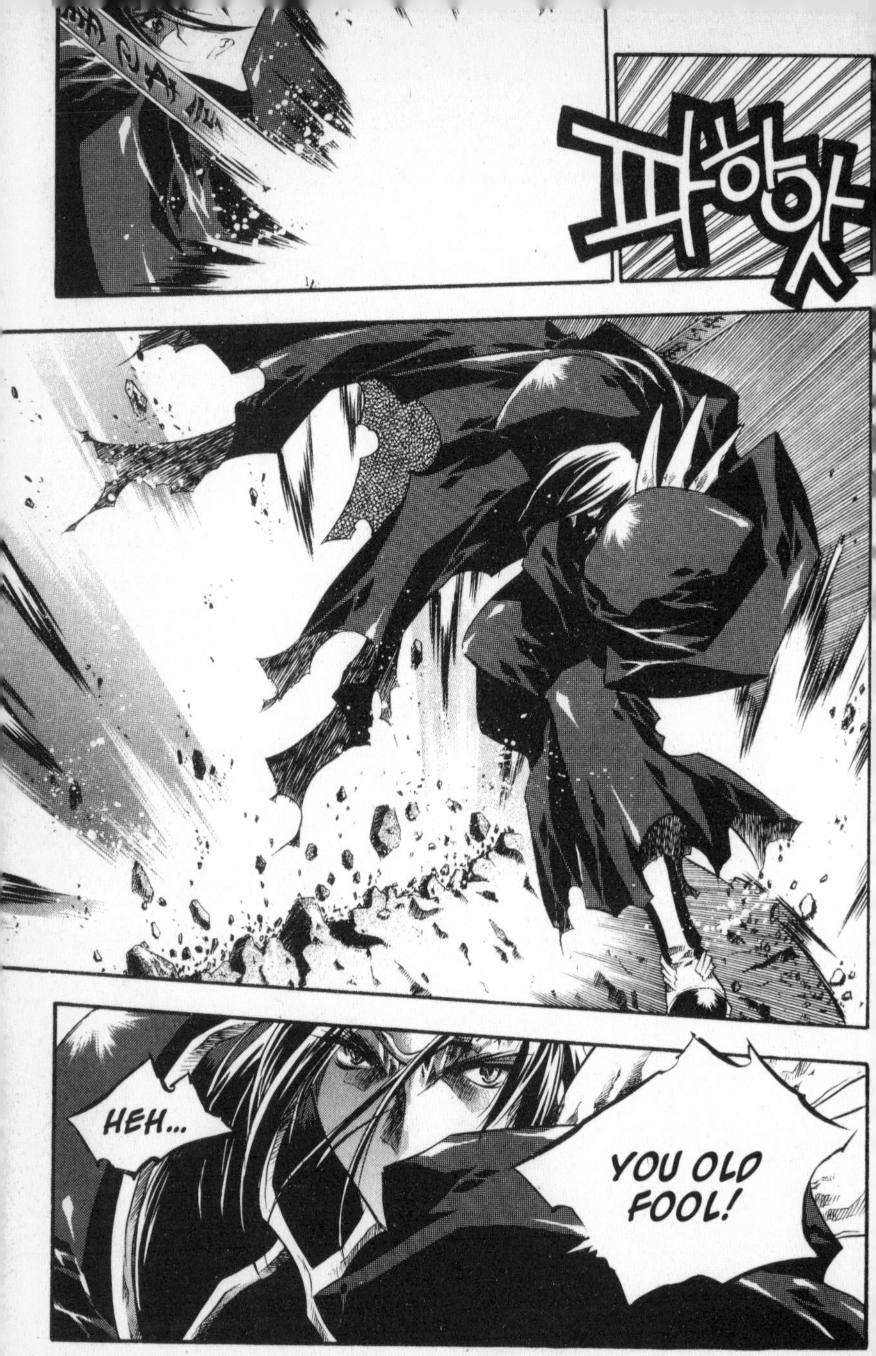
파아앗
HEH...
YOU OLD FOOL!

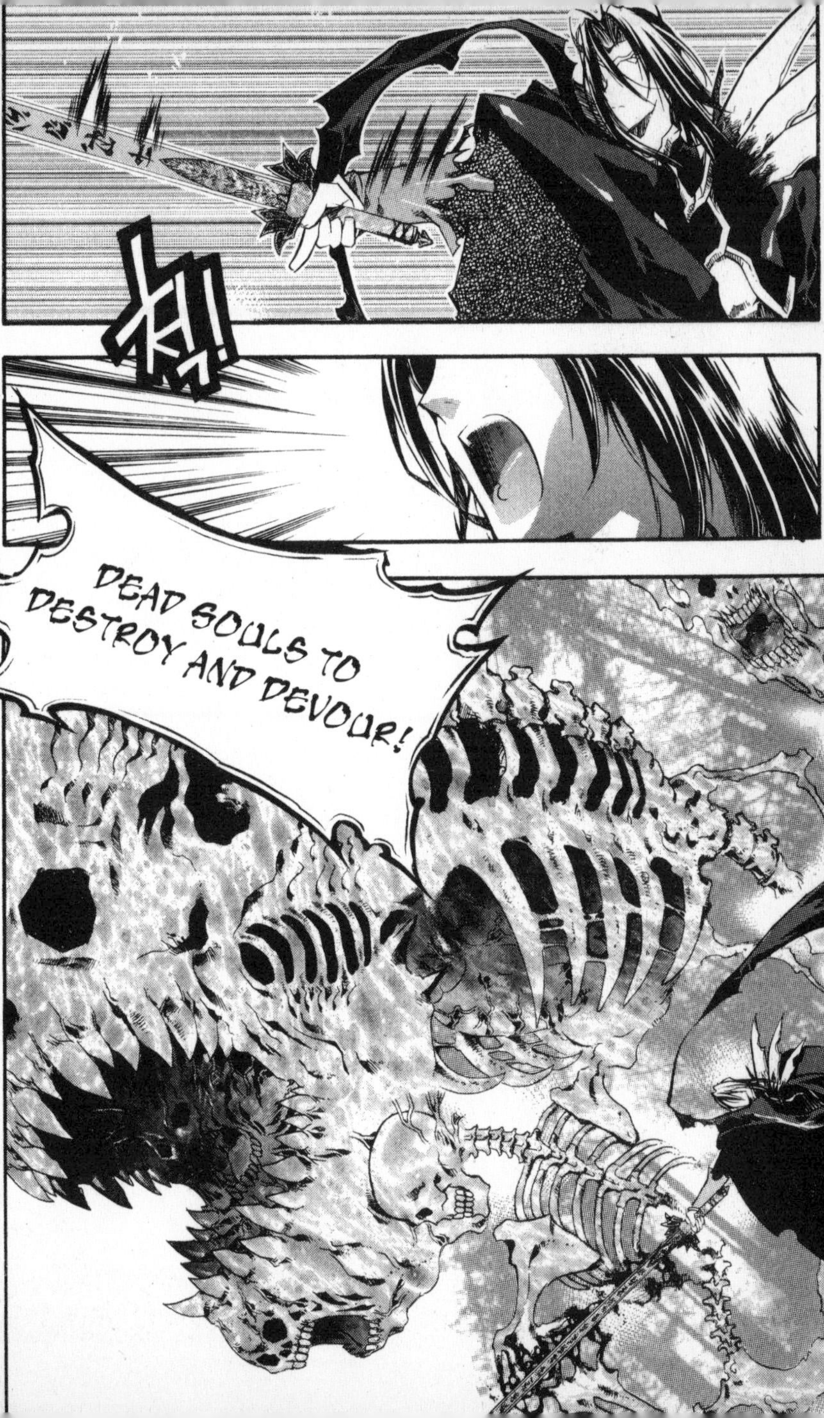
DEAD SOULS TO DESTROY AND DEVOUR!

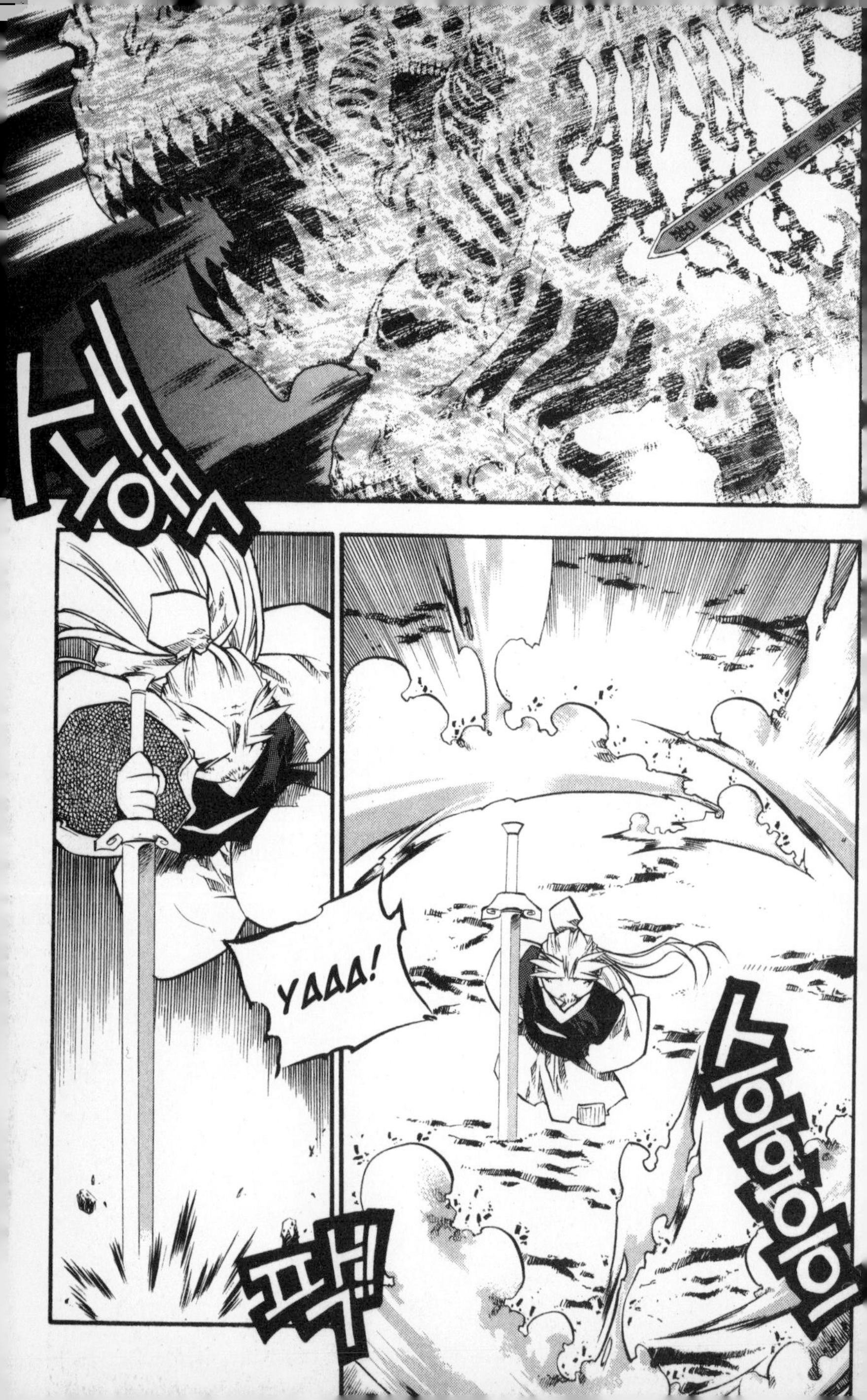
YAAA!

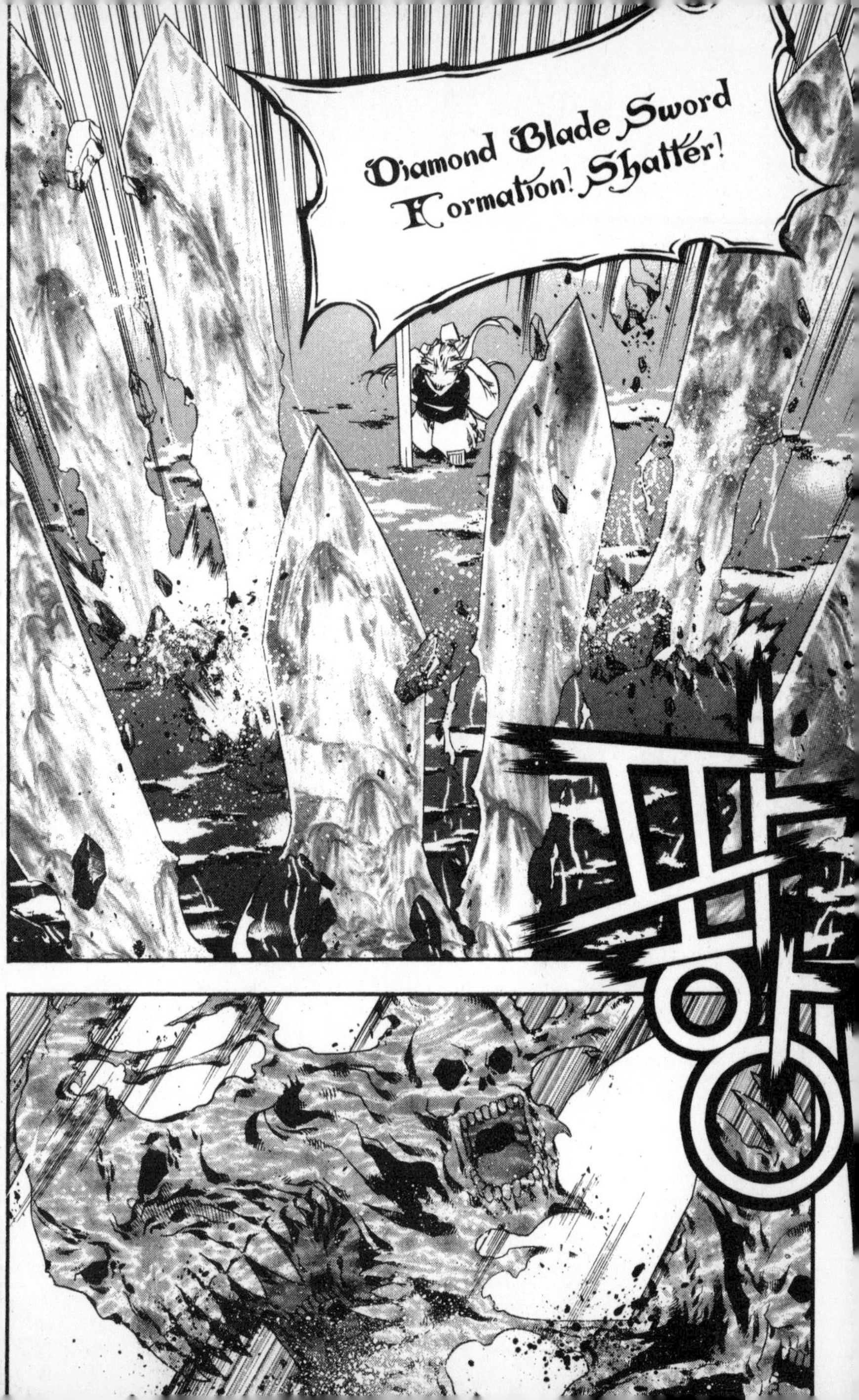
Diamond Blade Sword Formation! Shatter!

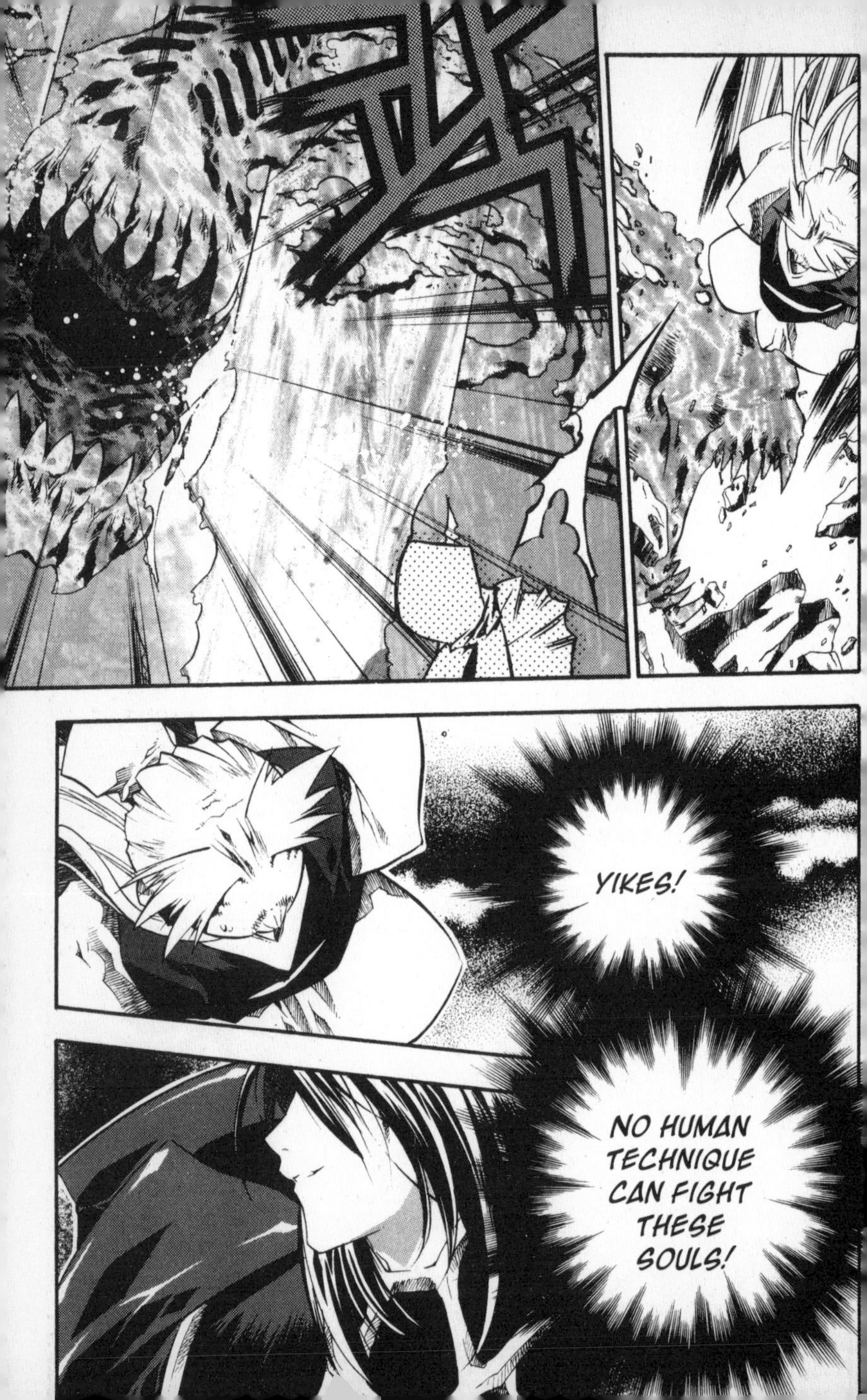
YIKES!
NO HUMAN TECHNIQUE CAN FIGHT THESE SOULS!

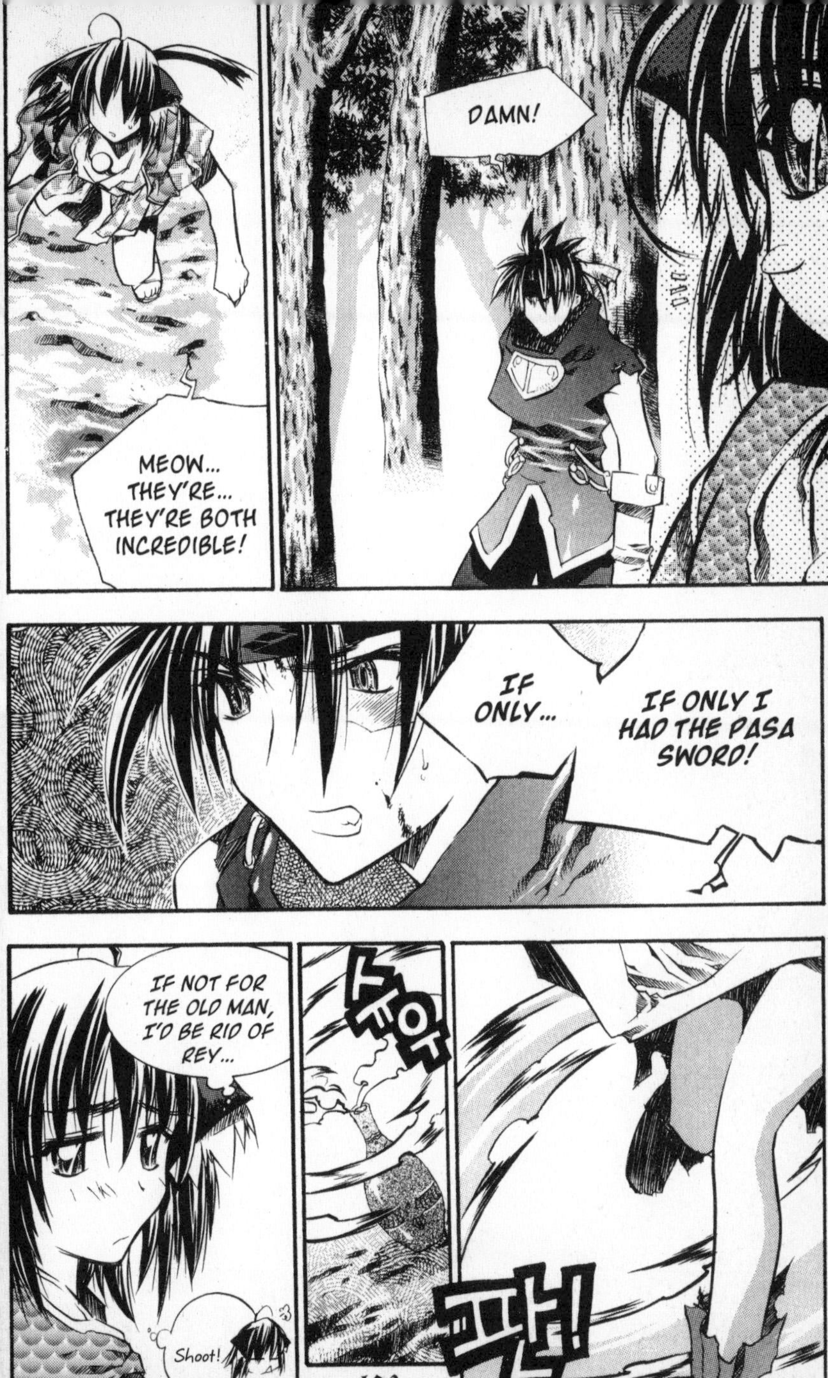
MEOW... THEY'RE... THEY'RE BOTH INCREDIBLE!
DAMN!
IF ONLY...
IF ONLY I HAD THE PASA SWORD!
IF NOT FOR THE OLD MAN, I'D BE RID OF REY...
Shoot!

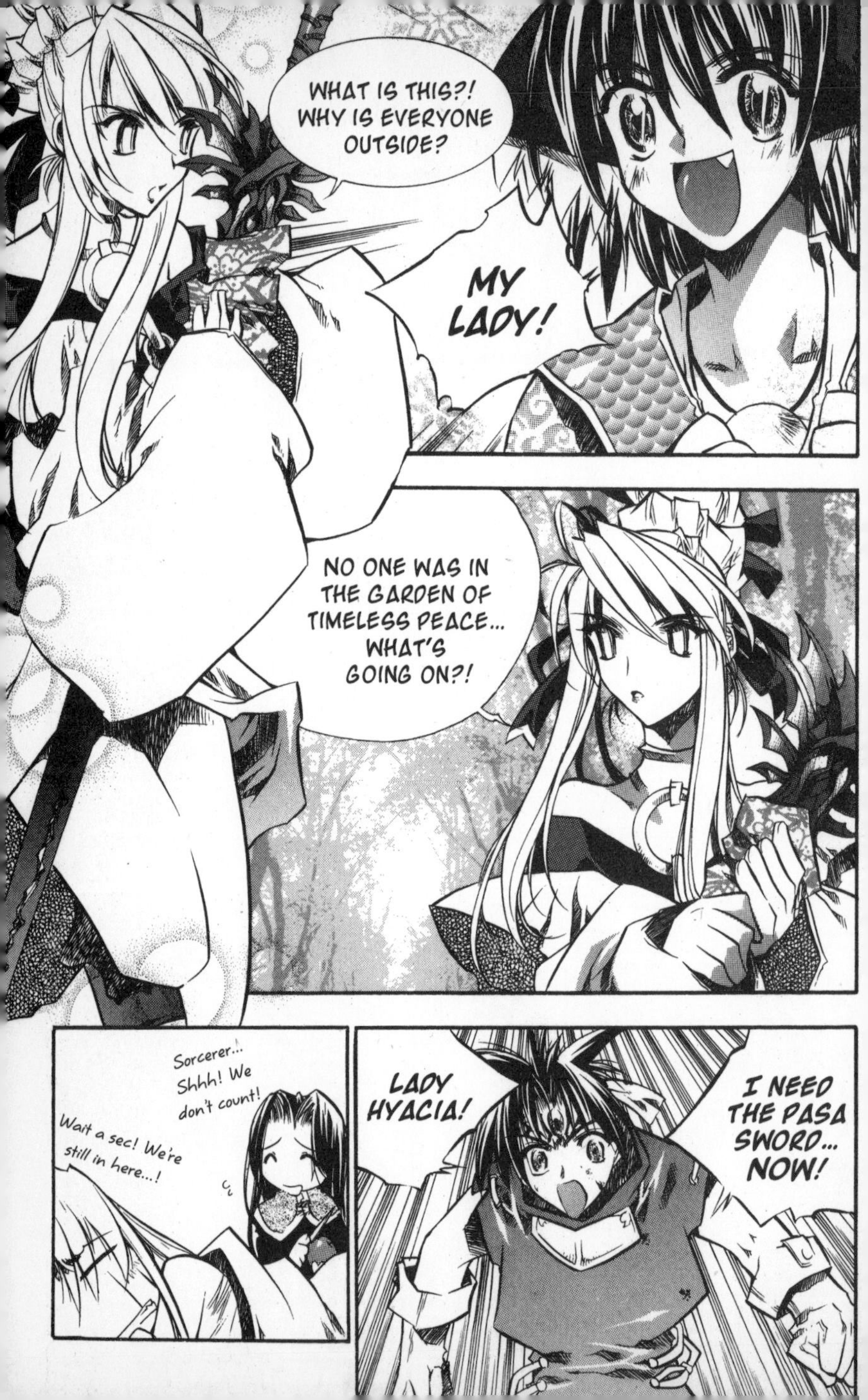
WHAT IS THIS?! WHY IS EVERYONE OUTSIDE?
MY LADY!
NO ONE WAS IN THE GARDEN OF TIMELESS PEACE... WHAT'S GOING ON?!
Wait a sec! We're still in here...!
Sorcerer... Shhh! We don't count!
LADY HYACIA!
I NEED THE PASA SWORD... NOW!

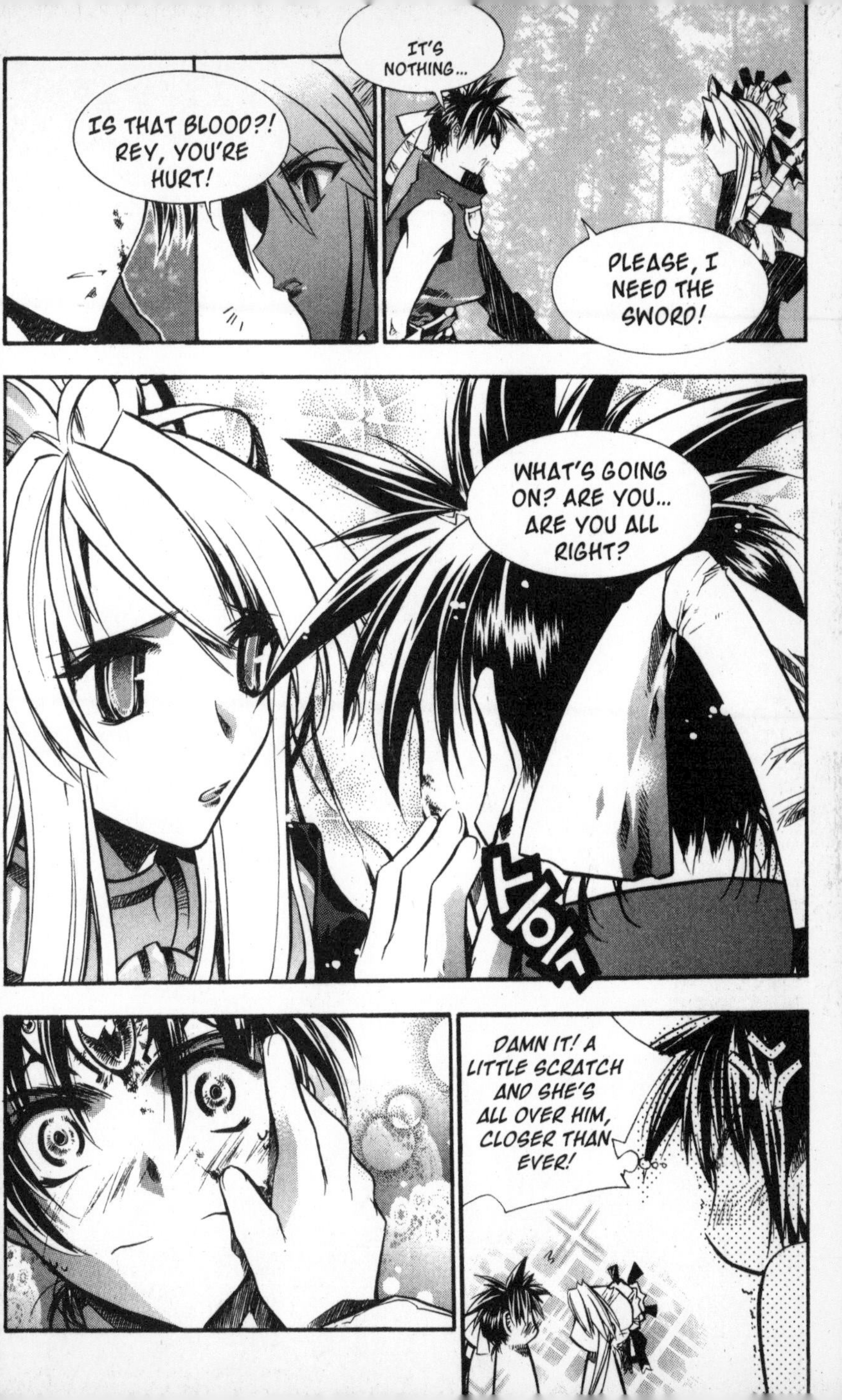
IS THAT BLOOD?! REY, YOU'RE HURT!
IT'S NOTHING...
PLEASE, I NEED THE SWORD!
WHAT'S GOING ON? ARE YOU... ARE YOU ALL RIGHT?
DAMN IT! A LITTLE SCRATCH AND SHE'S ALL OVER HIM, CLOSER THAN EVER!

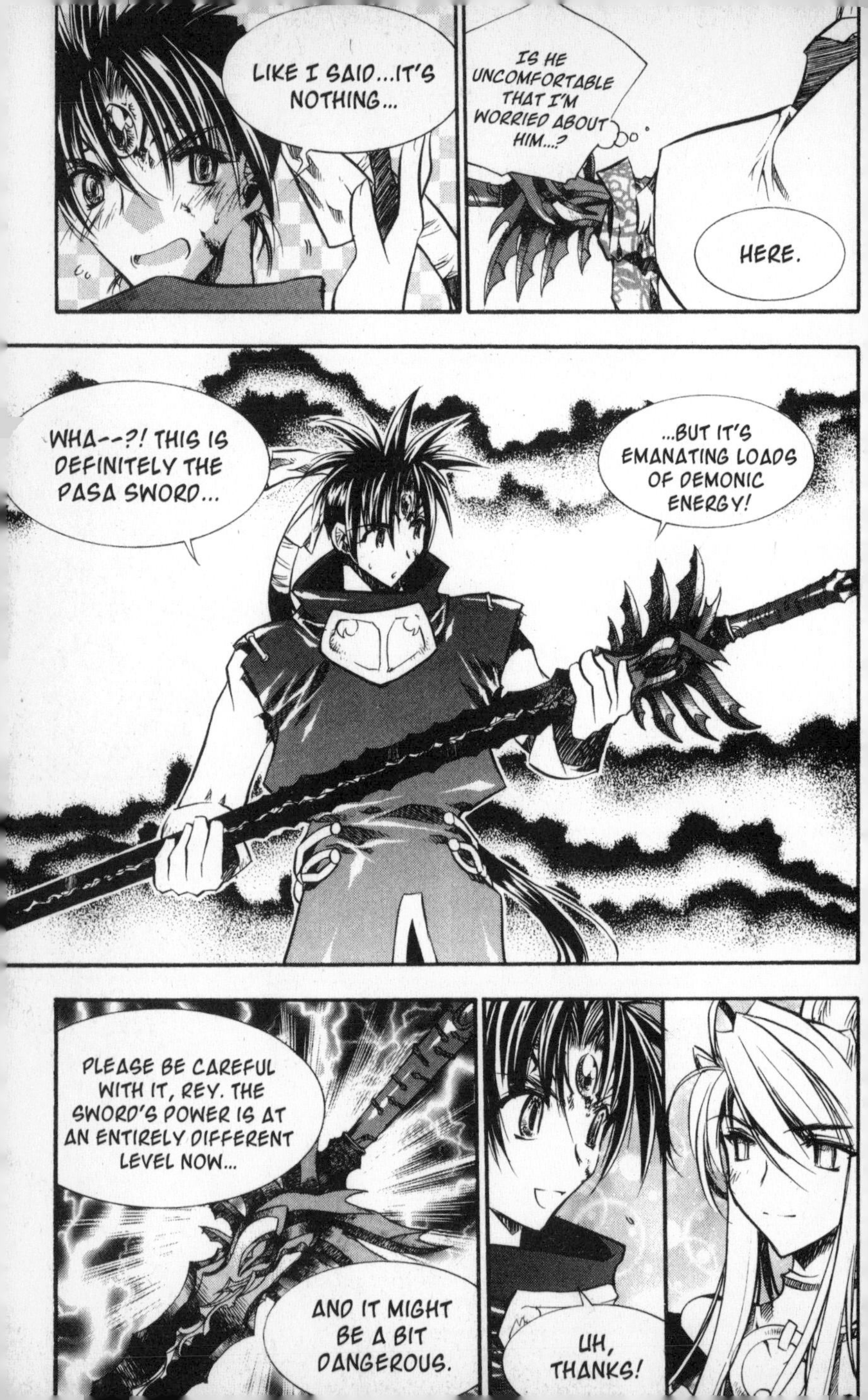
LIKE I SAID...IT'S NOTHING...
IS HE UNCOMFORTABLE THAT I'M WORRIED ABOUT HIM...?
HERE.
WHA--?! THIS IS DEFINITELY THE PASA SWORD...
...BUT IT'S EMANATING LOADS OF DEMONIC ENERGY!
PLEASE BE CAREFUL WITH IT, REY. THE SWORD'S POWER IS AT AN ENTIRELY DIFFERENT LEVEL NOW...
AND IT MIGHT BE A BIT DANGEROUS.
UH, THANKS!

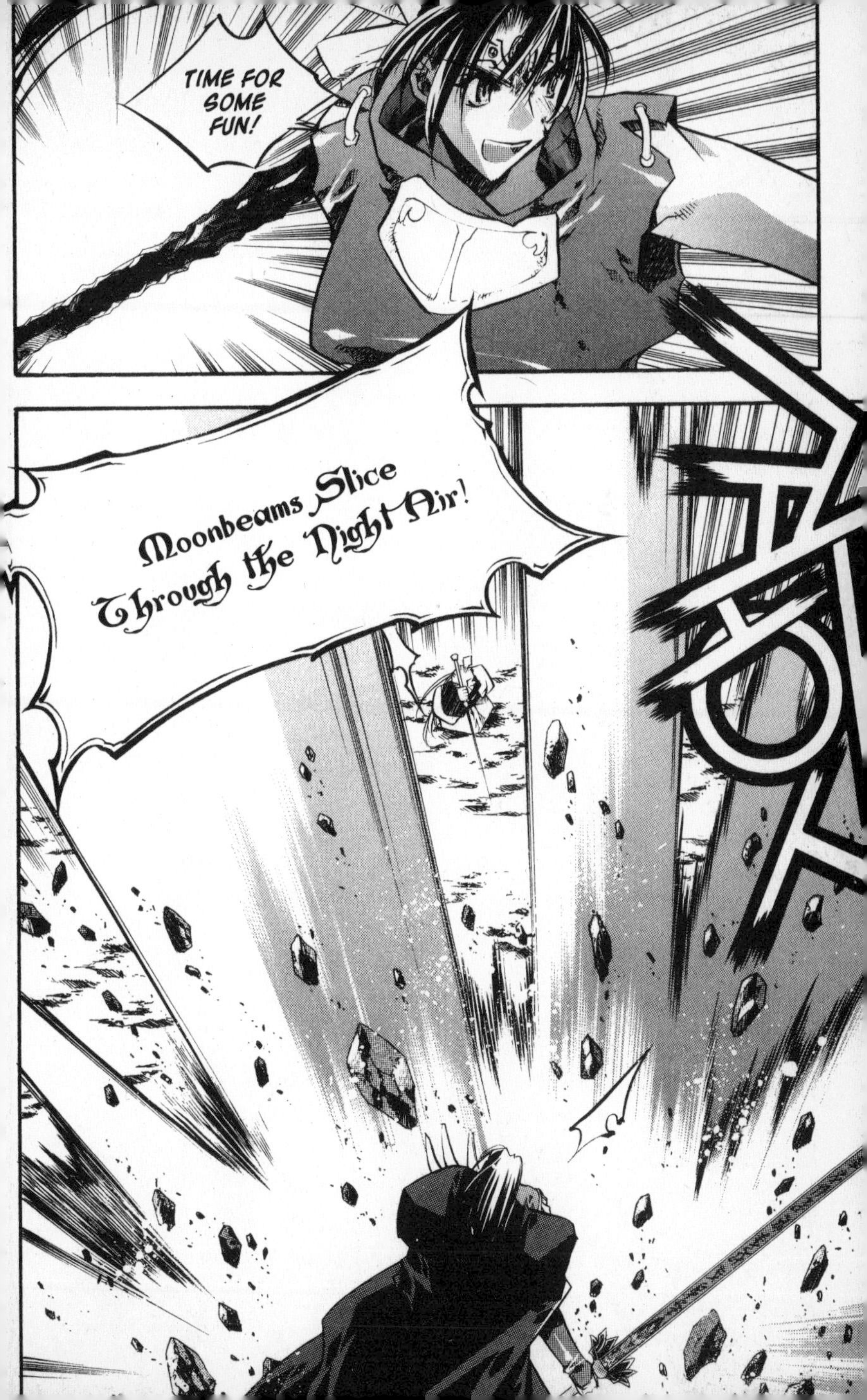
TIME FOR SOME FUN!
Moonbeams Slice Through the Night Air!

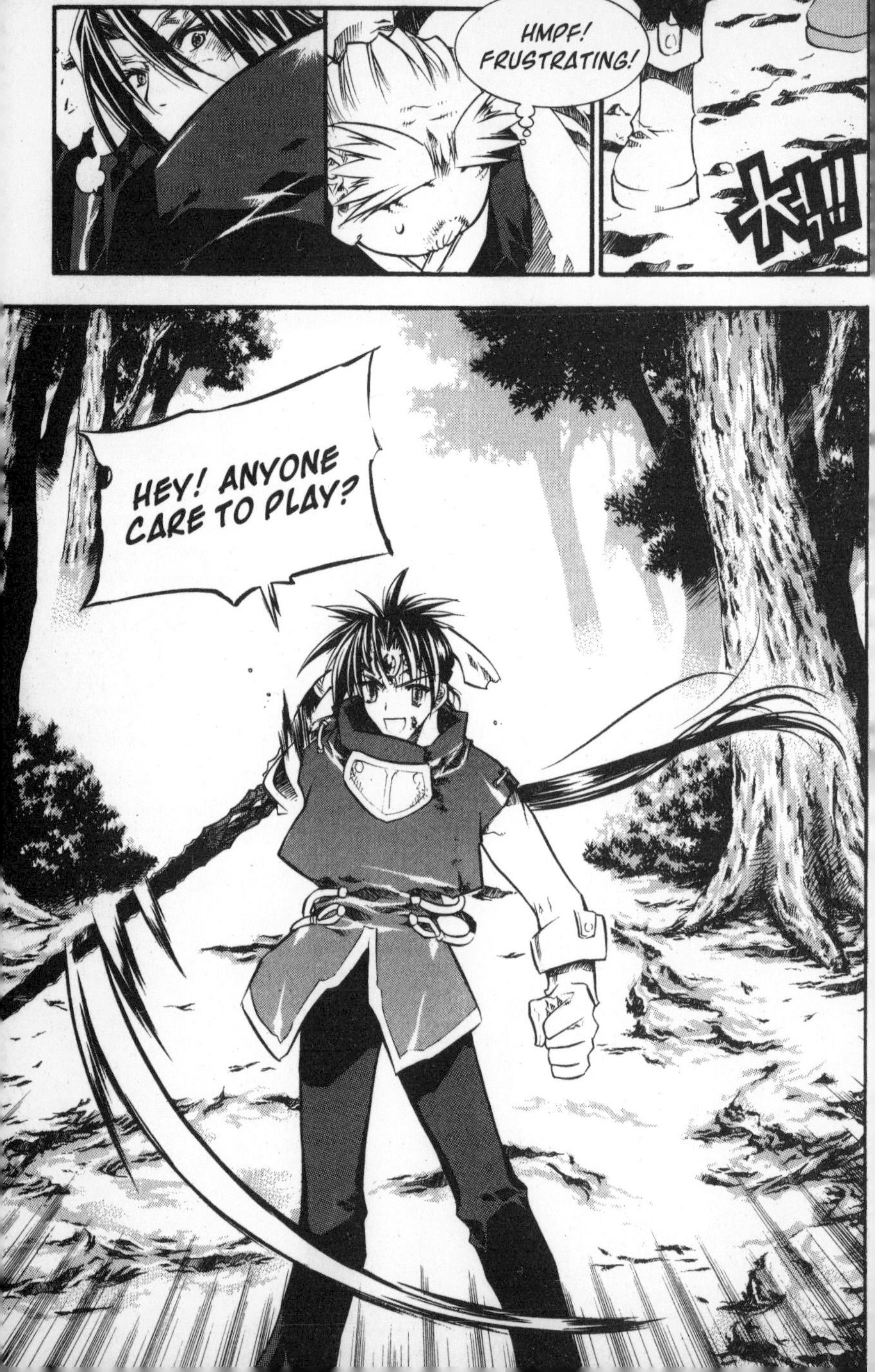
HMPF! FRUSTRATING!
HEY! ANYONE CARE TO PLAY?

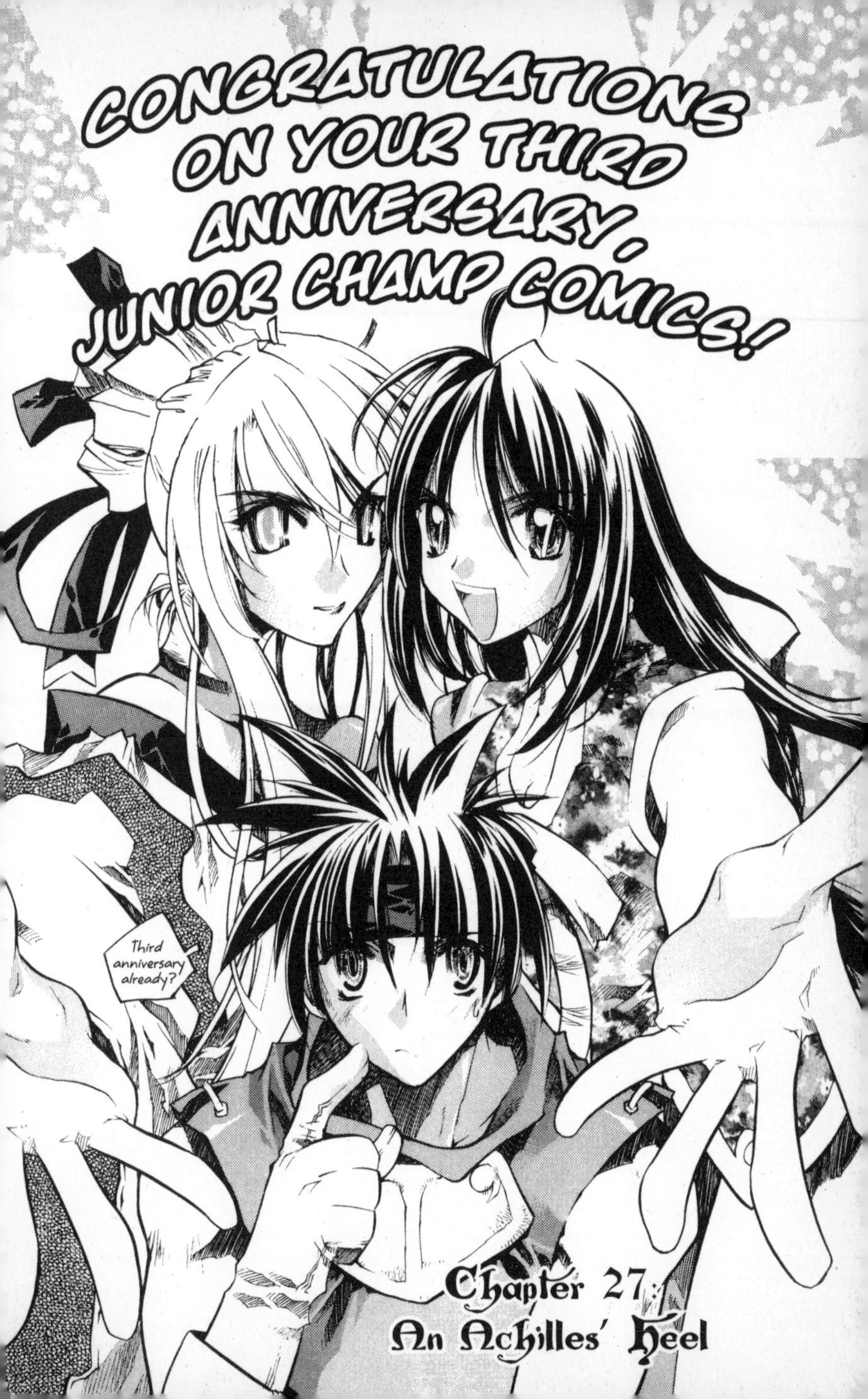
CONGRATULATIONS ON YOUR THIRD ANNIVERSARY, JUNIOR CHAMP COMICS!
Third anniversary already?
Chapter 27: An Achilles' Heel

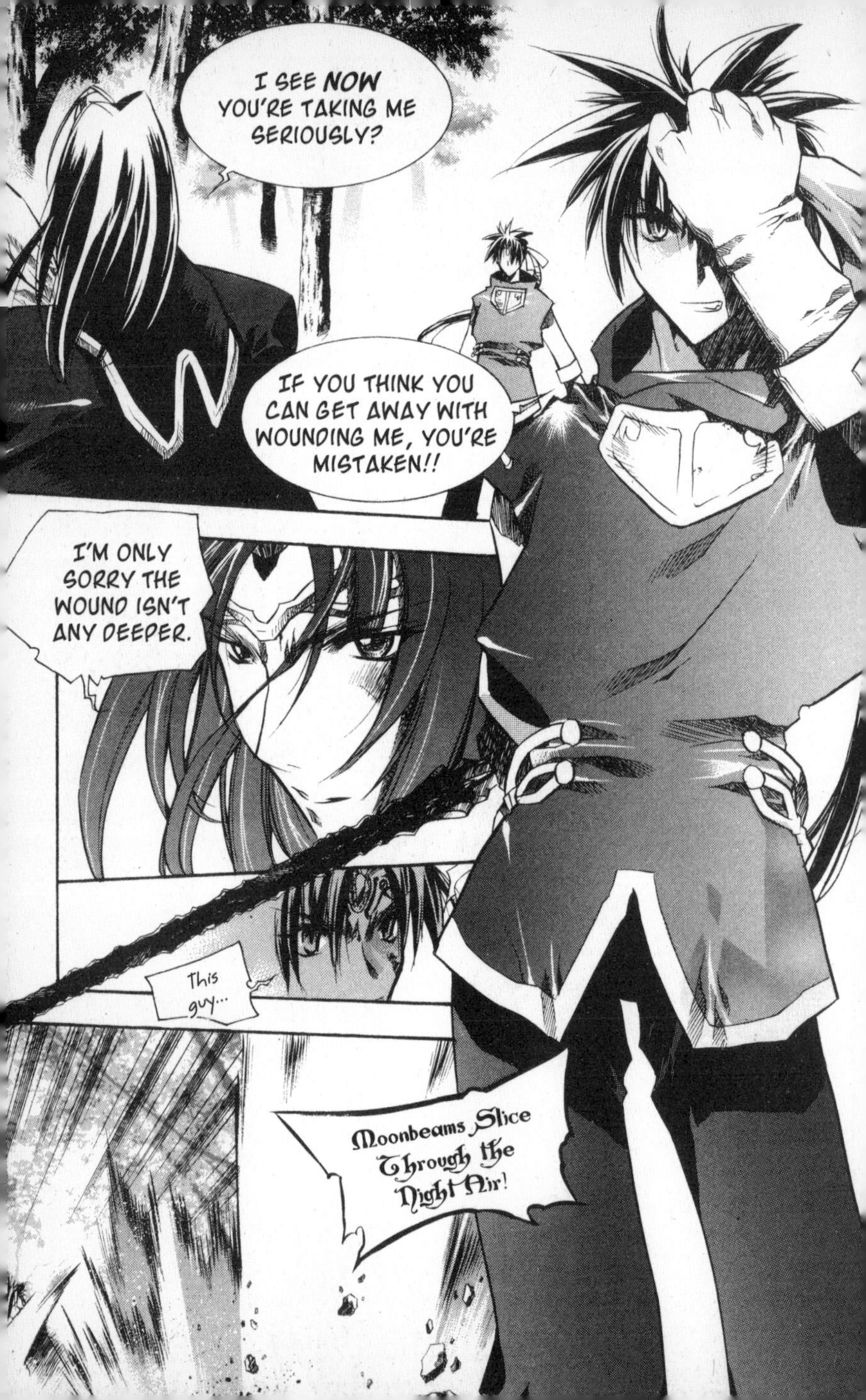
I SEE NOW YOU'RE TAKING ME SERIOUSLY?
IF YOU THINK YOU CAN GET AWAY WITH WOUNDING ME, YOU'RE MISTAKEN!!
I'M ONLY SORRY THE WOUND ISN'T ANY DEEPER.
This guy...
Moonbeams Slice Through the Night Air!

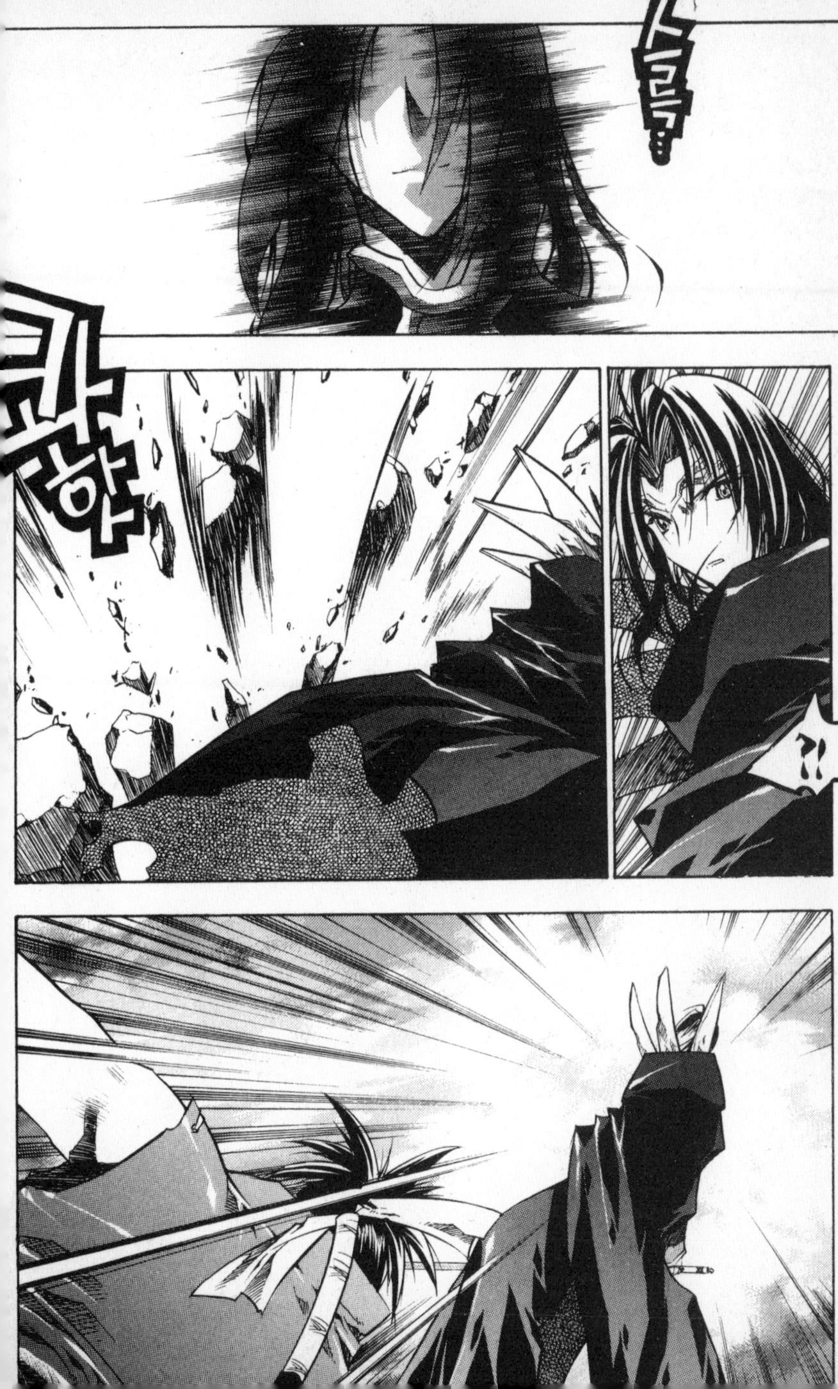
스륵...
콰앙
?!

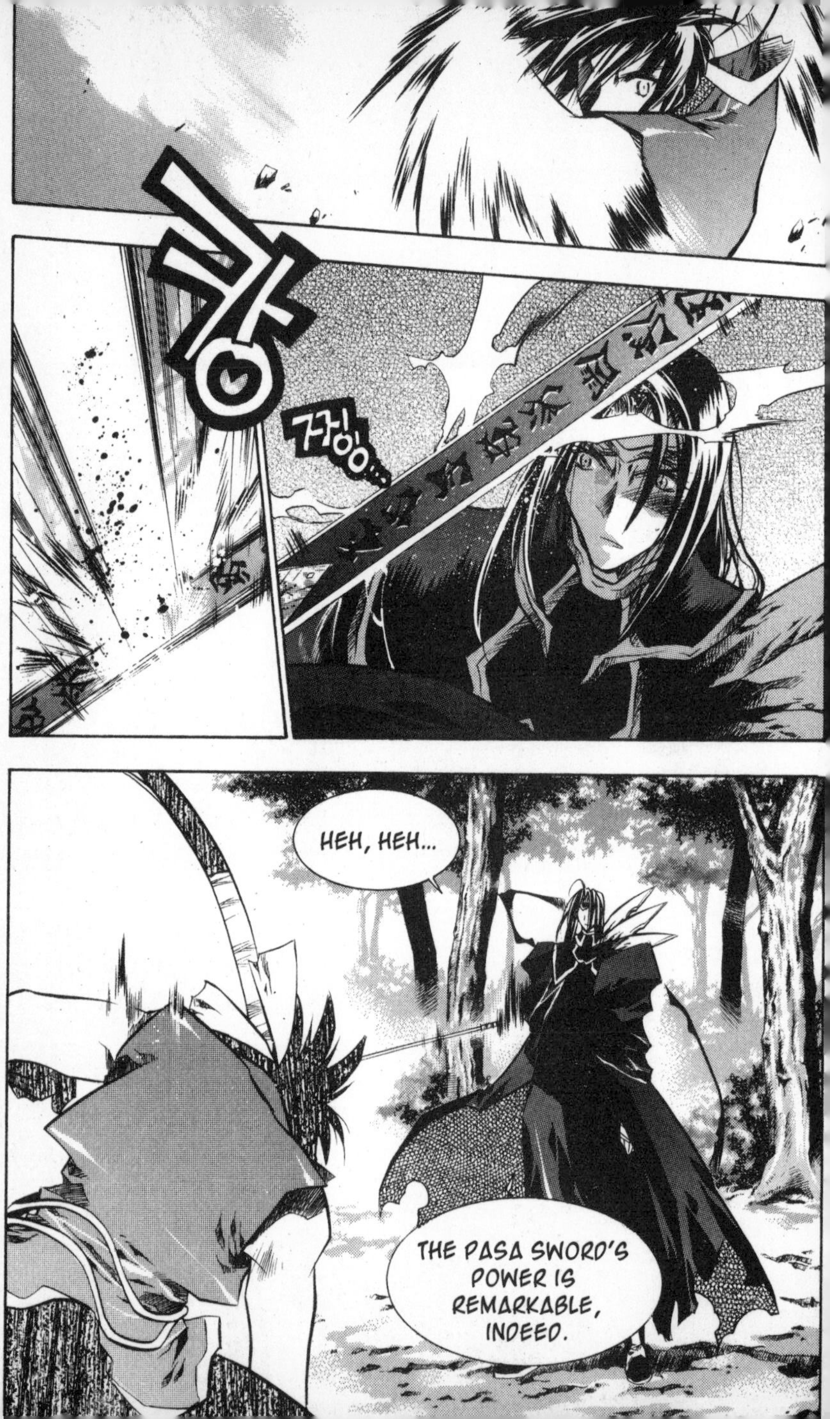
캉
HEH, HEH...
THE PASA SWORD'S POWER IS REMARKABLE, INDEED.

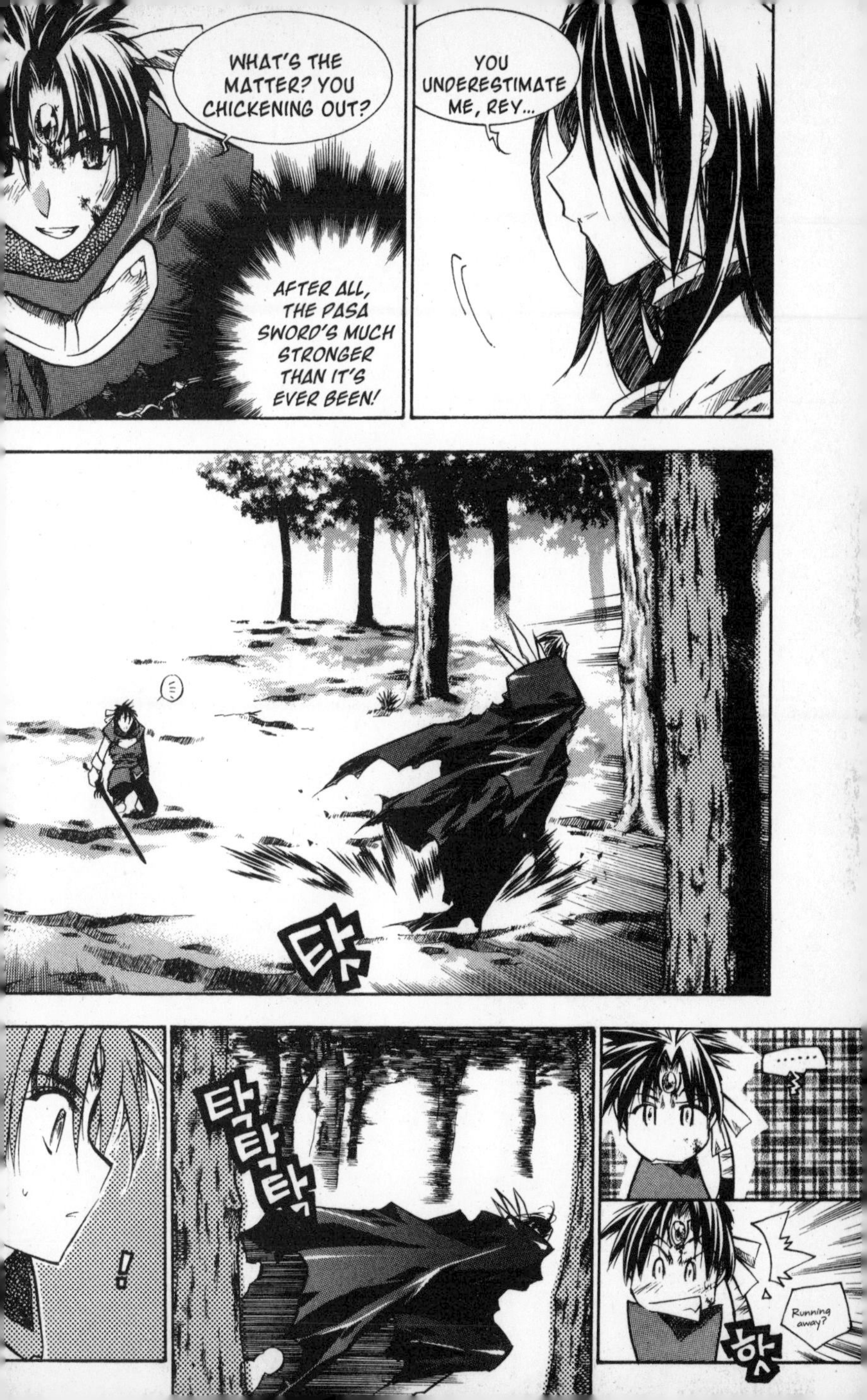
WHAT'S THE MATTER? YOU CHICKENING OUT?
AFTER ALL, THE PASA SWORD'S MUCH STRONGER THAN IT'S EVER BEEN!
YOU UNDERESTIMATE ME, REY...
탁
!
탁탁탁
......
Running away?
핫

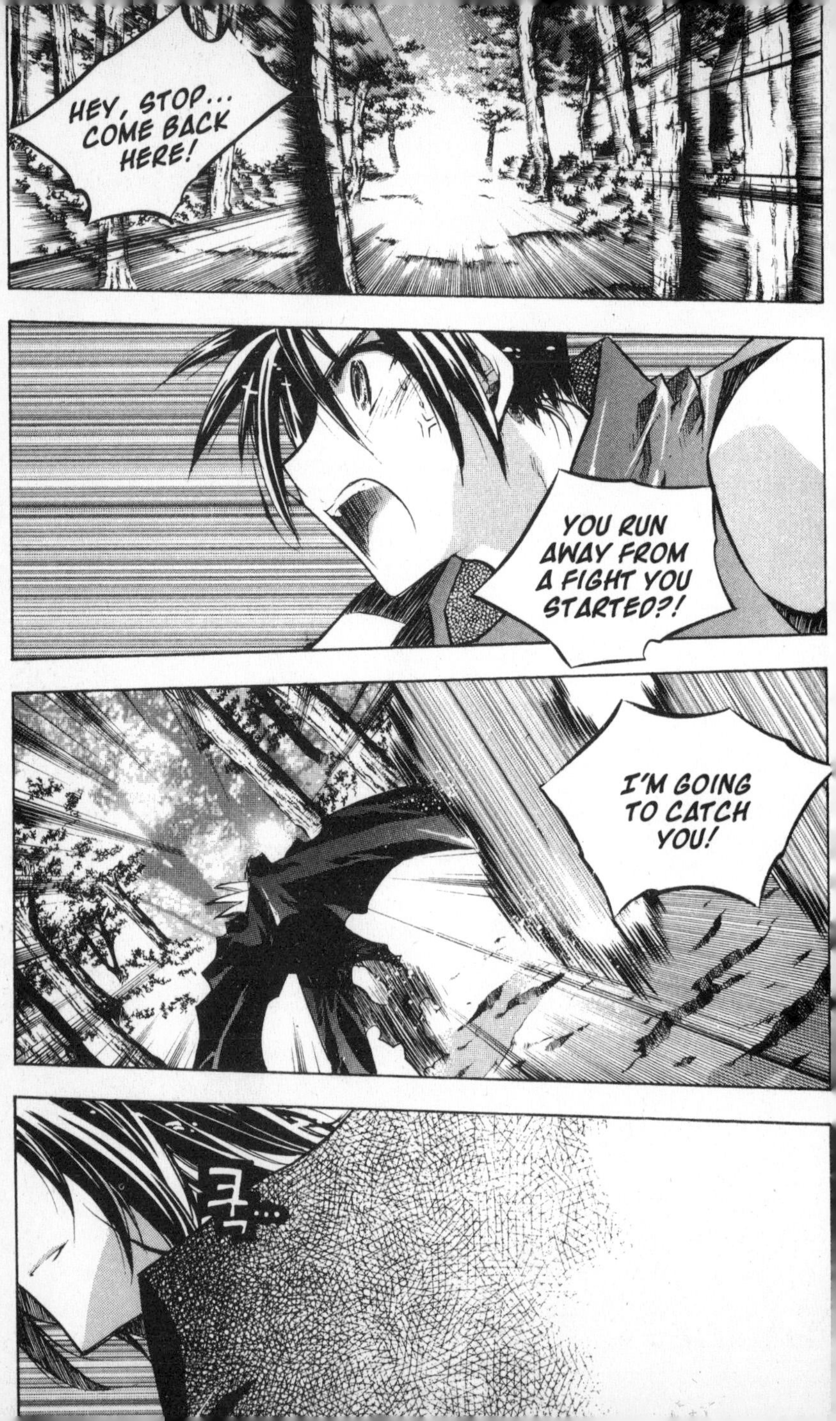
HEY, STOP... COME BACK HERE!
YOU RUN AWAY FROM A FIGHT YOU STARTED?!
I'M GOING TO CATCH YOU!
크...

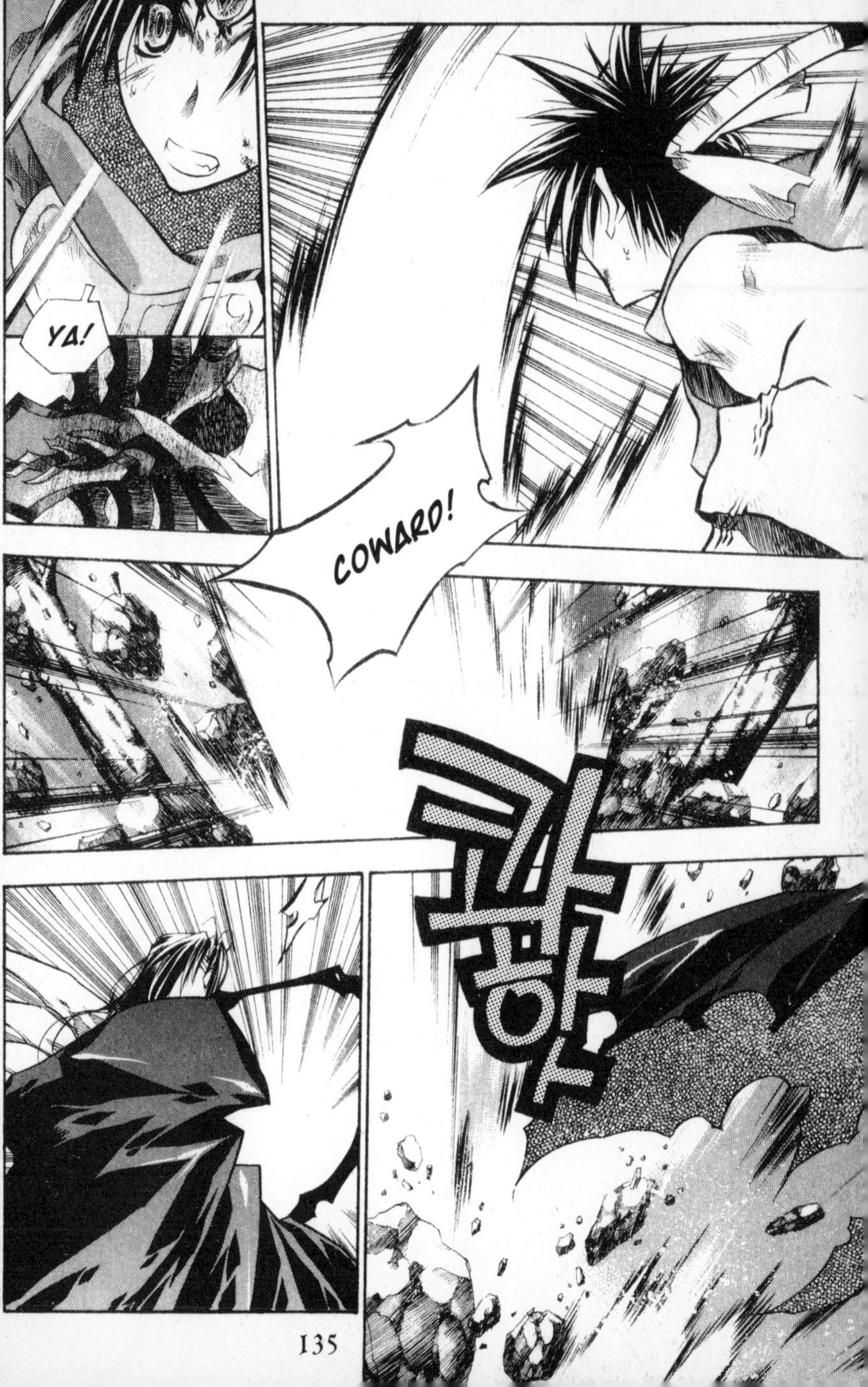
YA!
COWARD!
콰앙

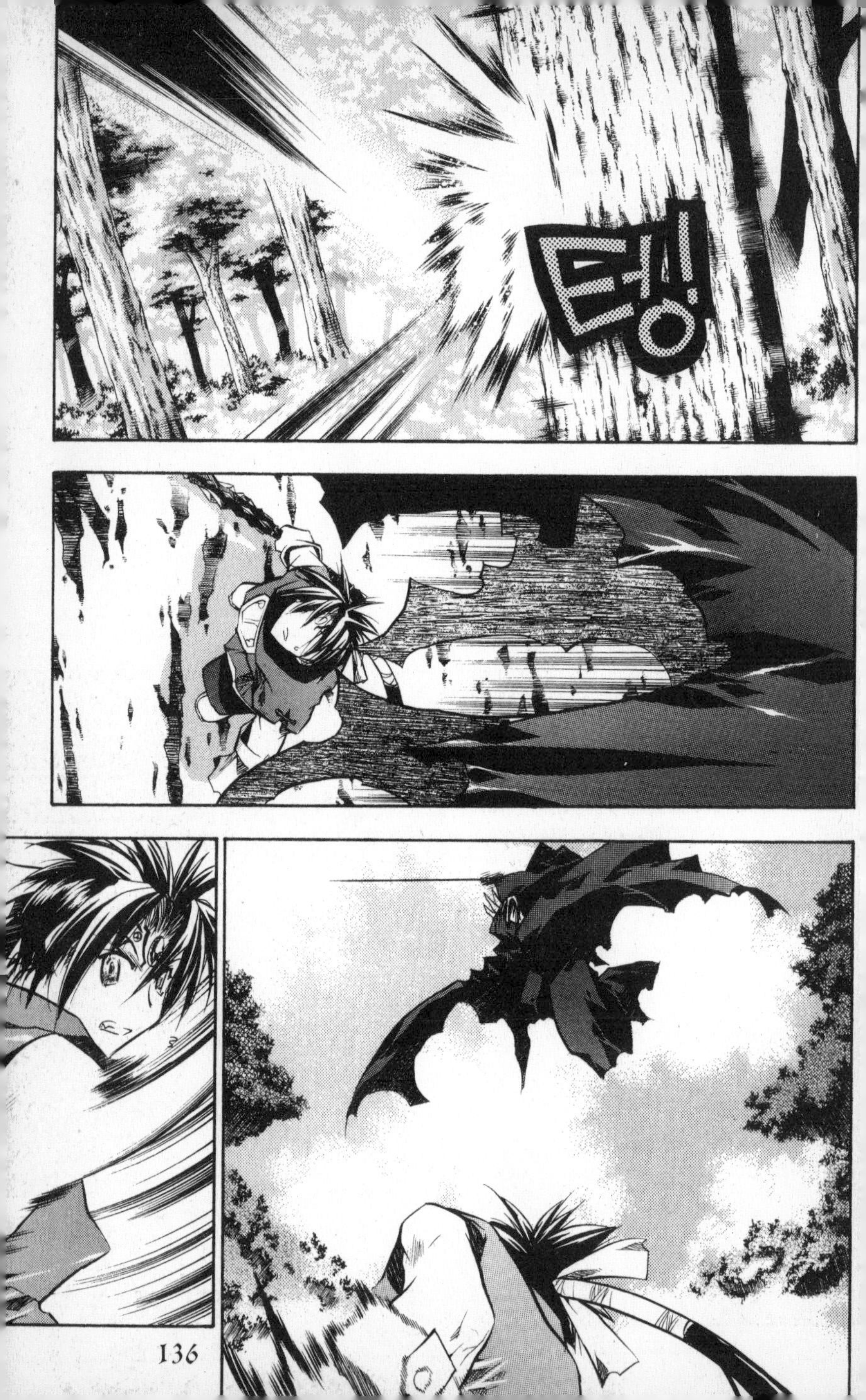
탱!!

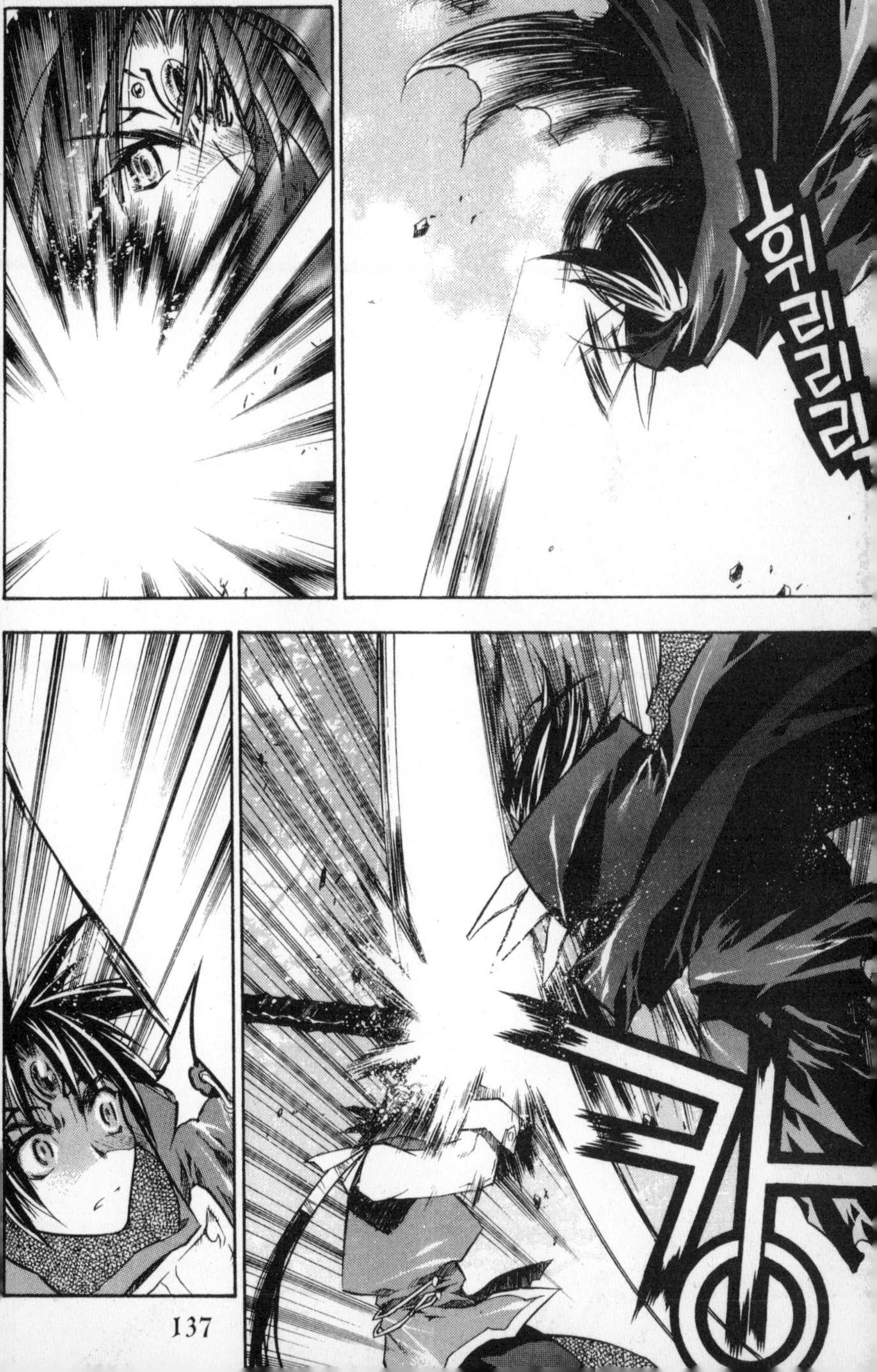
캉

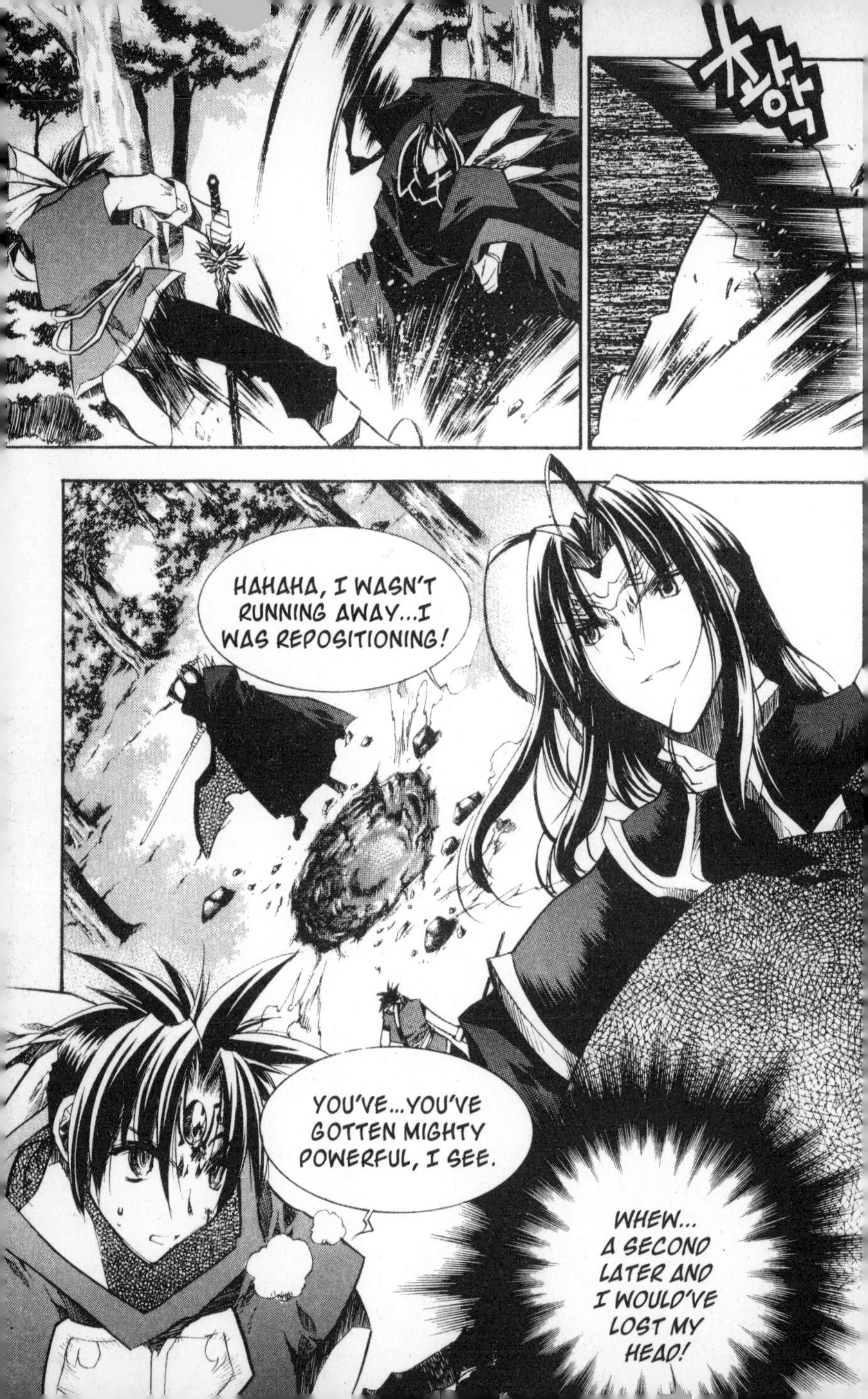
착
HAHAHA, I WASN'T RUNNING AWAY...I WAS REPOSITIONING!
YOU'VE...YOU'VE GOTTEN MIGHTY POWERFUL, I SEE.
WHEW... A SECOND LATER AND I WOULD'VE LOST MY HEAD!

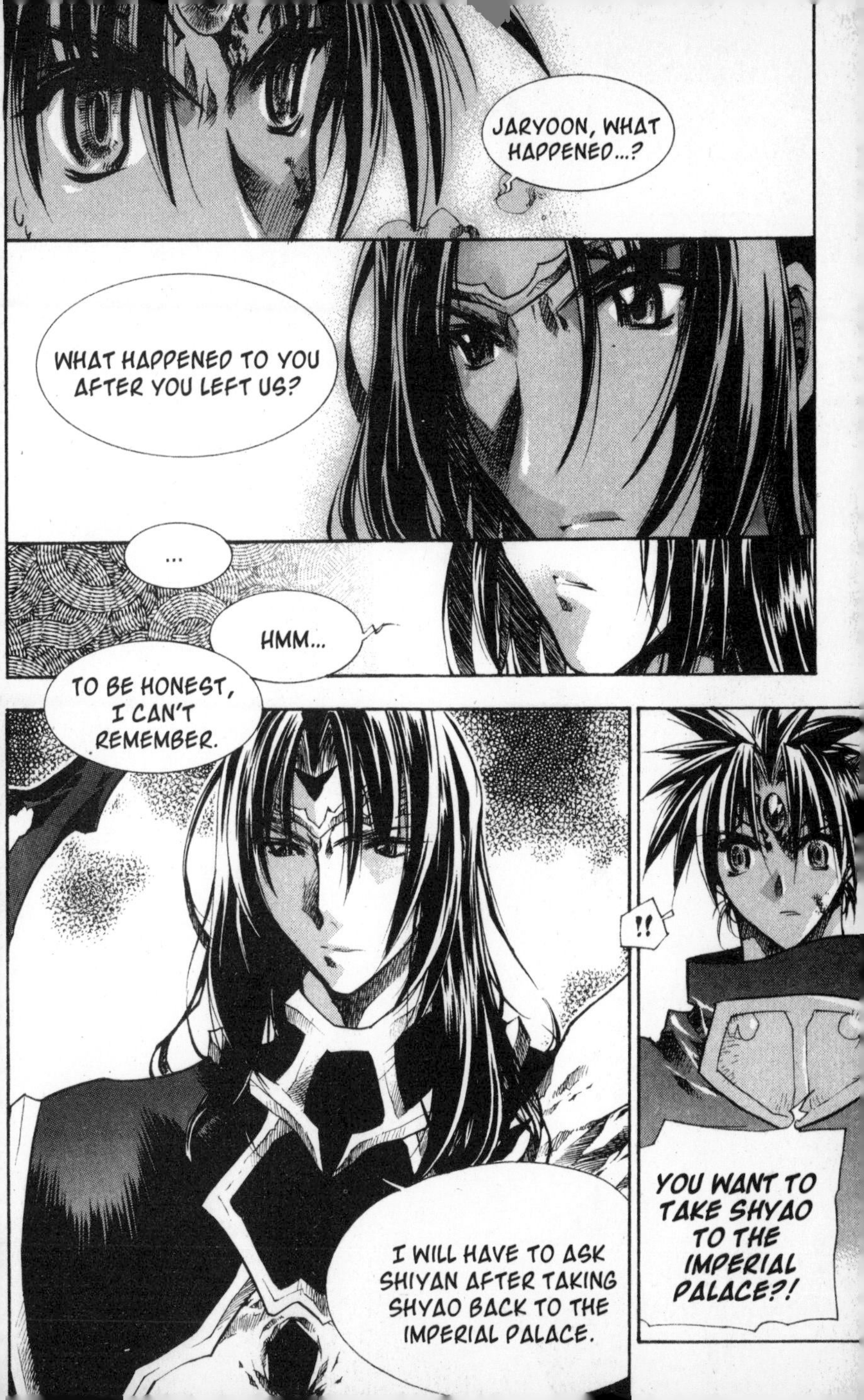
JARYOON, WHAT HAPPENED...?
WHAT HAPPENED TO YOU AFTER YOU LEFT US?
...
HMM...
TO BE HONEST, I CAN'T REMEMBER.
I WILL HAVE TO ASK SHIYAN AFTER TAKING SHYAO BACK TO THE IMPERIAL PALACE.
!!
YOU WANT TO TAKE SHYAO TO THE IMPERIAL PALACE?!

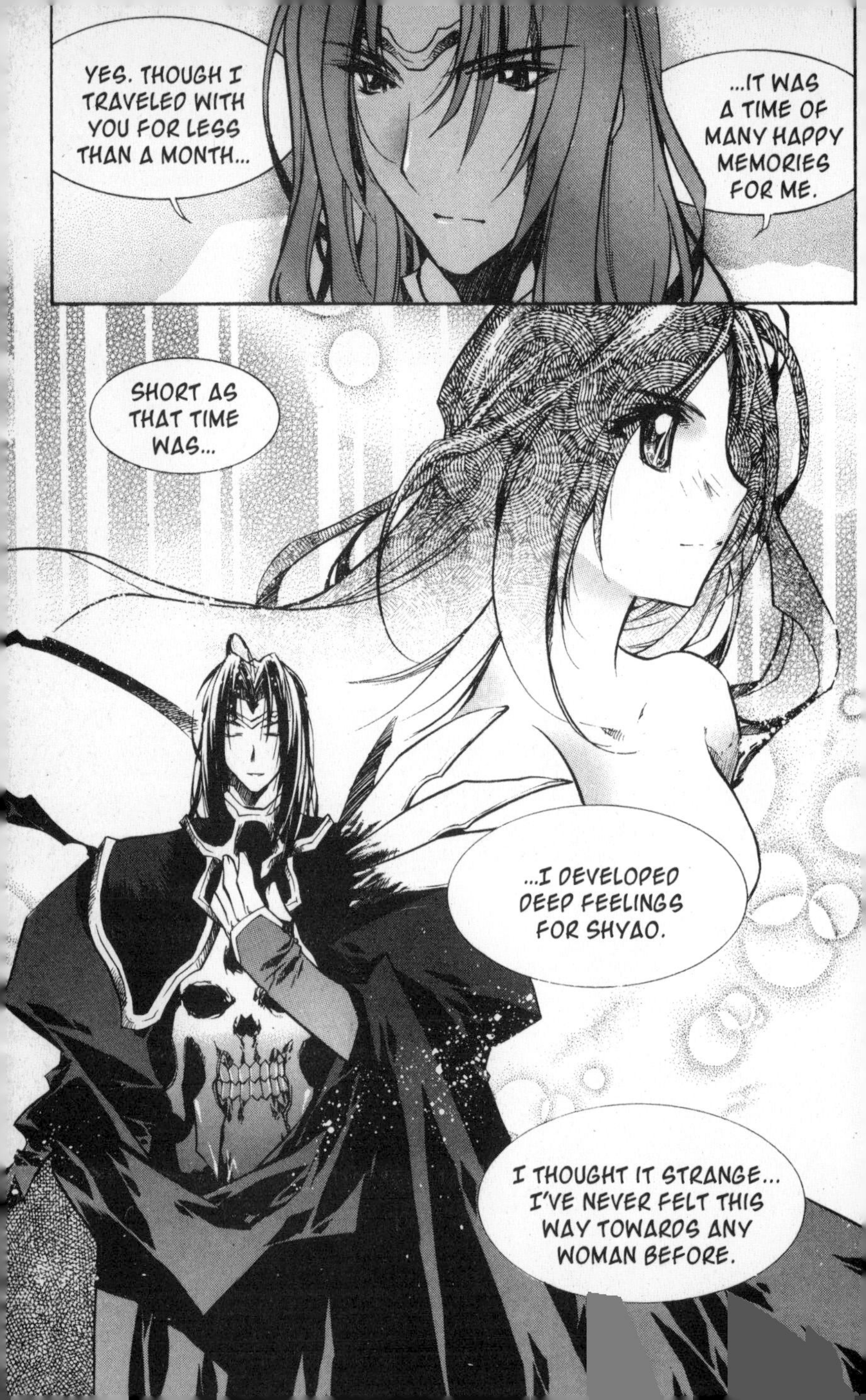
YES. THOUGH I TRAVELED WITH YOU FOR LESS THAN A MONTH...
...IT WAS A TIME OF MANY HAPPY MEMORIES FOR ME.
SHORT AS THAT TIME WAS...
...I DEVELOPED DEEP FEELINGS FOR SHYAO.
I THOUGHT IT STRANGE... I'VE NEVER FELT THIS WAY TOWARDS ANY WOMAN BEFORE.

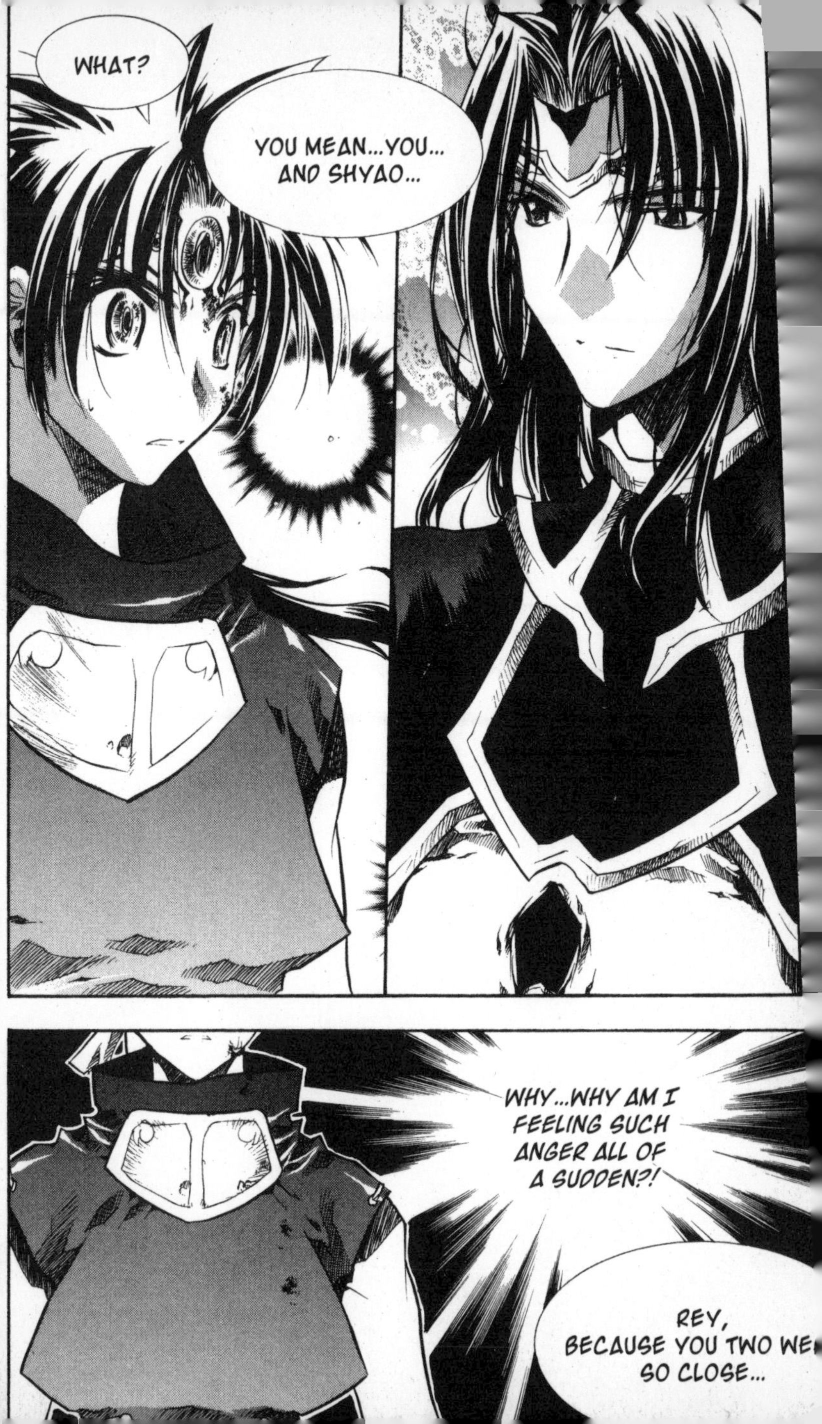
WHAT?
YOU MEAN...YOU... AND SHYAO...
WHY...WHY AM I FEELING SUCH ANGER ALL OF A SUDDEN?!
REY, BECAUSE YOU TWO WE
SO CLOSE...

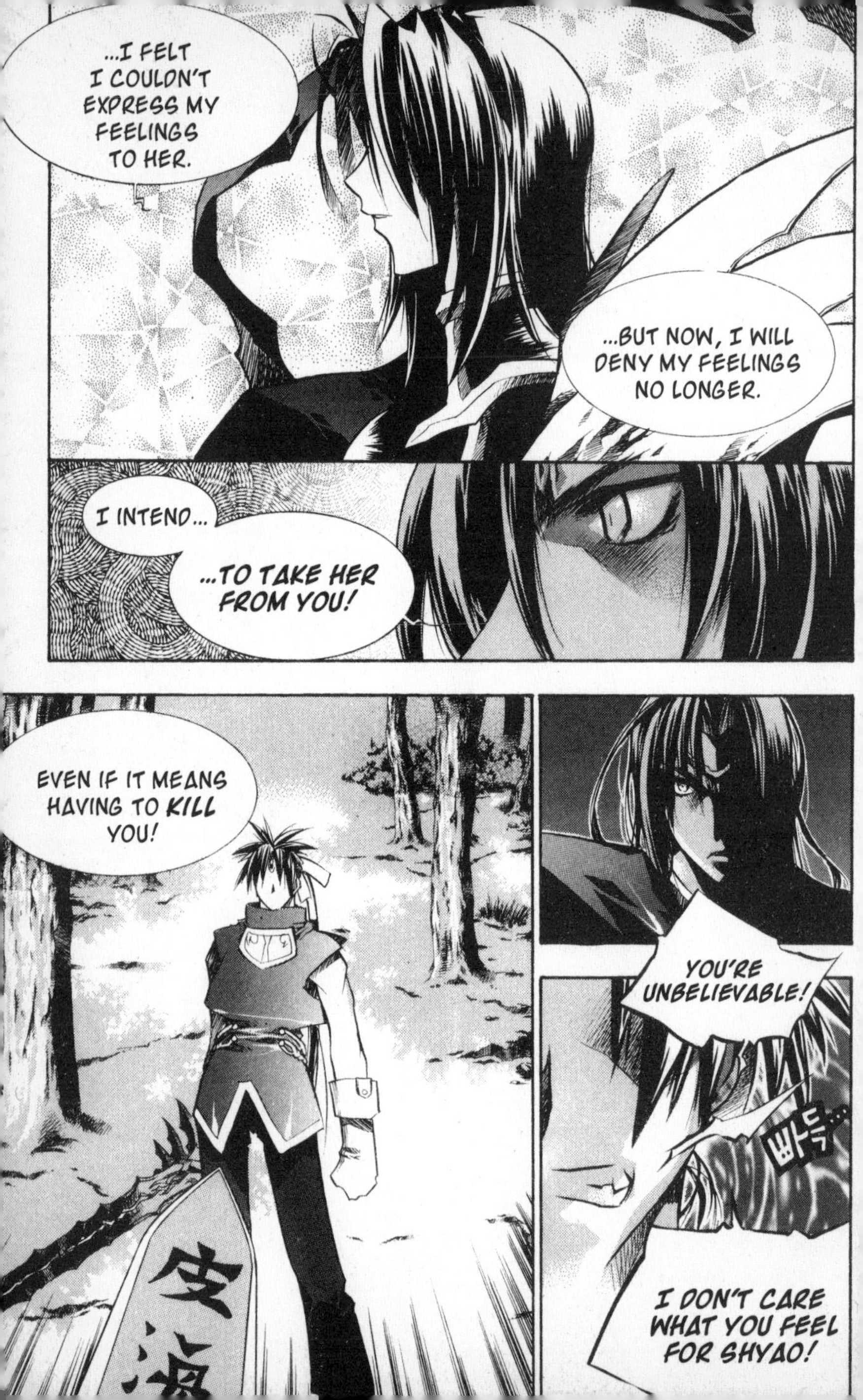
...I FELT I COULDN'T EXPRESS MY FEELINGS TO HER.
...BUT NOW, I WILL DENY MY FEELINGS NO LONGER.
I INTEND...
...TO TAKE HER FROM YOU!
EVEN IF IT MEANS HAVING TO KILL YOU!
YOU'RE UNBELIEVABLE!
I DON'T CARE WHAT YOU FEEL FOR SHYAO!

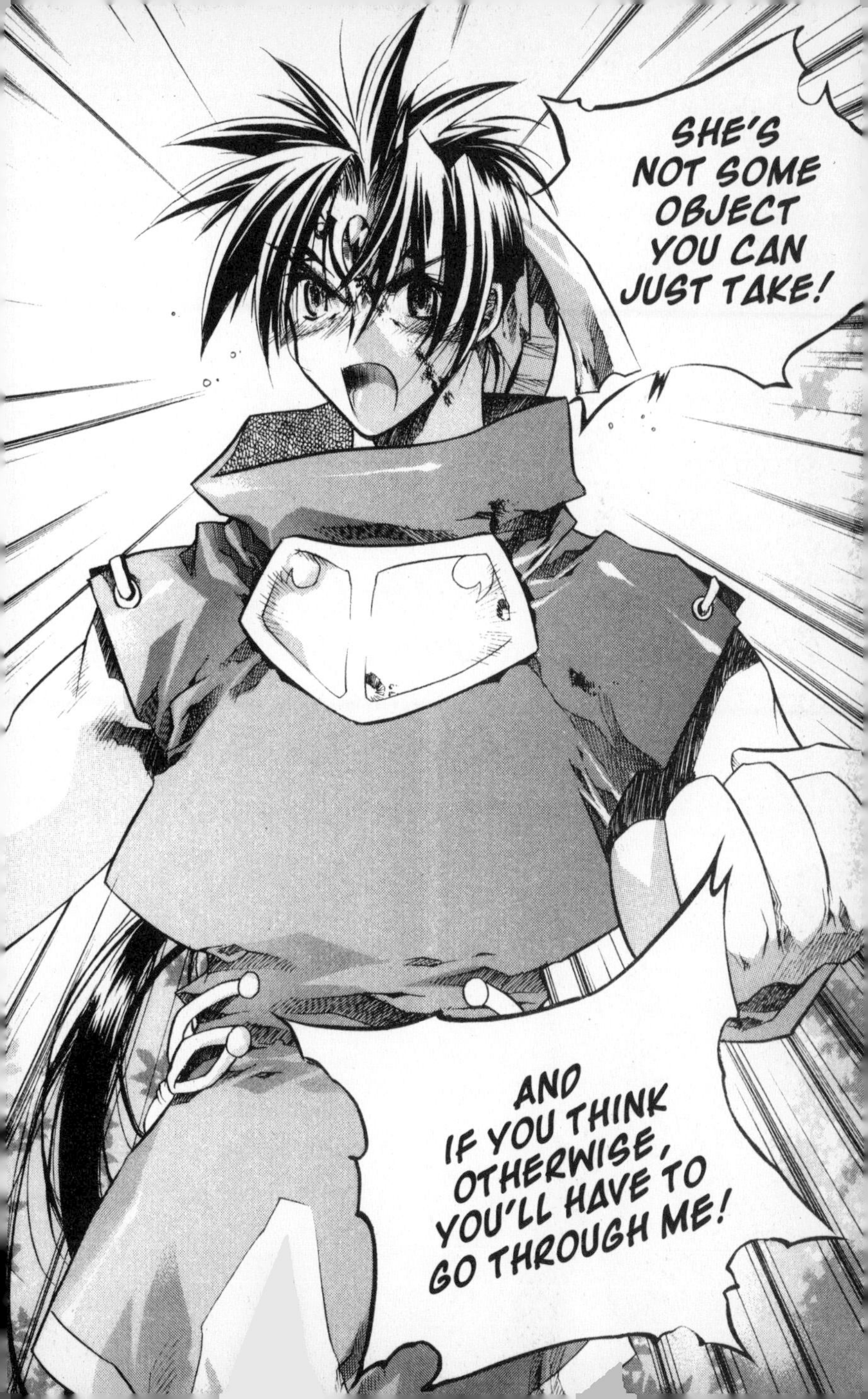
SHE'S NOT SOME OBJECT YOU CAN JUST TAKE!
AND IF YOU THINK OTHERWISE, YOU'LL HAVE TO GO THROUGH ME!

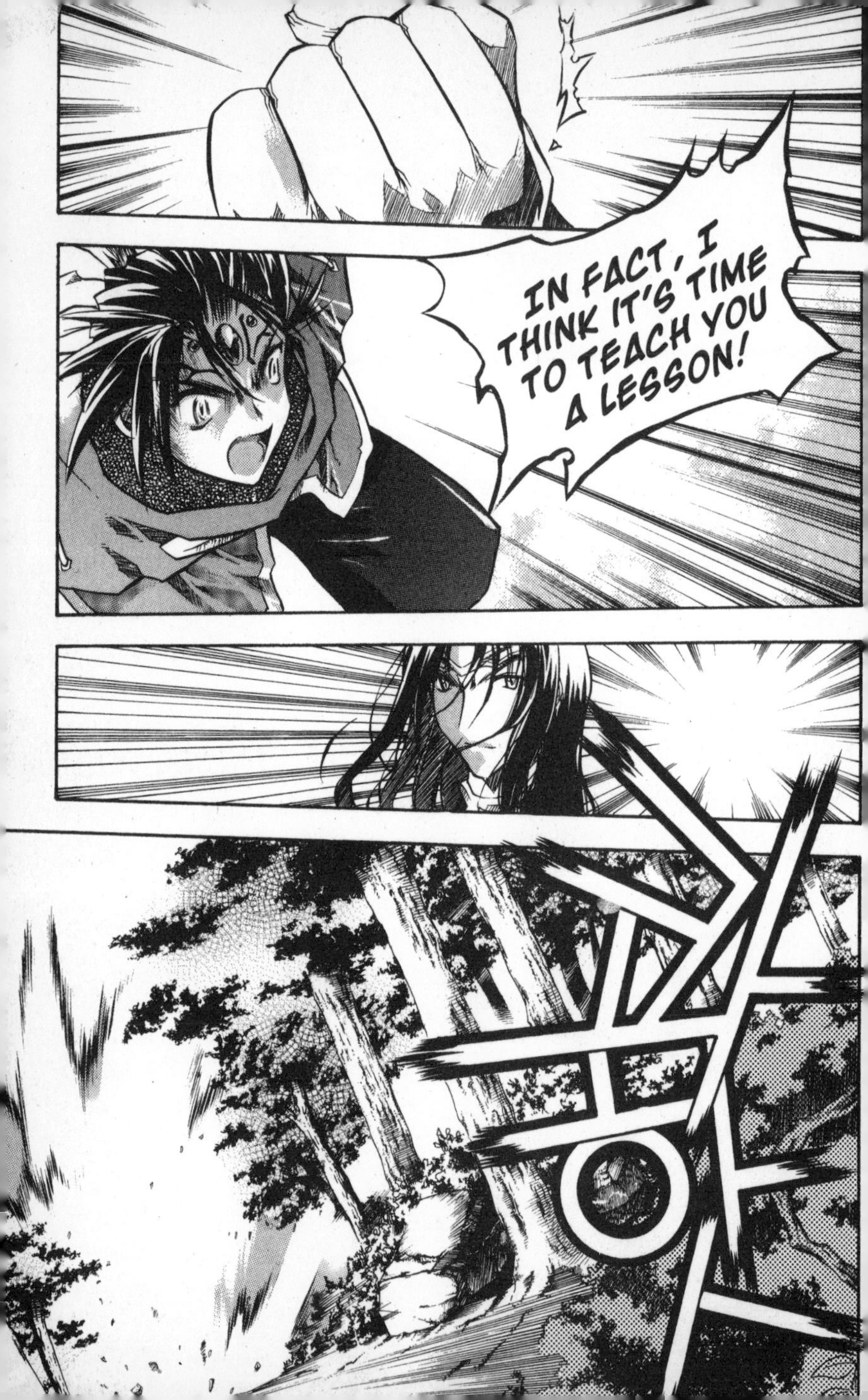
IN FACT, I THINK IT'S TIME TO TEACH YOU A LESSON!

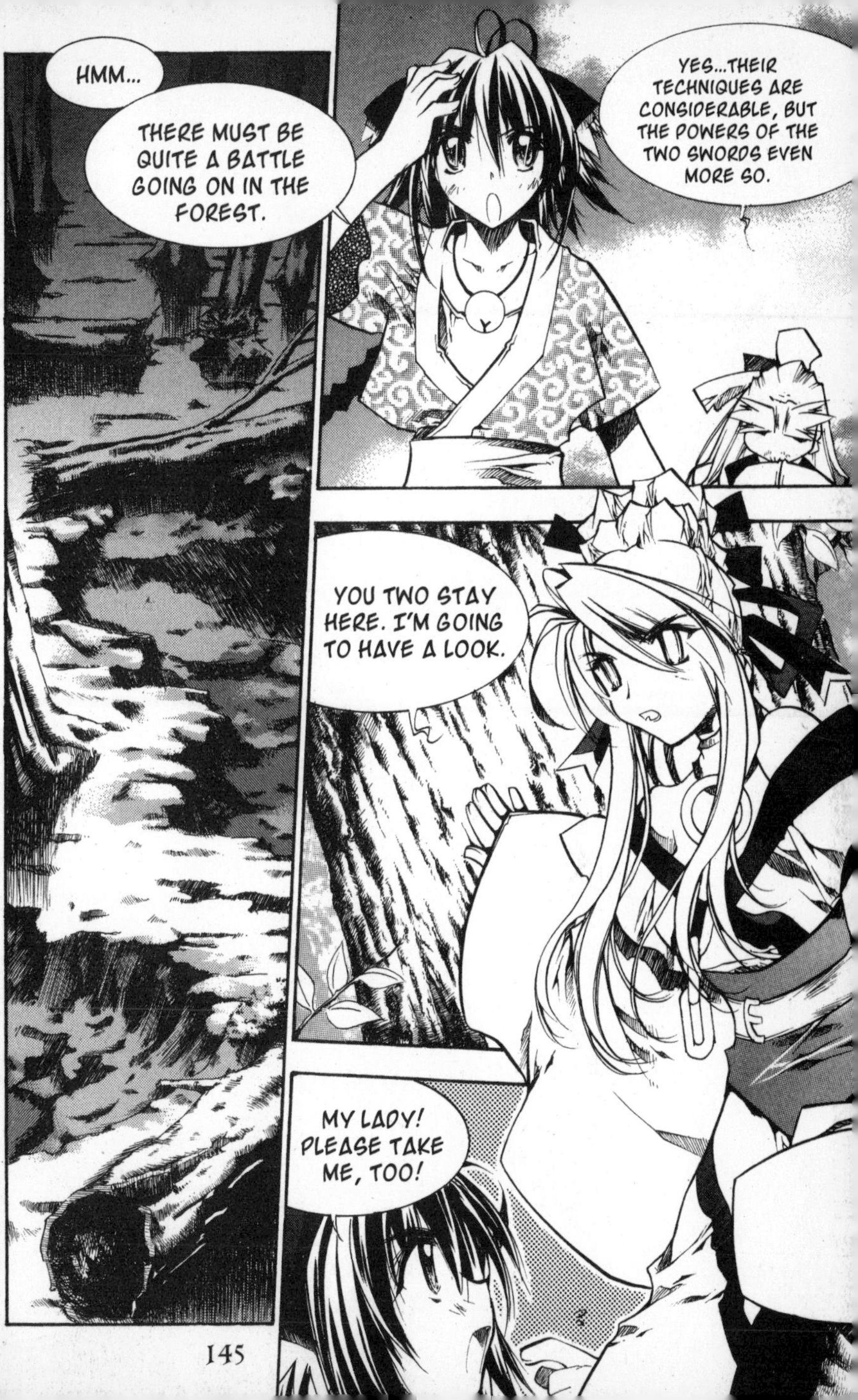
HMM...
THERE MUST BE QUITE A BATTLE GOING ON IN THE FOREST.
YES...THEIR TECHNIQUES ARE CONSIDERABLE, BUT THE POWERS OF THE TWO SWORDS EVEN MORE SO.
YOU TWO STAY HERE. I'M GOING TO HAVE A LOOK.
MY LADY! PLEASE TAKE ME, TOO!

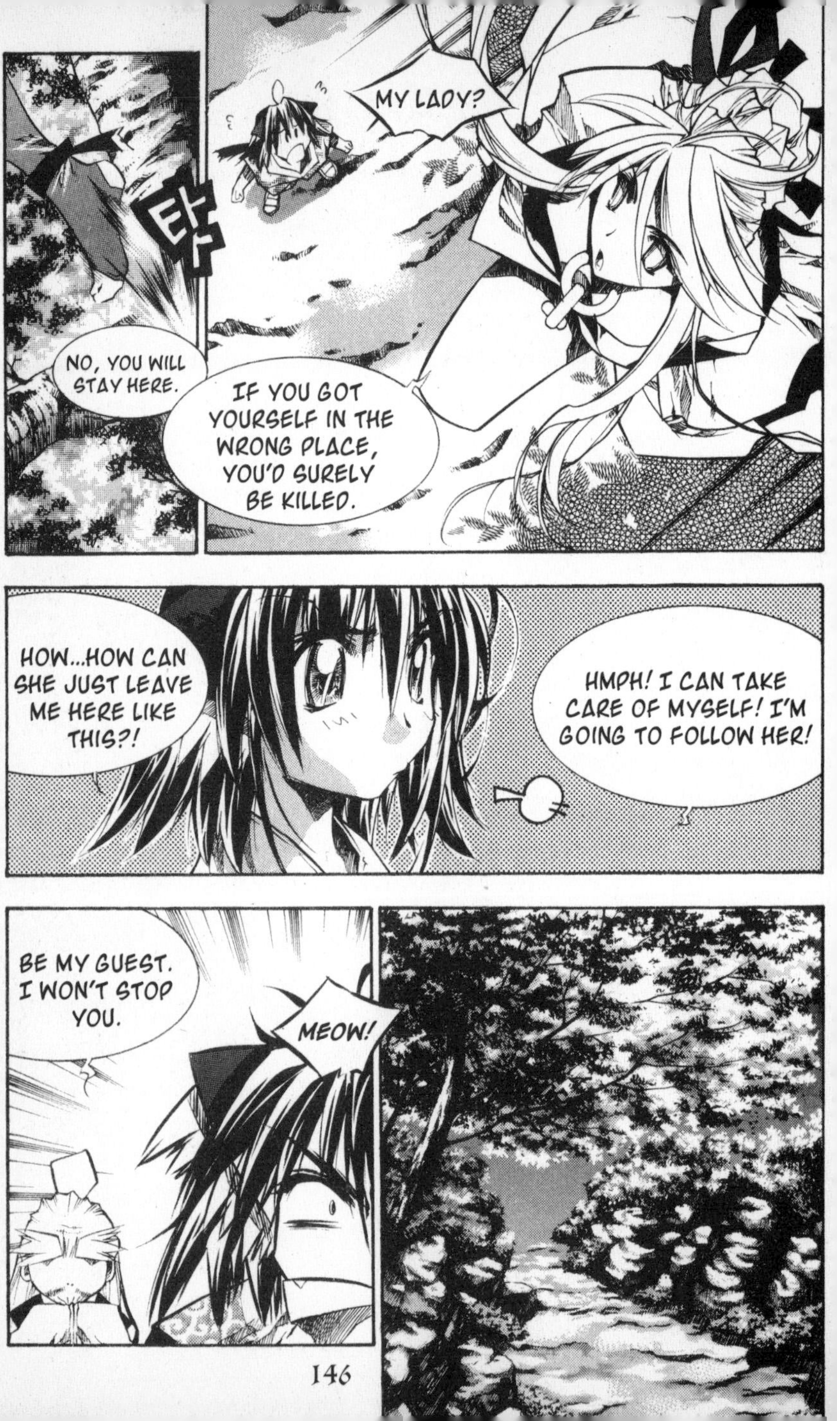
탁
MY LADY?
NO, YOU WILL STAY HERE.
IF YOU GOT YOURSELF IN THE WRONG PLACE, YOU'D SURELY BE KILLED.
HOW...HOW CAN SHE JUST LEAVE ME HERE LIKE THIS?!
HMPH! I CAN TAKE CARE OF MYSELF! I'M GOING TO FOLLOW HER!
BE MY GUEST. I WON'T STOP YOU.
MEOW!

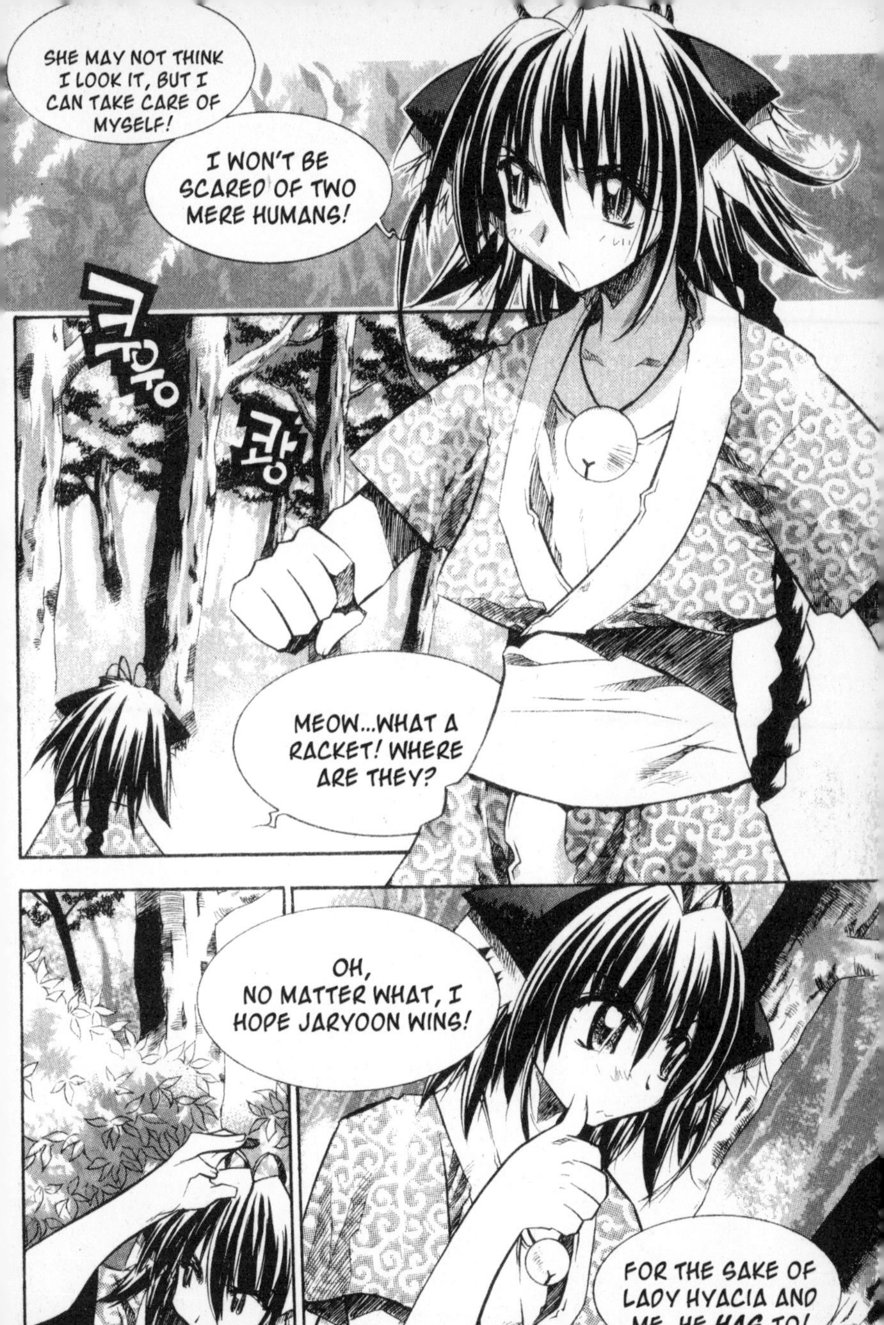
SHE MAY NOT THINK I LOOK IT, BUT I CAN TAKE CARE OF MYSELF!
I WON'T BE SCARED OF TWO MERE HUMANS!
쾅
MEOW...WHAT A RACKET! WHERE ARE THEY?
OH, NO MATTER WHAT, I HOPE JARYOON WINS!
FOR THE SAKE OF LADY HYACIA AND ME, HE **HAS** TO!

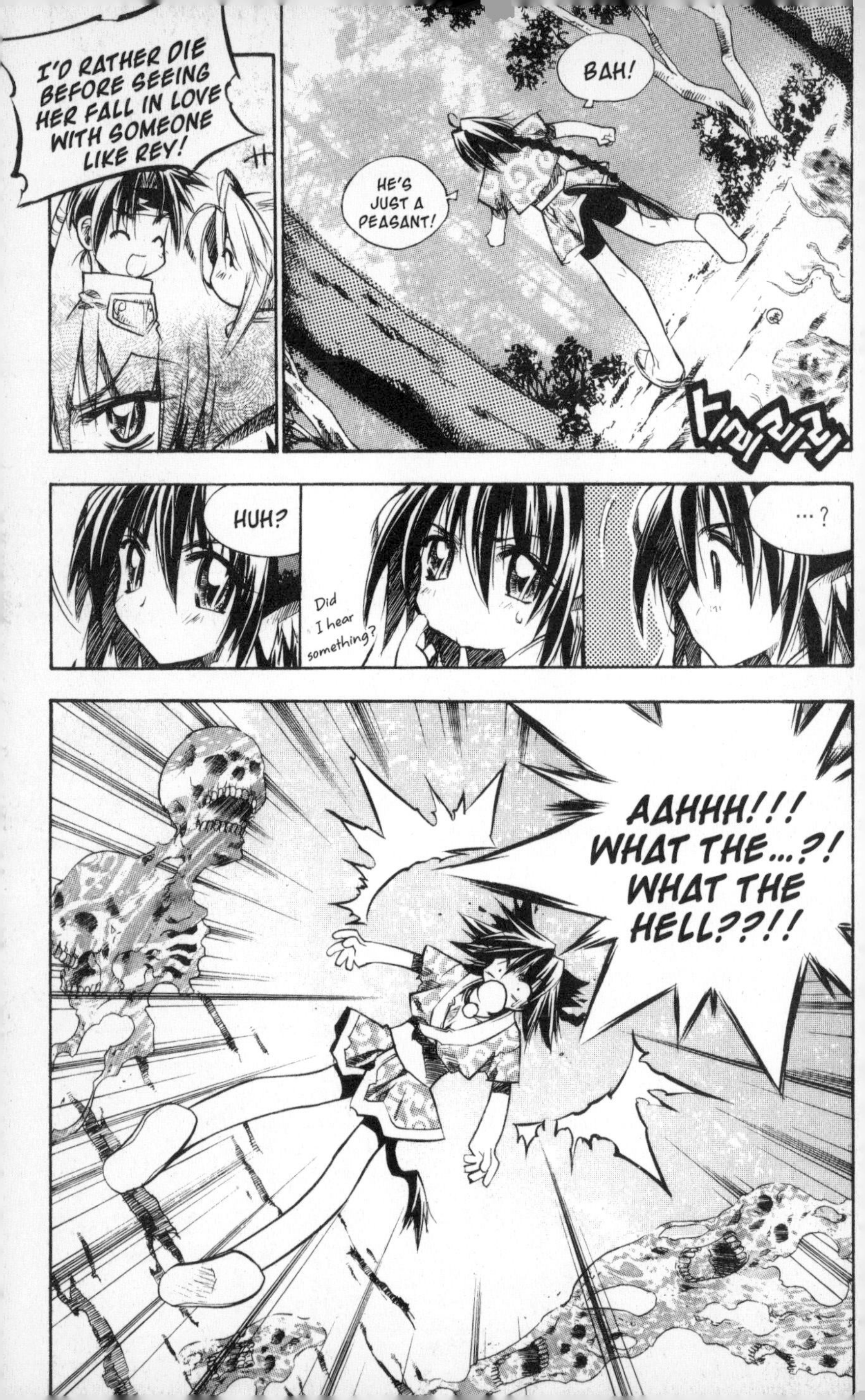
I'D RATHER DIE BEFORE SEEING HER FALL IN LOVE WITH SOMEONE LIKE REY!
BAH!
HE'S JUST A PEASANT!
HUH?
Did I hear something?
...?
AAHHH!!! WHAT THE...?! WHAT THE HELL??!!

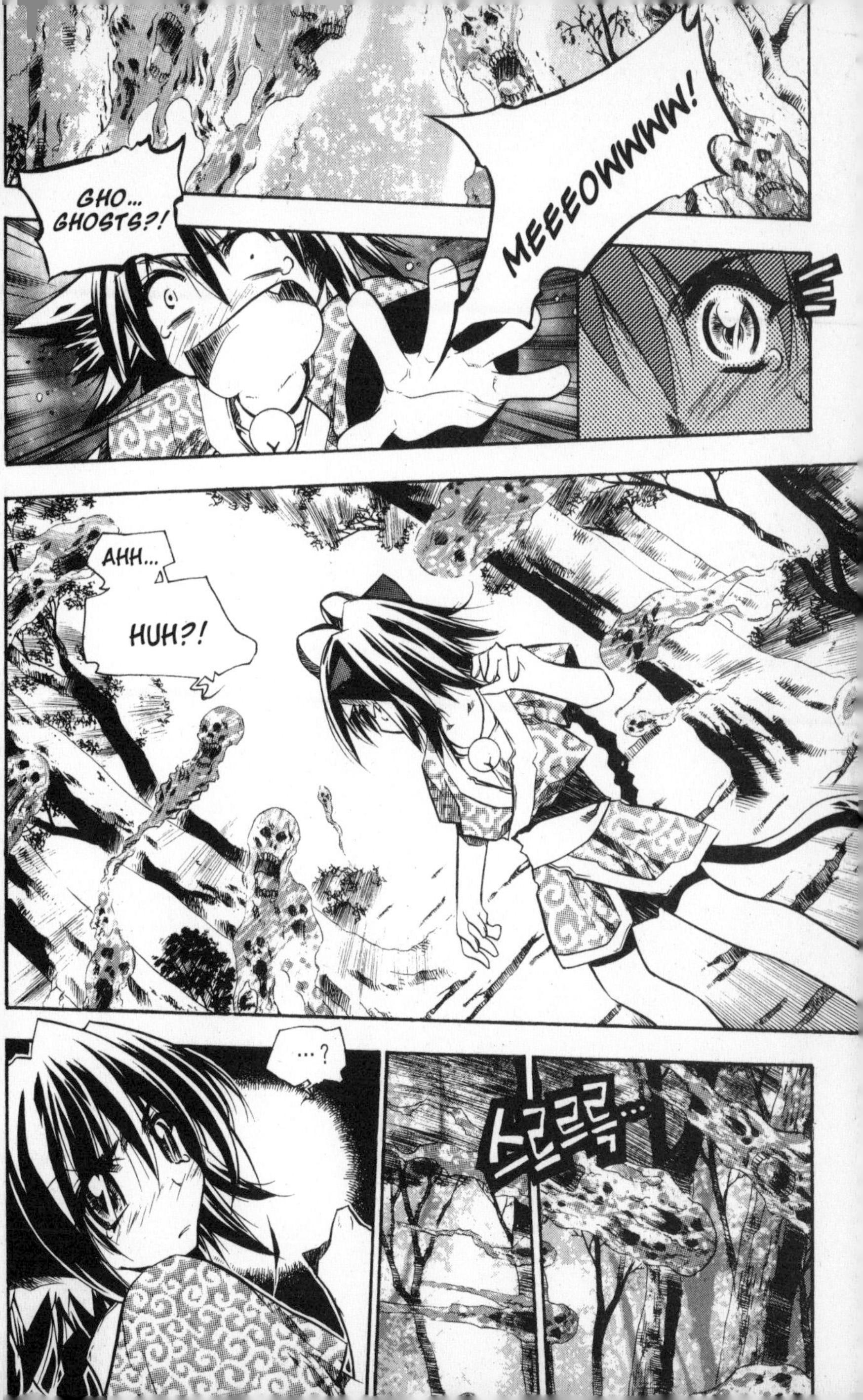
GHO... GHOSTS?!
MEEEOWWWWWW!
AHH...
HUH?!
...?
스르르륵...

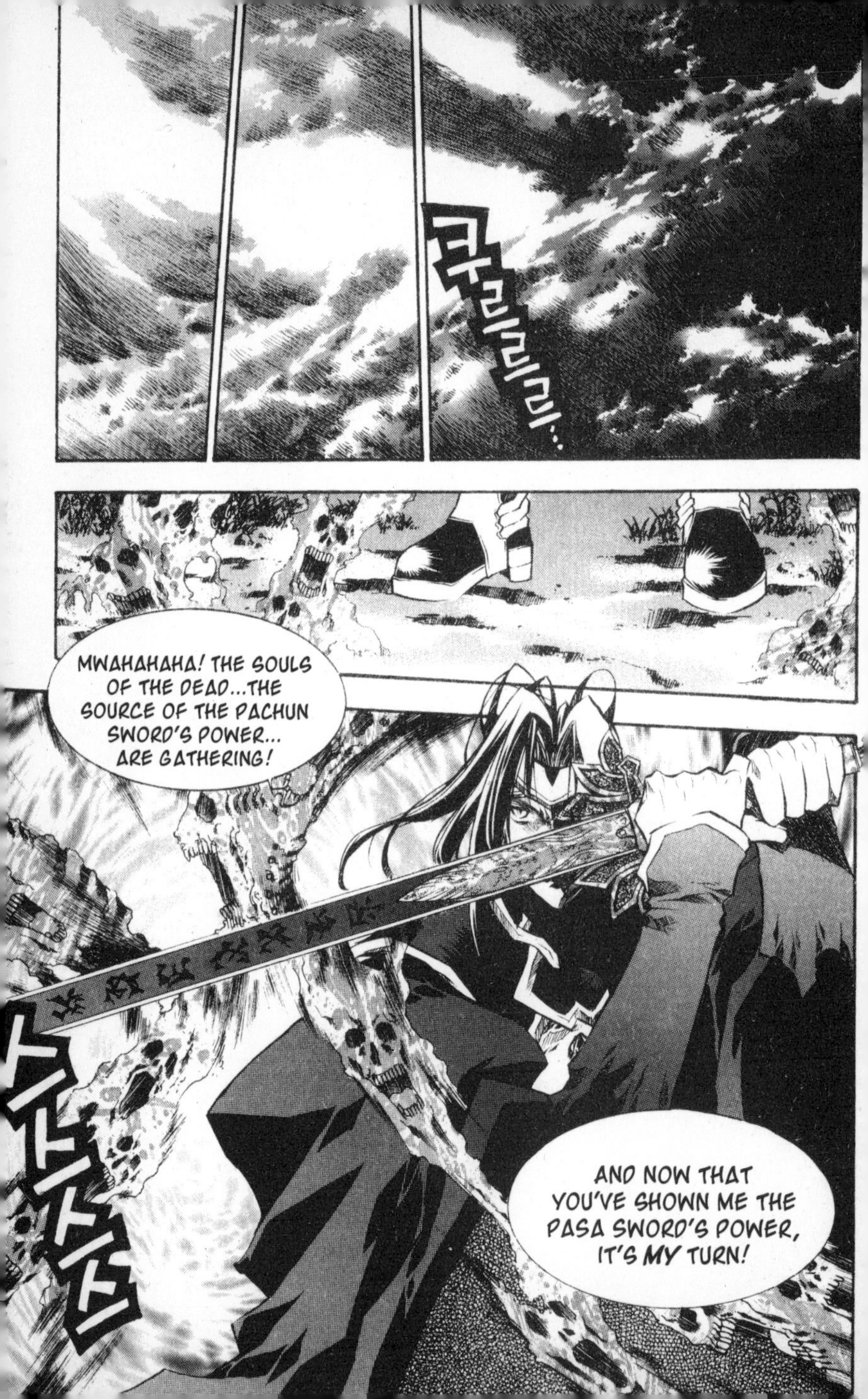
MWAHAHAHA! THE SOULS OF THE DEAD...THE SOURCE OF THE PACHUN SWORD'S POWER... ARE GATHERING!
AND NOW THAT YOU'VE SHOWN ME THE PASA SWORD'S POWER, IT'S MY TURN!

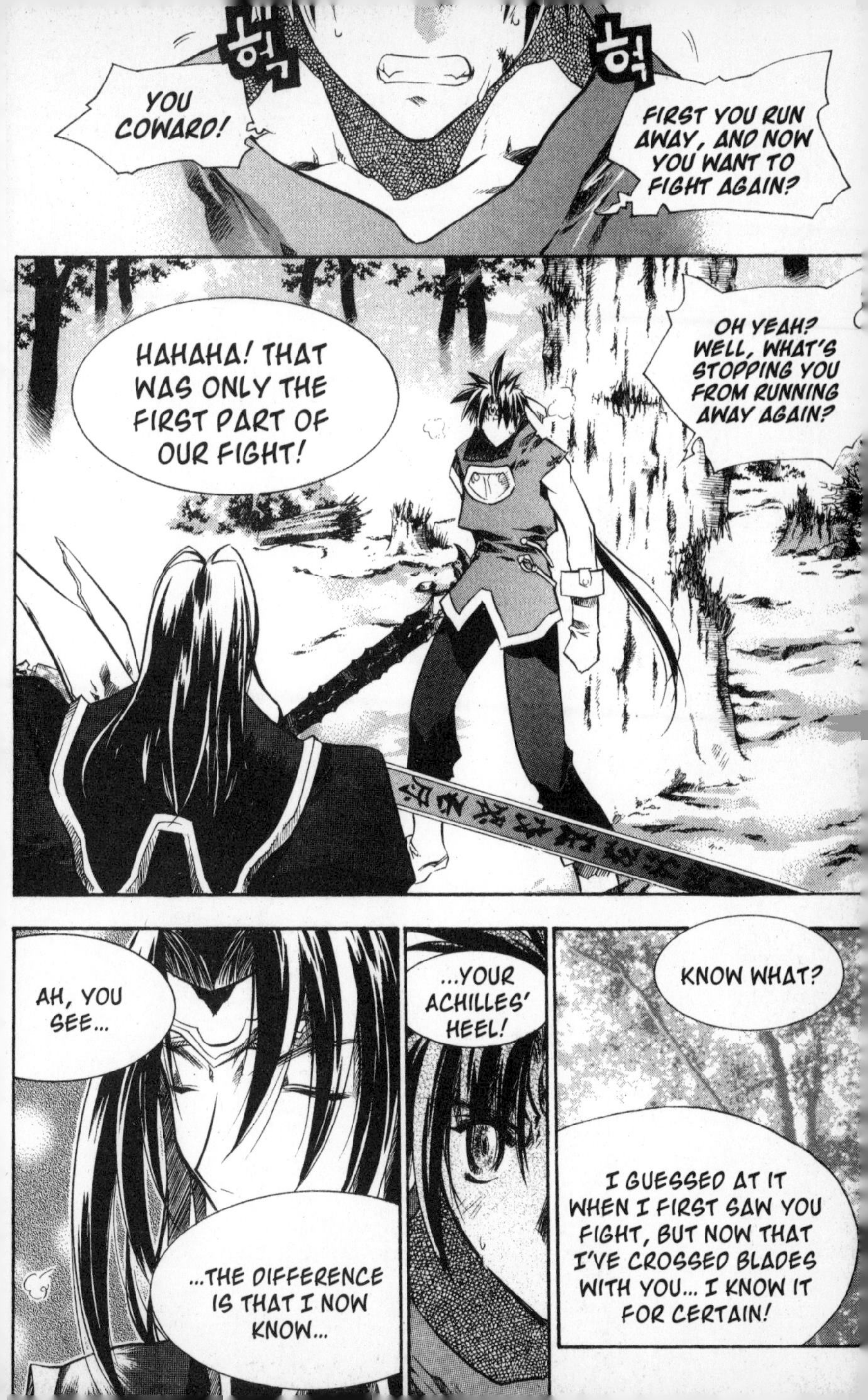

헉
헉
YOU COWARD!
FIRST YOU RUN AWAY, AND NOW YOU WANT TO FIGHT AGAIN?
HAHAHA! THAT WAS ONLY THE FIRST PART OF OUR FIGHT!
OH YEAH? WELL, WHAT'S STOPPING YOU FROM RUNNING AWAY AGAIN?
AH, YOU SEE...
...THE DIFFERENCE IS THAT I NOW KNOW...
...YOUR ACHILLES' HEEL!
KNOW WHAT?
I GUESSED AT IT WHEN I FIRST SAW YOU FIGHT, BUT NOW THAT I'VE CROSSED BLADES WITH YOU... I KNOW IT FOR CERTAIN!

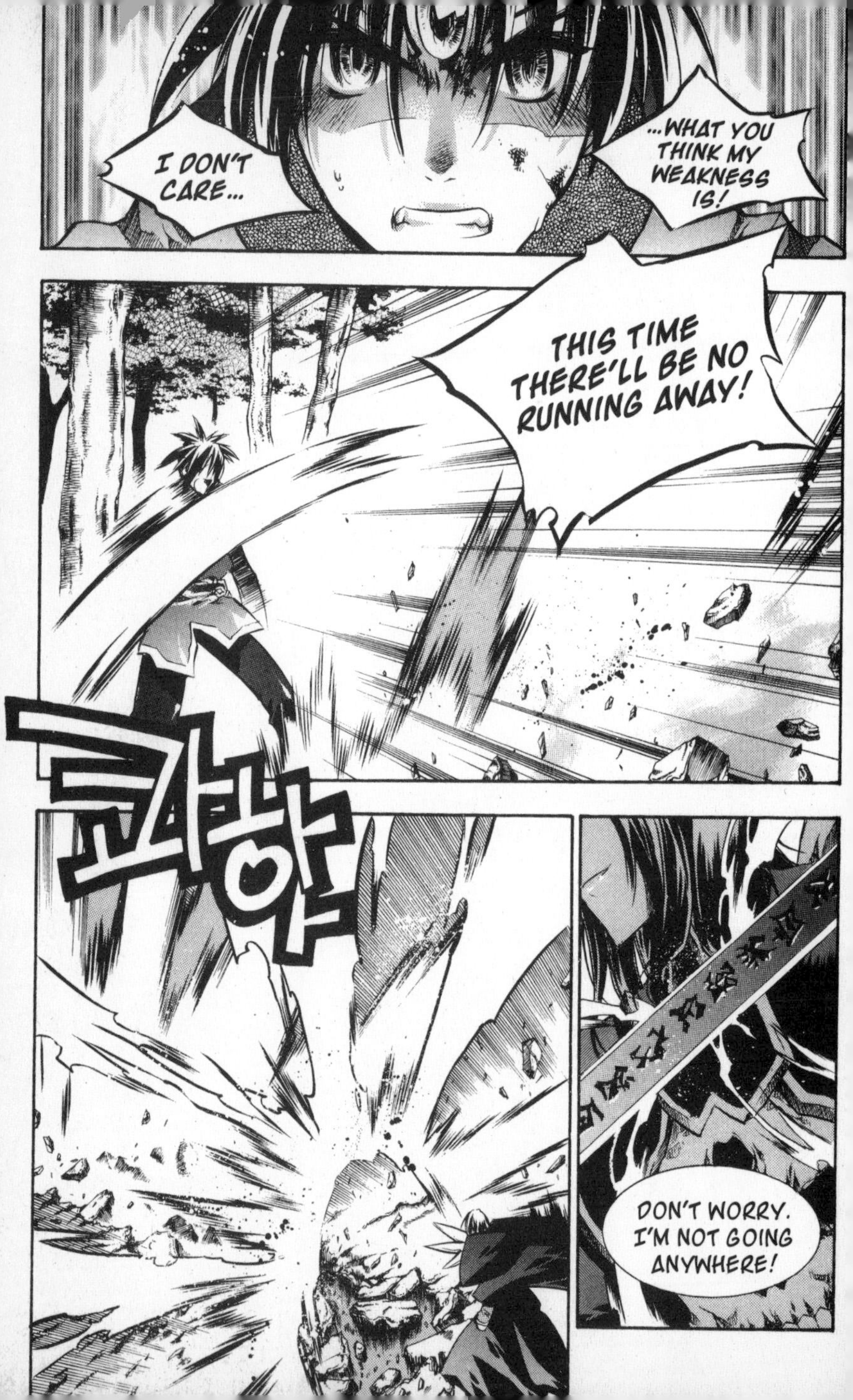
I DON'T CARE...
...WHAT YOU THINK MY WEAKNESS IS!
THIS TIME THERE'LL BE NO RUNNING AWAY!
콰쾅
DON'T WORRY. I'M NOT GOING ANYWHERE!

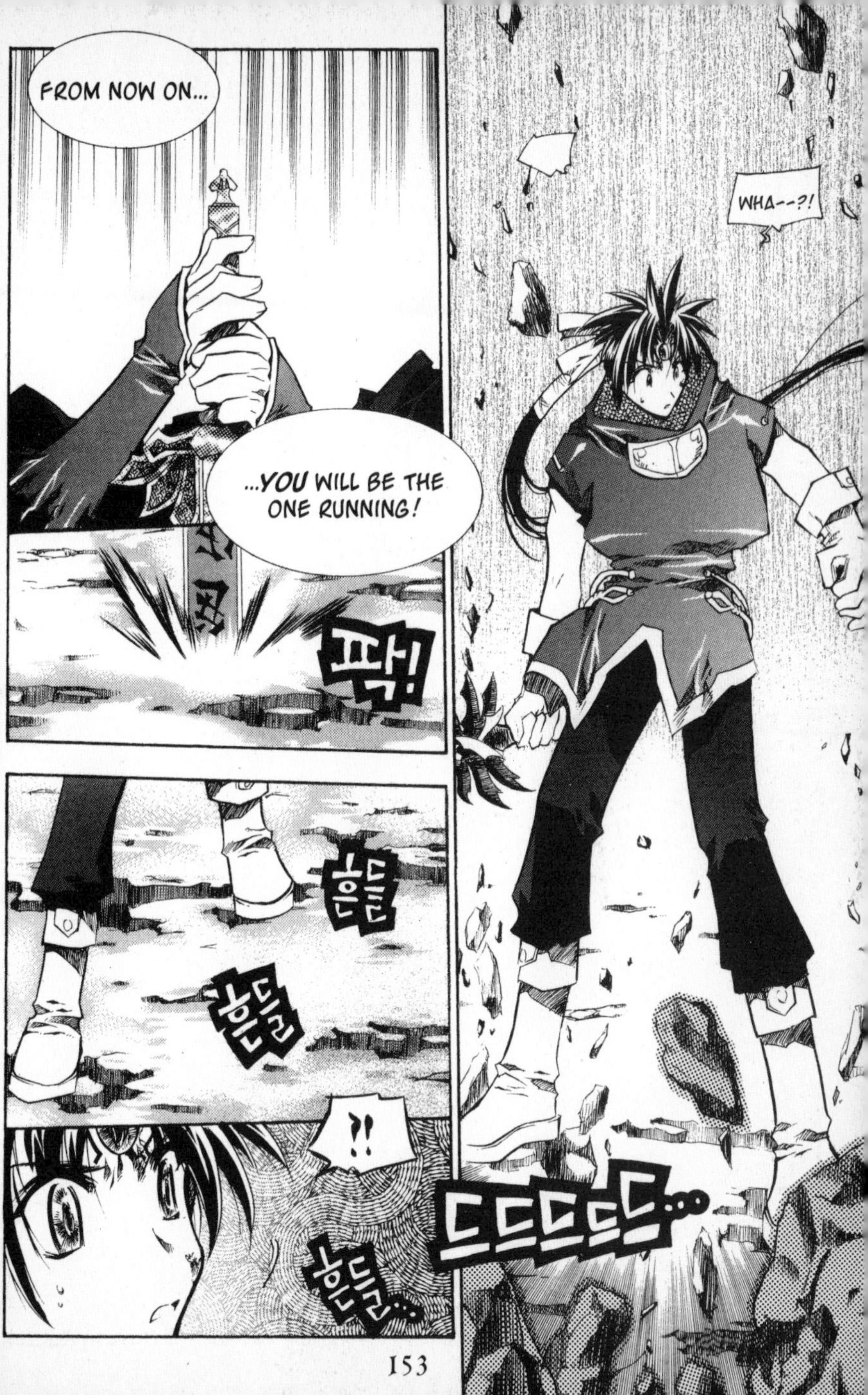
FROM NOW ON...
...YOU WILL BE THE ONE RUNNING!
팍!
흔들
흔들
?!
흔들...
WHA--?!
드드드드드...

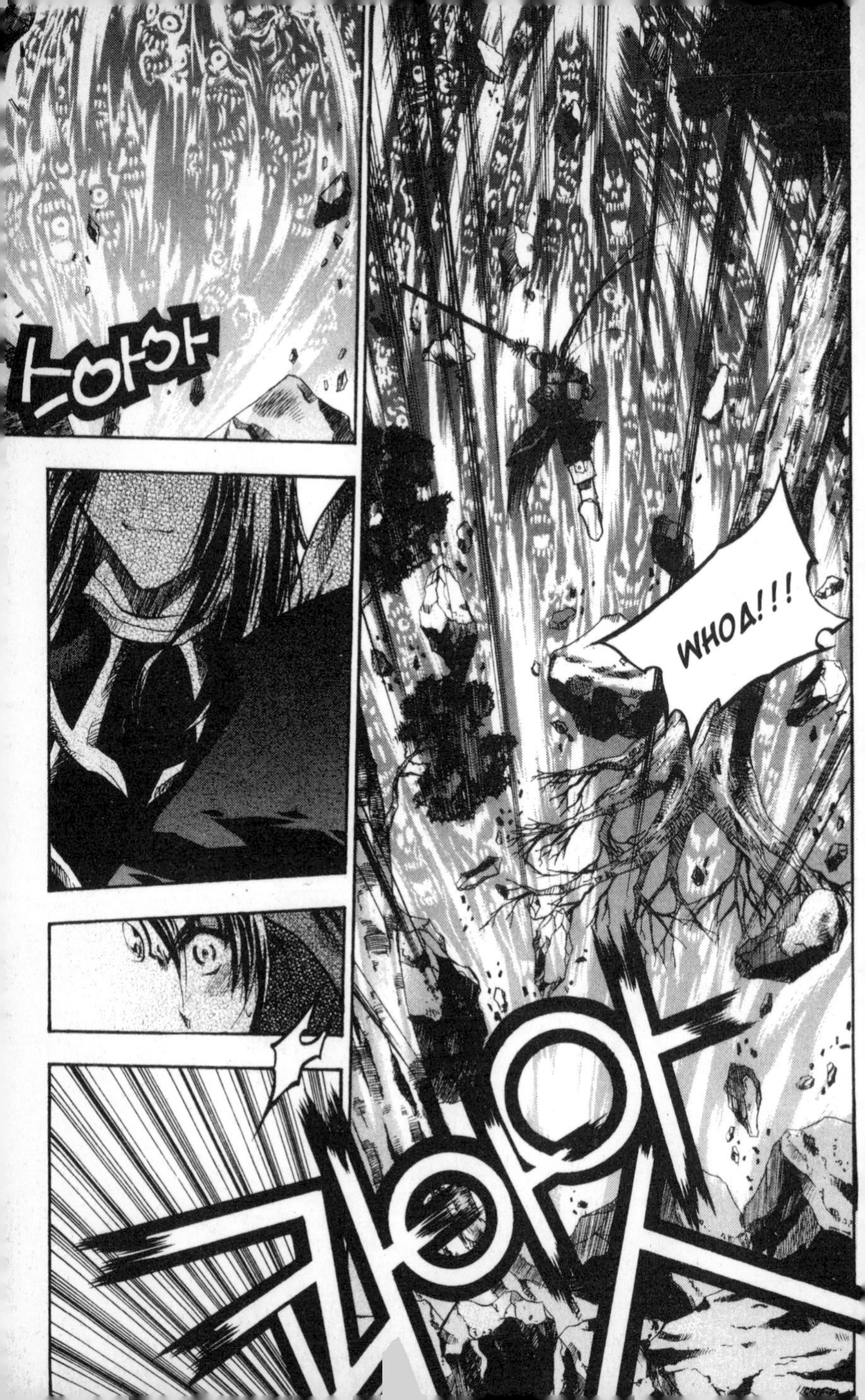
느아아
WHOA!!!

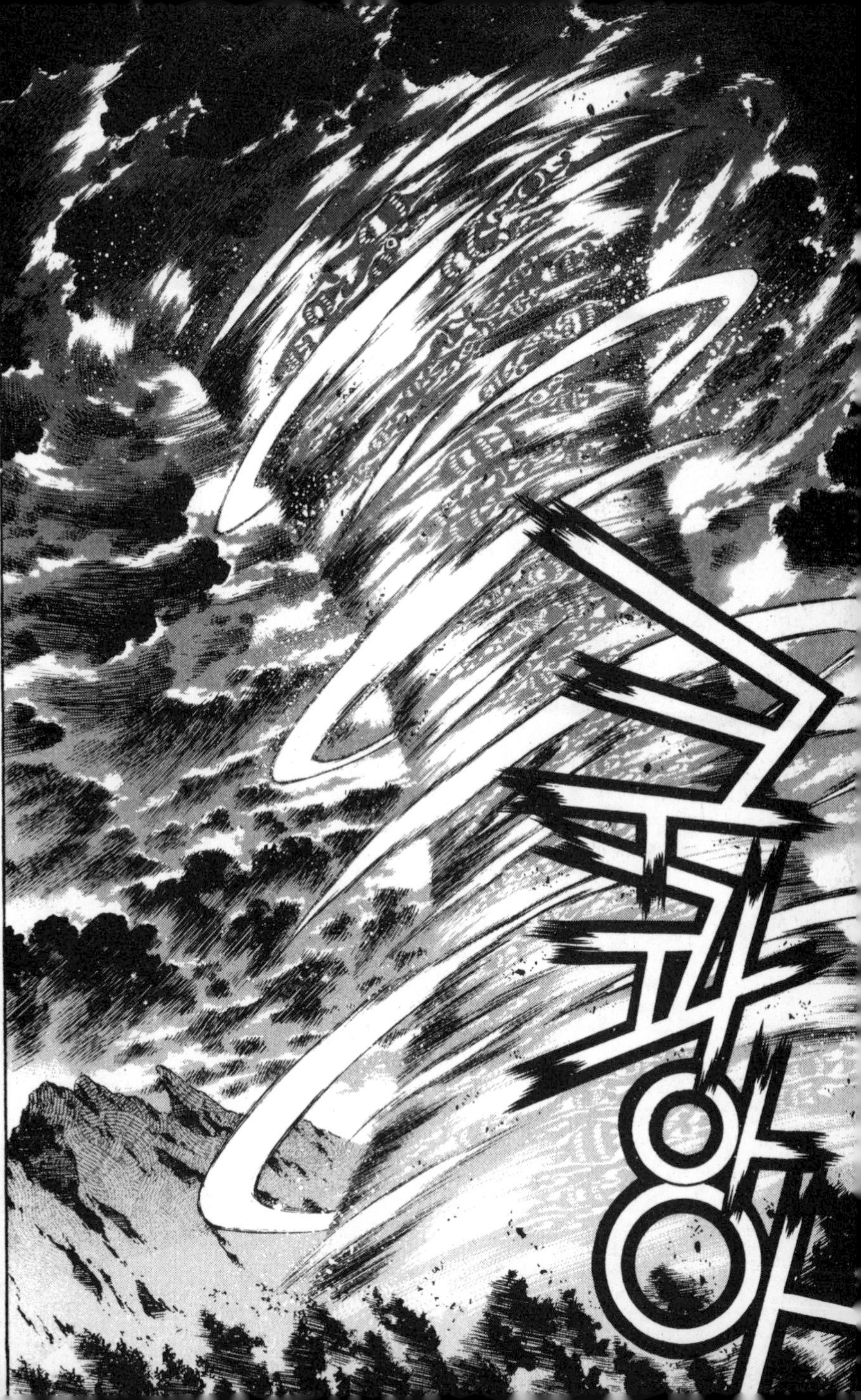

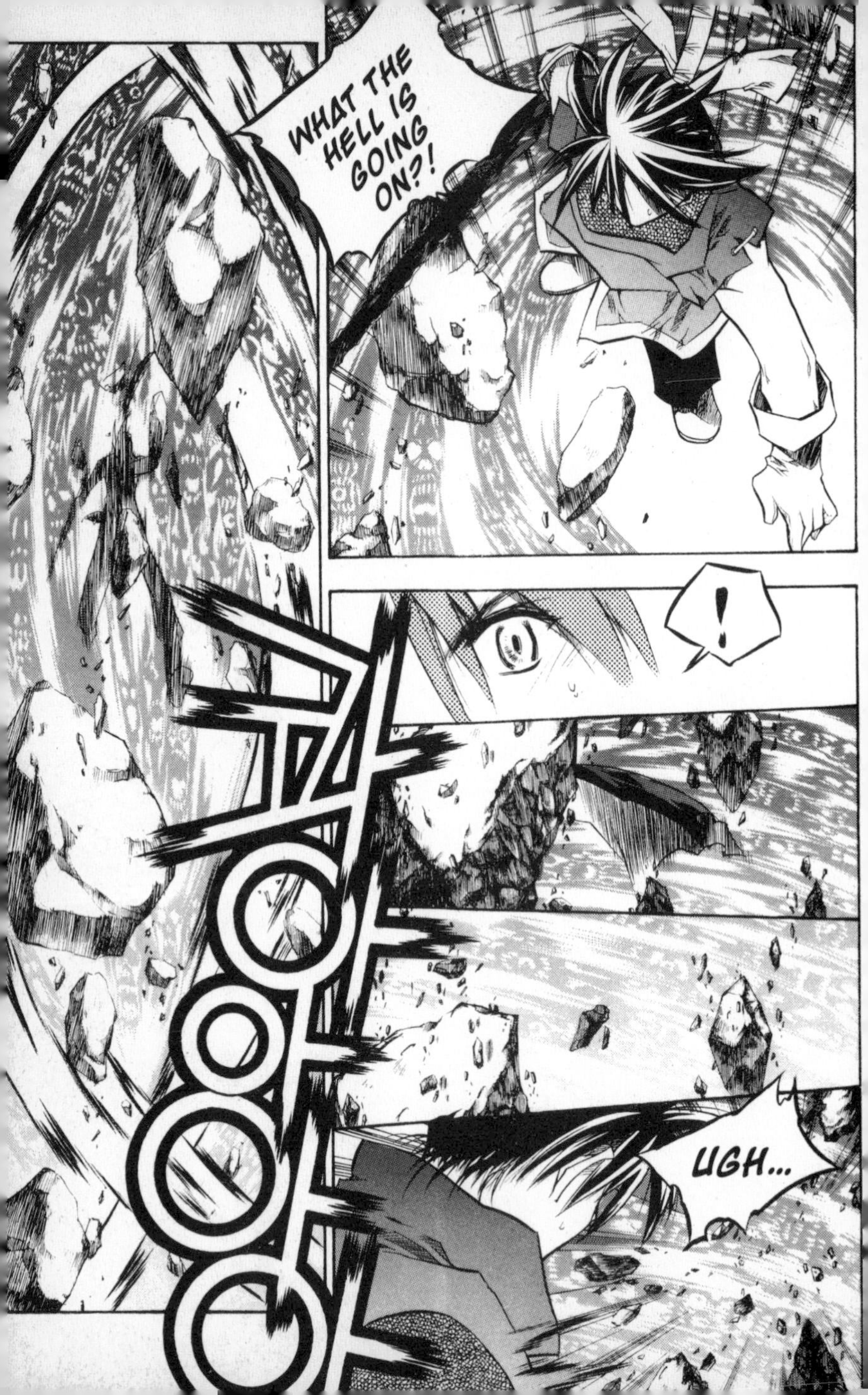
WHAT THE HELL IS GOING ON?!
!
GOOOOOOH
UGH...

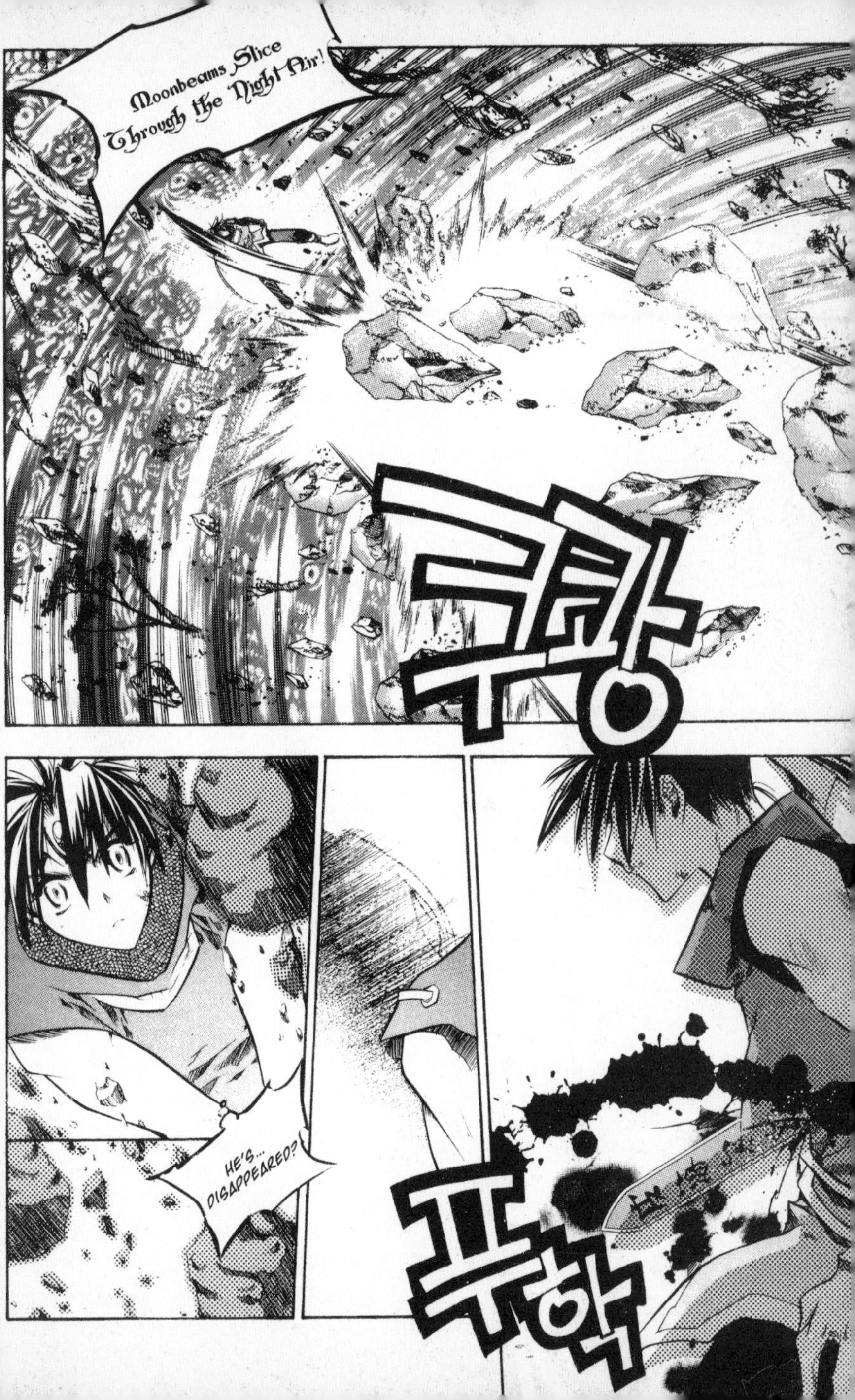
Moonbeams Slice Through the Night Air!
쾅
HE'S... DISAPPEARED?
푸학

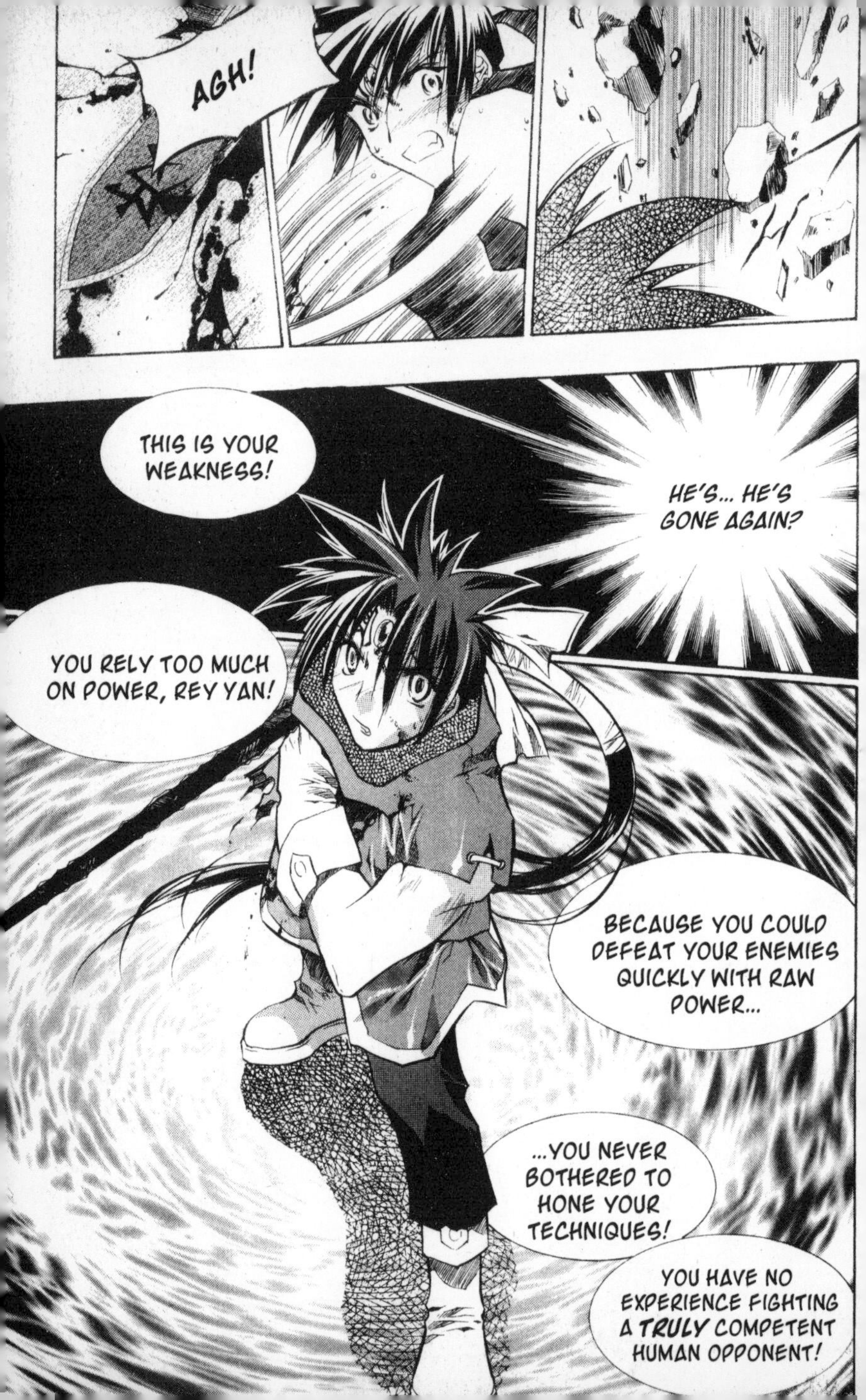
AGH!
THIS IS YOUR WEAKNESS!
HE'S... HE'S GONE AGAIN?
YOU RELY TOO MUCH ON POWER, REY YAN!
BECAUSE YOU COULD DEFEAT YOUR ENEMIES QUICKLY WITH RAW POWER...
...YOU NEVER BOTHERED TO HONE YOUR TECHNIQUES!
YOU HAVE NO EXPERIENCE FIGHTING A ***TRULY*** COMPETENT HUMAN OPPONENT!

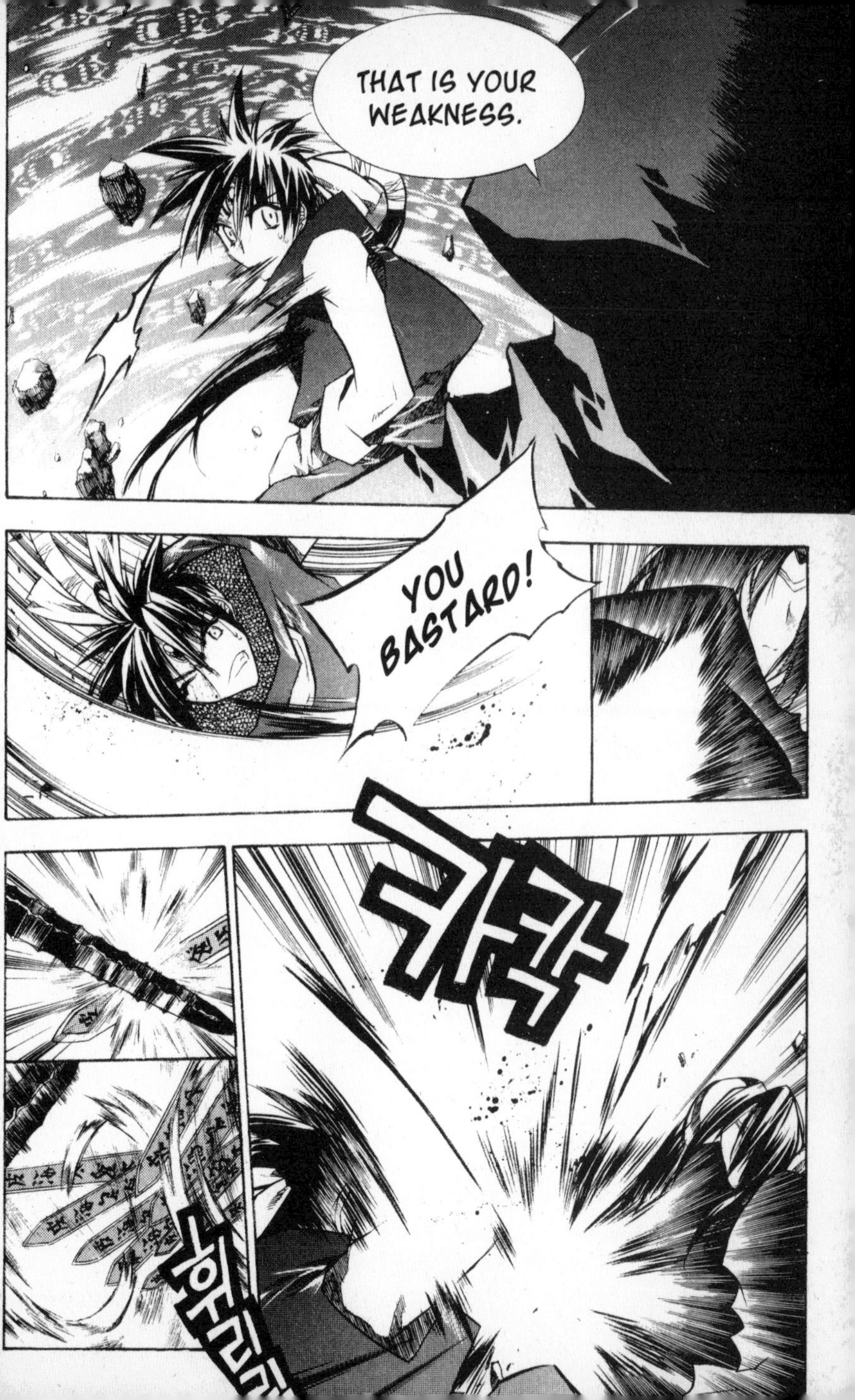
THAT IS YOUR WEAKNESS.
YOU BASTARD!

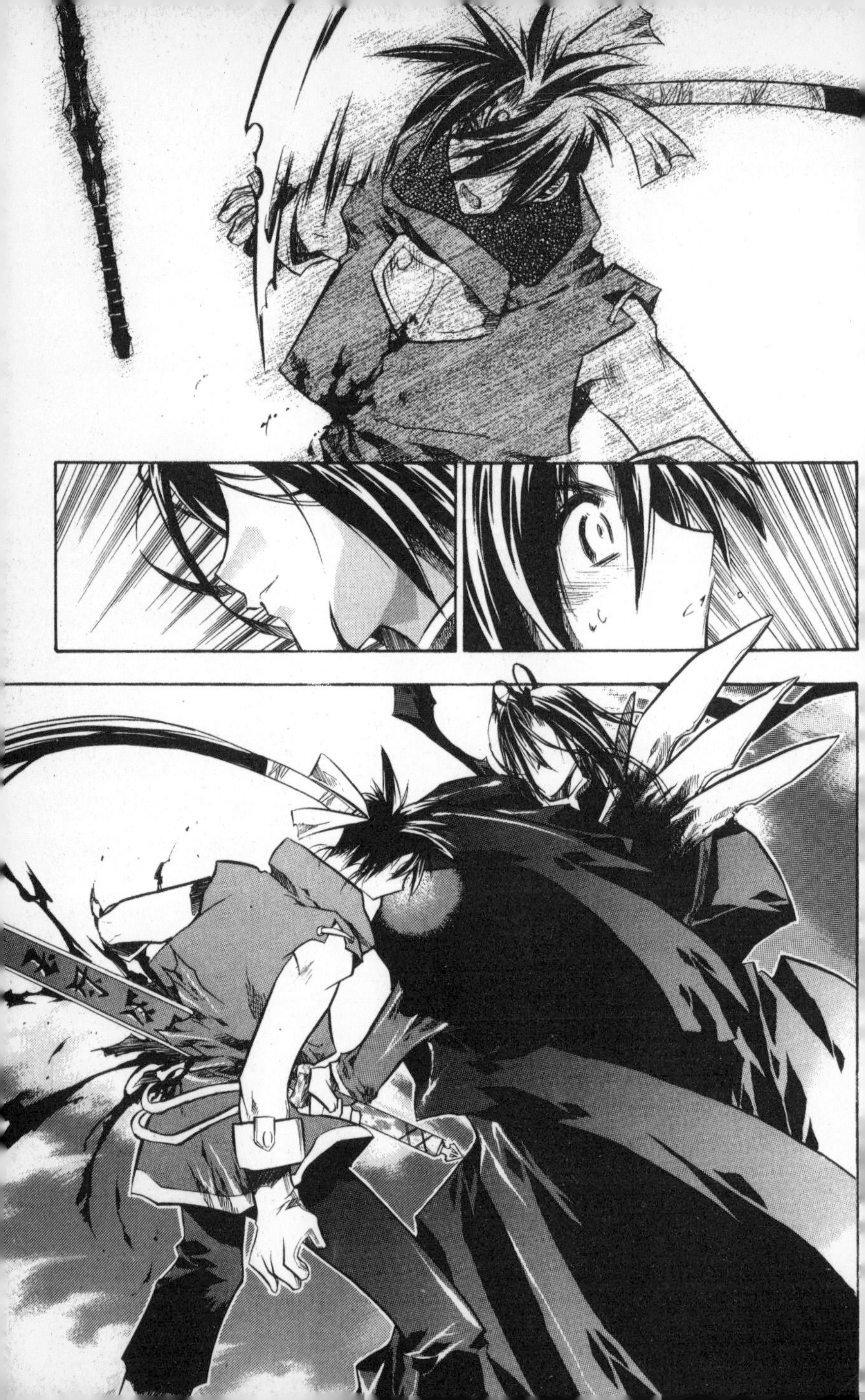

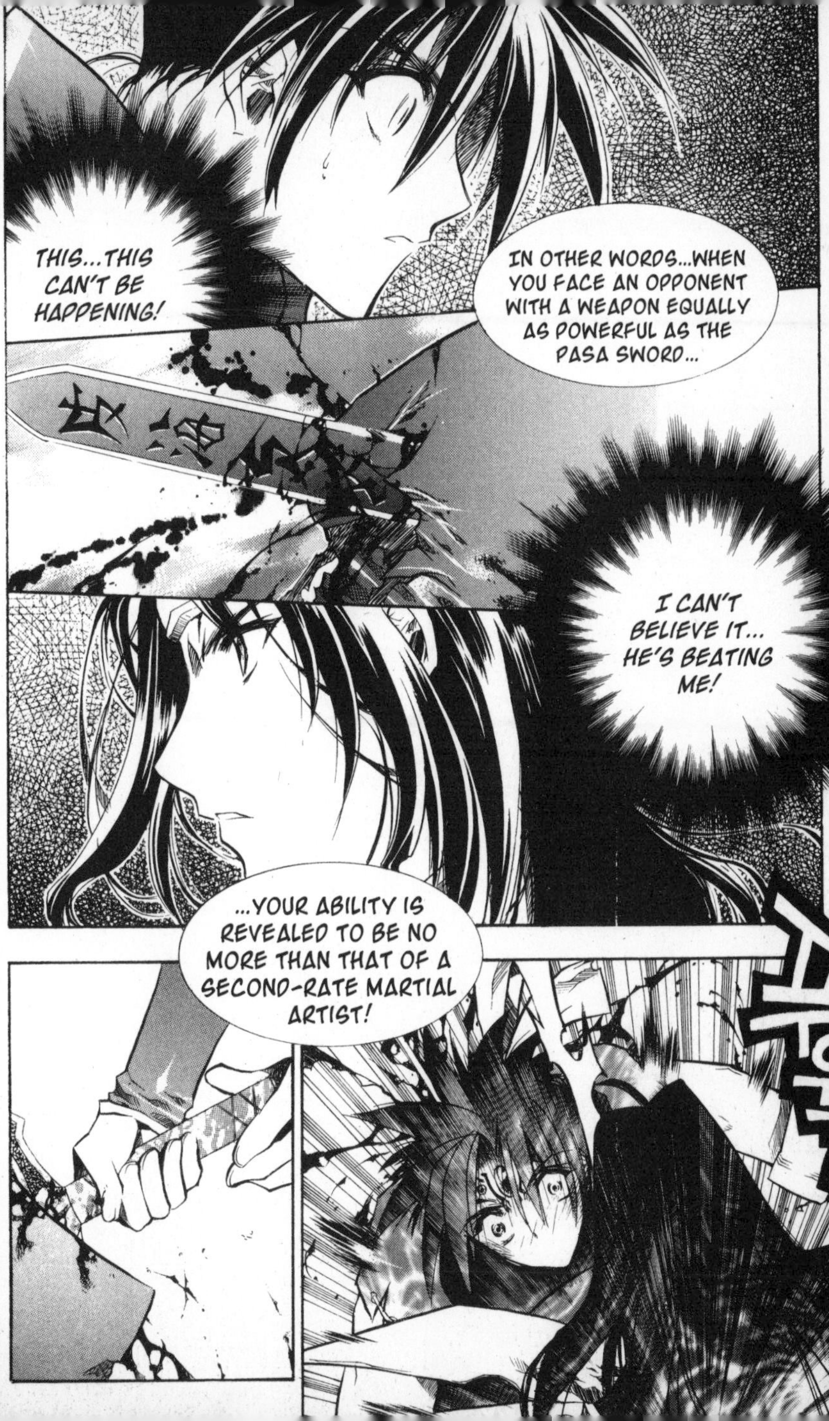
THIS...THIS CAN'T BE HAPPENING!
IN OTHER WORDS...WHEN YOU FACE AN OPPONENT WITH A WEAPON EQUALLY AS POWERFUL AS THE PASA SWORD...
I CAN'T BELIEVE IT... HE'S BEATING ME!
...YOUR ABILITY IS REVEALED TO BE NO MORE THAN THAT OF A SECOND-RATE MARTIAL ARTIST!

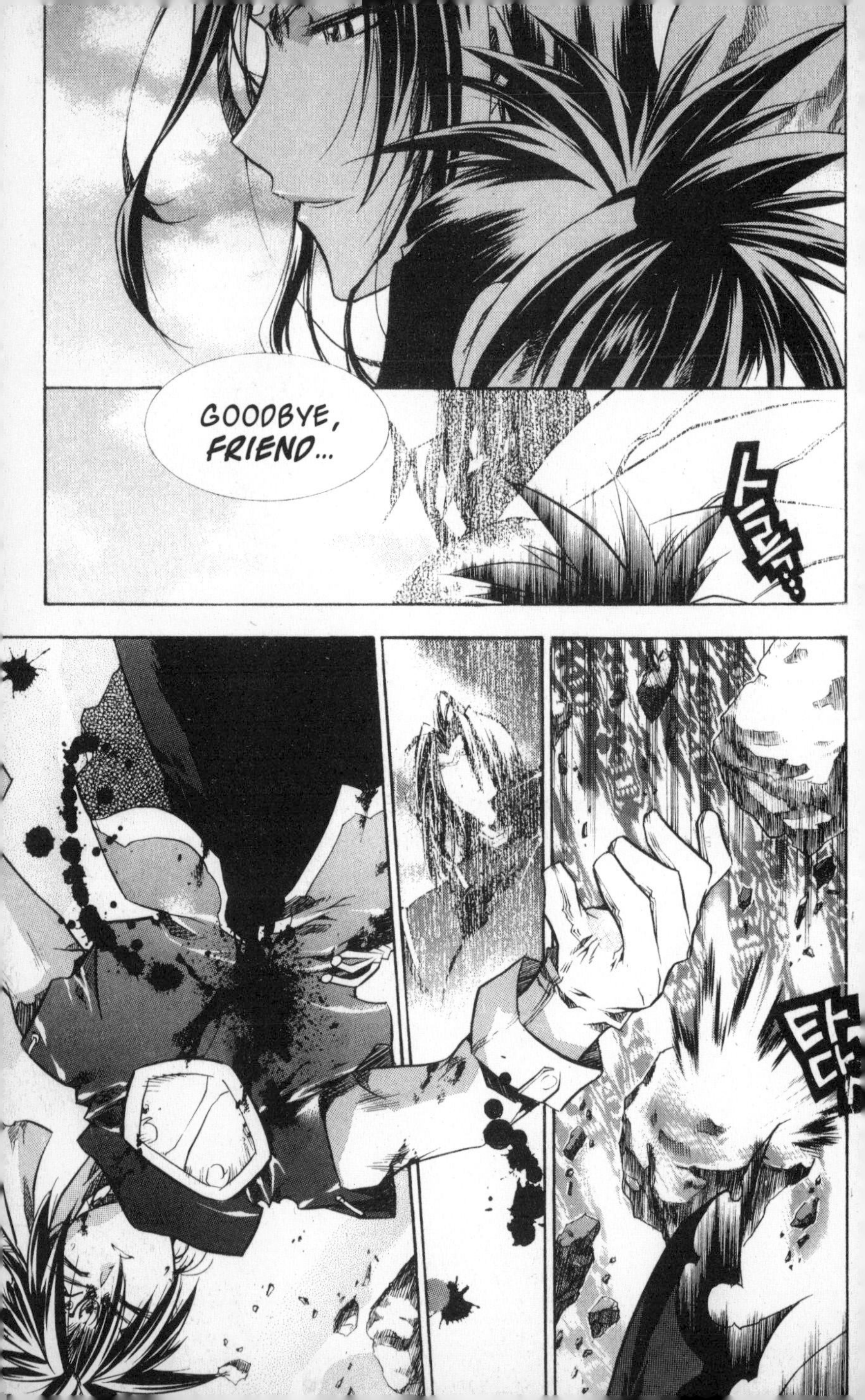
GOODBYE, FRIEND...

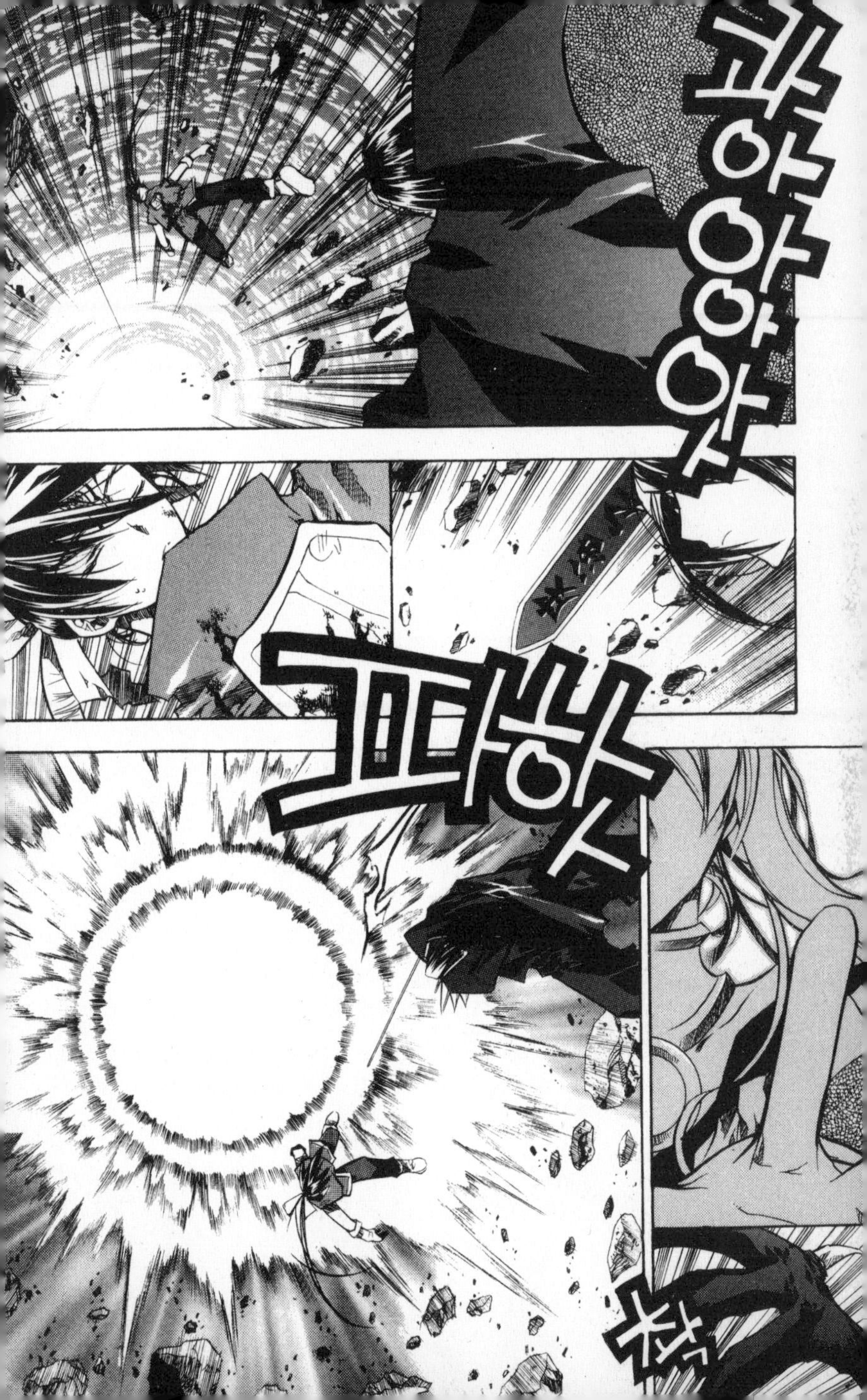
콰아아아아앗
파앗
착

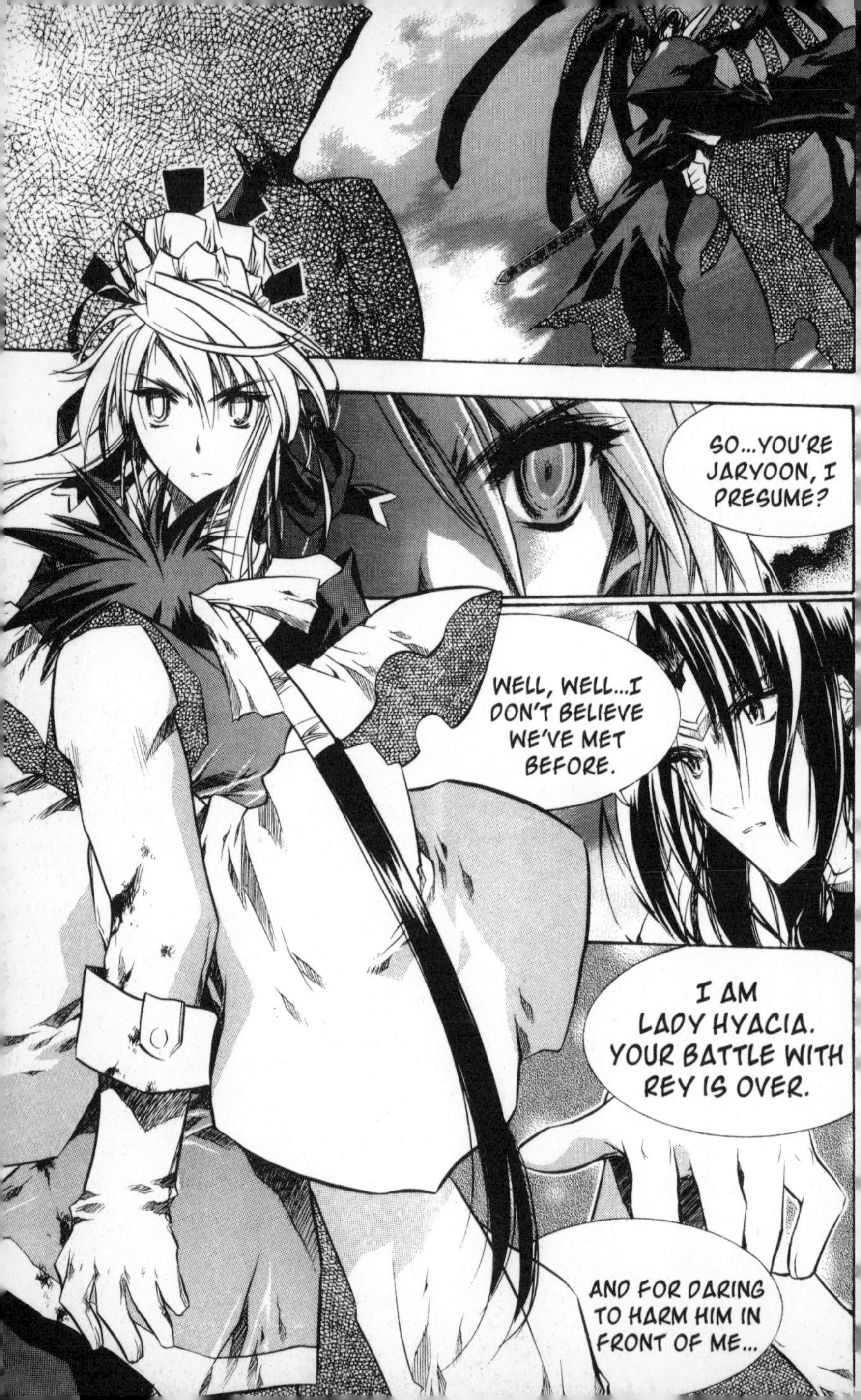
SO...YOU'RE JARYOON, I PRESUME?
WELL, WELL...I DON'T BELIEVE WE'VE MET BEFORE.
I AM LADY HYACIA. YOUR BATTLE WITH REY IS OVER.
AND FOR DARING TO HARM HIM IN FRONT OF ME...

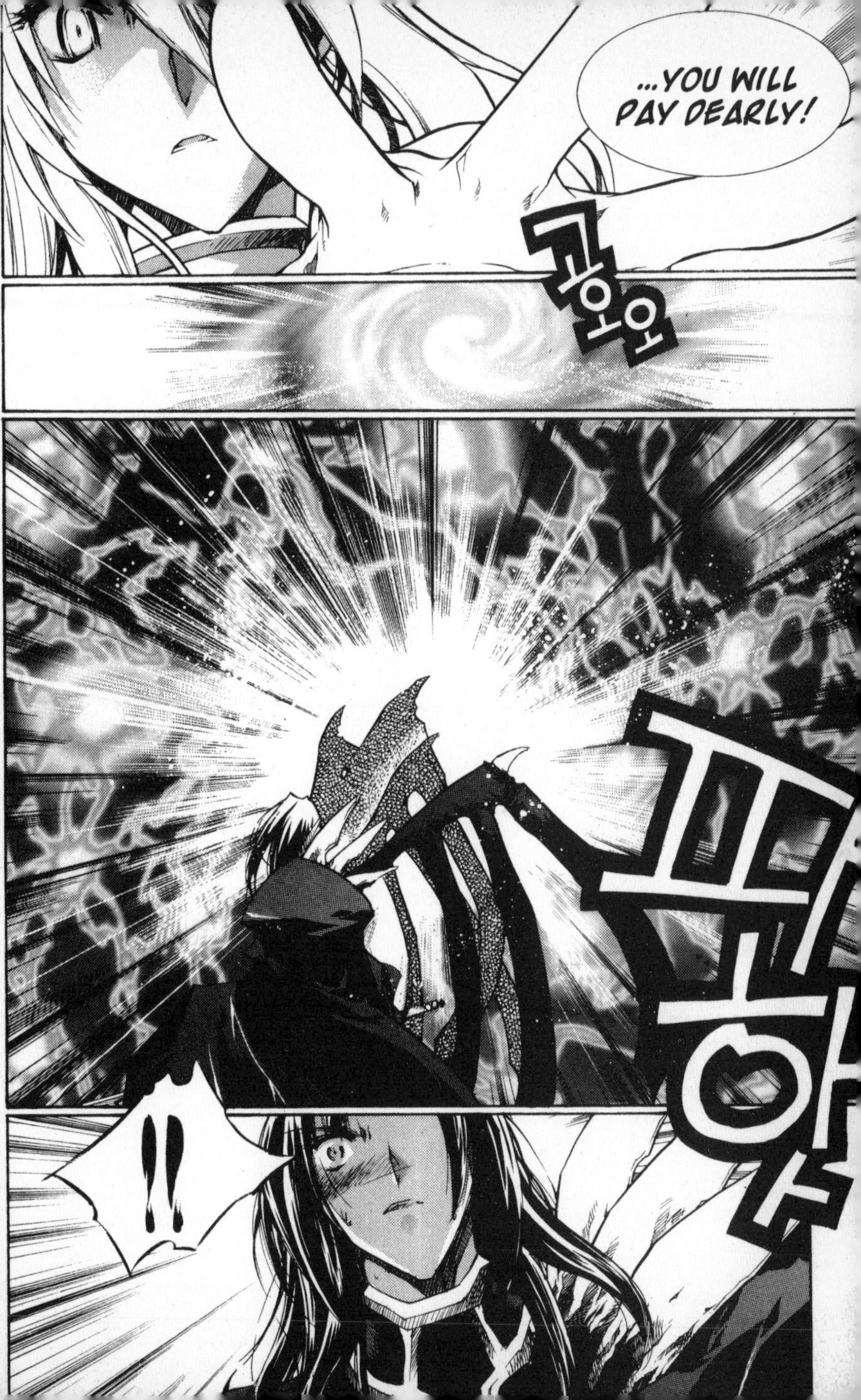
...YOU WILL PAY DEARLY!
!!

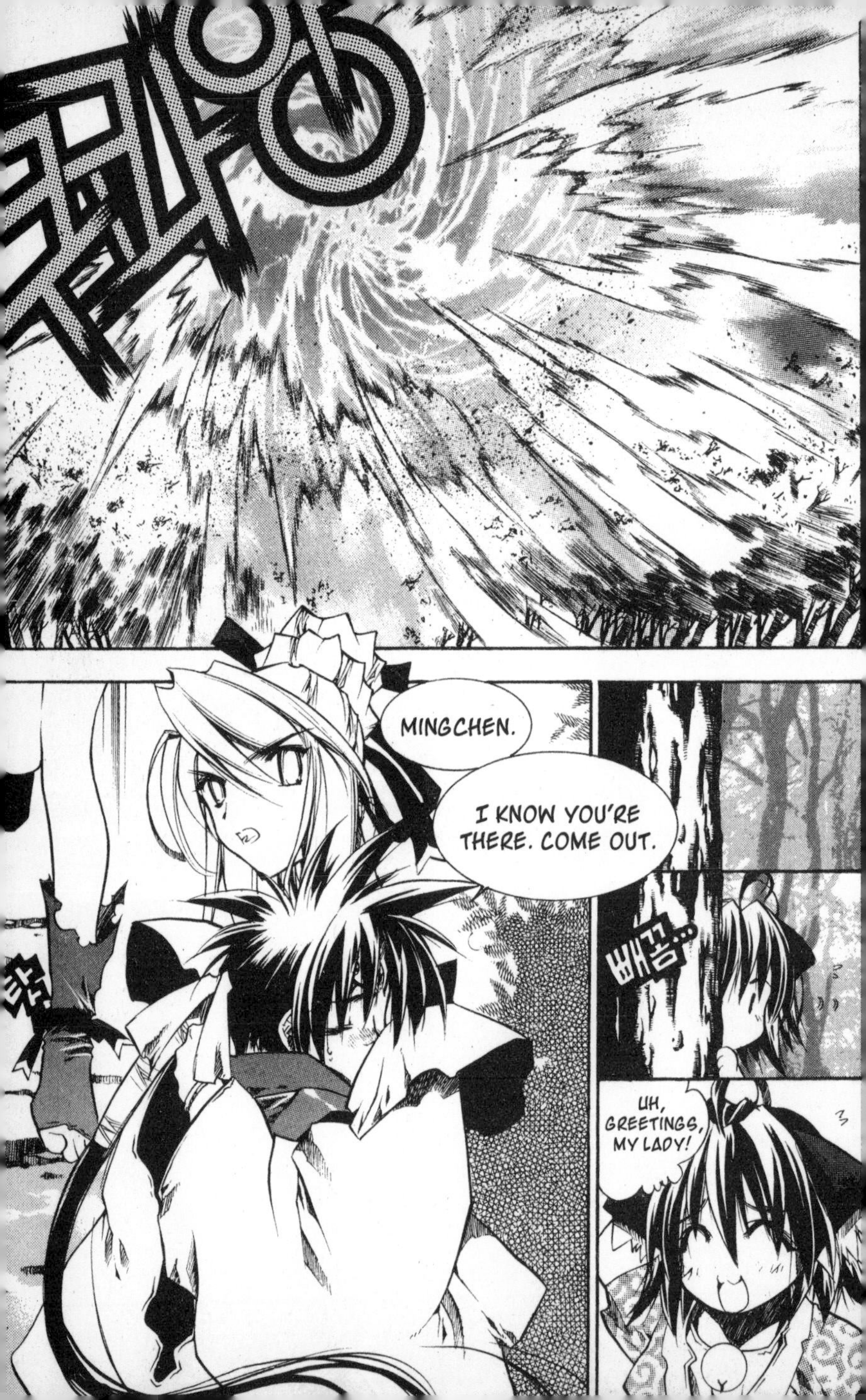
MINGCHEN.
I KNOW YOU'RE THERE. COME OUT.
빼꼼...
UH, GREETINGS, MY LADY!

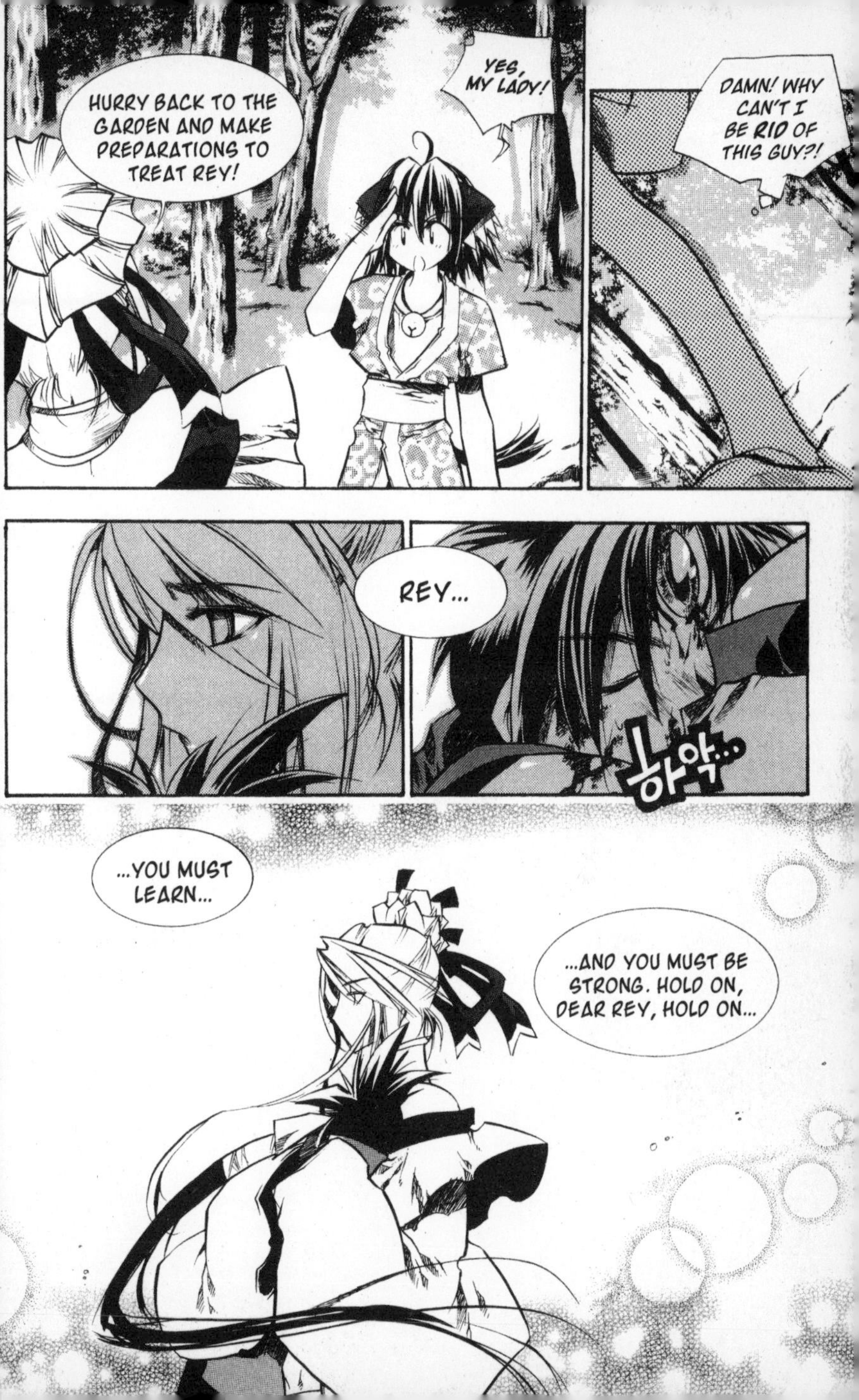
HURRY BACK TO THE GARDEN AND MAKE PREPARATIONS TO TREAT REY!
YES, MY LADY!
DAMN! WHY CAN'T I BE RID OF THIS GUY?!
REY...
하악...
...YOU MUST LEARN...
...AND YOU MUST BE STRONG. HOLD ON, DEAR REY, HOLD ON...

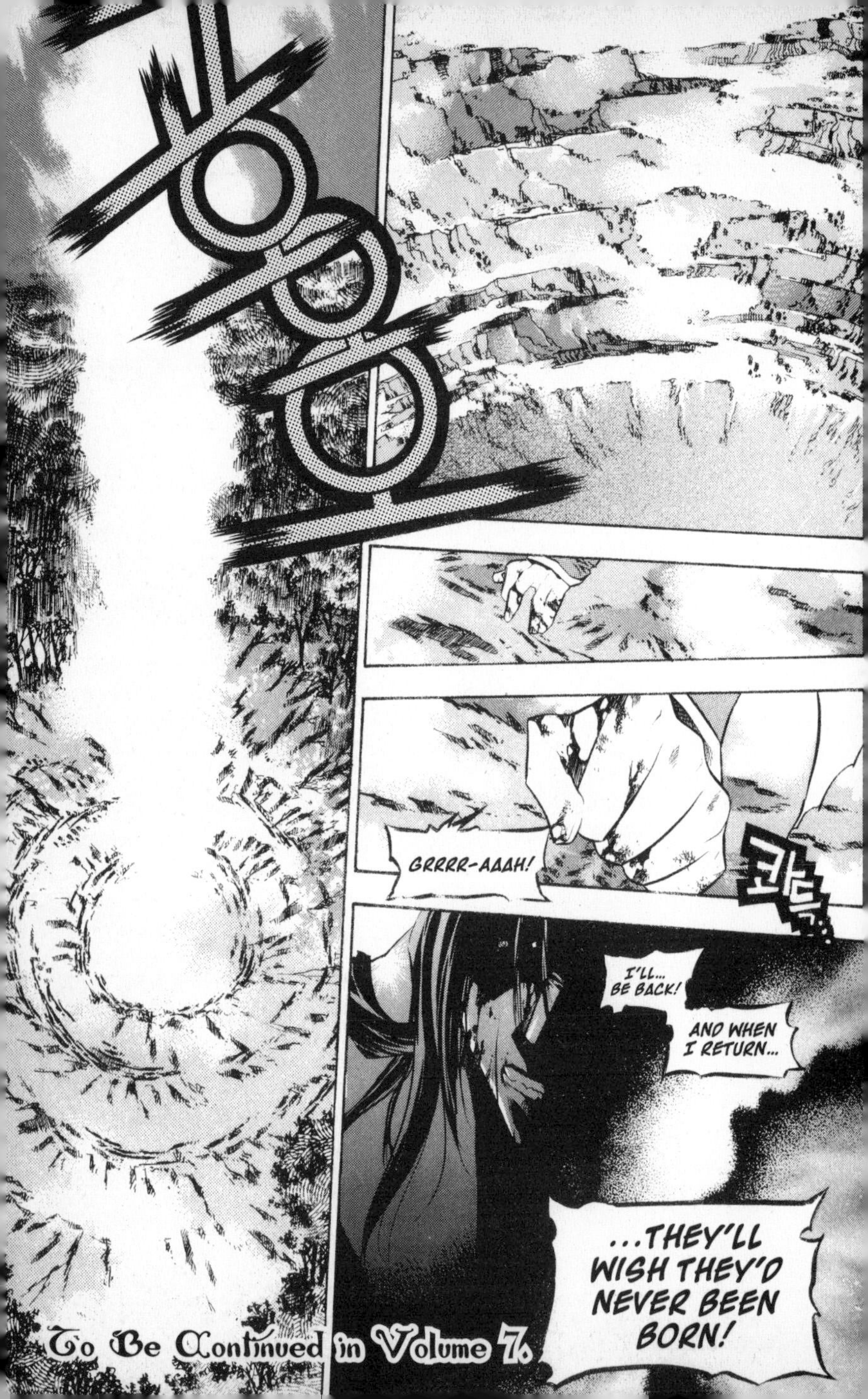
GRRRR-AAAH!
I'LL... BE BACK!
AND WHEN I RETURN...
...THEY'LL WISH THEY'D NEVER BEEN BORN!
To Be Continued in Volume 7.

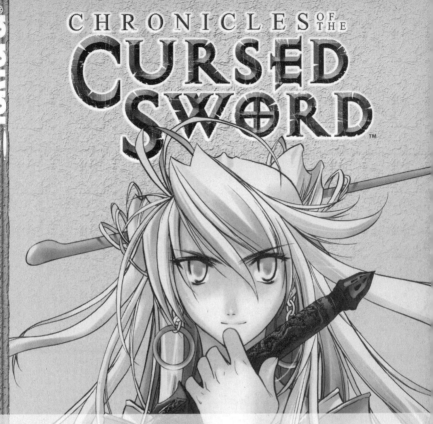

CHRONICLES OF THE CURSED SWORD

When Shyao journeys to the realm of the sages she undergoes a god-like transformation...and a secret is revealed that will decide whether or not Rey should be permitted to continue living! Meanwhile, Rey brings his combat skills to the infamous Muijin Fortress, where humans and demons alike battle for martial arts supremacy. There's just one catch—few ever make it out alive...

Chronicles of the Cursed Sword Vol. 7
Available July, 2004

AUTHOR: **YEO BEOP-RYONG**
ILLUSTRATOR: **PARK HUI-JIN**

7

ALSO AVAILABLE FROM 🐌 TOKYOPOP®

MANGA

.HACK//LEGEND OF THE TWILIGHT
@LARGE
ABENOBASHI: MAGICAL SHOPPING ARCADE
A.I. LOVE YOU
AI YORI AOSHI
ANGELIC LAYER
ARM OF KANNON
BABY BIRTH
BATTLE ROYALE
BATTLE VIXENS
BRAIN POWERED
BRIGADOON
B'TX
CANDIDATE FOR GODDESS, THE
CARDCAPTOR SAKURA
CARDCAPTOR SAKURA - MASTER OF THE CLOW
CHOBITS
CHRONICLES OF THE CURSED SWORD
CLAMP SCHOOL DETECTIVES
CLOVER
COMIC PARTY
CONFIDENTIAL CONFESSIONS
CORRECTOR YUI
COWBOY BEBOP
COWBOY BEBOP: SHOOTING STAR
CRAZY LOVE STORY
CRESCENT MOON
CULDCEPT
CYBORG 009
D•N•ANGEL
DEMON DIARY
DEMON ORORON, THE
DEUS VITAE
DIGIMON
DIGIMON TAMERS
DIGIMON ZERO TWO
DOLL
DRAGON HUNTER
DRAGON KNIGHTS
DRAGON VOICE
DREAM SAGA
DUKLYON: CLAMP SCHOOL DEFENDERS
EERIE QUEERIE!
ERICA SAKURAZAWA: COLLECTED WORKS
ET CETERA
ETERNITY
EVIL'S RETURN
FAERIES' LANDING
FAKE
FLCL
FORBIDDEN DANCE
FRUITS BASKET
G GUNDAM
GATEKEEPERS
GETBACKERS

GIRL GOT GAME
GRAVITATION
GTO
GUNDAM BLUE DESTINY
GUNDAM SEED ASTRAY
GUNDAM WING
GUNDAM WING: BATTLEFIELD OF PACIFISTS
GUNDAM WING: ENDLESS WALTZ
GUNDAM WING: THE LAST OUTPOST (G-UNIT)
HANDS OFF!
HAPPY MANIA
HARLEM BEAT
I.N.V.U.
IMMORTAL RAIN
INITIAL D
INSTANT TEEN: JUST ADD NUTS
ISLAND
JING: KING OF BANDITS
JING: KING OF BANDITS - TWILIGHT TALES
JULINE
KARE KANO
KILL ME, KISS ME
KINDAICHI CASE FILES, THE
KING OF HELL
KODOCHA: SANA'S STAGE
LAMENT OF THE LAMB
LEGAL DRUG
LEGEND OF CHUN HYANG, THE
LES BIJOUX
LOVE HINA
LUPIN III
LUPIN III: WORLD'S MOST WANTED
MAGIC KNIGHT RAYEARTH I
MAGIC KNIGHT RAYEARTH II
MAHOROMATIC: AUTOMATIC MAIDEN
MAN OF MANY FACES
MARMALADE BOY
MARS
MARS: HORSE WITH NO NAME
METROID
MINK
MIRACLE GIRLS
MIYUKI-CHAN IN WONDERLAND
MODEL
ONE
ONE I LOVE, THE
PARADISE KISS
PARASYTE
PASSION FRUIT
PEACH GIRL
PEACH GIRL: CHANGE OF HEART
PET SHOP OF HORRORS
PITA-TEN
PLANET LADDER
PLANETES
PRIEST

02.03.04T

ALSO AVAILABLE FROM TOKYOPOP®

PRINCESS AI
PSYCHIC ACADEMY
RAGNAROK
RAVE MASTER
REALITY CHECK
REBIRTH
REBOUND
REMOTE
RISING STARS OF MANGA
SABER MARIONETTE J
SAILOR MOON
SAINT TAIL
SAIYUKI
SAMURAI DEEPER KYO
SAMURAI GIRL REAL BOUT HIGH SCHOOL
SCRYED
SEIKAI TRILOGY, THE
SGT. FROG
SHAOLIN SISTERS
SHIRAHIME-SYO: SNOW GODDESS TALES
SHUTTERBOX
SKULL MAN, THE
SMUGGLER
SNOW DROP
SORCERER HUNTERS
STONE
SUIKODEN III
SUKI
THREADS OF TIME
TOKYO BABYLON
TOKYO MEW MEW
TRAMPS LIKE US
TREASURE CHESS
UNDER THE GLASS MOON
VAMPIRE GAME
VISION OF ESCAFLOWNE, THE
WARRIORS OF TAO
WILD ACT
WISH
WORLD OF HARTZ
X-DAY
ZODIAC P.I.

NOVELS
CLAMP SCHOOL PARANORMAL INVESTIGATORS
KARMA CLUB
SAILOR MOON
SLAYERS

ART BOOKS
ART OF CARDCAPTOR SAKURA
ART OF MAGIC KNIGHT RAYEARTH, THE
PEACH: MIWA UEDA ILLUSTRATIONS

ANIME GUIDES
COWBOY BEBOP
GUNDAM TECHNICAL MANUALS
SAILOR MOON SCOUT GUIDES

TOKYOPOP KIDS
STRAY SHEEP

CINE-MANGA™
ALADDIN
ASTRO BOY
CARDCAPTORS
CONFESSIONS OF A TEENAGE DRAMA QUEEN
DUEL MASTERS
FAIRLY ODDPARENTS, THE
FAMILY GUY
FINDING NEMO
G.I. JOE SPY TROOPS
JACKIE CHAN ADVENTURES
JIMMY NEUTRON: BOY GENIUS, THE ADVENTURES OF
KIM POSSIBLE
LILO & STITCH
LIZZIE MCGUIRE
LIZZIE MCGUIRE MOVIE, THE
MALCOLM IN THE MIDDLE
POWER RANGERS: NINJA STORM
SHREK 2
SPONGEBOB SQUAREPANTS
SPY KIDS 2
SPY KIDS 3-D: GAME OVER
TEENAGE MUTANT NINJA TURTLES
THAT'S SO RAVEN
TRANSFORMERS: ARMADA
TRANSFORMERS: ENERGON

**For more
information visit
www.TOKYOPOP.com**

02.03.04T

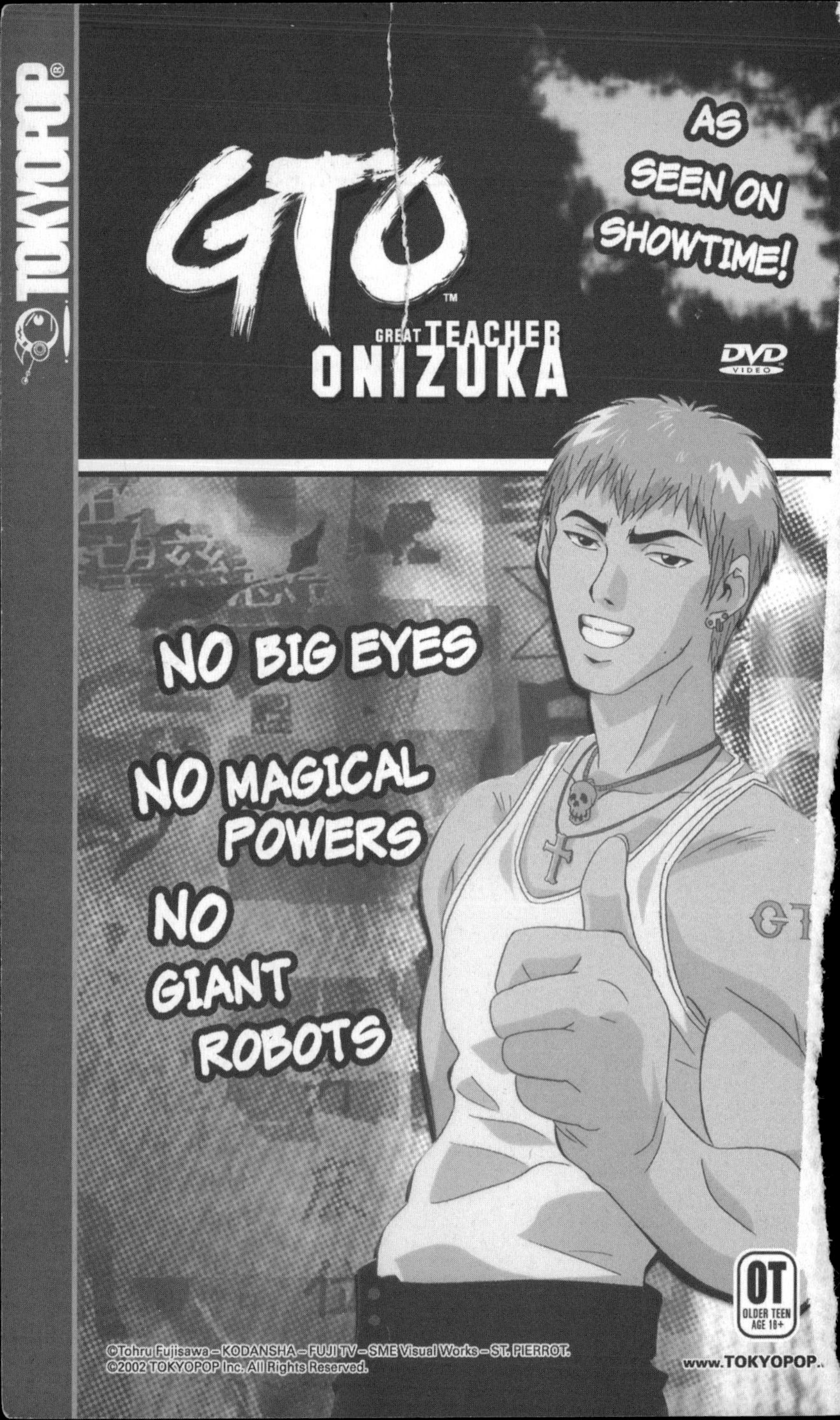
TOKYOPOP®
GTO™
GREAT TEACHER ONIZUKA
AS SEEN ON SHOWTIME!
DVD VIDEO
NO BIG EYES
NO MAGICAL POWERS
NO GIANT ROBOTS
OT OLDER TEEN AGE 16+
©Tohru Fujisawa – KODANSHA – FUJI TV – SME Visual Works – ST. PIERROT.
©2002 TOKYOPOP Inc. All Rights Reserved.
www.TOKYOPOP.

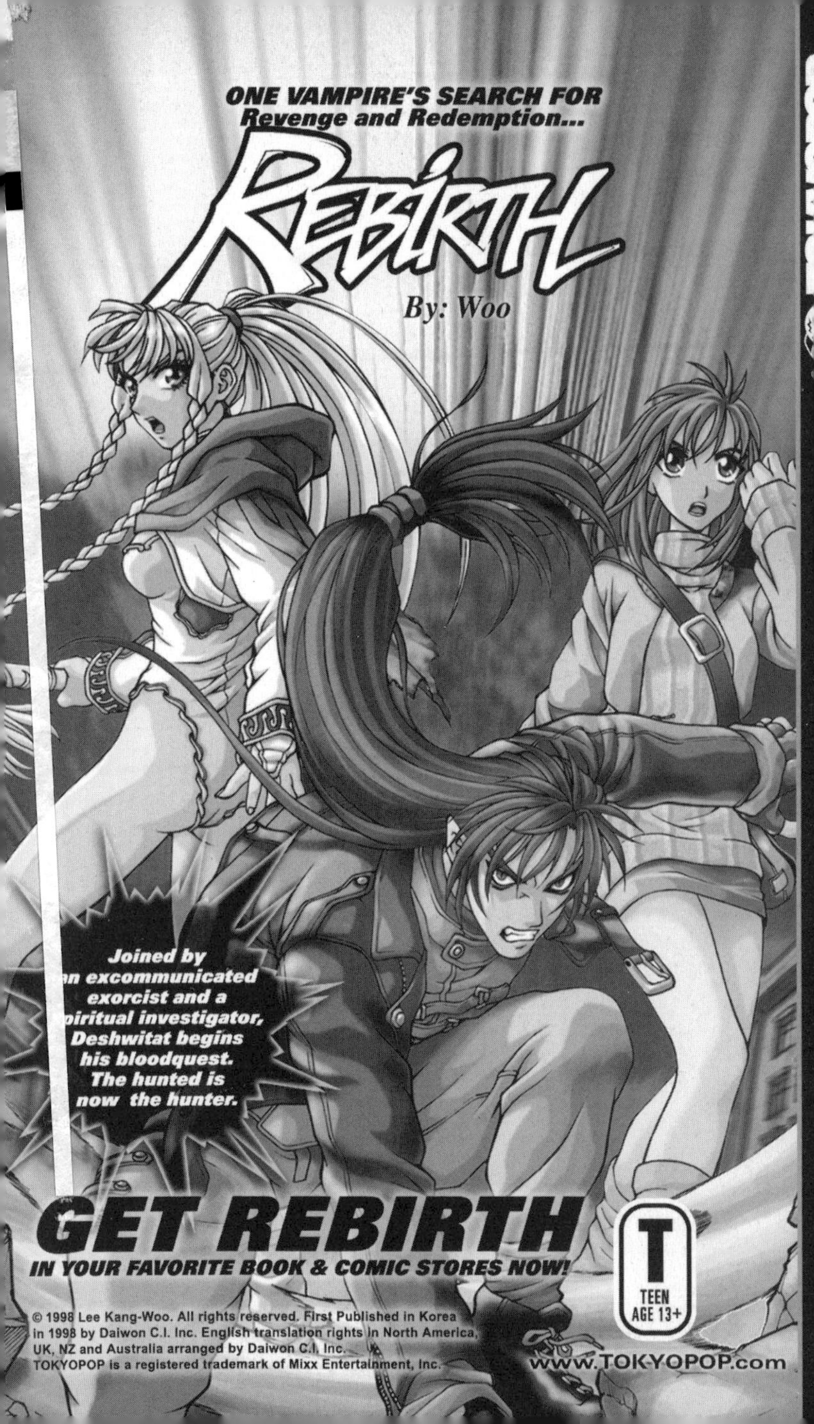
ONE VAMPIRE'S SEARCH FOR
Revenge and Redemption...
REBIRTH
By: Woo
Joined by
n excommunicated
exorcist and a
piritual investigator,
Deshwitat begins
his bloodquest.
The hunted is
now the hunter.
GET REBIRTH
IN YOUR FAVORITE BOOK & COMIC STORES NOW!
T
TEEN
AGE 13+
© 1998 Lee Kang-Woo. All rights reserved. First Published in Korea
in 1998 by Daiwon C.I. Inc. English translation rights in North America,
UK, NZ and Australia arranged by Daiwon C.I. Inc.
TOKYOPOP is a registered trademark of Mixx Entertainment, Inc.
www.TOKYOPOP.com

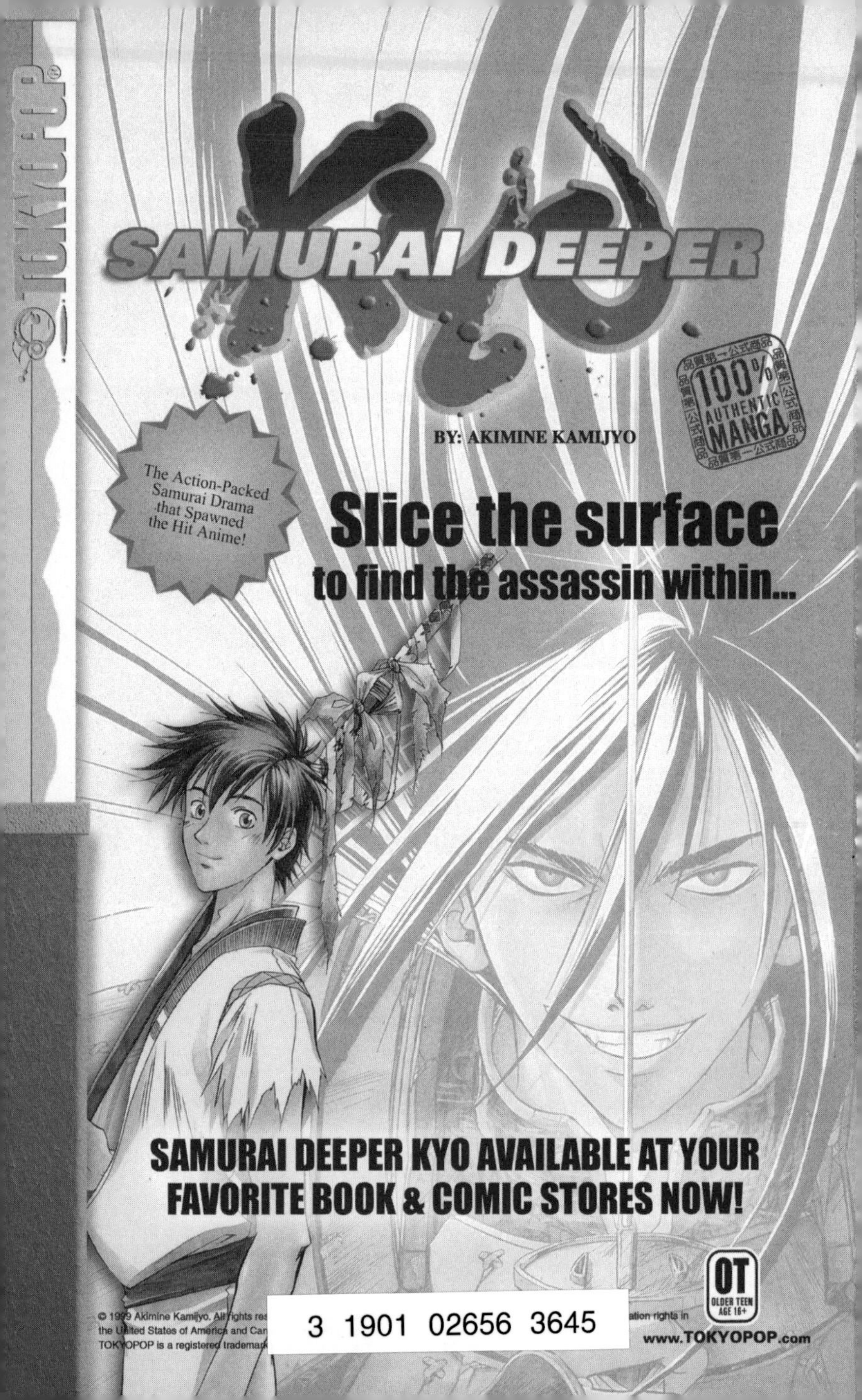
TOKYOPOP
KYO
SAMURAI DEEPER
100% AUTHENTIC MANGA
BY: AKIMINE KAMIJYO
The Action-Packed Samurai Drama that Spawned the Hit Anime!
Slice the surface
to find the assassin within...
SAMURAI DEEPER KYO AVAILABLE AT YOUR
FAVORITE BOOK & COMIC STORES NOW!
OT
OLDER TEEN AGE 16+
www.TOKYOPOP.com